The Seventies Now

NEW AMERICANISTS, A SERIES EDITED BY DONALD E. PEASE

THE SEVENTIES

NOW Stephen Paul Miller

CULTURE AS

SURVEILLANCE

DUKE UNIVERSITY PRESS   Durham and London 1999

For Maria and Noah

List of Illustrations

Acknowledgments

Many people made this book possible. Perry Meisel encouraged me to lengthen a brief essay I had written relating Watergate with seventies abstraction in poetry and painting. Reynolds Smith, my editor at Duke University Press, gave me the opportunity to expand my observations into a more general study of the seventies. Don Pease, W. J. T. Mitchell, John Brenkman, Eve Kosofsky Sedgwick, and Ross Chambers helped me refine my methodology. Thomas Fink, Hortense Spillers, and Thomas Kitts deepened my understanding of seventies literature; Mick Taussig spurred me to new concepts about seventies politics; and Molly Mason and George Sliwa enlarged my purview of seventies film.

Anita Feldman, Monica Duchnowski, and Tom Fink edited various manuscript versions. In the final writing stages, my wife, Maria, and Hugh Watts gave me crucial advice. Other people who read all or part of the book and offered suggestions include David Shapiro, Ernest Gilman, Mary Cross, Krystyna Mazur, Eric Miller, Kenneth Deifik, Barbara Willak, Shavaji Sengupta, Chris Debicki, Katarzyna Wywial, Albert Duchnowski, Rita Miller, Eva Moskowitz, Mary Carlson, Andrew Lawrence, Taylor Mead, Marc Dolan, Peggy Escher, Linda D'Angelo, Carla Kaplan, Willard P. Gingerich, Paul Baker, Susan Schultz, Kenneth Silverman, Ed Davenport, Myrna Nieves, Marie Umlah, Jonathan Schell, William Spurlin, Jonathan Arac, Stephen Greenblatt, Daniel Morris, Margueritte Murphy, Jeffrey Williams, Julie Mathis, Arthur Lawrence Miller, Harold Bloom, Michael Kampinski, Peter Baker, Lynn Crawford, Nikki Stiller, David Cagan, Samuel Miller, Kenneth Daley, Mary Lawlor, Elizabeth Mazzola, David Alfred Miller, Monika Szwagrzyk, Barbara Johnson, Duke University Press's anonymous readers, my colleagues at Jagiellonian University's English Institute, where I spent a year as a Fulbright scholar, fellow participants in John Brenkman's NEH seminar, and my cultural studies seminar students at Jagiellonian and St. John's University.

A travel and research grant from the President Gerald R. Ford Foundation to visit his presidential library in Ann Arbor helped me to research many aspects of seventies culture. The MLA, Narrative, German Fulbright, NEMLA, Integrative Studies, and Popular Culture conferences, as well as the American consulate in Cracow and American Studies Center and English Institute of the University of Warsaw, gave me forums to present and modify this work. St. John's University assisted me with several research reductions and grants. I am indebted to Reynolds Smith, Sharon Parks Torian, Paula Dragosh, Alma MacDougall, and others at Duke University Press for their acuity and care. I wish most to thank my wife, Maria, for her constant support.

The Seventies Now

Introduction

The seventies was the decade when Americans brought self-surveillance to a high level. The decade began with Nixon spying on Ellsberg "spying" on Johnson—with a culture and a counterculture fearful of one another's external surveillance, and it ended with virtually all aspects of American culture adapting themselves to a barely questioned corporate reality. It was almost as if Richard Nixon's overt surveillance and self-surveillance were ingested by the nation as a whole during Watergate and shortly thereafter internalized.

This book identifies a movement from external to internal surveillance throughout the seventies. We came to question the foundations of our society and government, yet our sense of what was possible diminished. We stopped short at the threshold of political awareness. In the early seventies, the "new politics" still implied grassroots strategies that promoted the sharing of wealth. By the late seventies, many political pundits had discarded as old-fashioned any means of redistribution of wealth that did not privilege the super-wealthy, and most Americans resigned themselves to this new formulation of the new politics. In the seventies, America's view of itself was arrested, its sense of social progress upended.

Nixon's presidency was merely the most visible part of an unconscious organizing mechanism that codified the sixties and innovatively helped more fully to commodify American culture. Discrete codifications of identity and of cultural energies came to dominate our lives. Of course, the seventies was a crucial period, if only because during this decade initiatives from the sixties in the women's movement, civil and voting rights enforcement, affirmative action, and environmental regulation were established. Progressive forces brought into play in the sixties had their effect at national and grassroots levels. However, these forces were also brought under control. For example, desegregation suits initiated in the sixties made their way through the courts in the seventies, and as a result more schools were desegregated in the seventies than the sixties. But at the same time Richard Nixon instructed the Justice Department to make the least possible desegregation effort permissible under law. Hence, the seventies saw a slowing of aggressive civil rights enforcement and a strengthening of de facto segregation, in schools and throughout society.

I define surveillance broadly as the monitoring and regimenting of an object, an institution, an area, a group, or a person, and self-surveillance as a self-monitoring and a self-regimenting that sometimes reinforces identifications put into place by external surveillance. This study maintains that surveillance and self-surveillance were dominant traits, or tropes, of seventies culture, and this introduction demonstrates this thesis with a wide array of seventies phenomena. Chapter 1 further historicizes the book's thesis, presents historical tools that inform the rest of the book, and supplies a chronology of seventies events. The next chapter uses films to explain how the seventies evolved from year to year and phase to phase. Chapter 3 examines in detail a mid-seventies analogue composed of poetic, painting, and political phenomena, and tracks American culture by considering a similar mid-eighties analogue. Each of the concluding three chapters looks more deeply into, respectively, seventies literature, art, and politics.

In the seventies, thinkers such as James Rule and Michel Foucault, with his novel interpretation of the panopticon (the prison control tower), explored the use of cultural institutions and the individual as self-surveying mechanisms. Foucault took surveillance seriously as an integral part of our seemingly free lives, as more than a *1984*-like nightmare of totalitarian control or a James Bond fantasy of international game-playing. If Watergate emphasized an increase in political and business espionage, the seventies also brought a surveillant organization of marketing and commodity information that increasingly expressed itself throughout every facet of our lives and in many cultural areas where one would least expect it.

As the seventies become material for nostalgia, we still overlook the sociopolitical import of the decade. The seventies "repackaged" the sixties. In a sense, surveillance took many new forms in the seventies. Credit checks became more centralized. Governmental agencies first used tools such as computer matching to cross-reference computer files, thereby identifying inconsistencies and finding lawbreakers. Body identification tools, which became more available to law enforcement agencies, eventually made it impossible to supply an unidentifiable Vietnam War victim's corpse for the Tomb of the Unknown Soldier. In this regard it might be said that advances in ultrasonography made it easier to monitor us from the womb to the grave. Perhaps more importantly, the silent majority as well as consumer-culture dropouts were canvassed and enlisted in the increasingly centralized marketplace. All manner of retail franchises became more pervasive. The advent of twenty-four-hour automated teller machines and more available credit-card debt lines made purchasing power more accessible. By the eighties, the terms "yippies" and "hippies" were comfortably replaced by the term "yuppies."

In the early eighties, fashion and popular music evoked the sixties at the same time that Reagan appealed to a nostalgia for an idealized pre-sixties reality. However, a more "revolutionary" version of the "sixties" could not be fully repressed. Public opinion hedged between ideology and practice. For instance, if the electorate believed in Reagan's notion of "military supremacy," the nation would also not support the possibility of sustained military conflict in Nicaragua. Similarly, a consensus assumed, as Reagan put it in his first inaugural address, that government was the problem, but another consensus did not want to end governmental social safety nets or industrial regulations. Americans entertained the euphoria of the notion of a freedom from governmental rules and inhibitions, but this sentiment oddly co-opted a more sixties and seventies counterculture elation at the thought of a return to basics. Reaganesque wish-fulfillment promised an idealized pre-sixties simplicity, but, with a sixties-like flourish, the Reagan administration billed itself as a "movement" and a "revolution," promising to negate the values of the sixties as it co-opted traces of its spirit. Reagan's landslides reflected a wish for the "happy days" of the Eisenhower fifties, a nostalgia without a hint of Eisenhower's farewell warning about excessive armament expenditures and, in the general's words, the growing "military-industrial complex."

If this kind of wish-fulfillment was seen with more skepticism in the nineties, it was because its downside, a less equitable sharing of wealth, became more obvious and relevant to America's middle class. The nineties brought a new return of the "real" that reacted against the wish-fulfillment of "official" government and political party rhetoric. As in the eighties, "unreal" government was vilified, but without overlooking the national debt incurred since 1981, as particularly expressed in how Ross Perot virtually ran against the federal deficit in his strong 1992 third-party showing, and in the 1994 and 1996

Republican congressional victories, in that many voters perceived that a Republican Congress and a Democratic president would offset one another and prevent "out-of-touch" eighties-like federal spending. The reality factor also figured into a Democratic presidential candidate winning both nineties presidential elections. Bill Clinton seemed more in touch with middle-class voters than George Bush, who admitted unfamiliarity with a supermarket scanner, and Bob Dole, who ran on a half-century-old war record and a seemingly irresponsible campaign promise to cut taxes by fifteen percent. Both nineties Republican contenders did not seem "real." Like the seventies, the nineties was characterized by the impulse to return to the "real," whereas the sixties and eighties brought differing cultural discourses of escapes from accepted realities.

"Reality" in post–World War II America was difficult to separate from the federal government and the Cold War, to which the nationally consuming project of World War II was eventually transferred in the late forties. What government reported had seemed real. With the problematic exception of the Korean War, from the end of World War II to the Vietnam escalation, government played a primarily positive role in the lives of most citizens. The federal government provided benefits, drove the economy, and helped institute civil rights. For the most part, only seeming fringes on the right and the left doubted the government. Although this is debatable when considering the differently motivated skepticism of many southerners, African Americans, and new leftists, these doubts never penetrated the overwhelming majority of Americans. For instance, even when Eisenhower was caught in a lie about the air surveillance of the Soviet Union during the U-2 incident, the nation had no way of contextualizing the information, and the incident did not affect Eisenhower's reputation.

During the Vietnam War, the credibility gap fostered the generation gap, which can roughly be defined as a gap between those who still identified themselves, if somewhat nervously, with "official" reality and those who did not. In the seventies, Nixon's eighteen-and-a-half-minute tape gap symbolized these prior "gaps." Indeed, Nixon provided a concentrated domestic symbol for the foreign "other" of the Vietnam War. Through Watergate, Nixon indirectly and unwittingly took the heat for the failed war. If official reality did not vanish with the Vietnam War, it nonetheless was no longer revered in the same way, and Watergate registered this adjustment.

Of course, reality is a general concept, but it is difficult to comprehend a historical era without grasping the "general." In the context of this book, the general is not a statistical term. I use it rather to convey how the dominantly characteristic features of an era's discourse, that is, the features that could be said to fuel an era, function within the entirety of cultural phenomena during that period. For instance, in terms of the sheer general population, the late sixties did not concern a rebellious, visionary youth culture. However, such a culture became a focus of the era in terms of the opposition and emulation it engendered, and the discomfort that many Americans felt about the conflicts in which some sixties youths found themselves. In other words, sixties alternative culture dominated the mainstream discourse, and still shapes our cultural memory of the period. Although more Americans subscribed to alternative culture in the seventies, adapting lifestyles that at least attempted to come to terms with individual freedom and growth, the general seventies discourse shifted into a different tenor and acquired a new set of issues. Key among these issues was a trend toward disinterest in the government that helped bring about deregulation and privatization, which was also assisted by a growing corporate funding of congressional elections. Politics became less "modernist"—a less self-contained "text" that is "authored" by relatively unaccountable political bosses. The antiwar movement of the sixties and politicians such as Allard Lowenstein first recognized this, and McGovern's attainment of the 1972 Democratic presidential nomination with a masterful student-based organization proved it. However, with the successful Nixon, Carter, and Reagan campaigns, big money, which could easily buy television and radio time, as well as political organizations and workers, replaced volunteer power as the most efficient way of circumnavigating entrenched political powers.

A Washington outsider like Jimmy Carter seemed populist because he did not have backing from the usual powers within the Democratic Party, but he had other big-money backers, such as Coca-Cola. "Populism" began to have little to do with popular-based programs. Carter sold an oxymoronic kind of candidate-based populism, populism that proceeds from trust in a candidate. However, this trust is not based on dedication to populist programs. A lack of social agenda in the Carter presidency reinforced an aversion to facing national problems. Reagan and other proponents of this aversion rationalized that America would need to face the "realities" of a less regulated market and a curtailed welfare state.

Tight-fisted Federal Reserve and budgetary monetary policies that sustained an ongoing seventies recession were rarely called into question, while Democrats were severely punished for inflation, which was quite arguably an ancillary problem. After all, the sharp rise in inflation began in 1973 and had three direct causes: Nixon taking the dollar off the gold standard (for which the public rarely holds him accountable), a 1973 worldwide crop shortage, and a slowdown in the rate of the production of goods and economic growth brought about by the 1973 oil embargo and subsequent price increases. The embargo was the most long-lasting cause of inflation; the resultant slowdown in production induced price markups brought about because money was chasing fewer goods. Economic stagnancy plus inflation—stagflation—occurred and, at the time, seemed difficult to explain. However, the government, in Herbert Hoover–like fashion, did increasingly little to combat the recession itself. This economic shortsightedness has not changed. Even in a period of the nineties when the economy is termed "good," it is only good in terms of a hampered economy's post-1973 oil embargo standards, in which the average American works harder for less security and income. Mysteriously, avenues of protest seem less and less effective.

In the seventies, many working Americans saw their economic anxieties in a social mirror. A dizzying proliferation of sixties culture caused a cultural overload and an urge to return to a more grounded "reality," turning attention away from both the Vietnam War and alternative culture. Phenomena throughout American culture such as Richard Nixon's successful 1968 presidential campaign and the art world's growing emphasis upon the minimal indicated a concern with slowing the speed of cultural consumption.

During the seventies, "reality" was once again "faced," after the "unreality" of the sixties, albeit with much ambivalence. This can be seen in the development of a writer such as Thomas Pynchon, from the relentless systemic complications of *The Crying of Lot 49* (1967) to "the final arch" and "end of the line" in the opening of *Gravity's Rainbow* (1973). The sixties are generally depicted as a time of cultural expansion and indeterminacy, in contradistinction to the seventies, which are portrayed as a decade of assimilation, containment, and delimitation. Relatively reserved minimalism and conceptualism dominate our accounts of the art and music of the seventies. Whereas the avant-garde theater of the sixties and the sixties minimalism of artists such as Donald Judd and Dan Flavin promoted an intermingling of all manner of sense perception and audience participation, the characteristic performance events of the seventies, such as the works of Robert Wilson, stressed the endless contemplation of spectacle and repetition. Of course, minimalist techniques were pioneered in the sixties, but whereas sixties minimalism tested the limits of painting, music, and other disciplines, seventies minimalism seemed more formal and ritualistic.

Seventies social codification was often exciting. In the seventies, women demystified their bodies with an exhilarating sense of exploration, as they articulated its phenomena in, for instance, *Our Bodies, Ourselves.* Public television surveyed and broke down into episodes the life and disintegration of a seemingly cohesive family in *An American Family.* On *The Brady Bunch,* children were demographically represented by age and gender, as if inhabiting the grid at the beginning and end of each program with its *Hollywood Squares*—like simultaneous portraits. We began to codify ourselves through fashion statements, such as wearing corporate logos on our T-shirts and other apparel. Ecology presupposed nature to be a closed system, or, in any case, a somewhat understandable one. However, notions of scarcity were intermingled with notions of limits and codification. In 1979, President Jimmy Carter discussed limits on American power, as he did throughout his presidency: "We have a keener appreciation of limits now, the limits of government, limits on the use of military power abroad, the limits of manipulation without harm to ourselves or to a delicate and balanced natural environment."[1] Countering this mind-set, the 1980 election of Ronald Reagan rejected limits on everything but social spending.

The Iranian hostage crisis became a symbol of American limitation that buried the Carter presidency, even as its earlier resolution might possibly have saved it. It was almost as if Americans identified with these political prisoners and saw the possibility of their salvation through them. Walter Cronkite noted the number of days that the hostages were in captivity at the end of each newscast. For months, almost every *ABC News Nightline* devoted itself to the hostage crisis, even when there was little to report.

The hostages were a constant reminder of America's sense of its own limits. We surveyed them daily in a manner that was as troubling as it was fixating. We focused on our apparent humiliation, and chose to read mightily into the event while wishing to will the problem away. Seeming to fall into this mind-set, the Carter administration desperately planned to rescue the hostages by sending soldiers into the center of Teheran to carry the hostages safely away. The mission never reached the city.

By the end of the seventies, the interests of Americans were effectively divided. The working class was content to have little leverage on its well-being.

By and large, the standard of living decreased, yet Americans had themselves, so to speak, politically and socially under control. Traditionally, the dire requirements of waging the Cold War facilitated such control.[2] The Cold War called for an ideological pose of supreme power, arguing that the Soviet Union was an ultimate threat. However, the Vietnam War had the odd effect of relieving tension with the Soviet Union and with China because the United States could not risk bringing the two other major powers further into the war. This served to make Vietnam and the entire Cold War less relevant to American national interests, since the Communist threat began to appear less menacing, even though, at the end of the seventies, the Soviet engagement in Afghanistan strongly reasserted the Cold War. Predictably, the American post–Vietnam War discussion of national limits increasingly lost impetus. It became more desirable to express American strength and ostensible limitlessness.

Ronald Reagan noted exasperation with limitations in his 28 October 1980 debate with Carter: "The country does not have to be in the shape that it is in. We do not have to go on sharing in scarcity."[3] Whereas the anger of the 1968 majority (the combined Nixon and Wallace votes) was directed at a displacement of limits, a dissatisfaction, that is, with the counterculture's defiance of limits (in terms of Vietnam, Cold War realities constituted a kind of limit defied by the counterculture) that seemed to negate their realities, the 1980 majority revolted against limits. Moreover, this revolt was not necessarily stated in partisan terms. We may point to a 1976 *Saturday Night Live* episode in which a Dan Aykroyd editorial rebutter character cautions America against the "inevitable perilousness" of an energy-wasting nation "sick with self-indulgence" while Chevy Chase's newscaster character brandishes an electric razor and makes faces at Aykroyd when he is not looking. The Aykroyd character is convincing yet pompous as he warns his audience:

> The energy crisis is upon us and yet most citizens are unaware of its implications and ultimate impact. The average Joe reads about and hears about it yet continues to ignore its inevitable perilousness. We live in a mechanized and electric society in the United States. We have been taught from generation to generation about the endless abundance of America's wealth, both in her natural resources and in her ability to take care of her own and others. We know in our collective subconscious that it cannot continue yet we go home, turn on the lights instead of burning a candle, turn on record players instead of singing to ourselves, blow-dry our hair instead of using a towel, and shave with a machine instead of a blade.

1. *Saturday Night Live,*
courtesy of Photofest

> We must get back to basics, a basic understanding of life's real values and a basic way of living that life. This means me, this means you learn to conserve. The term "wasting energy" is no longer a vestigial anachronistic cliché. It is an ominous and insidious prognosis for a nation sick with self-indulgence and ultimately a portent for an American Armageddon.

Humor here comes from a visual expression of what is verbally difficult to argue. This routine signals a growing counterculture tolerance of right-wing viewpoints. After all, the extreme right wing has long been skeptical of the federal government and "official" truth, seeing conspiracies in acts such as fluoridating water.

Skepticism about the oil companies' role in manufacturing a scarcity of oil confused the calls for conservation by Nixon, Ford, and Carter. Indeed, the oil companies had been arguing and advertising the notion that there was an energy crisis since the start of the seventies. They suggested a rise in oil prices that would subsidize the development of domestic oil, which would have been developed earlier in the century if foreign oil development were not cheaper.

Nonetheless, the 1973 embargo by OPEC, the Organization of Petroleum Exporting Countries, shocked the oil companies, even if they did try to capitalize on it. The skepticism of *Saturday Night Live* was justified, if somewhat misleading, because it made light of the ecological desirability of finding alternative energy sources.

In general, however, *Saturday Night Live* introduced a mildly subversive humor to mainstream American television culture. *Rowan and Martin's Laugh-In* and *The Smothers' Brothers Comedy Hour*, two sixties comedy programs, had politically dissident stances but were not particularly identified with youth culture. The "live" factor of *Saturday Night Live* gave the show an unpredictable and seemingly uncensored edge. Entertainment elements that seemed radical in 1975 seemed less and less so as the decade progressed. If Reagan was a much less memorable target of the program than Gerald Ford, it should be remembered that at times Reagan seemed more cutting-edge than *Saturday Night Live*. The program itself seemed less anti-establishment as its humor became more baselessly disjunctive and devoid of Republican targets, trends that were solidified when a new cast retooled the program in 1980.

A large part of *Saturday Night Live*'s success rested on the seventies marketing and media trend of forefronting personalities. ABC Sports revolutionized sports coverage with its "up close and personal" introductory features, close-ups, and narratives about what was personally at stake for individual athletes. A sense of the personal also became more prominently organized within the marketplace. During the seventies, the categorizations of *People* replaced the open vistas of *Life* magazine, which died before being reincarnated as a monthly. Interestingly, a rise in postal rates, typical of a then decaying American infrastructure, heavily contributed to the demise of *Life* magazine. Eventually, in the mid-seventies, sales of *People* magazine from supermarket checkout-line magazine racks (one reason why *People* is smaller than *Life*) caused *People* to become Time Incorporated's leading supplement for *Time* magazine.

Seventies marketing strategies more effectively reached virtually all Americans. Improved computer bases and direct mail and telephone operations and narrowcast media venues "found" almost everyone. The importance of finding new consumers grew as the economy slowed down, and locating new markets became paramount. Matrix management, the prevailing seventies business philosophy, preached the consideration of all available resources, and consumers were of course business's most crucial element. Few remained unsurveyed by the economy.

Culture at large codified what had been unaccounted for in the sixties. Block-buster bestsellers and films like *The Godfather, The Exorcist,* and *Jaws* posited hidden, unified, and seemingly uncontrollable forces that are met and de-feated. The "surface of reality" was recuperated. Indeed, Steven Spielberg's and George Lucas's major innovation, dating to the mid-seventies, may be their proclivity for contriving contraptions and technological masks that reaffirm humanistic assumptions.

"Deconstruction," which had its first American boom in the mid-seventies, played the role of a kind of mechanistic Jaws within literary criticism, dis-playing an ambivalence toward unity by confining all literature to a semiotic and textual realm while questioning the nature of the sign and the existence of unified texts. Although deconstruction may not seem like an enterprise that "faces reality," its critical works are nonetheless often organized around close readings that are even closer than those of the New Critics, and, in this respect, we can note a desire to cling to a given "reality," even as that reality is undermined. Deconstruction "surveys" and undoes its text by paying inor-dinate attention to tropological contradictions. Previously undetected biases are revealed. "Gonzo" first-person journalists, such as Hunter S. Thompson, similarly "ground," in the sense of both anchoring and grinding, their sub-jects, although in the "text" of their own lives. The reporter spends a great deal of space surveying him- or herself. Predispositions and prejudices must be announced, even if they ultimately seem harmless. Minute details of a re-porter's personal life defuse the official reality of a journalistic subject such as a presidential campaign. Despite his self-absorption, Thompson maintained that he "writes as close to the bone as [he can] get"[4] and that he attempts to produce "a cinematic reel-record" that can "record the reality."[5] Whereas de-construction undermines the unified reality of the text through critical self-surveillance, gonzo journalism devalues established versions of reality through the reporter's self-surveillance, even if this self-surveillance is ultimately en-dearing and self-serving. Ambivalently seeking the real, seventies American culture was similarly resolutely irresolute. We increasingly saw ourselves in terms of the recent past and our respective identity positions, but this past and these identities gradually lost explorative energies.

When I told a historian that I was writing a book about the seventies, she asked me how I could do it. "Wasn't Watergate the only thing that happened during the seventies?" she asked. Of course, much else happened during the seventies, but her reaction had an interesting validity. A conventional history of the seventies might have difficulty accounting for the vast sea change that the nation underwent during the decade. In typically positivist terms, it is difficult to account for how the decade of Watergate set the stage for the Reagan administration. Indeed, the seventies were the uncanny decade, the undecade, and to understand it requires an uncanny methodology. Hence, chapter 1 addresses this need by analyzing what I will characterize as "rippling epistemes." The concept of rippling epistemes allows us to utilize the sixties and the eighties while dealing directly with the seventies. Since I consider the theme of self-surveillance throughout many facets of seventies American culture, this chapter also justifies a field theory of culture. Chapter 1 ends by proposing the tool of "micro-periodizing," which the rest of this book applies to the seventies.

ONE

Rippling Epistemes

The uncanny feeling that one gets . . . is that we all define ourselves, constantly, as if we were Warhol's cultural symbols. —Henry M. Sayre, *The Object of Performance: The American Avant-Garde Since 1970*

Something like living occurs, a movement
Out of the dream into its codification.
—John Ashbery, "Self-Portrait in a Convex Mirror"

Self-definition is a kind of prison. —Margaret Atwood

1 The Post-Sixties

American culture as a whole has yet to experience another transition like the one the sixties put into play. I say "put into play" because we are still undergoing this transition. Since the sixties, periods lap together without the same discernible change that the sixties marked. While many important events have occurred since the sixties—from the 1973 oil embargo to the 1996 ending of federally assured welfare—no other post–World War II period so effectively divided what came after from what came before. It is almost as if mind-boggling world events like the endings of the Cold War, a political state of war in the Middle East, and South African apartheid; the technical advances of the so-called information age; and American political milestones like the 1980 election of Reagan and the 1994 election of a Republican majority in both houses of Congress occurred in an ever-broadening "post-sixties." No subsequent era has rivaled the sixties as a surprising cultural break that challenged previously embedded social conventions and, indeed, the premises of how reality, as a kind of validating mechanism in itself, was used.

"The sixties" conveys a sense of total cultural rupture that most Americans perceived at the time or have later come to sense. Although most Americans were not "cultural players" in the sixties, the notion of reality that was posited in the sixties—that reality needs to be justified and is only truly authenticated and accommodated by intimations of a visceral super-reality—touched nearly everyone to some degree, if only as a notion that needed to be denounced, repressed, or simply put out of mind. Traditional scales of measurement were not enough. Perceptively, Andy Warhol devised the hyperbole "superstar," and it was used widely without irony. Similarly, in 1967, the sports public insisted upon calling the first National Football League–American Football League Championship Game the Super Bowl, despite professional football's more functionally descriptive name.

More significantly, in the sixties, seemingly essential economic and social power relations of "reality" were called on to account for themselves. What the sixties was had so much to do with new possibilities that at times it verged on the rejection of recognizable reality. For instance, the central motif of a memorable anti-Vietnam protest was an attempt to levitate the Pentagon. Of course, this aspiration was one of absurdist political protest theater. Nonetheless, it bespoke an urge to transform America completely by mysterious means. After all, it seemed as if this had already happened. In *Armies of the Night,* Norman Mailer's contemporaneous account of the 1967 march on the Pentagon, Mailer is most swayed by the mystical possibilities of the younger, less overtly political marchers. An endorsement of the "real" powers of imaginative living leads Mailer to substitute forms of the fictional novel and historical writing for one another.

Underlying sixties protest was a notion that Cold War ideology, which could be seen as informing most of the American economy, was more fictitious than even the possibility of raising the Pentagon. Justifications for the Vietnam War did not seem credible or real. Perhaps more than anything else, the Vietnam War injected the surreal into sixties America. The war seemed outside reality. It appeared unjustifiable, since it was waged in the service of an intrinsically unstable South Vietnamese government. Certainly it was not worth the loss of so many lives. Official, government-sanctioned reality seemed a bad dream, an undesired unreality.

A small minority's questioning of established modes of thought was, of course, not the only thing that occurred during the sixties. However, this questioning and suspension of seeming realities provided the central spectacle (sometimes literally as demonstrations, happenings, be-ins, and teach-ins) that elicited severe animosity from many in the working class and the government, who were invested (often literally in terms of their capital and jobs within the military-industrial complex) in Cold War reality. Conflicting views of what happened and who was to blame for the violence at the 1968 Democratic convention in Chicago and the fatal shootings of students at Kent State and at Jackson State in 1970 testify to this division. The war in Southeast Asia and protest against it hinged upon a difference concerning what constituted authenticity. Many in the counterculture assumed that reality more reasonably resided in a new collective, psychological fashioning of American abundance than in war. Escalation seemed more plausibly descriptive of a culture experiencing its growing abundance than of the necessities of war.

Other historical moments in the Western world, such as in pre–World War I Europe and revolutionary Russia, brought widespread expectations of an imminent utopic future that seemed just around the corner. Since the Russian Revolution, however, the sixties is unique in its vision. Pre–World War II Americans did not live through futuristic visions such as those of the 1939 New York World Fair's "World of Tomorrow" in the same way that many young people of the sixties lived through sixties music. In the sixties, the sense of a reality suspended was lived more than it was viewed.

Experiences do not translate intact from one period to another. It is impossible to understand a phenomenon such as drug use, for instance, apart from different periods' contrasting approaches toward reality. An ideologically generated suspension of reality influenced how we think of the use of hallucinogenic drugs in the sixties. Drugs, even the same drugs, were used and thought of in very different ways in the sixties than in the post-sixties because a certain kind of escape from reality had more noble than naive connotations. Historical periods modify the "reality" of drugs. Interestingly, in the late sixties and seventies, law enforcement used drug use to code and survey a counterculture that the Nixon administration wished to destroy while at the same time, one often smelled marijuana in public places, such as parks and movie theaters. Society was full of mixed messages, leading to the bifurcated mind-set of the eighties that I discuss in chapter 3.

Fredric Jameson attempts to "periodize" the sixties, to discuss and analyze that time period as a problematized entity.[1] He conjectures that the sixties can be explained as a break between two capitalist modes. Jameson speculates that during the sixties our economy was stuck in a prolonged transition from industrial to post-industrial, service, and multinational modes. Economic systems lost regulatory power. A sense of economic reality was thus suspended, and all things appeared possible. American culture, which had expanded in the fifties with a "Cold War reality" in the background, expanded in the sixties outside the guidance of that vision. This break produced a sense of unlimited expansion, through a variety of economic, political, cultural, and social means, since economic and other manner of accountable authority were, during the sixties, unclear and indeterminate. Hence, a "referential gold standard" was temporarily lifted, inducing a euphoric sense of freedom. By the mid-seventies, however, reality had irrefutably returned, even if it no longer worked.

Because a sense of reality was so problematic in the sixties, it is not surprising that in many ways the seventies concerned a return to reality. But what reality? Was it possible to forget how political realities had been discredited by the Vietnam War, the string of sixties assassinations, and the electoral system's inability to run an antiwar presidential candidate in 1968? The sixties had succeeded in discrediting official, government-sponsored reality, but it was the sixties itself that most Americans were trying to recover from. As American culture, during the seventies, was incorporating sixties mores, it was also disavowing the subversive content of those mores.

If we have definitely left the sixties, it is sometimes difficult to characterize what has replaced them. Sixties music is still played on a full, codified spectrum of radio stations from hard rock to easy listening (perhaps more sixties and sixties-related post-sixties music, music recorded in the wake of the sixties or by musicians who became prominent then, is played on the radio now than in the sixties), and many young people know sixties songs better than recent ones. We still debate the Vietnam War and how politicians avoided fighting in it. Sixties politicians like the Kennedys and Nixon enamor us, and at times it has seemed that the Kennedy assassination and the Watergate scandal interest us more than contemporary events.

And yet, for all this, no one would dispute that the sixties are over, not even its seemingly ageless proponents. Jerry Garcia is dead (to some it might seem as if he merely died in the post-sixties, just like Janis Joplin and Jim Morrison, even if Garcia died twenty-five years later). If the import of the sixties is still debated, we have nonetheless certainly moved into a different cultural mindset, a different historical set of conditions. The sixties' sense of political and social possibility has vanished, and it is difficult to muster very much hope that our class, race, and social problems will be resolved, as many people reasonably hoped at various times throughout the early, middle, and late sixties. By the 1972 presidential election, it became obvious that the baby boomer "youth vote," enlarged by the lowering of the voting age from twenty-one to eighteen, would not effect a radical change in the nation's power relations.

And yet chronological, political, and social distance from the sixties oddly increases its value and currency. Many who were not alive during the sixties, or even the seventies, are curious about the sixties and feel as if they missed something necessary for coming to grips with the present. Who is to say that the sixties will not outlive the baby boomers? (Perhaps after we see past the promises of the new millennium, this may be all the more probable.) Apparently more prevalent than any cultural changes brought about by mere technological innovations or surface political changes, the sixties is still hanging, unresolved and unfinished.

After all, the sixties was a rip in reality, and once the basis of what a society assumes is severely questioned, how can a society feel comfortable with those assumptions again? A majority of Americans were not willing to "buy" sixties reality, nor could they put it aside. Generated by these two ambivalent currents, the sixties ripples into the present. The post-sixties lives together with seemingly uncontested, international capitalism. Indeed, it is difficult to see the difference. It is almost as if the culture of the sixties/post-sixties continuously expands so as to contain each new incarnation of the new, as if "the sixties" and a kind of postmodern, late-capitalist sieve through which all culture is overwhelmed by the omnipresent feel of capital and disarmed and co-opted, are two sides of the same coin, as if the sixties and late-capitalist fluid capital are part of the same infinitely absorbent cultural sponge, the same unanswerable question. Indeed, as the triumph of capitalism affects virtually everyone in the "developed" world, an increasing number of the world's citizens find themselves negotiating with the sixties.

The sixties metaphorically occupies the inner core of post–World War II reality. The Cold War realities prior to it must now answer to it. For instance, in the Persian Gulf War, George Bush claimed that one of his aims was to overcome the United States' militarily cautious "Vietnam syndrome" (as if Reagan had not already been celebrated for doing that), and then also said that he could not send troops to Baghdad for fear of getting America caught in another Vietnam conflict. In a sense, our entire society now fears being lost in the "unreality" of the sixties, expressing itself in an almost irrational fear of justified domestic expenditures and investments. Perhaps we fear uncovering an unfair distribution of wealth and utilization of public resources that will demand a traumatic readjustment.

The sixties shape our ontological horizons. The decade is the inner space we are unable to escape, within which we wire and survey ourselves, in which we lay out and order our ever-changing present. Since the sixties are the post–World War II epoch's central conflict between reality and non-reality, it engages us in our diurnal sense of things, shifting our sense of household, work, recreation, and gender behaviors. In the words of John Ashbery's "Self-Portrait in a Convex Mirror" (1974), in the seventies, "something like living occurs, a movement / Out of the dream [of the sixties] into its codification."

The unanswered sense of the sixties is captured as our historical sense of the seventies. Because the sixties is not quite over, and it is difficult to tell what comes after it, the sixties is where contemporary history loses its linearity. However, if the sixties is at the center of our culture, the codifications of the seventies are tantamount to our culture's central wiring. In the seventies the malleable identities and consumer patterns that we use to survey ourselves were put in place.

In the late sixties and seventies, a hegemonic mind-set gained force from an impulse to codify the sixties' breaks in reality and unaccounted for and surplus consumer production. This codification enabled distributors to charge for previously inexpensive services. Cable and pay television made their presence felt throughout the country. Gas stations charged for air. The telephone company charged for information. In 1951, C. Wright Mills's *White Collar* pointed out the increasing centralization of property in the United States. Mills, however, emphasized the effects of this centralization in the world of work. In the seventies, we saw this trend extended to the consumer life of Americans.

The consumer increasingly replaced the factory as the linchpin of production. It was not until the Great Depression and the New Deal that industrial capitalism unacknowledgedly appropriated Marxist perceptions concerning the veritable production of consumption. By the thirties, in the midst of the Great Depression, it was apparent that capitalism would need to either risk its collapse or facilitate mass means of consumption. Consumption would paradoxically need to be produced. Capitalists accepted the necessities of government work projects, federal business and financial regulations, Social Security, and the place of unions within industrial production.

The Democratic Party coalition from the thirties to the sixties was based on group identities that were codified by production roles, race, religion, region, and ethnicity. However, by the seventies, post-industrial emphases upon consumer conditions fostered a cultural environment in which identity-positions were, so to speak, seen in quotation marks. "We *decided* [emphasis added] to hold on to separate cultural identities," Marge Piercy's *Woman on the Edge of*

Time (1976) says of a utopic future that is fashioned in a seventies mirror, "But we broke the bond between genes and culture."[2] In the seventies, for instance, a woman could take on the identity of a feminist, and her consciousness could be raised by a heightened awareness of that identity. A wide array of other "identity prisms" were identified and used to survey the self and its culture. Such revelations were and are obviously invaluable to personal and social development. They indicate the power of the individual to try on and "buy into" identity. "Passing" from one identity to another does not seem to be the veritable, or actual, crime that it might well have been before the sixties. In this regard, the 10 October 1993 *New Yorker* commented upon the "radicality" of 1969 and 1970 fashions:

> It was about then, after all, that women's clothes went from being mostly a register of social propriety to being a public means of self expression and—this is not unrelated—women (re)discovered feminism. Deciding what and how to be would henceforth be all tied in with what to wear and how to look.
>
> The true legacy of 1969-70 . . . is the freedom to imagine the part and then to dress for it—the courage, on the part of women, to write the narratives, sartorial and otherwise, of their daily lives.[3]

The undermining of a pre-sixties American consensus enabled, by the early seventies, a hopping from one performative identity-position to another. For instance, a Native American feminist woman might shift emphases between her Native American and feminist identities. Of course, this absence of a deeply felt epistemological given in an individual's life also eventually led to the lasting impression we have of the seventies as a vapid decade that could not fulfill the social visions of the sixties, even though much of America experienced the sixties during the seventies. If what we think of as the sixties has left us with perpetually unfinished business—business, indeed, that is perhaps undoable—the same cannot be said about what we think of as the seventies because it is less clear what the business of the seventies was. It might be maintained that the seventies never began accomplishing its business. Nevertheless, I would argue that the business of the seventies completed itself before we were aware of what was happening. Before we knew it, most Americans learned to survey themselves, to the extent that they could fit a new formulation of an internationally corporate consumer system by putting a limit on how far they might imagine alternatives. For instance, despite the seventies novelty of "stagflation"—economic stagnation together with inflation—inflation was the only problem that was politically acceptable to address, even though the recession end of the equation seemed to generate the inflation—money was chasing fewer goods since the 1973 oil embargo. Nonetheless, progressive efforts to stimulate the economy, such as public works projects, increasingly became political anathema. Of course one might note exceptions among us, but the point is that there was little hope for group action that might offer economic or social alternatives. Although during the seventies consumers gained by imposing new manufacturers' safety and quality guidelines, it was nonetheless clear that corporations most influenced production and work legislation. Government and American consumers were, in a sense, held hostage to threats of drastically higher consumer prices attached to every progressive proposal that would regulate the marketplace or save the environment.

In the seventies, franchises began to dominate retail markets. Whether one shopped at a convenience store or the mall, one apparently participated in a corporately intermeshed international market cash flow. And every job that one might have, from teacher to carpenter to doctor to executive, seemed increasingly associated with this burgeoning international marketplace. If there were any alternatives, any valid answers to the sixties and the early seventies, somehow we held ourselves at bay. Unwittingly, we could not see alternatives because they would have implied government action at a moment when government lost its credibility and momentum. Even from a new leftist perspective, our various self-identities split us apart and seemed to make collective group action obsolete for all but Nixon's "silent majority," as northern whites became less embarrassed about asserting themselves as a group who identified with southern whites.

We must burnish into our historical senses the seventies as a significant period. The seventies are in large part remembered as somewhat annoying, the oil lines and the seizing of American hostages in Iran coming to mind, and also perhaps inconsequentially amusing, largely perhaps because of artifacts such as eight-track tape players, earth shoes, waterbeds, and disco music scenes. The decade's characteristic pop musical styles—punk, metal, and disco—are reminisced about but not usually taken seriously. Even the key historical event of the seventies, Watergate, is often delegated to the sixties as the prior decade's symbolic culmination. Indeed, the seventies is often recalled as more the aftermath of the sixties than anything in its own right. In retrospect, even in the eighties, the nuclear freeze movement was arguably caught up in an inability to get past sixties methods of protest.

There is a remarkable "lag" time in our feeling of historical progression since the sixties. A critical mass of adolescents in every decade since the sixties has felt as if it has missed out, or, in some cases, is noticeably resentful about the implication that it has. It behooves us to comprehend the seventies so as to move past the sixties. This will only be possible through grasping the seventies as something in itself, as something more tangible than the idealized punk and disco renditions of much seventies nostalgia. We must understand the seventies as it touches and arrests us. We must deploy the lessons of the seventies or we will never know where the sixties went. Oddly, the seventies can lead us to the unfinished business of the sixties and, by a circuitous route, to the present.

2 Uncanny Criticism

The political unconscious, according to Fredric Jameson, is the ideological limitation embedded in a society's cultural mind-set. Jameson demonstrates the Greek etymology of the word "politics" as meaning the affairs of the city when a city can be defined as everything within a wall. For Jameson, this wall is a trope for the limitation of tropological and imaginative powers. Because of these cultural limits, or, as Jameson calls them, horizons, all cultural phenomena are ideological and political. Additionally, they are primarily political because it is only through the language of culture, in its broadest sense, that the contradictions and inequities of economic and political power can be dynamically yet unconsciously reconciled. Put simply, culture is a cover-up. However, this does not necessarily involve a conspiracy or even a cause and effect relationship as much as a "structural causality,"[4] Louis Althusser's term, cited by Jameson, for a system of causality in which the whole of a culture expresses itself in its parts.

In this sense, I believe, the critic walks a tightrope over an uncanny void, a void that does not exist until it is recognized.[5] One might feel an uncanny horror when working outside cause and effect relations. Causality, after all, constitutes our most comfortable mode of accountability. It allows us to identify what is "outside" a recognized chain of causes and effects. But causal analysis also allows us to evade cultural responsibility and to narrow ourselves and our cultural lives unnecessarily. It privileges systems of narrow influence and does not encourage illuminating interdisciplinary interfaces, the non-reductive merging of political and artistic considerations, or the application of cultural analysis to the diverse products of cultural consumption to which we are all subject.

For both Jameson and Althusser, the absent totality of a culture is found everywhere in that culture. In a radical departure for Marxists, economic considerations are no longer chief determinants. How culture produces itself must help account for any given part of the whole. Jameson argues that it is no longer possible to understand cultural and literary phenomena distinct from the cultural and social powers that hold them in place. Althusser lists every conceivable manner of culture as "ideological state apparatuses."[6] Every function that it is possible for culture to fulfill, such as education and entertainment, is an ideological state apparatus because cultural phenomena serve the limits of conceivable reality so that this reality does not threaten the existing social order. This order is deeply entrenched, protecting the most essential workings of social division, inequity, and repression. Althusser bases his notion of culture as an aggregate of ideological state apparatuses on Jacques Lacan's category of the "real order." For Lacan, the real is the always unknowable yet linguistically enabling limit on our imaginations and symbolic workings, what Wallace Stevens might call the nothing that is.

In the face of such reality, what purpose can criticism serve, especially when it concerns art and literature? For Althusser, even "revolutionary" art assists ideological limits, or horizons, on thought. Yet such art does so in a way that betrays the political realities that underlie it. Similarly, what virtue remains for art in a culture wherein all cultural phenomena serve repressive ends? A work of art is effective, Althusser posits, because it "accounts" for modes of cultural production. To perceive art is to distance oneself from the ideological horizons of reality so as to make that reality visible. Althusser elaborates on the relationship between art and ideologically determined reality:

> This relationship is not one of identity but one of difference. I believe that the peculiarity of art is to "make us see" [*nous donner à voir*], "make us perceive," "make us feel," something which alludes to reality. . . . What art makes us see, and therefore gives to us in the form of *"seeing," "perceiving,"* and *"feeling"* (which is not the form of knowing) is the ideology from which it is born, in which it bathes, from which it detaches itself as art, and to which it *alludes*. . . . They make us "perceive" (but not know) in some sense *from the inside,* by an *internal distance,* the very ideology in which they are held.[7]

Successful art, even abstract art, offers its audience the opportunity to see the absent workings of culture. Thus an artwork can be a kind of spy. Indeed, since art is inescapably political, overt content is unnecessary, and abstract art, better camouflaged, can be a successful double agent, or put differently, a two-way mirror.

The poet John Ashbery expresses this concept in an essay about Frank O'Hara published soon after O'Hara's death in 1966. "Unlike the message of committed poetry," wrote Ashbery of O'Hara's work, "it incites one to all the programs of commitment as well as to every other form of self-realization: interpersonal, dionysian, occult or abstract."[8] When Louis Simpson attacked Ashbery for his seeming lack of a committed stance against the war in Vietnam, Ashbery replied, "All poetry is against war and in favor of life, or else it isn't poetry, and it stops being poetry when it is forced into the mold of a particular program."[9] Through poetry, a poet acts politically. Of course, a great deal of poetry supports war and "particular program[s]." Ashbery, however, suggests that any poem that is worth being called one offers an opportunity to see into ideology and propaganda. If a poem did not, if it were not a kind of two-way mirror or double agent, it would not be a poem because it would indeed be unconsidered ideology or propaganda and, as Ashbery implies, good writing creates an excess that cannot be neatly controlled; its message cannot be easily contained. Indeed, the aesthetic is not on an entirely different plane from any other category. Quoting Ashbery, Charles Simic maintains that "each self, even in its most private concerns, is representative, that the 'aesthetic problem' . . . is a 'microcosm of all human problems,' that the poem is a place where the 'I' of the poet, by a kind of visionary alchemy, becomes a mirror for all of us."[10]

Indeed, as I will discuss in chapters 3 and 4, an Ashbery poem is effective as a poem and as a cultural product because it clarifies the workings of that poem's historical period and our present understanding of that period. Jameson observes that "history is inaccessible to us except in textual form."[11] Historical events themselves are rewritings, or, we might just as easily say, repicturings: "The whole paradox of what we have here called the subtext may be summed up in this, that the literary work or cultural object, as though for the first time, brings into being that very situation to which it is also, at one and the same time, a reaction."[12] "As though for first time" suggests the freedom that can be experienced within a confined, historical horizon. It is the critic's job to bring the political unconscious to consciousness in a manner that must be unique and seemingly fictional because it has never existed as consciousness before. According to Jameson, history is text. Yet history is not a text until it is made so by those who interpret it, who draw it out.[13] A critic acting on this premise will always be faulted when a strong, creative reading is thought to be a false reading. Jameson's words in this regard bear citation:

> I happen to feel that no interpretation can be effectively disqualified on its own terms by a simple enumeration of inaccuracies or omissions, or by a list of unanswered questions. Interpretation is not an isolated act, but takes place within a Homeric battlefield, on which a host of interpretive options are either openly or implicitly in conflict. If the positivistic conception of philological accuracy be the only alternative, then I would much prefer to endorse the current provocative celebration of strong misreadings over weak ones. As the Chinese proverb has it, you use one ax handle to hew another: in our context, only another, stronger interpretation can overthrow and practically refute an interpretation already in place.[14]

"The age," says Jacques Derrida, "already in the past is in fact constituted in every respect as a text,"[15] and it sometimes seems that we must strenuously labor to keep history and poetry like Ashbery's from articulating one another.

This is particularly true when discussing a relatively undefined era such as the seventies. Like the 1973 comet Kahoutek, the decade of the seventies (one wonders if the comet's nonappearance would have had quite the same impact in another decade) is only vaguely sighted, and the seventies may be equated with what Ashbery, in "Self-Portrait in a Convex Mirror," calls the "question[ing]" for "what we need":

> It may be that another life is stocked there
> In recesses no one knew of; that it,
> Not we, are the change; that we are in fact it
> If we could get back to it, relive some of the way
> It looked . . .
> (SP, 196: 16, 22, 28–32)[16]

I address seventies culture to provide a springboard to face how "we are" "the change" that the seventies now is, even if one is too young to remember the seventies.

Henry M. Sayre speaks about an uncanny experience that one has when looking at the shifting theatrical personae within Cindy Sherman's oeuvre of photographic self-portraits. According to Sayre, we "buy into" and identify with Sherman's dramatic and media poses and realize that we have surveyed and organized ourselves into entities as established and ephermeral as War-hol subjects.[17] We experience ourselves as the products of surveying a void or break. Similarly, the sixties were a break in reality, and in the seventies, we codified this break, the break that, in a sense, we are.

To know the seventies we must reconceive and reimagine it. Foucault main-tains that through the "basis of a political reality" we "fiction" history.[18] One might colloquially liken this basis to a fluid epistemological building code, a DNA underlying the construction of much of an epoch's most significant cul-tural phenomena. When I say "DNA," I mean to suggest a kind of fictive other life of an era that determines the ontological horizons of that era, that is, what cannot, even in the imagination, be escaped. What "works" as an evocative cultural articulation does so because it accounts for, reconciles, and manifests the era's predominant and constitutive means of semiotic production and dis-tribution.

Distinctions that we ordinarily make between seemingly authored and non-authored works need not preclude analogies between the two. For Foucault, all phenomena are discourse:

> What, in short, we wish to do is to dispense with "things." To "depresen-tify" them. To conjure up their rich, heavy, immediate plentitude. . . . To substitute for the enigmatic treasure of "things" anterior to discourse, the regular formation of objects that emerge only in discourse. To define these objects without reference to the ground, the foundation of things, but by relating them to the body of rules that enable them to form as ob-jects of a discourse and thus constitute the conditions of their historical appearance. To write a history of discursive objects that does not plunge them into the common depth of a primal soil, but deploys the nexus of regularities that govern their dispersion.[19]

In other words, a "thing" cannot be understood without a condition, context, or system, that makes its understanding possible. We need to understand the manner in which understanding is produced. In terms of a historical study, this means coming to grips with a period's prevalent ways of knowing. This is done by decoding the nexus of discursive regularities that govern the disper-sion of discursive phenomena. For Foucault, a historical study seeks to com-prehend the "conditions of historical appearance," that is, to understand how certain pheonema have entered the historical discourse within an epistemo-logical system that is constitutive of our understanding of an epoch. All forms are constituents of the epistemological systems (or, in effect, enabling rules of discourse) that are at work in a given period. A basis is thus established for synchronic cultural studies and periodization.

Foucault's "ungrounding" of his historical study might be considered historically as characteristic of the sixties. Lacking an empirical ground, all categories are open to question and comparison. A historian can find unexpected significance in her or his objects of study:

> However banal it may be, however unimportant its consequences may appear to be, however quickly it may be forgotten after, however little heard or however badly deciphered we may suppose it to be, a statement is always an event that neither the language [*langue*] nor the meaning can quite exhaust.[20]

From the postulation of this kind of plenitude, surplus, or inexhaustibility of meaning to be garnered from statements, the extremely close readings[21] that we normally associate with literary criticism can be applied to all manner of cultural artifact. For Foucault, many diverse kinds of cultural output may be discussed as "documents."[22]

These documents need not be considered as the work of a single consciousness, since Foucault likens documents, in the broad sense of the term as he uses it, to "archaeological" artifacts that have been abstracted from an unfamiliar culture.[23] This deliberately estranged perspective promotes a more adequately close "reading" of each object of study.

The use of this kind of estranged reading perhaps offers our only escape route from ideological constraints. It is through these close readings that ideology can be opposed, played upon, and resisted, if not entirely escaped. Ross Chambers's *Room for Maneuver* (1992) stresses the inevitability and desirability of the misreadings of texts. These misreadings are based upon misinterpreted influence, reminiscent of Foucault's characterization in *La volonté de savoir* of psychiatrists predetermining the discovery of the hysteria that they have diagnosed and Tzvetan Todorov's observation that explorers "discovered" the America they needed to discover.

Chambers appropriates Harold Bloom's theories to a more potentially political end. Power, Chambers reminds us, is shifting, and deferential yet aggressive readings can provide perspectives on power. I thus use an emancipative strategy here that spasmodically swings between extremely close readings and the testing of relatively large hypotheses. The smallest details are sometimes on the same writerly plane as the largest cultural generalities. One might say that my method promises to recuperate paranoiac surveillance by recognizing the methods of Nixon and by using those methods for ends that strengthen both diversity and interactivity in our social fabric, instead of pitting strands against one another.

Putting this "paranoid mind-set" in a nineties context, Independent Counsel Kenneth Starr may be said to have inappropriately used analogic and metaphoric bases for the Whitewater and Monica Lewinsky investigations. In other words, the basis of, for example, the possibility of Clinton trying to arrange a job for Lewinsky to influence her testimony was enough *like* a similar possibility concerning former Associate Attorney General Webster Hubbell to justify Starr's investigation. The arguable legal irrelevance of the Lewinsky matter in itself did not bother Starr, since he was primarily trying to prove a pattern. However, Starr wanted it both ways—he was not only investigating a pattern, he also wished to prosecute the law about perhaps irrelevant specifics by selectively (in the sense that the possible perjury of others than Clinton and Lewinsky in the Paula Jones case did not concern him) whenever his targets might be responsible for relatively minor violations. Hence, small matters were isolated from larger contexts and relevant patterns. While I also hope to open metaphoric "trapdoors"[24] in the texts and phenomena that I study, I place them in the context of other possible readings, and I do not exclude other justifiable interpretations in the name of an investigation after "the truth." Perhaps, even outside academic and artistic audiences, deconstruction has helped make such searches seem hopelessly naive and inherently biased, which in part would explain Starr's unpopularity in public opinion polls.

Deconstruction clears a space to reexamine the givens of American culture through close reading. New Historicism and other relatively new and vital adaptations of close reading flow through the critical space of deconstruction, by showing how we are constructed as subjects by various ideologies and discourses.[25] Deconstructionism at its best offers tools that can help to unlock the "inversely dynamic" antithesis implicit in, for example, an economic term that comes into vogue in America at about the same time as deconstruction, "stagflation," and its cultural parallels, that is, the economy's and the culture's inability to expand while its financial currency is not so paradoxically devalued. In a sense, the next subchapter deconstructs Foucauldian epistemes by noting their inherent instability. I hope that the next subchapter's working hypothesis concerning the episteme applies the resources of much already existing critical energy and sheds light on the seventies by bringing to bear upon the era itself the uncanny criticism the decade directed toward itself.

3 Epistemes

Michel Foucault's *The Order of Things* (1967) uses the term "episteme" to de-scribe an era's prevailing mind-set, its epistemological horizons. "By episteme," says Foucault in *The Archaeology of Knowledge,* "we mean, in fact, the total set of relations that unite, at a given period, the discursive practices that give rise to epistemological figures, sciences, and possibly formalized systems. . . . It is the totality of relations that can be discovered, for a given period."[26] Like a fractal or DNA strand, all patterns within one part of an episteme can be found within any other part of that episteme. For instance, according to Foucault, in the Middle Ages, knowledge proceeded from a literal relation between language and thing. This literal manner of association helps to explain how all kinds of knowledge are formulated. In a similar fashion, *The Order of Things* identifies several epistemes for other historical eras and the "breaks" between them.

Later in his career, Foucault, mindful of their reductive limitations, placed epistemes in the background of his work. He shied away from the concept of epistemes in favor of considerations of cultural "discourses" that change during particular historical moments. Foucault examined social phenomena as progressions of discursive formations. In particular, he studied the "dis-cursive" phenomena of social regimentation and sexuality. Using the avenues of his chosen objects of discourse, Foucault likened these explorations to ar-chaeological digs into history. This method allowed Foucault more adroitly to consider shorter increments of time.

This book employs both Foucauldian objects of study: the episteme and the matrix of the discursive subject. I study discourses and disciplines such as the nature of the state, the presidency, spatial reality, and the individual. However, to detect and connect small changes among discourses, I apply Fou-cault's notion of the episteme to shorter periods of time, micro-periods, to coin a term, of only two or three years, whereas *The Order of Things* considered epistemes that lasted considerably more than a century. Epistemes graduate through micro-periods without losing their dominant discursive characteris-tics. For instance, roughly speaking, I micro-periodize the seventies into 1970–71, 1972–74, 1975–77, and 1978–79. As important as Foucault's larger divisions might be, shorter divisions seem valid and important to our ability to under-stand how different facets of post–World War II culture relate. The different periods of post–World War II America "read" like important distinctions within an unclearly connected story.

As with Foucault, the spans that I discuss in this book have indefinite beginnings and endings. However, whereas Foucault considered these periodic border times and hybrid moments as breaks that indicate shifts between epistemes, I employ this indefiniteness in distinguishing epistemes, this juxtaposition of epistemes, as constituent of the epistemes themselves. Notably, Foucault never could explain changes between epistemes. Perhaps this is paradoxically because change is so prevalent. As Darwin employed changes in the features of species to reassess the Aristotelian notion of a species even though the changelessness of each species was crucial to Aristotle, I use change as a way of unhinging the ostensibly fixed category of the episteme. Like species, epistemes are always in transition. Epistemes change as our present perspectives change. An episteme is distinguishable but shifting and admixed. Epistemes use synchronic perspectives but are not limited to synchronic views. After all, a narrative, which all historical explanations must in some sense be, must suggest change.[27]

I use the term "rippling epistemes" to convey how the mind-sets of eras intertwine with one another and make each other possible. This ripple, or relational space between eras that occupies no fixed time, actually composes eras. Relations between eras *are* eras. For instance, the "eighties" could not exist as we know it without an appeal to the informing realities of a socially compliant aspect of the fifties and a laissez-faire, commercially deregulated aspect of the pre-Depression, New Deal twenties—both seen through a sixties sense of malleable reality. Each era in this eighties cocktail has other characteristic features. Seemingly contradictory phenomena within an episteme interrelate. Although of course very related, the epistemic notion of a period is not the same as the chronological period. Epistemes fashion and are fashioned by the informing contents of other epistemes. Epistemes might express themselves through and depend on chronological time, but epistemes nonetheless have a life of their own. They ripple. A theory of rippling epistemes will clarify how the totality of one era, its mind-set or episteme, affects another era and the phenomena within that era.

As much as the analysis of data, epistemes are the material of historians, the clay of historical sense. They are the virtual clay that allows us to sculpt an era, the intermediary between an era's reception and the active "writing" of an era, where history and writerly creation come together. Epistemes give historians a base from which to sift data. They form a ground for the sense that history ultimately is.

Rather than maintaining a monolithic unity between events, artifacts, and documents, I am putting forth frames that permit dialogue and that when drawn together present a dramatic illusion that is always open to revision. In a sense, this is no different from what any critic or historian is called upon to do. This study's method merely accounts for the inevitable writerly nature of any history, as it insists on the strong possibility of history's own writerly nature—that is, a period's strong connections with certain oppositions, conditions, and features that shape its semiotic production.[28]

History, therefore, can be treated in a semiotic fashion, by conceptualizing years, eras, decades, periods, epochs, and cultures not as definitive but at least as heuristic devices and at best as ripples in the fabric of the current episteme carried by the zeitgeist. Keeping in mind these complications, I offer this sketch with the proviso that its value depends on its use in the reading of cultural phenomena.

Broadly speaking, I posit a rift in American mind-sets during the sixties that other aspects of American culture appropriate for diametrically different ideological ends in the seventies, laying a ground for the Reaganism of the eighties. The "seventies" surveys and catalogs the influence of the "sixties" through trial and error, ambivalently reconsidering older (ostensibly pre-sixties) organizing mechanisms. To risk oversimplifying, the sixties and a naive sense of the fifties, or pre-sixties, are reimagined through one another. Note the sense of discovery in "The Task," the first poem in Ashbery's 1970 volume of sixties poetry, The Double Dream of Spring:

> And the way is clear
> Now for linear acting into that time
> In whose corrosive mass he first discovered how to breathe.[29]

During the seventies, prior periods begin, in a sense, to be syndicated like television reruns. Time seems to slow down. It almost seems as if recent history were being surveyed and cataloged.[30] In the early seventies, the comedian George Carlin, alluding to cultural phenomena such as the television program Happy Days and the various hit remakes of fifties rock singles, said that if there were a seventies revival it would need to include a fifties revival. In fact, ongoing nostalgia for and cynical mockery of the seventies, such as nostalgia for the mid-seventies heavy metal that is appreciated at a Texas high school in the film Dazed and Confused (1993) and renewed interest in mainstream disco music as depicted in new style seventies bars and in the November 1992 two-hour NBC special "A Seventies Celebration," center on the middle and late seventies, when it was possible to recycle the sixties, if only, at times, as a turn from or reaction against it. Although decades tend to distinguish themselves most in their latter years, it is nevertheless difficult to imagine the same intensity of nostalgia for the early seventies as the early sixties and the early fifties because the sixties too powerfully overshadow the early seventies. By the mid-seventies the influence of the sixties was increasingly experienced as stifling, and the latter half of the decade is thus more identifiable. However, we paradoxically remember the late seventies with early seventies styles. (The media associates the seventies fashions that have recently been revived with the mainstream disco culture of the late seventies. However, platform shoes, extreme skirt lengths, lace-up boots, and chokers in fact became prominent during the very late sixties and the very early seventies.) Seventies nostalgia thus asserts a kind of anxiety of influence with the sixties by using but not acknowledging the nearness of its influence. If the late seventies, having cleared a space from the influence of the sixties, forecast an eighties repression of an awareness of bad times for most Americans and an assertion of the "These Are the Good Times" attitude of the 1979 Sister Sledge song, the sixties ambivalently engage the early and mid-seventies. In brief, the early seventies nervously tangle with the romantic influence of the sixties, and the mid-seventies open territory for an alternative to the sixties with the sacrifice of a presidency and all its attendant ontological baggage, while the late seventies, through simultaneous Carteresque melancholy and the unrelenting elation of disco grooves, is drawn to a new and stronger denial—a wish for something both industrial and non-capitalistic. Neither the gap in reality (a kind of sixties reality) or pre-sixties certitudes cancel one another out, but both rather exist unintegrated side by side.

To grasp the overlapping epistemes of the sixties and the seventies means better understanding epistemes and focusing upon them as phenomena in themselves, although, significantly, interrelated. This does not deny that everyone's sixties and seventies are different, but merely maintains that there are certain "family resemblances" in these perspectives, and these family resemblances are, although open to interpretation, not tepid generalities but intense, if dialogic, cultural signifiers. Causal explanations are not in themselves sufficient to explain these epistemes. Nor are demographics. Rather, the phenomenon of the sixties is part of the general logic of the Cold War and a not entirely repressed ambivalence about accepting it.

Often the long shadow of the sixties is attributed to the post–World War II baby boomer generation's nostalgia for its youth. However, even if the baby boomer generation is still demographically dominant, it does not follow that it should have fixated upon its youth. The generation that was born after World War I did not cling as much to the culture of its youth, and neither did it have the same pervasive influence or succeed in imparting its culture to its young.

The preponderance of so many young people in itself does not explain the sixties. After all, all youths are not alike. If sixties culture is noted for its social and artistic innovations and "youthful" protests, there is nonetheless no reason why the young are necessarily characterized by these qualities since young people are also known for deferring.

It might be argued that aging baby boomers fixate on the sixties when they have more disposable income and time. However, this does not explain why their children still relate to sixties-based music and live in an anxiety of sixties' influence. Should not then post-sixties youth have taken over as a more leading consumer group in place of the boomers? Stylistic revolts by nineties youths still employ fifties-dominated punk styles that apparently opposed sixties styles. At times they seemed to be protesting the central place of the sixties in a marketplace they have little hope of leaving.

For example, the film *Reality Bites* (1994), marking out an epistemic turf for twenty-somethings in the nineties, posits itself in contradistinction to the heritage of the sixties. The film begins with a valedictorian's indictment of the ideals and practices of the baby boomer generation, and then goes on to claim the music of and nostalgia for the seventies as its own. The film refers to such seventies phenomena as the television situation comedy *One Day at a Time*, the theme song to the Saturday morning program *Schoolhouse Rock*, and various hits of the decade like "My Sharona." The film's characters, however, would have been young children during the seventies. Of course, *Reality Bites*, like the seventies period piece *Dazed and Confused* (1993) that was marketed to nineties youth, represents an urge for members of another generation to find comfort in reminders of their childhoods. And yet by this same logic, college students and recent college graduates of the late sixties would have valorized fifties culture. Even the teenagers of the mid-seventies, as indicated by the characters of *Dazed and Confused*, consume recent cultural productions. Seventies youth culture indirectly revolted against the sixties by endorsing contemporaneous cultural productions that were rawer, in terms of style and attitude, such as punk, than the preceding idealisms of the sixties. The characters in *Reality Bites* still oppose the sixties, which anchors a kind of pre-history for the so-called Generation X as depicted in the film. *Reality Bites* is marketed to offer a demographic group's consolidated historical perspectives on each period that it lived through since infancy. It is a kind of prepackaged archaeological dig. The enabling yet anxiously felt unconscious of the mind creating this dig could be said to be the sixties and agons, or conflicts, between the sixties, the fifties, and the seventies. The grunge look that the film fixes on as contemporaneously early nineties can be said to layer and to codify stereotypical beatnik, hippie, and punk styles. Similarly, the Seattle-style rock that the band of the moment plays pays homage to sixties-style studio sound, the driving beat of seventies punk, and early sixties and fifties "unplugged" sounds, reminding us that to become unelectronic is just one choice of switches among many upon current electronic instruments. The eighties witnessed the bloom of the synthesizer; nineties music absorbs its antithetical impulse within that bloom.

After the sixties an immense cultural archive was put into place. Fortunes were made in the syndication of old television programs and the marketing of old records. The "new" now invariably invokes various aspects of a sixties-marked archive. The nineties grunge look would seem to demonstrate that the sixties do not age as much as put on layers. However, while the terms of the nineties "Generation X" may have been set in the sixties and seventies, the sixties are perhaps more an outgrowth of World War II than the fifties. The sixties were made possible by middle and late forties federal planning, such as the highway system and the GI Bill, that facilitated the dominance of nuclear families. The post–World War II generation was to be relatively stress-free and privileged, something new and special. In the words of Dalton Trumbo's script for *A Guy Named Joe* (1943), Americans saw their offspring as something like "a generation of angels" for which World War II was being fought.

If the youth culture had been facilitated by forties federal planning, it was distinguished as a group in the fifties as a prime advertising market of unformed consumer preferences and ready cash. Hence, the sixties was a surprise because this youth culture seemed suddenly to speak for itself in a manner that commanded "official" attention. Although mediated by activists and artists, the episteme of the sixties was derived from consumer culture and was in fact immediately merchandised. But in itself it was something else. The forces of the marketplace helped bring sixties culture together and then sold that culture, but the phenomenon of the sixties was a kind of Frankenstein monster that defied the commercial codifications that helped constitute it. Youth culture identified with the American artistic counterculture (which became the world's preeminent avant-garde after European artists fled Europe), the world disarmament movement, and the black civil rights movement. Sixties yearnings for alternatives to a capitalist-driven society seemed too real, and it is easy to see why, to leaders like Nixon, the youth counterculture of the late sixties and early seventies conveyed anarchy. Dominant epistemic trends changed in the seventies. The seventies inevitably refer to the sixties and, since much of America experienced "the sixties" in the seventies, in a sense *were* them, but, because commercial codification was such a central aspect of the seventies and a peripheral quality of the sixties, the seventies also broke from the sixties as it gave the sixties a kind of demographic weight. The sixties take shape as they lose impetus. For sixties counterculture, the sixties seem to concern an almost apocalyptic hope and potential, but, since the seventies, the sixties must to some degree be seen as a historical climax and, paradoxically, the stuff of nostalgia. In a sense, the chronological sixties itself were lived after the fact. The Haight-Ashbury Diggers mourned "the death of the hippie" and commercialization of their community and movement ("if you are going to San Francisco, be sure to wear some flowers in your hair," love beads, head shops, etc.) in the spring of 1967, before the summer of love.

Unable to find a convincing historical resolution, the culture of the baby boom generation remains largely associated with its youth status. Prefiguring this, Bob Dylan's 1967 song "Tears of Rage" notes, "We pointed out a way for you to go / But you thought it was nothing more than a place for you to stand." Somehow the sixties have come to mean an era that did not fructify. An era that was to be a beginning of the end of history becomes the beginning of a rather cool, indefinite kind of history.

We often think of the "the sixties" as the late sixties, but it could have been predicted that the hopes of the sixties were doomed as soon as Robert Kennedy was assassinated with a year and a half of the sixties remaining. Caught between its front and rear views, its expectations and its aftermath, the sixties is a ripple between them. Because the expectations and the aftermath of the sixties are so incommensurate, this ripple does not subside.

Eras are inextricably linked to their documentations, that is, how they are registered both at the time and in the future. After all, the word "era" is derived from the Latin for a counting device that was used to record quantities of money, commodities, and sporting scores. As Sonny and Cher, in the midsixties, sang: "History turns another page / Electronically they keep a baseball score / The beat goes on," noting that the concepts of counting and accounting are mutually generative. We must either account for our historicizations or mindlessly historicize, to, as David Jauss says in *For a Theory of Reception,* bump our heads against our "horizons of expectation."

The etymology of "era" sheds light on why eras seem to fit all too nicely into decades. We use the turning of decades to note previously perceived, desired, and feared cultural changes. For instance, in his 1960 presidential campaign, John F. Kennedy explicitly played upon expectations for the beginning of what was already termed "the sixties" to render his vision of the New Frontier more credible and attractive. "We stand today on the edge of a new frontier— the frontier of the 1960's, a frontier of unknown opportunities and paths, a frontier of unfulfilled hopes and threats,"[31] said Kennedy in his acceptance speech at the Los Angeles Democratic National Convention. "We are moving into the most challenging, the most dynamic, the most revolutionary period of our existence—the 1960's," the candidate elaborated later in his campaign. "The next ten years will be years of incredible growth and change—years of unprecedented tasks."[32] Not only is it difficult to separate the era from its documentations; it is also difficult to separate it from its expectations.

Noting the rippling effect of epistemes is particularly important in understanding the seventies, a decade that is commonly seen as a bridge between the sixties and eighties. But this bridge is crucial to the composition of what it connects and how we understand these entities. We need to account for the quivering ripple within the more recognizable waves of epistemes. The difficulty in this is that the connecting ripple between eras is an action with an indefinite beginning and end, if any beginning and end. It is more difficult to describe than the eras themselves. "The spaces between things keep getting bigger and more important,"[33] says the poet John Ashbery. Indeed, since the entire seventies is sometimes seen as something like a connecting ripple, or an undecade, an "uncanny criticism" is called for. "Uncanny criticism" is not so concerned with cause and effect as it is with readings that become possible by noting relationships between phenomena. It is, for example, only by noting the relationships between characteristic means of "escaping from reality" in the sixties and escaping from reality as we understand it in terms of the eighties that we can see how committed the seventies was to its own formulations of the real. "Uncanny criticism" does not exclude discussions of the agency of "cause" but merely incorporates cause and effect into the total picture. Cause and effect exist more as inflections than as dominant keys. For example, the credibility gap related to the Vietnam War may well be the most important underlying "cause" of Watergate. Nevertheless, this formulation will be misleading if we do not see the war and the scandal as related phenomena that enunciate relevant discourses related to government and the populace's responses to its workings. Watergate shaped how we might understand the significance of our prior involvement in Southeast Asia. Only by understanding the seventies as a ripple can we come to grips with the decade.

4   Rippling Nixons

A brief discussion of Richard Nixon will illustrate this rippling effect. More than the Cold War itself, Nixon helped fabricate and manipulate a Cold War episteme. If the Cold War can be called an actual series of events, its episteme is the Cold War's informing potential. The Cold War occurred within an enabling state of mind I am calling the Cold War episteme. A Cold War episteme puts notions of existence and nonexistence into binary opposition, to wit, nuclear annihilation versus the survival of humankind.

The Cold War episteme is different from the Cold War in that the episteme describes the Cold War stance as a dominant configuration of knowing. This episteme plays on and is in some sense a part of the sobering calls to reality of the episteme(s) of World War I, the Depression, and World War II. However, the Cold War episteme contains an indefinite sense of a pervasive *unseen* enemy. The post–World War I Communist scare was more tied to overt xenophobia and anti-labor interests, and it did not produce the same search for spies and unlikely suspects as post–World War II anti-Communism. Causally speaking, the development of nuclear weapons and the production of apparently deadly secrets about them made more plausible the threat of a total catastrophe that could be perpetuated by a few spies. The United States developed the bomb out of a commitment to its necessary involvement in world affairs, and a World War II state of mind subsequently carried it into the Cold War.

Each post–World War II period—the late forties, the fifties, the sixties, the seventies, the eighties, and the nineties—in some way reinterprets this Cold War episteme and correspondingly seems to call for another Nixon. New Nixons correspond to new phases of the Cold War and, reciprocally, Nixon's career is a thread through which post–World War II America intertwines. In the late forties, Nixon helped imprint the Cold War upon electoral politics with an innovative red-baiting congressional campaign that equated New Deal progressivism with socialism and Communism. Nixon understood that the Soviet Union gave Republicans the perfect enemy with which to pry middle-class voters from the

New Deal coalition. Then Nixon's Alger Hiss investigation introduced the Cold War into the internal workings of American government, unnerving the liberal foreign-policy establishment.

Nixon used the Cold War to search for an appropriate national enemy and judiciously oscillated between domestic and foreign enemies. As we shall soon see, he deepened the ideological ends of the Cold War. Preceding the anti-Communist efforts of Senator Joseph McCarthy, Nixon did not allow himself to get mired in a grossly overdetermined anti-Communism. Red-baiting and Cold War dread were rather tools for Nixon to signify urgency and crisis[34] that he could be called on to counteract in a more than hysterical fashion. The Cold War constructed the stage that Nixon could play upon, and as vice-president, Nixon played with relish the roles of statesman and foreign policy expert.

If the Hiss case put the young Nixon in the vanguard of articulating how America's enemies might be among us, later in his career, by focusing on the threat from the outside, he could be less divisive, give his patriotism a more positive team-oriented tone, and stress the successes rather than the failures of the United States. For example, Nixon jumped at the chance to celebrate American consumer abundance by parrying Nikita Khrushchev's doubts in their famed 1959 Moscow trade exposition "Kitchen Debate." Nixon was able to make Khrushchev appear naive for not being able to imagine the veracity of America's household consumer accomplishments.[35]

In a sense, Nixon helped change an accent in the relationship between normality and the Cold War. For Nixon, the negative became positive. We might think of extreme Cold War peril as enforcing the norm in American society and behavior (fifties counterculture lying outside the norm and fifties youth culture lying outside the official) for the supposed purpose of more easily detecting those who might place the nation in peril. However, the Cold War also gave an oppositional term for a positive sense of freedom to rally itself around. Many Americans saw the nation as a kind of peaceful army of predominantly "nuclear" families. A more peaceable Cold War stance with the post-Stalinist Soviet Union unconsciously recognized that Americans were more normally preoccupied in a loosely controlled organization of official, consumer reality than in war.

Like Nixon, John Kennedy also perceived a two-pronged Cold War application. In 1960, Kennedy "out-Cold Warred" Nixon on the front of peace, by promising to make the economy grow faster than Eisenhower thought it wise, and on the front of war, by blaming the Republicans for the United States' supposed nuclear missile disadvantage to the Soviet Union—the famously trumped up "missile gap."[36] It is important to note that Kennedy simply played his Cold War hand better. He made the Cold War seem more vibrant.

Nixon was momentarily stunned by his Cold War demotion. If his decision to run in the 1962 California gubernatorial election was less than inspired, he nonetheless later applied what he learned in an unusual context. Edmund Brown defeated Nixon by questioning his credentials as a local politician.[37] Interestingly, when Nixon ran for president again in 1968, he centered his campaign on what had previously been thought to be a local issue—law and order, but, as we shall see, with a Cold War twist.

A prolonged overheating of the Cold War gave Nixon his opportunity to return to electoral politics when, while not overtly backing the war in his 1968 presidential campaign, and downplaying his long-standing and strong commitment to the Vietnam War, Nixon was able to find the enemy in Vietnam War dissenters, youth culture, "drugs," and, in general, the enemies of "law and order." To many Americans, these groups were out-of-control forces of confusion that were somehow intermingled with the war itself. For Nixon, the enemy was once again within America.

As president, Nixon knew that if he could use the Cold War he could use the sense of an end of it. He tested the horizons of the episteme. Seeing that the original conditions of the Cold War (Communism vs. the Free World) had served their purpose, it was almost as if Nixon had one foot in and one foot almost but not quite out of the Cold War. By the seventies, Americans tired of the Cold War together with the Vietnam War. If the Cold War's major fruit was the Vietnam War, the Cold War must have been somewhat overblown. And if China could be a hated enemy one minute and virtually an ally the next, the Cold War must have been somewhat contrived.

Nixon was able to divert many Americans' attentions from the Vietnam War by promising that it, along with the draft and the captivity of Vietnam prisoners of war, would end in the foreseeable future. He neutralized dissent by gradually removing the draft issue[38] and declaring new American war initiatives top secret. Secrecy and the control of information became more important than powers of persuasion. As Nixon wished to turn our gazes away from Vietnam, he turned his gaze to his "personal" enemies and in the process became both America's model self-surveyor and self-enemy. Eventually, he virtually unified America in opposition to him. Nixon was a kind of human sacrifice to a shift from perceiving Communists as the chief American enemy to casting the federal government in this light. After all, what could Americans say about a system that caused them to vote overwhelmingly for a disgraced president like Nixon?

The subtlety of Nixon's game of shifting enemies caught up to him. Nonetheless, it was because of his subtlety that his career did not expire like that of his imitator Joseph McCarthy. Nixon noted a dialectic in the Cold War between the internal and external enemy that in turn helped shape the characteristic periods of post–World War II America. His last writings implore us to extend Cold War fears and crises into every corner of the globe. The prospect of terrorism renders Cold War dualism unnecessary. If terror can erupt anywhere at any time, we cannot object to the powers that will inevitably protect themselves as they protect us. Surveillance is justified as being against them and not us. This urgency means that government as a national security state must supersede government as a care and service provider. In a sense, the Cold War does not end; it becomes more vigilant.

If Nixon alleviated tensions with the Soviet Union and China and, after five years in office, brought American troops home from Vietnam, he never conveyed a sense that the crisis at home was over. Moreover, he insisted on tighter and tighter controls over foreign policy. Interestingly, the possibility of future challenges to Nixon's foreign policy, in the wake of the release of the *Pentagon Papers* that in itself did not concern him, led to the formation of the "plumbers," who perpetrated the Watergate break-in and indirectly precipitated Nixon's fall. Nonetheless, even after his humiliation, exile, and death, he is continually evoked as a marker of presidential scandal and failure while in some ways also being a model of the last state-of-the-art, self-motivated, world-affecting president. Perhaps this is because no one more than Nixon embodied the Cold War while not being contained by it.

5   America Self-Identified

Perhaps it was unfortunate, perhaps it was not inevitable, but Nixon was our secret self. In an uncanny fashion, he came to represent America. He undid himself through self-surveillance. One might say he found himself to lose himself. In the same way and at the same time, the great American middle class gradually lost its New Deal tradition of social and economic progress in favor of stronger identifications with narrow self-definitions and interests.

Nixon helped halt the progressive thrust of the sixties by weakening such Great Society–related programs gathered under the umbrella of the Office of

Economic Opportunity as the Job Corps, Neighborhood Youth Corps, VISTA, Head Start, Upward Bound, and the Community Action Program. Nixon allocated fewer and fewer funds to OEO in his budget recommendations, underspent funds passed in the final budgets, and appointed administrators to scuttle the office. His nominee for OEO director, Howard Phillips, actually began dismantling OEO because Nixon's fiscal year 1974 budget omitted all OEO funding. A federal court needed to order Phillips to stop the destruction on the grounds that budgets must first, of course, be passed by Congress.

In effect, the Nixon administration sacrificed the workings of government to the virtual fetishizing of information about its own control and production. Drawing only from those groups it needed to form an easily addressed majority, the administration narrowed its constituency and frame of reference. In this process, Nixon helped to coalesce a so-called silent majority of various white ethnic groups into their white, respectively ethnic, *and* American majority identities. He helped make it fashionably American to "return" to "white" self-identities that earlier in the century American society only problematically accepted as white. We may note that Michael Novak's *The Rise of Unmeltable Ethnics* (1972) stressed both a pride in Polish, Italian, Greek, and Slavic ancestries and flag-waving American patriotism, maintaining that they reinforced one another as important group identities.

The school busing issue served to mobilize forces to protect the dominant ethnicity of many school districts. In 1956, although Eisenhower did not favor forced integration of public schools, he spoke for a consensus when he ordered federal troops into Little Rock to enforce the Supreme Court's anti-segregation ruling. Eisenhower simply could not stomach the Court being disobeyed. In the fifties, for Eisenhower, the reality of the law was sacrosanct. He would not allow the law to be so publicly ignored. However, in the seventies, for Nixon, the law was less important than observing the reality of popular convention, and he declared a 1972 moratorium on the enforcement of court-ordered busing. When busing was finally implemented again in 1974, Irish and Italian ethnicities in Boston vigorously asserted themselves against the court mandate and African Americans.

Nixon also indirectly reinforced minority self-identifications. Since the "majority" seemed increasingly intractable, there seemed to be little alternative but to practice minority politics. Focusing upon a group's chosen interests seemed more practical than an appeal to the higher sentiments of the American people. With the 1964 Civil Rights Act's outlawing of Jim Crow, overt discrimination became less of a civil rights issue than covert discrimination, and most Americans had little interest in proactively addressing deep-seated issues of economic inequality and veiled bigotry. Hence, if a minority group did not sensitize the nation to its problems and interests, no one else would. Indeed, the work that was done in identity-politics was obviously beneficial if we concede that there is in some respects more appreciation of non-dominant cultures.

If minority identity is good and necessary, it becomes limiting when it works against the forming of beneficial coalitions. As I argued in the second section of this chapter, it makes sense that every identity-position would in some way mediate every other identity-position. After all, we are all connected to a marketplace that does not allow absolute divisions between groups.

Every identity is a site upon which the culture at large works. Identities influence one another, as the many "powers" that follow black power testify to. Baby boomers (those born up to ten years after World War II) are also a minority that has significantly affected the marketplace. If a pervasive theme of the seventies was the finding of identities, on another level, during the seventies, the baby boom generation assimilated itself into the marketplace at the same moment that it changed the nation's mores. Of course, in terms of marketing, the baby boomers are a statistically important consumer group, but they are still a minority with an effect even beyond its numbers. They affect our concepts of "identity" and "lifestyle." Since "lifestyle" is a word coined in the seventies to describe a contextualized sense of self-identity, lifestyle connotes malleable identity and identity as a kind of consumer item. Indeed, helping produce consumer groups is a kind of primary production of capitalism. If capitalism feeds off the production of demand, cultural diversity should serve it well. Ultimately, capitalism and diversity tend to form a symbiotic relationship, and this awareness strengthens diversity's lever upon capitalism.

If many baby boomers got to know who they were as seemingly mainstream, perhaps mall-frequenting American consumers, nonetheless, mainstream America could be dissected into diverse demographic groups. Demographics flourished in the seventies. Americans were broken up into urban professional singles, young suburban housewives, retired senior citizens, and so on. Others who identified themselves outside the mainstream were easier to find and address through their more distinctive media selections. They could be narrowcast to with more affordable press and media-time purchases. Paradoxically, as Americans became more "identified" with fixed identities (black, white, lesbian, gay, straight, women, men, physically challenged, ethnic white, athletic cultured, girl cultured, boy cultured, deaf cultured, Native American, single cultured, Latino, Asian American, preteen cultured, urban, and *ad nauseam*), they became easier to address as members of a loosely unified American economy. How one fashioned oneself became a decision that dictated one's activities. Often, exploration has ceased to matter except to corroborate one's prior conclusions or to valorize oneself over other groups.

We cannot afford the illusion of entirely "privatized" self-identities. This plays into the hands of large market forces by making us easier to reach and manipulate. Limiting self-identity traps us. The Nixon administration's surveillance operations demonstrated a similarly somewhat short-sighted self-absorption. If Americans turn away from the government and privatize their identities and means of information gathering, so did Nixon. The "plumbers" group was put together because Nixon needed his own private surveillance outfit. He could not twist the FBI and CIA entirely to his own ends, although he tried to gain greater control over them. Indeed, Nixon's surveillance operations were unique. Past presidents had made Oval Office recordings, but Nixon was the first president to record everything. His recording system was voice-activated.

Presidents generally need to negotiate with entrenched Washington career politicians. After Nixon's reelection, he would not accept this, wishing to have unchecked power over every facet of the administrative branch of government, using the threat of IRS audits and other pressures to accomplish this. Even though his ambitions were "grand," he was subsumed by the narrowness of his own sense of who he was. It is important to note that had Nixon become president in 1961 and acted similarly, his behavior might never have come to our attention. In a sense, the seventies was Nixon's time, the time for his narrow all-inclusiveness to be profoundly representative, not just merely a symbol of a dominant group, as he might have been in the early sixties.

Like Nixon, Americans undid themselves through self-surveillance. An illusory ethos of self-sufficiency developed that inhibited meaningful coalitions from forming. Questions of identity hindered less debatable issues of vested interests. Seemingly natural economic allies were divided. More and more Americans turned from an interest in broadly collective action, and throughout the seventies, progressive politics increasingly lost its agency—a unified government that the electorate trusts to help the poor, regulate the marketplace, educate and train Americans of all ages, guarantee health care, and credibly protect American domestic and international security. When, in his first inaugural address, Ronald Reagan said that government was the problem rather than the solution, it had a strong ring of truth for most Americans. Strangely, government itself became the government's scapegoat. Even if Jimmy Carter had been reelected in 1980 (putting aside that he lost in a landslide), many Americans clearly expected less from their federal government. By the end of the seventies, a white majority previously nurtured by Nixon felt that the government could not represent it. It is almost as if they abandoned a national project that sustained itself from World War II until the Vietnam War. Oddly, the late sixties lie in the dead center of the Cold War era.

In the seventies, America moved toward a resolution of the Cold War "realities" of itself as the world's only good and potent nation-state, theoretically holding a place for all its citizens and threatened only by citizens and residents who, for unfathomable reasons, would not accept that place. This Cold War put modes of self-definition into play that were eventually somewhat suspended in the sixties and returned to in complicated fashions during the sixties' denouement in the seventies and the eighties, when identity-politics were instituted by minority groups to consolidate and further civil rights gains, as well as by "whites" who posited themselves as ideologically unmarked so as to fight minority politics.

At the Cold War's inception, much ideological work that centered around the expanded role of American citizenship in the world was required to sell expenditures for the Cold War to a post–World War II America that was weary of international confrontation. It was not difficult to pass the black hat from the time of the Nazis to the Communists, or, for intellectuals, "Stalinists." The prewar purges, the murder of Jan Masaryk, and other Communist brutalities contributed to this casting. (Western brutalities, of course, in Latin America, Asia, Algeria, and elsewhere went unreported.) However, an even larger dose of Communist villainization was required in the face of the demand for demobilization that followed World War II and the unwanted costs of arming for and fighting against foreign Communist foes. It was much less expensive to invent American Communist spies and other internal security threats (even during World War II, there was little opposition to the racially motivated Japanese internment camps), coinciding with a redefinition of American citizenship and the seemingly perverse dangers of those who seemed to oppose its values, as exhibited, for instance, by President Harry Truman's 1947 Executive Order 9835, setting up secret "loyalty boards" to pass judgment on federal government employees accused of disloyalty. This redefinition of citizenship culminated, during the Korean War, with the emerging prominence of the as yet unnamed military industrial complex. The American World War II effort, which, especially during and after its ending, had come to replace a New Deal sense of national cooperation and definition, was in turn replaced by a hope for and view of postwar prosperity in the light of the Cold War.

Eventually, the military industrial complex was able to reuse the dire good-versus-evil confrontation of World War II. This application created a prevalent illusory world outlook that, with the Soviet Union's explosion of its first atomic bomb in 1949, was paradoxically predicated on the "bottom line" need to prevent the world's nuclear destruction through the stockpiling of thermonuclear devices and the unacknowledged public works project of defense spending. However, in the sixties, the Vietnam War threw into doubt the Cold War impulse to contain Communism.

This undermining of Cold War reality could not help but cause Americans to question who they were and what they identified with. To be "American" no longer meant the same thing. If intellectuals and the counterculture questioned who they were in the fifties, this questioning was clearly more pervasive in the sixties. Not surprisingly, the seventies saw a trend toward at least temporarily clarifying identities. However, economically, socially, and politically, seventies America did not recapture the imagined security of the fifties, and there were complications.

It is almost as if, in the seventies, American culture, to steady itself after the sixties, walked toward a metaphoric wall of relative certainty and self-identity, only to find itself walking through that wall. Ambivalence about surer realities predominated. Past certainties were again accepted, but with qualifications. "I know it's only rock and roll," ruminated the Rolling Stones in 1974, "but I like it." "Two out of three ain't bad," argued Meatloaf—it is enough that he might love and need you—you shouldn't want to possess him. Reflective of the rising divorce rate of the seventies, the Carpenters, who performed the most popular early-seventies wedding songs, approached marriage uncertainly. "For all we know," Karen Carpenter mulled, "Love may grow." Stephen Stills sang, "If you can't be with the one you love, love the one you're with." From a transatlantic vantage point, Elton John bid good-bye to the yellow brick road, and John Lennon, resettled in New York, announced with a depth and grace of tone unparalleled in any other recorded vocal of his that "the dream is over." "I was the Walrus," he sang in "God," "But now I'm John . . . You'll just have to carry on." The collective fantasy of the Beatles was replaced by the minority politics of allegiances to particular ex-Beatles.

Identity-positions drove seemingly irrefutable awareness of one's place in the world, but were also seen as fringe. As various "others" were formulated into seventies politics, a self-avowed mainstream politics organized itself around an opposition to these so-called others. At the height of the sixties, the consensus of conservative national power in the United States was forged through an alliance between the ruling class and the working middle class. In the thirties, Walter Benjamin similarly noted, "fascism attempts to organize the newly created proletarian masses without affecting the property structure which the masses strive to eliminate."[39] Hegemony increasingly appropriates newly charged minority politics that seek reality in the individual's identification with a distinguishing feature. For instance, the seventies saw the establishment of individual desire to wear apparel with prominent consumer product logos. The inverse—the organized circulation of personalized graffiti on subway cars and other public spaces—was repressed. By the eighties, graffiti-proof cars were standard.

In the seventies, identity took on a special meaning within gay politics wherein self-identification was in itself, before Stonewall, an unusual and somewhat radical act. And yet, in the nineties, Eve Kosofsky Sedgwick and others have demonstrated the improvisatory, ephemeral character of coming-out itself. Various feminist critics seek to theorize female identity within a loose system of cultural differences. Identity-politics are increasingly less shielded from deconstructive, detotalizing critical energies. For instance, by the early nineties, seminars abound devoted to problematizing minority identifications, and *October* and *Social Text* devote entire issues to the subject.

Nonetheless, it remains to be seen whether or not these questionings about identity are not testaments to how entangled we are in it. To tell the story of the seventies is difficult because it requires the relating of seemingly unrelated identities. If the seventies was the decade of "definite identities," the decade itself is particularly hard to identify. After all, no one identity seemed representative. Moreover, the seventies were caught between two more identifiable decades. In the sixties, youth culture seemed prominent although not representative, and in the eighties a paradoxically free-spending conservative culture seemed dominant. But what were the seventies? Half sixties and half eighties? The seventies were the undecade that was perhaps the most important decade. It will require an inventive history that can see agency dispersed between phenomena and eras and an uncanny criticism that can interpret relationships to get the seventies to yield its cultural relevance. Paradoxically, we need the problematic of cultural theory to concretize the seventies and the present. To accomplish this, I call for "theory" that is concrete since it can rely upon close reading that is tied to a synchronic view of period that can be further historicized through the concept of epistemes that ripple. As Richard Rorty has declared the death of philosophy as a discipline that is insulated from general questions of culture, perhaps we are beginning to recognize that literary criticism, though it may contain valuable analytical tools and fields of reference, is misleading when confined to its own discipline and literature— just as a particular identity-politics agenda may be a dead end when its concerns are limited to one "identity."

6 Personal Perspectives

"The seventies—weren't they the Reagan years?" asks Ralph Berger, a retired liquor store owner and newspaper advertisement salesman in his own seventies, when I ask for his impressions of the decade. I remind him that the eighties were the Reagan years, and he recalls that the seventies were "that nothing time." Nevertheless, he characterizes the period positively. The seventies, he says, was "an even-keeled time" in which the nation recovered from "the revolutions of the sixties." Then, says Ralph, inflation ruined the refreshing calm. He blames inflation on Jimmy Carter's governmental overspending in his vain attempt to be reelected.

I disagree with some of Ralph's facts and perspectives. Nonetheless, I hope that my history of the seventies accommodates Ralph's views. I have tried to write a cultural history that layers historical perspectives and touches the limits of our historical perceptions. Anyone's views are relevant to my study, not because of a democratic impulse but because all historical perspectives are part of what "happened" in the decade. Moreover, despite how different personal perspectives of the seventies are, they are related. For most, the seventies proceeded from a complex fabric of events, trends, and fads to a malaise of possibilities.

Ralph believes that "the craziness" returned with Carter and that we have not yet recovered, and, similarly, Mario Mezzacappa, a poet who was born in 1973, believes that "everything is retro." Everyone who is his age, he says, wants to know what happened. The past is still doing the work of the future. The future becomes the business of copying the past. However, like Ralph, Mario recalls the seventies pleasantly. For Mario, it was a time of "sweatshirts with zippers, big brown Zenith color TVs, and Big Wheel" toy bicycles. However, Mario feels that there is now "newer money," which makes it easier for young people to open their own skateboard businesses.

Mario looks back upon the surveillance controversies of Watergate as obsolete. He notes that it is now difficult to distinguish the culture from the counterculture or kitsch from high art. The young poet maintains that "everything is so blended. There is no need for surveillance. Everything is out." Similarly, Madeline Roberts, a social worker who was born in 1963, says that surveillance became less intrusive after the seventies.

Because of the seventies, Madeline says that she now "wants to make movies." "VH1," she notes, has made us "visually oriented." We are in a state of "watching" in which we all watch and "think about how" we are watched. She is resigned to "computer banks" that "can check up on you." She feels that "people" might as well "listen to everything you say" and that "boundaries have broken down" so that "everything is connected up globally." There is "no mystery." She says that "feminism" has taught us the significance of "looking at the other. We become aware of sexual surveillance." She observes that after the seventies she felt "no guilt in looking into people's houses" because "if the president taps people's phones, I can do it." In general, the seventies disappointed Madeline. She remembers it beginning with fun trends like macramé and ending with reduced expectations—"being glad to be bored," as Madeline puts it. Similarly, Carole, a fiftyish clerk in a law office whom one might think of as culturally opposite from Madeline, characterizes the seventies as the hinge between optimism and pessimism, between a time when she and her family felt good about the economic strength and world position of the United States and a time when they doubted them.

I remember going to Times Square as a kind of joke with a couple of friends on New Year's Eve 1970 and feeling empty as the ball dropped. I anticipated anticlimax without end. On New Year's Eve 1980, I felt a similar yet more gnawing emptiness in a Soho, New York restaurant. In 1986, I picked Ashbery's "Self-Portrait in a Convex Mirror" as an object of close reading. The subject of Watergate seeped in. Then I could not keep the flood of the seventies out.

7 Micro-Periodizing

Micro-periodizing considers small temporal changes within a historical period. These changes articulate the period's prevalent episteme. For instance, the seventies episteme is composed of alternations between the doubting and the privileging of established modes of reality. Watergate is the key event in this ambivalence about seemingly outmoded organizing mechanisms, as I discuss further in chapters 3 and 6, and I break the seventies into four micro-periods: pre-Watergate, 1970–71; Watergate, 1972–74; post-Watergate, 1975–77; and pre-Reagan, 1978–79. These micro-periods oscillate between different dominant overtones. The pre-Watergate period culminated in Nixon's reelection and a new sense of the "reality" of presidential authority. Watergate undermined this reality. However, in the wake of Watergate, it became increasingly apparent that no widespread "sixties"-style reform would be forthcoming. Nonetheless, the pre-Reagan micro-period prefigured a new national wish-fulfillment when it was posited that such problems as the energy crisis were not real problems at all.

While maximizing an internal surveillance in which meaningful political change would be imagined as an "unreal" possibility that fructified as a dominant mode in the eighties, American society incorporates cultural liberalisms, such as our increasing concern with cultural diversity. Since the seventies, politics and cultural factors bifurcate. While conservatives dominate political agendas and elections, prevailing cultural attitudes seem to have liberalized. The conservative values that are so crucial to Newt Gingrich's vision of "American Civilization" do not prohibit him from writing and marketing a sexy novel. Typical talk-radio stations balance their patently insensitive star conservatives with open-minded, understanding therapists. Libertine radio entertainers such as Howard Stern co-opt the styles of sixties subversiveness. In general, we have learned to draw the line between significant political innovation and cultural novelty. Our surveillance becomes more a function of a consensus about what is possible.

The nation's politics became dominantly conservative in a short period. Whereas mid-sixties Gallup polls showed the nation evenly split about the touchstone liberal issue of capital punishment, by the mid-seventies an overwhelming majority supported its reinstitution, and a 1976 Supreme Court decision obliged them.[40] Liberalism began to seem unreal, certainly not as real as the simple retribution of capital punishment. A consensus formed against Great Society aims despite many Great Society successes. After all, the economy had never been better than in the mid-sixties. The popular media rarely pointed out that the Vietnam War and not the Great Society caused the Johnson administration to dip into Social Security funds that otherwise might have still been self-paying. Great Society programs could have been, and still can be much improved. More attention could be paid to their implementation, and programs could be better and more efficiently coordinated. But the Great Society's fruits are not more evident because our leaders valued the Vietnam War over Great Society initiatives. The war contributed to a focus on governmental, more than corporate, limitations.

What accounts for the free fall of traditional liberalism? A free exchange of ideas is most necessary in an economically expansive society, and America's growing conservative disposition since the seventies can partially be explained by a lack of growth throughout the American economy. Although the economy's production at least doubled between 1970 and 1990, only about one of every two hundred Americans gained in real income. Moreover, the mid-nineties economy can only be considered burgeoning when severe underemployment of many Americans, lack of security, and prevalent requirements to overwork are accepted.

So why are the loudest cries for social change ones that would curtail government activism? If we, on some level, chose economic stagnation, it may be for many of the same reasons that are reflected in the electoral process serving up a political leftover, Richard Nixon, in the late sixties. We could not sustain the euphoria and disorder of the sixties. It is almost as if we unconsciously chose a lack of balanced growth and well-being over a potential situation in which a plentiful economy might challenge a work ethic that holds a powerful American reality in place. Mysterious Federal Reserve Board interest-rate hikes between the seventies and nineties sometimes seem more culturally than economically motivated, even if these motivations are unconscious.

We grew content with corporations, businesses, and the super-rich paying less in taxes and contributing less to a vibrant educational support system for the general population. After all, corporations can much more easily trade in their work forces for other ones around the globe, and they have less need for a flexibly skilled work force. The virtues of diversity have been, in effect, cornered. As the standard of living ceases to expand, there is less need for powerfully free, or liberal, thought. However, since Watergate, voters have grown more suspicious of "big government" than of the big corporations for which they work and from whom they buy. Watergate helped unleash a faction of the American electorate that would rather oppose the federal government than join Nixon's opponents. Government has become a straw dog. Conservatives may feel surveyed and policed by government but corporate realities shape our lives. Indeed, the term "the sixties" primarily conveys an escape from conventional corporate forces. We have learned from this sixties stance to self-police ourselves.

In 1982, *It Seemed Like Nothing Happened* sounded like an appropriate title for Paul Carroll's history of the seventies. If the book's name still sounds apt, this may have more to do with our perception of the seventies than with any empirical reality. As the following chronology demonstrates, much happened in the seventies. History as social progress, however, appeared to end in the seventies, thus undermining what might seem the point of history. The decade began with the flounderings of the Nixon administration and ended with the floundering of its antidote—the Carter administration.

Perhaps we require new historical apparatuses and webs of historical associations to record the seventies. Even if the seventies are still familiar, we need a history degree-zero to work from. I do not arrange the following account by subject because I wish to give a flavor of the headlines and media atmosphere of the times. I place the following news blips in paragraphs to blend them. My continual use of the phrase "on such and such a date" supplies a formulaic spine for this blending. I also characterize each micro-period and year of the seventies.

First Micro-Period: Pre-Watergate

Generally speaking, in each seventies micro-period, the rift between accommodating the sixties socially and culturally and not accommodating it politically widens. Nonetheless, even from a social perspective, the pre-Watergate micro-period marks an end to sixties cultural escalation. The war was relatively out of the news, so Nixon's bombing of Cambodia shocked the left into a renewed sense of itself and a kind of last gasp of sixties-style protest that resulted in the deaths of several students. These deaths in effect functioned as a forbidding warning. In the face of the deadly possibilities of protest, this micro-period promoted a spirited domestication and codification of sixties attitudes. Identity-positions took on more credence, and the United States decreasingly was seen as a whole, except by the majority white identity-position.

1970 "A New American Reality." The generational reconciliation that Woodstock was touted to be proved empty. The student deaths at Kent State and Jackson State functioned alongside Nixon's calls for less government to chill social protest and progress.[41] And yet the Great Society, along with its government spending "double," the Vietnam War, was still in place. However, in 1970, Nixon drastically cut the Office of Economic Opportunity, the centerpiece of Great Society programs.

Here are some of the major news stories of 1970:

■ *President Nixon's 22 January State of the Union address describes a new American reality—a "new American experience." Nixon says that governmental bureaucracies are out of touch with America's current mood. To replace welfare, Nixon surprisingly proposes a negative income tax in the form of a minimum family income. He also asks Congress to make environmental "reparations" contingent on ending the Vietnam War. On 18 February, a Chicago jury clears all seven defendants of charges of conspiring to riot during the 1968 Democratic convention, but Rennie Davis, David Dellinger, Tom Hayden, Abbie Hoffman, and Jerry Rubin are convicted on the relatively minor offense of crossing a state line with rioting intent. On 8 April, the Senate turns down Nixon's Supreme Court nomination of appellate judge G. Harrold Carswell from Florida because of his segregationist background and undistinguished record. After rounding the moon, a powerless Apollo 13 heads toward Earth, and the astronauts splash down in the Pacific Ocean on 17 April, the same day that Nixon announces the withdrawal from Vietnam, before 1971, of 150,000 more troops. However, on 30 April, Nixon announces an "incursion" into Cambodia to cut supply lines. All manner of antiwar demonstrations break out throughout the nation, particularly on college campuses. National Guardsmen, on 4 May, kill four students and wound nine others at Kent State University. Nixon offers no condolences, galvanizing his base and polarizing the nation.*

During the next week, Nixon finally is able to fill Abe Fortas's empty Supreme Court seat with the Senate approval of Harry Blackmun, who would author the majority brief for the Roe v. Wade decision. On 12 May, state police kill two students at the mostly black Jackson State College. On 12 June, Richard Nixon's older daughter, Tricia, marries Edward Cox. As a prelude to the Twenty-sixth Amendment, President Nixon, on 18 June, signs a bill lowering to eighteen years old the eligible age for voting in federal elections. On 1 July, the state of New York legalizes abortions during the first twenty-four weeks of pregnancy. Nixon semiprivatizes the U.S. postal system by granting the Post Office autonomy within the federal government. On 15 September, United Auto Workers mount the automotive industry's largest strike since the early fifties. The 3 November elections are a wash. Democrats win nine seats in the House of the Representatives but lose two seats in the Senate. ■

1971 "National Security and Revenue Sharing." The Watergate scandal began with the Nixon administration's response to the publication of the Pentagon Papers. In 1971, Nixon began to pin 1972 reelection hopes on foreign affairs. He needed to control the way his initiatives in the Soviet Union and China would be shown to the American public, and to this end external surveillance by the Nixon administration would soon flourish. Although *the Pentagon Papers* primarily concerned the Johnson administration, a lack of control of information dissemination threatened Nixon and his Secretary of State, Henry Kissinger.

Nixon was frustrated by his lack of a clear and attractive domestic program and wished to begin globalizing the 1972 election. By more fully identifying the presidency with foreign affairs, Nixon was creating a context to shrink the domestic domain of the federal government—a context that would inevitably reverse gains made in civil rights after World War II.

■ *Nixon's 22 January 1971 State of the Union message stresses revenue-sharing with state and local governments. On 8 February, South Vietnamese forces, under the cover of American air attacks, invade Laos. Apollo 14, on 9 February, splashes down after a successful lunar landing. On 23 March, the Senate votes not to fund development of a high speed supersonic plane. Charles Manson receives a capital punishment sentence on 29 March. The Supreme Court upholds busing as a tool of school integration on 20 April. On 24 April, 200,000 people demonstrate in Washington against the war in Vietnam.*

On 10 June the Nixon administration legalizes trade with mainland China. On 30 June, the Supreme Court rules against the Nixon administration's right to block publication of the Pentagon Papers. *Nixon, on 15 August, institutes ninety-day wage and price controls. Forty-three people die on 13 September when New York state troopers confront prisoners who are holding guards hostage at Attica State Prison. The Nixon administration, on 2 October, calls for the admission of Communist China into the United Nations. On 12 October, Nixon announces his intent to visit the Soviet Union, the first presidential visit since World War II. On 14 November, Nixon announces phase II of his economic program—a more flexible and voluntary wage and price control. On 18 December, Nixon devalues the dollar by more than 8.5 percent.* ■

Why did not Watergate revitalize the sixties? In fact, Watergate was too successful. In a sense, the spectacle of a president "caught in the act" *was* the sixties. The idea of a "naked" president was an incredible truth that underscored the credibility gap. However, Nixon was his own best argument against big government, and he oddly did more to discredit the federal government than to discredit himself. The political system was widely credited with "working" in the "constitutional crisis" of Watergate, yet the system came together in doing little else than driving Nixon out of office. Without Nixon, the nation's lack of a political agenda was apparent. In the aftermath of Watergate, government was as lusterless as it was inefficient. Gerald Ford's WIN buttons (Whip Inflation Now) became an object of derision. Ironically, in the aftermath of Watergate, an energy supporting Nixonian aims of privatization was unleashed throughout the nation.

1972 *"Pandas, Ping-Pong, and Third-Rate Burglaries."* Nixon's reelection was in jeopardy before his trip to China. However, Nixon's foreign policy initiatives do not in themselves explain his 1972 landslide. As with George Bush's failure to convert his Gulf War popularity into reelection, foreign policy coups do not always guarantee presidential success. More significantly, Nixon's 1972 campaign success carved out the present political landscape. Nixon was able to marginalize liberal opposition. Of course McGovern helped by waiting until three in the morning to deliver his Democratic Party presidential nominee acceptance speech, due to the fact that he could not control an endless flow of vice presidential nominations countering his ill-advised choice of Senator Thomas Eagleton. Unlike many political insiders, McGovern somehow did not know about Eagleton's extensive record of mental health problems and treatments that had included electric shock therapy. Nixon easily established McGovern's lack of credibility, linking him to the "unreality" of sixties counterculture.

Watergate was emblematic of a movement in American society from the issue of external surveillance to the subsequent non-issue of internal surveillance. News of the Watergate burglary led the CBS News and, given McCord's, Hunt's, and Liddy's involvement with the operation, it appeared tied to the Nixon administration. However, mere appearance was not enough, and the story dropped from the view of most Americans. The White House's containment of Watergate was successful until the election. The story needed to remain disconnected from both the White House hierarchy and all of the other actions by the covert Gordon Liddy–devised Gemstone operation.

■ *On 5 January 1972, President Nixon approves NASA's plans to develop the space shuttle. On 21 February, Nixon begins his historic visit to China. On 17 March, the president announces a moratorium on the enforcing of court-ordered school busing. On 22 March, the Senate approves the Equal Rights Amendment by a vote of 84 to 8, sending the measure to state legislatures. The North Vietnamese army, on 30 March, crosses the DMZ. On 16 April, Apollo 16 is launched, the last manned moon mission. J. Edgar Hoover dies on 2 May. On 9 May, the United States begins to mine North Vietnamese harbors. On 15 May, George Wallace is shot in a shopping mall in Laurel, Maryland. Nixon in Moscow, on 26 May, signs a nuclear agreement with the Soviet Union to hold nuclear arsenals at present levels. On 8 June, Congress passes a bill delaying court-ordered busing yet also providing two billion dollars to help elementary and high schools desegregate. On 17 June, Nixon addresses the people of the Soviet Union on Soviet television, and, on the same day, five employees of the Republican National Committee are arrested in the Democratic national headquarters at Washington's Watergate hotel. Furman v. Georgia, on 29 June, establishes that capital punishment, according to the Supreme Court, can constitute cruel and unusual punishment. Executions are put on hold. On 8 July, the Nixon administration announces the sale of huge amounts of wheat to the Soviet Union. On 12 July, the Democrats give George McGovern their presidential nomination, and, on 1 August, Democratic vice presidential candidate Thomas Eagleton resigns because of his admission to receiving electric-shock treatment. Eagleton is replaced on 8 August by R. Sargent Shriver. On 12 August, the last American ground forces leave Vietnam. On 11 September, eleven Israeli athletes are killed by Arab terrorists at the Munich Olympics. On 7 November, Nixon is reelected in a landslide, and on 18 December he resumes bombing North Vietnam.* ■

1973 *"Privacy and Hearings."* Senator Sam Ervin's televised Senate Watergate hearings and the oil embargo were the year's biggest ongoing stories. However, the most culturally undigestible news event of 1973 was the Supreme Court's *Roe v. Wade* decision, because the Supreme Court based its decision on rights of privacy rather than the equal rights of women. The privacy foundation of Judge Harry Blackmun's abortion rights decision—based on an extrapolated, constitutionally unstated "zone of privacy" that he derived from several amendments, made it easier to deny women, particularly poor women, access to abortions because abortion choice was not viewed as a right but a possible "freedom." (The Supreme Court would later uphold federal prohibitions against funding abortions.) In no way could *Roe v. Wade* be viewed as a kind of affirmative-action decision correcting systematic imbalances against women, and the option of abortion continues to be heavily weighted toward the economically privileged. A ruling based on equal rights protection would have made abortion on demand a more arguable right. Overtly, *Roe v. Wade* kept the government from women's bodies, while more subtly exercising almost as much surveillance and control through economic pressures. Hence, *Roe v. Wade* exemplifies a trend toward subtle surveillance. Here are the events of 1973:

■ *On 11 January, Nixon begins voluntary imposition of most phases of wage and price controls. Nixon's 20 January State of the Union address asks Americans to consider a federal government with less effect on their lives. The Supreme Court hands down* Roe v. Wade *on 22 January. Five days later, the United States signs a cease-fire with North Vietnam. It will withdraw its troops from Vietnam in sixty days. On the same day, the draft is ended. In a prelude to subsequent executive privilege battles, on 5 February, the director of the Office of Management and Budget announces that the Nixon administration is withholding eight billion, seven hundred million congressionally appropriated dollars. It is not clear that the administration has such power. On February 7, the Senate Select Committee on Presidential Campaign Activities is established. It will be chaired by Senator Sam Ervin of North Carolina. The United States devalues the dollar by 10 percent five days later. Three hundred members of the American Indian movement "retake" Wounded Knee in South Dakota on 27 February. On 23 March, convicted Watergate burglar James W. McCord writes his famous letter to Judge John Sirica. McCord notes pressure exerted on all of the burglars to maintain silence. He identifies John Mitchell as an "overall boss" and warns that "all the trees may fall." On 20 April, FBI Director Patrick E. Gray admits to destroying Watergate evidence and resigns. On 30 April, Nixon's chief of staff, H. R. Haldeman, domestic affairs assistant John Ehrlichman, Attorney General Richard Kleindienst, and presidential counsel John Dean III resign. Nixon claims no knowledge of any "wrongdoing." On 11 May, charges against Daniel Ellsberg for pilfering the Pentagon Papers are dismissed after it is disclosed that E. Howard Hunt and G. Gordon Liddy and other "plumbers," in a kind of Watergate rehearsal, burglarized Ellsberg's psychiatrist's office and tried to steal his file. (Some "plumbers" intentionally left traces of their visit so as to demonstrate their efforts to their superiors.) On 13 June, Nixon announces a price freeze on retail goods. On*

16 June, Nixon and Brezhnev announce terms for negotiating the Strategic Arms Limitation Treaty. On 21 June, by a five to four vote, the Supreme Court allows for community standards as criteria for determining what is pornographic. On 25 June, John Dean charges Nixon with complicity in a Watergate cover-up, and with authorizing hush-money payments to the Watergate defendants. On 1 July, Nixon signs a bill increasing Social Security benefits by 20 percent. On 16 July, Alexander Butterfield reveals the existence of a White House taping system, and a week later the Nixon administration does not comply with a Senate subpoena of the tapes, citing executive privilege. On 14 August, the United States stops bombing Cambodia. On 6 October, Egypt invades the Israeli-held Sinai Peninsula. On 10 October, Vice President Spiro Agnew resigns. On 15 October, the United States announces that it will supply Israel with needed arms. On 16 October, Henry Kissinger and Le Duc Tho win the Nobel Peace Prize. Also on 16 October, Maynard Jackson is elected mayor of Atlanta, the first black mayor of a major southern city.

On 20 October, the Saturday Night Massacre occurs: President Richard Nixon orders Attorney General Elliot L. Richardson to fire Special Prosecutor Archibald Cox; Richardson refuses and resigns; Deputy Attorney General William D. Ruckelshaus becomes acting attorney general and he also resigns without firing Cox, enabling Solicitor General Robert H. Bork to dismiss the special prosecutor. OPEC announces an embargo of oil imports to the United States and a 10 percent cut in production on the same day. Two days later the mideast conflict ends. On 23 October, the Justice Department appoints Leon Jaworski as the Watergate special prosecutor. On the same day, the House Judiciary Committee is charged with investigating possible impeachment charges against Richard Nixon. Nixon says that he will obey subpoenas for the tapes. On 30 October, the White House says that two tapes do not exist. On 7 November, Nixon addresses the nation about the energy crisis and Congress passes the War Powers Act over a rare Nixon veto. On 9 November the Watergate burglars are sentenced: Liddy receives twenty years. On 13 November, employees of Gulf and Ashland Oil companies plead guilty to making illegal contributions to Nixon's reelection campaign fund. On 16 November, Nixon signs the Alaska pipeline appropriation bill. On 21 November, an eighteen-and-a-half-minute tape gap is revealed. On 30 November, Bud Krogh pleads guilty to breaking into Daniel Ellsberg's psychiatrist's office. On 6 December, Gerald Ford takes the vice-presidential oath. ∎

1974 "Resigned." The 1974 resignation of Richard Nixon was the key event of post-sixties America. However, Watergate is probably more associated with

1973 than 1974. In 1973 the nation witnessed a surreal middle-game of astonishing blunders and ill-advised exchanges, whereas, in 1974, it saw a relatively neat and thoroughgoing end-game. In effect, the impeachment process was reversed. Constitutionally, the House of Representatives indicts and the Senate conducts the trial. However, the Senate aired the indiscretions of the 1972 campaign and the House, in 1974, established the concrete charges and "smoking gun" that effectively convicted Nixon and forced him to resign. Nixon's resignation speech was the neat culmination of Watergate. Oddly, however, Americans were given a more conservative president, Gerald Ford. Watergate helped alienate a significant segment of the American electorate, creating the tyranny of the radical center as we have come to know it. If many people wanted less from the government, those in government were increasingly happy to oblige. External surveillance was becoming less necessary.

■ *On 1 January 1974, Nixon signs the Supplemental Security Act. On 4 January, Nixon refuses to deliver tapes and documents to the Ervin committee. On 15 January, experts testify that the eighteen-and-a-half-minute tape-gap was not accidental. On 4 February, Patty Hearst is kidnapped. On 12 February, the Symbionese Liberation Army demands that William Randolph distribute food to the poor in exchange for the release of his granddaughter. On 1 March, Haldeman, Ehrlichman, and Mitchell are indicted for obstruction of the Watergate investigation. On 18 March, OPEC ends the oil embargo against the United States. On 3 April, Nixon says that he will pay over four hundred thousand dollars in back taxes, admitting that two huge deductions are questionable. On 29 April, Nixon issues his Watergate tape transcripts. On 1 May, the Judiciary Committee rejects these transcripts. On 16 May, Kleindienst becomes the first attorney general convicted of a crime when he pleads guilty to not testifying in complete compliance with the Senate committee investigating ITT antitrust violations. On 12 June, Nixon is hailed as a hero in Cairo. On 21 June, Judge W. Arthur Garriety rules that the Boston School Committee consciously maintained a segregated school system and orders school busing to cure this situation in September. On 27 June, Nixon visits the Soviet Union for nuclear disarmament talks. On 24 July, the Supreme Court rules that Nixon must surrender the tapes, and the White House says that it will comply. On 27 July, the House Judiciary Committee forwards two articles of impeachment to the full House: obstruction of justice and repeated violations of the oath of office. Later it will add a third article of impeachment: defiance of committee subpoenas. On 5 August, Nixon releases transcripts of the 23 June smoking-gun conversation with Haldeman, in which* he instructed Haldeman to initiate the obstruction of the FBI's investigation. Nixon delivers his resignation on 8 August, which becomes effective on 9 August at noon when Gerald Ford is inaugurated. On 21 August, Ford nominates Nelson Rockefeller to be his vice president, and, on the same day, Ford signs a twenty-five-billion-dollar education bill that makes school busing more difficult. On 8 September, Ford pardons Nixon for any possible crime he may have committed as president. On 12 September, Boston school busing between Roxbury and South Boston begins. Ford announces his disagreement with the ruling. On 16 September, Ford announces a conditional amnesty for Vietnam draft evaders and deserters. On 11 December, Michael Faith is stabbed in a South Boston high school. On 17 December, the Senate Foreign Relations Committee begins investigations into the CIA's role in the 1973 overthrow of Allende in Chile. On 15 October, Ford signs a campaign reform bill that sets limits on congressional and presidential spending. Public funds are given to major presidential candidates. On 5 November, Democrats make substantial gains in the Congress due to dissatisfaction about Watergate and the faltering economy. On 24 November, Ford and Brezhnev sign an arms agreement in Vladivostok. On 19 December, Nelson Rockefeller is sworn in as vice president. ■

Third Micro-Period: Post-Watergate

If the narrowing of spheres of interest by groups and individuals can be equated with a self-codifying force within American society, the other side of this force is a trend toward abandoning the collective engine of social improvement. This trend became pronounced after Watergate. In the wake of Watergate, government understandably was most active in attempting to enact campaign finance reform—attempts that in retrospect have failed. In the third micro-period, proactive government no longer seemed relevant. The end of the Vietnam War made even the national security aspect of government seem impotent. In terms of domestic issues, Gerald Ford blocked more legislation than Nixon, and Jimmy Carter's central mission was initially framed as a kind of negative—energy conservation. Although these years take place in Watergate's aura, this micro-period was oddly rudderless. There seemed to be little basis for anything but a bread and circus approach toward government, and a kind of Reaganism was probably inevitable. Indeed, Jimmy Carter forefronted the symbolism of his 1976 candidacy—a candidate who would not tell a lie, carried his own luggage, smiled broadly, wore blue jeans but read philosophy, and so forth—in a manner that seemed excessive for politicians at the time.

2. Vietnam evacuation 1975, courtesy of AP/Wide World Photos

Emblematically, in the mid-seventies, *All in the Family* was replaced as the number one television program, a position it had occupied throughout most of the early seventies, by *Happy Days*. A critical nostalgia for a pre-sixties gave way to the fantasy of one.

1975 "Helicopters and Pilots." The national news showed South Vietnamese helicopter pilots ditching their half-million-dollar helicopters in the South China Sea as they jumped from their crafts ten or twenty feet above the water. The pilots would then swim to an American aircraft carrier that had no space for the copters. The U.S. evacuation from Southeast Asia brought home to many Americans the war's ultimate futile absurdity. However, this lesson translated more into a distrust of government than into a distrust of the military or of industry. The inability of the Congress that was elected in the wake of Watergate either to capture the imaginations of many voters or to enact legislation demonstrated that effective progressive government would not soon return. Somehow liberals were in more disarray after Watergate than before.

■ *On 1 January 1975, Haldeman, Mitchell, Ehrlichman, and Robert C. Mardian are convicted of obstruction of justice. On 8 January, Ford announces a committee headed by Nelson Rockefeller that will investigate illegal domestic activities of the* CIA. *Ford's 15 January State of the Union address calls for a sixteen-billion-dollar income tax cut to battle unemployment, inflation, and energy dependence. On 12 March, Maurice Stans pleads guilty to violating campaign laws. On 22 March, Kissinger gives up on his efforts to bring peace between Israel and Egypt. On 30 April, South Vietnam falls to North Vietnam. On 14 May, the U.S. cargo ship* Mayaguez, *seized by Cambodia for alleged spying, is ordered to be recovered by Ford. The ship and crew are returned but fifteen marines die. On 10 June, the Rockefeller Commission on the* CIA *suggests a congressional committee to oversee the agency. On 9 July, the Ford campaign suggests that Nelson Rockefeller will not be on a 1976 national ticket. On 17 July, Soviet and American astronauts shake hands in space. On 31 July, James Hoffa is publicly reported missing. On 27 August, a federal commission finds Ohio Governor James Rhodes and all National Guardsmen involved blameless in the 1970 Kent State shootings. On 10 September, Congress enacts a near eight-billion-dollar education bill over Ford's veto. On 18 September, Patty Hearst is captured. On 22 September, Sara Jane Moore unsuccessfully tries to assassinate President Ford. On 12 November, Supreme Court Justice William O. Douglas resigns. On 26 November, Ford announces that he will help New York City avoid bankruptcy. On 4 December, the Senate Select Committee on Intelligence releases its findings that the* CIA *helped to create a context for the overthrow of democratic rule in Chile.* ∎

1976 *"Running against Washington."* With the end of the war in Vietnam, patterns of surveillance changed. Indeed, the 1975 Rockefeller Commission demonstrated that the CIA itself was now a vulnerable target. Jimmy Carter's victory over Washington-based Democratic candidates in Congress made it clear that discontent with Republicans had spilled over to discontent with government in general. Traditional Democratic coalitions could no longer win a Democratic presidential nomination, and the Democratic Party needed the novelty of a southerner running for president to capture the south and win a close election. By 1992, the Democrats would need two southerners on the national ticket to employ successfully their version of the Southern Strategy.

∎ *Ford's 19 January 1976 State of the Union address stresses spending curbs and the dangers of inflation. On 30 January, the Supreme Court outlaws provisions of the 1974 Federal Campaign Act that limit spending on the premise that they are incompatible with First Amendment free-speech guarantees. On 5 April, Howard Hughes dies. On 2 July, the U.S. Supreme Court, in a seven to two decision, rules that the death penalty is constitutional. On 4 July, the nation celebrates its bi-*

centennial. On 15 and 16 July, Jimmy Carter and Walter Mondale are nominated to the Democratic national ticket in New York. On 19 August, Ford is renominated, and he picks Robert Dole as a running mate. On 7 October, in his second debate with Carter, Ford says that Poland is autonomous from the Soviet Union. On 2 November, Carter defeats Ford in a close election. ■

1977 *"Death and Peace."* Gary Gilmore's execution and Menachem Begin's visit to Cairo were perhaps the two most dramatic 1977 events. On the one hand, primal realities were revisited with the reinstitution of capital punishment after its ten-year suspension. On the other hand, euphoric possibilities of world peace and unthinkable mergers, first taking the form in the seventies of Nixon's trip to China, were more dramatically displayed in the sudden image of Israel's and Egypt's leaders declaring their peaceful intentions toward one another. And yet peace appeared staged without Palestinian participation. In 1977, Carter was unable to sell the energy crisis "as the moral equivalent of war." No other vision seemed to be in the offing.

■ *On 17 January, Gary Gilmore is executed by a firing squad in Utah. The big news in Jimmy Carter's 20 January inaugural address is a pledge to seek the worldwide end of nuclear weapons. The next day Carter pardons draft evaders unconditionally. On 24 February, in an attempt to base his administration's foreign policy on issues of "human rights," Carter cuts foreign aid to nations that violate such rights. In April, the Senate Finance Committee looks into large, unbacked personal loans that Bert Lance, Carter's Office of Management and Budget director, had his bank make to him. On 1 May, massive arrests occur in Seabrook, New Hampshire, because of protests against a planned nuclear reactor. In July, Begin visits Sadat in Cairo. On 13 July, a blackout strikes New York City. On 20 July, Leon Jaworski is called upon by the House Ethics Committee to investigate "Koreagate," more prominently known as Abscam. On 4 August, Congress forms the Department of Energy. On 12 August, the space shuttle conducts its first successful test. On 7 September, the United States and Panama sign the Panama Canal Treaty. On 8 September, the United States and Canada agree to build the Alaska pipeline. ■*

Fourth Micro-Period: Pre-Reagan

The nation in some ways needed the ideological change of subjects that the 1980 election of Reagan would provide. The pre-Reagan micro-period produced

3. Jonestown, courtesy of AP/Wide World Photos

consistently terrifying news, such as the Jonestown mass deaths, the Three Mile Island nuclear threat, the Cambodian holocaust, stagflation, boat people, and the Iranian hostage crisis. In this last micro-period of the seventies, a lack of progressive leverage upon collective American identity was reflected in news eruptions that exceeded our ability to cope with them. It was almost as if there were a power vacuum at the center of American power and identity.

1978 "Bakke and Jonestown." The production of memorable news, which noticeably declined after Watergate, further slowed in 1978. The Bakke decision ruled affirmative action constitutional in principle yet found in favor of Alan Bakke, who was claiming that the University of California at Davis had discriminated against him because he was a white male, although he claimed that he was better qualified than some black women who had been accepted. Ambivalence was further institutionalized by one of the oddest and most deconstructed Supreme Court decisions. Justice Lewis F. Powell Jr. voted with four justices in one decision for Bakke, ordering him to be admitted to the Davis medical school, and then Powell voted with the other four judges in upholding the University of California's right to continue an affirmative action policy.

The mass suicide of hundreds of James Jones's followers was perhaps the most startling example of a time when the news turned grim. The last two years of the seventies were viscerally negative and made the electorate receptive to Ronald Reagan's incredibly positive message. For many, there seemed little point in resisting it. They self-surveyed themselves into a kind of covenant of expecting little government and business in exchange for a sunny ideology.

■ *On 7 April, 1978, Carter delays production of the neutron bomb. On 6 June, California voters overwhelmingly approve Proposition 13, curtailing real estate taxes. In August, the Native American Long March is held from San Francisco to Washington. On 17 September, Sadat and Begin sign the "Camp David Accords." On 6 October, the Senate extends the ratification deadline for the Equal Rights Amendment. On 31 October, huge losses on Wall Street cause the Federal Reserve to raise its prime rate to 9.5 percent. On 18 November, the 911 followers of Jim Jones commit mass suicide in Jonestown, Guyana. Representative Leo Ryan is murdered when investigating the cult. On 27 November, the United States allows fifteen thousand boat people to enter the country. On 16 December, Cleveland defaults.* ■

1979   "Nuclear, Oil, Hostage, and Spiritual Crises." The year 1979 continued a trend of less and worse news. Three Mile Island and the Iranian hostage crisis characterized the year. Both events concerned extreme anxiety about energy sources. The crisis in Iran created oil lines for the first time since the Nixon administration. Skylab, the crashing satellite, metaphorized global uncertainty and the untrustworthiness of experts in the sciences. As if to signal the decade's end, disco pervaded the nation's pop music charts and then suddenly fell off the charts near the year's end.

■ *On 1 January 1979, the United States establishes formal diplomatic relations with China. On 26 March, in a formal ceremony at the White House, Egypt and Israel declare a state of peace. On 28 March, the Three Mile Island nuclear reactor leaks radioactive steam and a nuclear meltdown almost occurs. On 25 May, 273 people die in a DC-10 crash near O'Hare Airport in Chicago. On 18 June, Carter and Brezhnev sign the SALT II treaty in Vienna. On 28 June, OPEC announces an oil price hike and inflation jumps. On 15 July, Jimmy Carter tells America of its "crisis of confidence." In July, Carter also fires Bella Abzug as the head of the President's National Advisory Committee, and twenty-six committee members resign. Arthur McDuffie is murdered in Miami, and the acquittal of the police accused of his murder leads to the 1980 Miami riots. On 27 September, the Department of Energy is created. On 4 November, Iranian students protesting the admission of the Shah to a New York hospital seize sixty-six Americans in the U.S. embassy. On 19 December, the Senate votes to approve a billion-and-a-half-dollar loan to bail out Chrysler.* ∎

In the defining speech of his presidency, Jimmy Carter did not use the word "malaise" when speaking of America's spiritual crisis. However, his noting of a "crisis of confidence" in America was roundly panned, when the media translated his speech to mean that all our problems stemmed from "malaise." After all, was not the president responsible for inspiring confidence, enthusiasm, and *real* solutions? And yet Carter had identified a problem. Americans did not believe him when he spoke about the benefits of energy alternatives and conservation. Indeed there was a massive "crisis in confidence," and most Americans, including Carter, had resigned themselves to things as they were while resenting that state of affairs. "Self-surveillance" was nearly complete. The next chapter uses seventies films to further articulate this trend and microperiodize the decade.

Two

Mystery Tain: Micro-Periodizing Seventies

Films from *Patton* to *Apocalypse Now*

As I first watched Quentin Tarantino's *Pulp Fiction* (1994), I wondered if the film was set in the seventies. Virtually all of the film's music, cars, styles, and cultural references are from the seventies or earlier. I only knew the action of the film was taking place in the present when the seventies was depicted as the past—as a flashback with Butch the boxer (Bruce Willis) as a boy receiving his dead Vietnam War POW father's gold watch. If the seventies were the past, it obviously could not be the present. However, the present seemed like the seventies, and the film conveyed an impression of a past and a present both entangled in that decade. The film displayed a time-space that could not move past the seventies. This impression was reinforced later when I saw Tarantino, interviewed on VH1, comment that he wished to create a cultural neverworld in which time could not be pinned down.

Interestingly, this neverworld ends in the seventies. The seventies haunts the motion picture. The film's "pulp fiction," its fantastic lexicon, is the seventies. Several of the film's key episodes hinge on appropriations from seventies films. When Mia (Uma Thurman), the wife of an organizationally powerful gangster, tells Vincent Vega (John Travolta) that he must compete in a dance competition with her so that they can win the dance trophy, we think of *Saturday Night Fever* (1977). Indeed, Travolta's mere presence reminds us of *Saturday Night Fever*. In *Pulp Fiction*, however, Travolta plays a kind of Tony Manero gone bad—a hit man hired by Mia's husband, Marsellus Wallace (Ving Rhames). While out of town, Marsellus has ordered Vincent to take his wife out and to do whatever she wants. Mia reminds him of her husband's request when he hesitates to dance in a twist contest at a fantastically nostalgic restaurant that Vincent calls "a wax museum with a pulse," much like Freud's metaphor for the unconscious—a magic slate that retains all impressions in its underlying wax surface. In a sense, Travolta is the seventies museum-piece. We wonder if this contest has not somehow driven Marsellus's and Mia's choice of Vincent as her date for the evening. Perhaps Mia scoped Tony out on her television monitors when he first entered her home. Was he indeed that famed man who could dance? Is this an inter-filmic revision in which Tony Manero will be forced to keep the trophy that he renounced seventeen years earlier in *Saturday Night Fever* when he did not feel that he won it fairly due to ethnic and racial considerations? Travolta's character feels no such anxiety in the nineties.

Whereas in *Saturday Night Fever,* the dance competition outcome drives Tony away from his partner, winning the contest brings Vincent and Mia closer together, and Vincent must convince himself not to become romantically involved with his boss's wife. Mia confirms Vincent's cautious attitude when, thinking it is cocaine, she takes Tony's heroin without his knowledge and overdoses from it. Her heart virtually stops, and she must be brought to life with an adrenaline injection in her heart. As in various seventies horror films, Mia moves with the needle in her breast. In *Carrie* (1976), which also features Travolta, Carrie's mother (Piper Laurie) lives for some time with a knife in her heart. However, she dies, unlike Mia, who, as a kind of reverse vampire, is revived by a blow to her heart. For Mia, life is found in death and nostalgia.

If the movie's fiction is trapped in the seventies, it is a fiction that is presumably stripped of sixties and seventies ideals. There is never any concrete hope established for a better society. At the end of the film, Jules (Samuel L. Jackson) interjects a positive note by leaving society, but a life of submissiveness to criminal authority is presented as the only alternative to being, as Vincent puts it, an unemployed "bum." (Indeed, as if to support Vincent's sense of responsibility, the audience has already seen a scene in which he dies because Jules was no longer there to back him up.) Since most Americans have been forced to compromise themselves in many ways to avoid unemployment, and we see little alternative, we are startled when we realize how easily we accept their profession and work. It is only when Jules questions his own job that we recall obvious moral problems involved with being a hit man.[1] Even the nomadic, wandering existence that Jules decides to live instead of working for Marsellus rings true as an appraisal of our status within the world's work force. As in westerns, Jules connects the roles of hired gun and displaced worker. *Pulp Fiction* presents the character of an alienated hit man rather than the more family-oriented Luca Brasi figure in the seventies film *The Godfather* (1972).

4. *Deliverance,* courtesy of Photofest

A glaring seventies reference occurs when Marsellus and Butch, in the midst of an apparent death struggle in a pawn shop, are apprehended by a clique of sadists. *Pulp Fiction* blunts the impact of its *Deliverance* appropriation by overtly referring to the 1972 film when Marsellus calls his rapist "Hillbilly." Marsellus seems to be thinking of the southern hill people of *Deliverance.* Marsellus's request of Butch, "Don't tell anybody about this," parallels the same request by Ned Beatty's character in *Deliverance.* However, the taboo of such knowledge in *Deliverance* far surpasses the telling of a tale that would severely embarrass Marsellus. The buggery perpetrated is not at all as shocking as it was in *Deliverance.* If the seventies is the film's pulp fiction, it is not a fiction for which we are asked to suspend our disbelief. The nineties film reduces seventies competition, horror, and taboo into an entertainingly subtle adrenaline play—a fiction, a pulp fiction.

Pulp Fiction relies on seventies references for its culminating statement. At the conclusion of the film, Vincent's fellow hit man, Jules, tells Vincent of his intention to leave his job and wander the earth looking for life's meaning like "Cane in *Kung Fu,*" the seventies television character. After Vincent warns him of the stigma attached to not having a job, the facilitating incident that allows Jules to make good on his promise to leave his job involves another seventies reference. When the diner where Vincent and Jules are having breakfast is held up by a pair of young lovers who display passionate affection toward one another while asserting control over the diner's workers and patrons, Jules negotiates what he wants from the petty thieves by invoking *Happy Days*. He keeps his wallet and a briefcase with mysterious, glimmering value so he can return it to Marsellus, and rather than kill the thieves, Jules gives them fifteen hundred dollars so that he can feel the worth of human life. To attain the proper atmosphere to resolve the film and avoid bloodshed, Jules asks the woman bandit, "What is Fonzie like?" and he receives the reflex answer, "Cool."

Does *Pulp Fiction* point toward a way out of the seventies, an escape from its pulpy, waxy cultural fiction? The impracticality of Jules's solution tells us that it most assuredly does not, as does the film's narrative time-sequence. The film actually ends only a few hours after it begins. However, the individual stories of Mia and Vincent and Butch are threaded into the central tale of the two hit men who ultimately encounter the two petty burglars whom the audience first meets before the film's opening credits and does not see again until the film's ending, this time from Vincent's and Jules's vantage point. In terms of its narrative time, the film ends with Butch's retrieval of the gold watch, which represents traditional, paternal American values, the values that are presumably why Butch cannot deliberately lose his prizefight as Marsellus demands and thus must flee Los Angeles to escape him. The watch can be interpreted as a keeping faith between generations, an overcoming of time and generation gaps. The watch has an influence, unlike the destabilizing influence of the gold glow of Marsellus's briefcase. In part because Butch so values the gold watch, he might be more in place as a forties character. And yet since *Pulp Fiction* ends with Jules and draws its central message from him, the film highlights Jules's mission. Like Jules, the audience never settles into a concrete reality. We become cultural surfers who handle time-periods like waves. For example, the opening credits' soundtrack punningly reflects the audience's role as epistemic surfers by switching from static to surfing music, as if the film were "surfing" on a radio dial.

The seventies are still, as the poet John Ashbery puts it, on an "unassigned frequency." In chapters 3 and 4, I describe how the backing of a mirror— the tain—functions as a symbol of the site of a regimentation of reality. In this sense "the backing of the mirror" of a reality that shattered in the sixties cannot be reconstructed in the seventies. *Apocalypse Now* (1979) fittingly concludes the films of the seventies by alluding to this tropology. Its opening collage of Martin Sheen's head—upside down and superimposed on a close-up of a ceiling fan that suggests a helicopter—connotes a lens that will no longer reverse its images. The subject is at odds with its objects of perception, and, as Slavoj Žižek says, "The subject is the tain of the mirror."[2] (The next two chapters discuss the tain's metaphoric relationship to the seventies in more detail.) *Apocalypse Now* is not about the Vietnam War as much as about the impossibility of any sane perception of reality incorporating the war. It concerns a subject that cannot be a subject.

Mainstream American movies were only free to discuss the war when it was too late to affect it. Hence, by the time *Apocalypse Now* was released, Vietnam was not its most resonating subject. *Apocalypse Now* has more to do with a certain psychic deadening that was occurring among Americans. The film begins with Sheen's character anguished and fighting with himself inside a Saigon hotel room, where the Vietnam War seems both remote and internalized. The film's moral dilemma centers on him rejecting the idea of killing another American, only eventually to find it unavoidable. As I discuss later in the chapter, the opening hotel room typifies the film, in that *Apocalypse Now* keeps the Vietnam War itself at a distance, as if it is in a frozen past that is nevertheless an absent presence.

Early seventies movies such as *Patton, Little Big Man,* and *Deliverance* in which Vietnam is not an overt subject but which involve Vietnam in an actively critical fashion are our most authentic Vietnam War films, in the sense that they approach the war as a living presence. Similarly, *The Conversation,* released before Watergate's climax, and the indirect treatment of the scandal and/or the historical contexts for it that are given in *Jaws, Serpico,* and other mid-seventies movies provide our greatest Watergate films. Vietnam is the absent subject of several key early seventies films, Watergate is close to the heart of many mid-seventies films, and significant late seventies films more overtly thematize the Vietnam War but point toward an eighties kind of apoliticalness. That the Vietnam War is the great absent presence of late sixties and early seventies films might not be surprising, but curiously late seventies films that need not consider the taboo against explicitly discussing the war tend not to engage with the war as a political issue.

I use film here as a way of adding "pulp" to the "fiction" of the seventies. Seventies films are a prime resource for concretizing and vivifying the decade. Mainstream cinema of the period is a barometer of the sensational, the authentic, and the institutionally unvoiced because, compared with television, films have a luxury and supplemental status. Popular films, which had been in commercial and artistic decline since the advent of television, are clearly rejuvenated by the late sixties. Relaxed censorship standards enable seventies movies to tap much sixties counterculture creativity. Sixties rock innovations modulate into film production as the Hollywood studio system continues to break down. While rockers begin to age past the music scene, other baby boomers mature into young film talent who confront the individuating energies animating American society.

At times, in the seventies, film seems more a cultural vanguard than music. Both assimilate the counterculture. Society at large, during the seventies, ingests and codifies phenomena that had fallen outside the purview of mainstream and official sanction, exemplified by the motorcycle police in James William Guercio's *Electra Glide in Blue* (1973) who lay "a head shop distributor's general hippie regalia—you know, the whole routine" from a counterculture van on the highway for inspection. This cultural codifying operation includes the self-identification of various groups, or subject-positions. Minority politics, including the constitution of a new "silent majority," work hand-in-hand with a demographic zoning of America. As the sociologist Niklas Luhmann observes, group-identification and self-identification refer to an individualizing energy that runs throughout society.[3] In the early seventies, what my preceding chapter terms the pre-Watergate micro-period, forces of individual self-actualization and fulfillment encounter these codifying forces as enemies. For instance, *Patton* can be seen as an artist's battle with bureaucracy. What makes the film interesting, of course, is that the artist here is a practitioner of war.

If in the following discussion I isolate seemingly inconsequential details, it is much as an interpreter of a dream might examine apparent minutiae to an end beyond the surface content of that particular dream. Hence, at times, my readings may be difficult to accept and may not resemble the filmmaker's aims. Rather than providing definitive readings of certain films, I intend to "walk" slowly through the seventies by selecting some mainstream feature films from each year as data from which to identify small epistemic shifts from year to year and micro-period to micro-period in a kind of slow, meditative performance.

Of course, since films take several years to write, plan, film, edit, and market, the actual "year" of a film is somewhat arbitrary. The actual release date of a film is a kind of negotiation between its planning and production and its distribution and influence. Nonetheless, since I am looking for a general ripple of the episteme, the year that a film is first consumed and makes a social impact is a good place to begin.

Among the chief topics that I discuss in each film, space functions as a perceptual material for surveillance and self-surveillance. In the course of the seventies the camera becomes more fixed, scenes are more deliberately set, and the camera frame is more carefully filled, as if to match a sense of the deliberateness and approval of surveillance.

I begin by discussing three 1970 films that revive apparently passé genres: *Patton* renews an American interest in war movies by rendering the World War II general's career, replete with its inherent love of war and political incorrectness; *Love Story* mainstreams the woman's romance by telling the story of a rich man's son's love of a young working-class woman whom he meets at Harvard, his father's opposition to the eventual marriage, and his wife's senseless death from a rare disease; and *Little Big Man,* based on Thomas Berger's 1964 novel, turns the American western into a post-sixties happening by adding many sixties trappings to the novel and linking the nineteenth-century plight of the Cheyenne with the plight of sixties culture. The film tells a tale about a boy who is captured by the Cheyenne and raised by them, his shuttling between the Cheyenne and white worlds, and his role in the Battle of Little Big Horn. These 1970 reformulations of traditional genres are on the cusp between the sixties and seventies. They bespeak a return of a dated reality that incorporates and contains a new awareness attained in the sixties.

Patton, the 1970 Academy Award winner, was the first film in several years to make vital use of the subject of World War II without shrinking from its overtones of glory. Whereas Mike Nichols's 1968 film version of *Catch-22* and Robert Altman's 1970 film about the Korean War, *M*A*S*H,* present war as a meaningless gridlock, Francis Ford Coppola's and Edmund H. North's screenplay for *Patton* depicts war as a means of self-expression. It is appropriate that *Patton* was one of the first major moneymakers of the seventies (following *Airport, M*A*S*H,* and *Aristocats*) because it promotes a recognition of the reality of the experience of World War II in a way that distinguishes it from the experience of the Vietnam War. Underscoring this point, President Nixon, viewing *Patton* with a mind apparently closed to its irony, watched the film repeatedly on his bedroom wall while planning the bombing of Cambodia. However, Nixon knew enough not to go public with his enthusiasm for making war, and he attempted, unconstitutionally, to hide his escalations of the war, realizing that it would be futile to try rallying the nation around the war effort.

In *Patton,* World War II is valid but obsolete. We have outgrown the reality that had sustained America. This painful realization is embodied in the film's

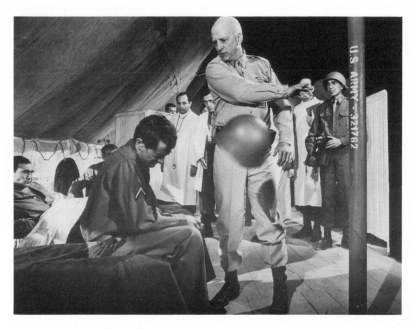

5. *Patton,* courtesy of Photofest

title character, who believes that he is reincarnated from another time. At a battlefield he comments: "The world grew up, hell of a shame. Dick, I want a twenty-four hour guard put around this area. If we don't the damn Arabs will dig them up just to get their clothes. Our graves aren't going to disappear like everyone else who fought here—the Greeks, the Romans, the Carthaginians. God, how I hate the twentieth century." The character to whom Patton speaks dies in the subsequent confrontation with Rommel, and Patton fittingly presides over his burial. The film often shows cemeteries and the burial of the dead. Indeed, unlike previous World War II films, *Patton* buries World War II as it displays it.[4]

Patton's dissemination of space captures this double perspective on World War II. *Patton* is filmed in a wide-screen process ("Dimension 150") in which seventy-millimeter prints are projected on a deeply curved screen, a process that lends itself to battle scenes. However, relatively few viewing audiences saw *Patton* in Dimension 150, and on normal screens the process flattens out close-ups and other scenes, creating an expectation that the flatness will be reversed and will bounce back. The use of mirrors also provides a double perspective. Patton can look directly into a mirror and gain inspiration from what the mirror has to say. As the camera shows his mirror image he says, "All my life I've wanted to lead a lot of men in a desperate battle. Now I'm gonna do it." In contrast, General Montgomery blows fog in a mirror so he can sketch a battle plan in the moisture. When Montgomery leaves the bathroom, he says that it is difficult to believe that this is where the Italian campaign was devised. Patton, unlike Montgomery, fights the power of secondary, enclosed spaces. Rommel and the other enemy German commanders are always shown deliberating inside a sophisticated command station. Open, sun-drenched spaces attract Patton, who is rarely seen sitting down. However, he is seen hunched and seated, as a reflection in a ceiling mirror, after being told that the operation he will command is a mere decoy. When he lobbies for his European invasion plan he does so in a way that he describes as "purely social, by that I mean purely political." He has no private life that does not project into a political realm, which is why diplomacy is so difficult for him.

The film is particularly memorable for its shots of Scott alone or with only one interlocutor, because of the relatively unused space that is a Dimension 150 by-product. Perhaps the most riveting scene of the film is its prologue before the opening credits, wherein Patton, in front of the backdrop of an American flag many times higher and wider than the general's figure, addresses his silent, unseen troops while looking directly into the camera. He seems to be talking to the theater audience and telling us that we are still partly in World War II even though that experience cannot be duplicated. "All real Americans love the sting of battle," he says. "Americans love a winner, and will not tolerate a loser. Americans play to win all the time. I wouldn't give a hoot in hell for a man who lost and laughed. That's why Americans have never lost and will never lose a war, because the very thought of losing is hateful to Americans." He thus comments on why it is difficult for Americans to accept the wars that follow. The film's relentlessly wide use of space describes the largeness of Patton's individuality and its projection on a nation-state. At the same time, however, it conflicts with an efficient use of focus. The uninspiring, bureaucratic forces that hound Patton throughout the movie appear justified by a new reality. Everyone cannot be as central as Patton. Omar Bradley, as played by Karl Malden, speaks for the GI. "He doesn't live out your dreams of glory," Bradley tells Patton, "He's stuck here." "There goes old Blood and Guts," says one foot soldier. "Our blood, his guts," qualifies another. And yet Patton is not after personal glory so much as the glory of an America whose army can beat its English allies out of conquests. Patton frames his one-upmanship by fulfilling a prophecy of an American empire that links it to the great empires of the past. The film's extremely wide screen bespeaks problematic imperialistic dimensions.

Director Franklin J. Schaffner and cinematographer Fred Koenekamp use much background space around Patton, as if to say that such aggrandizing space is a luxury that is now as anachronistic as Patton. The audience cannot imagine such space in Vietnam; television and photographic images of Vietnam, to which the American public was exposed daily, rarely conveyed such space.

A German officer in the film calls Patton a "marvelous anachronism." *Love Story* may have also seemed somewhat anachronistic. As *Patton* resuscitates the war film genre, *Love Story*, based on Erich Segal's 1970 book, reprises the woman's romance film of the thirties and forties for a general audience. The movie testifies to a renewed confidence in packaging. To paraphrase the film's famous definition of love, "Love means not doubting a brand name." The title signals that the film packages a love that exists for itself and not as a story that is cosmic or mystical in a sixties fashion. Rather, the film domesticates love for a self-conscious public.[5] Sixties love is tamed, and emotive expansiveness domesticated. Thus enclosed, outdoor public spaces figure prominently: the film is framed by shots of Oliver (Ryan O'Neal) reminiscing at the Central Park ice-skating rink; Jenny (Ali MacGraw) watches Oliver play ice hockey; Harvard appears as a confined academic theme park; and the many odd jobs Oliver takes during law school invariably are in such domesticated outdoor spots as Christmas tree lots or yacht-lined coves.

The film's preoccupation with rinks and arenas indicates an impulse to play out sixties phenomena in official, on-view mainstream America, while protecting America from the unrest of the sixties by marginalizing it. Although director Arthur Hiller and cinematographer Dick Kratina use a generally straightforward early seventies filmic style that relies on the relatively unadorned location shot, the film seems to be hermetically sealed against countercultural traces. Visually, it is almost as if the sixties had never happened. In one of three of the movie's only references to the sixties, Oliver tells his father that Jenny "is no crazy hippie." However, the sixties are also contained by assimilation into high culture when Jenny makes a point of grouping the Beatles with Bach and Mozart. In the film's only cryptic remark, Jenny seems to refer to the Vietnam War by using the phrase "bringing the troops home for Christmas" as a euphemism for her imminent death. It is as if the film ideologically ends our concerns with the Vietnam War before that war is actually over. Interestingly, although understandable given Hollywood's reluctance to mention Vietnam, Oliver's draft status is never a question or issue even though the story occurs in the latter half of the sixties.

In short, *Love Story* markets the sixties while maintaining a distance from it. The "free love" of the sixties turns into commodified forms of pleasure. No apologies necessary, the signifier separated from affect, "Love means never having to say you're sorry." Compassion and self-sacrifice are no longer relevant. Oddly, love asserts itself as a way of repressing the sixties. Unconditional love is here either mainstream family-oriented or hedonistic and singles-oriented, and both are divorced from sixties overtones of universal love. Love is rather enclosed, like the ice-skating rinks that frame *Love Story*, concentrated like the light in Ashbery's mirror[6] that the next two chapters discuss.

Universal love and acceptance are also relegated to the past in *Little Big Man*. The film uses a portrayal of Cheyenne society to depict both a nostalgia for and a fulfillment of a recent past. The Cheyennes, or "Human Beings," as they call themselves in the film, are thoroughly domesticated in an enlightened sense. They are generally sensible, tolerant, visionary, and pleasure-loving. Jack (Dustin Hoffman) chooses the Cheyenne, or Human Being, lifestyle over that of white society, in which "the world was too ridiculous even to bother to live in" and "we're all fools and none of it matters." In the white world, divisions of labor and roles are meaninglessly imposed, as when General Custer insists that Jack is a mule-skinner, and Jack must agree to placate Custer. Jack fails as a born-again Christian, medicine-show assistant, gunfighter, storekeeper, alcoholic, hermit, mule-skinner, and cavalry scout, and it is difficult to tell whether the problem lies with the worker or his society. Work is seen as a kind of anatomical violation. "Every business has its [body] part to lose," says a one-handed, one-legged, one-eyed, one-eared medicine-show man played by Martin Balsam.

Jack prefers his identity as Little Big Man. As a Human Being, his life adds qualities of dimension and transgression to the ideal of the pastoral, suburban American family man. His domestic space within the cozy enclave of his "geodesic" teepee allows him to roll from one of his four wives' beds to another, even if it is clear that Sunshine (Amy Eccles) is his real wife. In *Little Big Man*, the pastoral-suburban lifestyle of the Native Americans oddly leads to sixties-like hippie apocalyptic values. Jack lives to be 121 years old but his post-Cheyenne life clearly has no relevance. He even proclaims himself to be a "failure as an Indian" because he does not carry out his plan to assassinate Custer in order to avenge Custer's soldiers' murder of Sunshine and other

6. *Little Big Man,* courtesy of Photofest

Human Beings. The two My Lai–like (Arthur Penn used Asian American extras in the scenes to underscore the similarities) massacres of the Human Beings that the film depicts, in effect, mourn the passing of a kind of hippie relevance due to repressive, inhuman forces.

Little Big Man is framed as an oral transcription, a kind of revelation to the audience. At the film's beginning, Dustin Hoffman's character insists upon talking into a historian's tape recorder. His voice narrates the film, linking it to the present, and speaks for the unsatisfactory conclusion of the sixties, which can be viewed as the last gasp of modernism before postmodern realities set in. "A world without Human Beings," says the chief, "has no center to it." Like Jack, the chief has lost his "power to act," as he terms it, and cannot even die. The film's final close-up is particularly haunting; it shows the 121-year-old Jack slightly closing one eye as if to problematize both immortality and death.

This flicking of Hoffman's eye points to these 1970 films' use of ambiguity and of ambivalent characters at their conclusions. In *Patton,* all-out war is anachronistic but still sways our imaginations. There is little indication, in *Love Story,* of how Oliver will face the end of his perfect world. It is difficult to imagine the characters in *The Boys in the Band* (1970) (a film that I discuss in more detail in chapter 4) resolving their ambivalence about their homosexuality. *Little Big Man* presents a figure of cultural resentment sealed and virtually untouched for a century. Director Tom Laughlin's surprise hit, *Billy Jack* (1971), also uses Native American culture to display nostalgia for the sixties even as it is just ending by showing how a Native American saves a progressive school for wayward teenagers that supports sixties-like culture against repressive small-town forces by, ambivalently, cutting a deal with the police before being arrested.[7]

In *Little Big Man,* Native Americans are not seen as noble savages, but they are enviably "laid back." There are no problems except those posed by whites, who, as the chief says, see the living as dead instead of the inanimate as living, as the Human Beings do. The chief, played by Chief Dan George, is a kind of hippie president who leads by interpreting his dreams. Contrastingly, Custer leads by making uncompromising assertions. Needing one more victory against the Indians to consolidate his chances of being nominated for president, he refuses to see danger as he rides into Little Big Horn. This characterization of Custer thus echoes what many Americans had long ago intuited to be the Vietnam War's self-justifying bureaucratic logic, a perception later confirmed by the *Pentagon Papers* and more recently by Robert MacNamara's memoirs. Thus, after Custer's initial decision to save Jack from his soldiers' suspicion that Jack is a Cheyenne sympathizer, Custer explains why he will not execute Jack for plotting to assassinate him: "Your miserable life is not worth the reversal of a Custer decision." Then, expecting misinformation from the assassin, Custer relies on Jack to mislead him. The general would then know what not to do. However, Jack tells Custer that he would like him to march into Little Big Horn because he wants him dead, and Custer misinterprets his honesty. Since Jack becomes a personification of misdirection, his life is fittingly saved at Little Big Horn by a Human Being who does everything backwards. (The "backwards" Human Being had long resented Jack for saving his life in battle, thus seeming to belittle him, and now can belittle him in return.)

Jack/Little Big Man often saves himself from certain death by revealing himself to be a white man to Indians and an Indian to white men. With its leading character, the film's audience is privileged to shuttle between two worlds. *Little Big Man* opens an exhilarating space, an alternative reality such as the first moon landing and Nixon's 1972 trip to China, a *Dark Side of the Moon* as Pink Floyd's early seventies album puts it as opposed to *The Wall* of their late seventies album. As in *The Boys in the Band,* the audience is given access to a perhaps previously exotic reality. Both *Little Big Man* and *The Boys in the Band* provide a means for American culture at large to recuperate and yet further marginalize historically oppressed identities. Both films portray beleaguered, troubled demographic entities. Similarly, Melvin Van Peebles's *Watermelon Man* (1970), about a white character who mysteriously turns black (Godfrey Cambridge), demonstrates the social construction of race while also emphasizing race as a social limit because its protagonist finds no solution to his problems other than joining a militant black self-defense group. Other films directed by African Americans, such as Gordon Parks's *Shaft* (1971) and Gordon Parks Jr.'s *Superfly* (1972), also suggest the need to emphasize limited identity-positions (societal roles) despite an awareness of their limits. The title character of *Shaft* is a black private detective who works for the racketeer he is investigating, demonstrating the ambiguous position of the black professional. Just as ambivalently, the hero of *Superfly* is a black drug dealer who tries to leave the underworld by making one deal that is big enough to allow him to retire, and thus the remedy to his problem can be found in its intensification.

In 1971 films, a more profound state of almost liminal, haunting "in-betweenness" dominates. In *The Last Picture Show,* Polly Platt's scenic design depicts the public area of a small Texan town in 1951 and 1952 as a flimsy, ghostly facade, reducing public space to the merely residual and supplemental. The film's sharp, John Ford–like wide angles and black and white contrasts underscore the sparse landscape. Platt's design echoes the understatement of its hero, Sonny Crawford (Timothy Bottoms), who rarely initiates action. A consummate anti-hero, Sonny is manipulated by his best friend, Duane (Jeff Bridges), who, for instance, does not give him enough time in his own pick-up truck to make love with his girlfriend; by Jacy (Cybill Shepherd), the girlfriend, who contrives a marriage with Sonny so that it can, after her parents annul it, contribute to her small-town fame; and by his football coach, who hires him as an escort for his unloved wife (Cloris Leachman), who in turn offers Sonny an easy romance.

Both in terms of its central character and locale, Peter Bogdanovich's movie concerns an absent center. We become concerned with peripheral characters who are outside the old boy networks of oil well owners and football coaches, whom we meet only fleetingly. Moreover, Sam the Lion (Ben Johnson), Sonny's surrogate father and owner of the town's pool hall, diner, and movie theater (now closing because of television), dies halfway through the film. The impact of Sam's death is mulled over by characters throughout the film, yet it is never come to terms with.

Similarly, the narrative of *Klute* (1971) involves a father who has disappeared. Near the beginning of *Klute,* we see the silent unity of a suburban

7. *Klute,* courtesy of Photofest

holiday celebration in an upwardly mobile, small town Pennsylvania community followed by camera shots of an empty chair and a confused wife. A small audiotape player, hovering in a kind of hyper-space, appeared before the initial family scene and seemed to look over it. The machine plays a woman's voice advocating that "nothing is wrong" and one should "let it all hang out." We hear this tape six times throughout the film and soon guess that this is the professional advice that call-girl Bree Daniels (Jane Fonda) gives to her client, voyeuristic multinational businessman Peter Cable (Charles Cioffi). The film soon loses the traditional innocence of its opening and shifts to New York and a problematic relationship between the now ex–call girl and rural-policeman-become-private-investigator Klute (Donald Sutherland).

Cable, whose name suggests a shuttle-like shell game of international business, is in continuous transit between New York and Pennsylvania. He has disrupted a family that is not his by murdering the beneficent missing patriarch of the film's opening, Tom Gruneman, after Gruneman inadvertently witnessed his boss, Cable, with a prostitute (whom Cable also murders). Cable hires Klute as a subterfuge to mislead the FBI. However, it is through the uncovering of this cover-up (a cultural foreshadowing of Watergate from Alan J. Pakula, the future director of *All the President's Men*) that Klute discovers that Cable has tried to set up Gruneman. Cable has forged obscene letters allegedly written by Gruneman to Daniels. Through an analysis of typewriters, Klute eventually determines that Cable is the perpetuator of the cover-up and hence probably the murderer. Although the dead Gruneman is redeemed, the system as a whole is shaken because a higher-up in the system, his boss, who is indeed the initiator of the investigation, is responsible for the crime. We often see Cable in his high New York skyscraper office, and scenes of checking out possible surveillance operations on roofs and top floors associate the apparent menaces of boardrooms and surveillance.

Whereas in the sixties surveillance techniques tended to be seen from the point of view of spies and enforcers of world order, in the seventies the concealed tape recorder is the tool of the obsessed corporate stalker. Surveillance enters the lives of everyday characters.

The appropriately named Cable obsessively listens to his "let it all hang out" recording of Daniels and terrorizes her by playing it over the phone. Bree, however, is trying to move past this precept. She is trying to free herself of a compulsion to offer herself as a prostitute through on-screen therapy sessions that sometimes serve as the soundtrack for interactions between Bree and Klute. In the early seventies, one-to-one psychotherapy assumes a new validity (often in popularized forms such as Primal Scream therapy), after a sixties preference for less guided spiritual searches over psychotherapeutic experts. The overdubs of Bree's therapy sessions seem to "survey" her troubles and triumphs over her professed inability to feel. And yet Cable's terrorizing of Bree with her own "talk" uses a kind of predetermined variation of the talking cure against her.

In a sense, Bree is "stalked" by a society that traps her in a life without dignity. Bree says that when she tries to leave the "system" she finds herself "looking up its ass." Fashion being one of Bree's alternatives to prostitution, *Klute* introduces us to Bree in a demeaning fashion line-up, and Cable chooses a fashion industry loft for his final rendezvous with Bree. Bree goes to this loft, the office of her only remaining prostitution client—an old man for whom she does not mind merely dressing and playacting—because she cannot reach her psychotherapist, has alienated Klute, and wants someone to talk and be with.

We may consider *Klute* antifeminist because Bree is eventually rescued by a man. It is difficult to refute this view based entirely on the film's explicit content. However, although Bree needs Klute's help, it is clear if unstated that Klute needs Bree to help him negotiate the rural world that will never be the same for him. Cable, after all, comes from a small town. Sutherland plays off this unvoiced dimension of his role. Although business-like and stoic, he often has cool tears in his eyes when his talks with Bree validate his problematized experience. The film ends with Bree and Klute moving from Bree's New York apartment while we hear a voice-over of Bree telling her psychotherapist that she might move back in a week. It is difficult not to take this possibility seriously, although Bree's growth in therapy makes the positive ending of the film more credible. Like *Patton, Love Story, Little Big Man,* and *The Boys in the Band, Klute* does not provide a definitive or happy ending. Similarly, the unresolved ending of the sixties lends itself to individual solutions.

Some of the film's most moving moments show Bree trying to maintain a single person's domestic space that contains traces of sixties counterculture trappings. However, she is often seen from above, suggesting that she has no secure space because she can be surveyed. The early establishment of this space makes us aware of how eerily vulnerable Bree is to a stalker's incursions.

Klute, like *Play Misty for Me* (1971), prefigures the onslaught of horror films later in the decade. Horror is a prominent feature of seventies films, and I will discuss it throughout this chapter. I should note here that George Romero's *Night of the Living Dead* was first released in 1968, but since it was an independent, low-budget endeavor it was not widely seen until the early seventies. Its subject of being barricaded in a country house as the dead awaken with a vengeance speaks better for the return in the seventies of an outmoded reality that I have been discussing throughout this book than a late-sixties reality. Nonetheless, *Night of the Living Dead* also has a late-sixties subtext. The film's hero is Ben, a black man (Duane Jones) who must radicalize himself against antagonist, incompetent, and unhelpful whites. With a hammer and a gun, he copes with the reality of this unreal situation, in which dead bodies are recharged by radiation from a military satellite reentering the earth's atmosphere, prefiguring the media event of Skylab's falling to Earth at the end of the decade.

Of course, *Night of the Living Dead* is, in some respects, a revival of fifties schlock shock, and the army general's television discussion of military operations in the film echoes the often inevitable calling-in of the army in fifties horror films. However, *Night of the Living Dead* takes greater relish in mocking these military operations through the general's pompous demeanor.

Ben manages to save himself but is undone by paramilitary assistance. Misidentifying him as a ghoul, volunteer police forces shoot him. The film ends with macabre still-photos that seem to incorporate the hero's perspective, before the volunteers place him on a pile of dead bodies that are burned, preventing them from coming back to life. After all, if the hero were allowed to revive, we might identify with him.

In the sixties, we can see a kind of compromise with horror occurring in *Rosemary's Baby* (1968), wherein a woman's cosmic fears are justified when she finds that she really is pregnant with the devil's child. Nonetheless, she is still happy to love her child. The horror is incorporated into a somewhat functioning vision. However, by the late seventies, in, for example, *Eyes of Laura Mars* (1978), fear and horror have no lighter side and cannot be compromised. Laura Mars is a woman who cannot free herself from surveying the horror that will presumably overtake her. She sees through the eyes of someone stalking her, but she does not know who the stalker is.

If, in a somewhat uncritical fashion, the audience entertains the perspective of the unveiled rapist/murderer in *Eyes of Laura Mars,* the early seventies *Carnal Knowledge* (1971) requires its audience to be critical of its phallocentric leading character. *Carnal Knowledge* is memorable for its disturbing and unreconciled overtones. This film, like *Klute,* foretells the increased prominence that the notion of behavior as "scripts" and "tapes" and "games" takes on throughout the seventies via the reception in the decade of Eric Berne's *Games People Play* (1964), with its Transactional Analysis, in addition to Wayne W. Dyer's *Your Erroneous Zones* (1977) and other popular psychology books. Ritualized acts of prostitution occur in both *Klute* and *Carnal Knowledge.* At the end of *Carnal Knowledge* its central character, Jonathan (Jack Nicholson), so that he can attain an erection, hires a prostitute (Rita Moreno) to enact his script, which lauds his supposed male dominance. Jonathan must completely control his environment to arouse himself. "I just want it right," he tells Rita Moreno's character when she changes the script's wording. Correspondingly, Mike Nichols films *Carnal Knowledge* with a great deal of reserve and control. He uses few actors and shoots them from a frontal vantage point. *Carnal Knowledge* mainstreams Jean-Luc Godard's straight-into-the-camera documentary interview techniques of the sixties. Nichols's sets seem clean and clinical.

Jules Feiffer's script problematizes game-playing. Near the beginning of the film, Jonathan's college dormitory mate and best friend, Sandy (Art Garfunkel), is told by his future wife, Susan (Candice Bergen), that everything is just an act since we present ourselves differently to different people in our lives. Nevertheless, near the end of the film, Sandy has a relationship with a young hippie-like woman (Carol Kane) who, he says, teaches him that life is not a game and real behavior is possible. Although this already dated sixties authenticity seems dubious, Jonathan's alternative of rigid scripting seems even more unattractive.

Surveillance adds an insidiousness to the film's game-playing. Jonathan uses information that Sandy tells him about Susan to seduce her, his best friend's girlfriend. When Sandy tells Jonathan of Susan's sensitivity, Jonathan is able to manipulate it and feign sensitivity to her by speaking about his supposed insecurities about being like post–World War II "Communists." Interestingly, the film follows Jonathan from the McCarthy era to the more politically and sexually open early seventies but implies that progress is dubious.

It may seem incredibly far-fetched to claim that the Vietnam War is an important absent signifier in *Carnal Knowledge*. However, Jonathan's escalating persistence within his phallocentric logic to the point of merely paying for its affirmation might remind one of the United States's engagement in and financing of the Vietnam War. Indeed, in *Carnal Knowledge,* life-and-death guerrilla battles of college-age men and women could be said to mirror the quagmire in Vietnam. The engagements between the sexes, like Vietnam, seem to begin innocently enough but eventually subsume the film's leading characters. As in Vietnam, conflicts lying under the surface unexpectedly emerge and information is misdirected. When Jonathan tells Susan that he must be a "spy" because women always speak in "codes" and do not mean what they say, Susan counters by telling Jonathan that it is he who always "means something else" than what he says. The least credible characters are understandably the most skeptical characters.

The presence of the absent signifier of Vietnam is perhaps more recognizable in a film like *Deliverance* (1972). *Deliverance* takes middle-class southern men who have managed to avoid fighting in Vietnam through a swamp replete with circumstances that seem more like a set for a Vietnam War film than those of John Wayne's *The Green Berets* (1968), the only widely distributed mainstream film directly about the Vietnam War until *Coming Home* (1978) and *The Deer Hunter* (1978). (*Tracks* [1976], *Go Tell the Spartans* [1978], and *The Boys in Company C* [1977] were not widely released to general audiences.)

John Boorman's *Deliverance,* from James Dickey's seventies book and screenplay, begins with the survivalist premise of Burt Reynolds's character, Lewis, that we are selling away our connection to nature. He convinces his friends to canoe down a southern river that will soon be dammed and transformed into a "big lake." "They're drowning the wilderness," says Lewis. Like *Save the Tiger* (1973), *Deliverance* problematizes the romanticization of an apparently archaic authenticity.[8] Nevertheless, after members of the group are killed, dismembered, raped, or suffer a loss of faith in civilization, the film seems to say that these primal desires should not be taken too lightly.

Most of *Deliverance* revolves around a pre-Watergate need to cover up a justifiable act of self-defense that is committed in response to the acts of forced sodomy and degradation for which the film is most remembered. The vacationers decide that society will not believe the savagery perpetrated against them and will convict them of murder.

A confirmed survivalist, Lewis believes that the "law" and "machines will fail." Rambo's bow and arrow from the eighties films can be traced back to Lewis's reliance on the bow and arrow in *Deliverance*. The film also prefigures the Bernard Goetz incident in 1984, and the militia movement and can be compared to the more contemporaneous *Dirty Harry* (1971), *Death Wish* (1974), and *The French Connection* (1971). The latter film adds a fear of multinational economic arrangements to the mix.

William Friedkin's *The French Connection* is best remembered for its revitalized use of a dramatic car chase that is grittier than chases in sixties action films such as *Bullitt* (1968) since it occurs under the elevated subway tracks of a dilapidated section of Brooklyn. Detective Doyle (Gene Hackman) pursues a hijacked subway train with a car commandeered from a civilian. The lengths to which Doyle goes in the chase to maintain his tail is credible because it animates the surveillance activities that permeate the film. The audience often sees the subject of surveillance with the detectives' voice-over. Most of the film's action revolves around police tails and stake-outs.

The film contradicts all manner of sixties mind-set but one—a sense that cities are decaying. When Doyle visits a nightclub where the Three Degrees sing "Everybody's Going to the Moon," the "moon" of the song might be a metaphor for the suburbs. It is almost as if the rubble of the city must be surveyed and related to the federal government, as two federal agents bureaucratically oversee and impede Doyle's wiretapping activities. Doyle shows no remorse when he accidentally kills a federal agent, and Doyle never acknowledges that the federal government does after all help finance his elaborate surveillance operations.

Although Doyle and his partner manage to bust most of the main participants in a major drug deal, the film ends with a feeling of uncertainty in a flooded warehouse basement on Ward's Island off Manhattan. Ostensibly, this is because the French ringleader escapes. Underlying this uncertainty, however, is the inadequacy of the plot's premise to account for contemporary realities.

New York is supposed to be out of heroin and awaiting a multi-million-dollar shipment, but it is no longer credible to suppose that the United States can control its borders so as to cut off drug supplies so efficiently. Indeed, it seems impossible effectively to control crime at all. The pervasiveness of crime is demonstrated by how plausible it seems for ordinary citizens to be involved in the film's chase and shoot-up. Moreover, on two occasions, Doyle uses telephone booths as temporary "prisons" to detain a witness and a suspect, as if to symbolize the intertwining of our sites of public communication and police action.

It is important to note that *The French Connection* portrays a New York of the early seventies, when cities seem things of the past. By the late seventies, the idea of New York is gentrified and glamorized. It would be difficult to imagine Woody Allen's valorization of New York in *Manhattan* (1979) earlier in the decade. Indeed, it might be argued that the renewed credibility of New York is a crucial factor in making possible the "serious" Allen of *Annie Hall* (1977), *Interiors* (1978), and *Manhattan*.

If the reality of New York in *The French Connection* is crumbling, suburbia still seems an urban supplement. An illustrative image is the Lincoln Continental that the police methodically and obsessively tear apart and dissect to find the much sought mother lode of heroin, an image which portends an uneasiness with car culture, its hidden dangers, and a kind of "drugged" consciousness that seemingly fuels it and maintains its dominance. The police examination of the Lincoln is similar to the elaborate medical examination of the possessed girl in Friedkin's next major seventies hit, *The Exorcist* (1973), and both scenes associate clinical examination and issues of demonization.

Steven Spielberg's first film, *Duel* (released to international theaters in 1972 and shown on American television in 1971, but not viewed in American theaters until 1983), also treats the theme of survival in a lawless society. Like *The French Connection,* the film revives the excitement to be found in the closely surveillant car chase. *Duel* concerns the frantic efforts of a traveling salesman (Dennis Weaver) in a small automobile to avoid the sadistic impulses of a faceless oil-tanker driver to torment and murder him with his truck. The movie schools Spielberg in the treatment of ominous, seemingly all-powerful, mechanistically impersonal surveillant forces as they prey on everyday Americans, preparing the director for his quintessential achievement in this "genre," *Jaws* (1975). The character of David Mann, the frustrated salesman in *Duel,* represents the overburdened American working man stalked by impersonal corporate forces, and, since his calls for help to the police and others receive no response, unassisted by society. By 1972, the force of conventional institutionalized law does not appear adequate, and it is no coincidence that the release dates of *Deliverance, The Godfather* (1972), and *Serpico* (1973) are within a few months of each other.

Serpico marks a shift from the pre-Watergate to the Watergate micro-period. Like antagonists in pre-Watergate films like *Klute* and *Little Big Man,* Serpico (Al Pacino) seeks to actualize himself. However, as in Watergate-era films like *The Godfather* and *Pat Garrett and Billy the Kid* (1973), Serpico cannot ultimately differentiate self-development from a hopeless effort to affect a corrupt and unreformable system.

The film presents a crass urban landscape in which little separates the police and the criminals. Serpico's counterculture friends give him a perspective from which to question the corruption and bureaucracy of the New York Police Department. To a fellow partygoer who introduces herself as an "actor, singer, dancer, and Buddhist," Serpico answers, "I'm a cop." Serpico wishes to be a cop with culture, but he is prevented by counterproductive police regulations and corruption. "If they would take all that energy, see, put it into straight police work, we'd have the city cleaned up in a week. It would be cleaned up. We'd have no crime," he declares. "Who can trust a cop who don't take money?" one of Serpico's colleague's comments, and Serpico is thus ostracized for refusing to take bribes.

Whistle-blowing brings Serpico into contact with another layer of corruption. He is misled into thinking that action is being taken concerning his complaints while in fact they are being ignored. By going public, Serpico triggers an independent investigation. However, if, as Serpico maintains, "the whole fucking system's corrupt," what guarantee is there that outside investigators will be uncontaminated? Thus the film's contradictory ending—Serpico courageously testifies at the Knapp Commission but also resettles in Switzerland and leaves the police department.

The audience is never led to believe in the effectiveness of Serpico's testimony, or of the power of testimony in general, and Serpico refuses to be decorated for merely "being a good cop," putting his gold shield aside by his hospital bed after being shot in an apparent set-up. He halfheartedly testifies, but his testimony dwells on a moral order that he believed in when he left the police academy, where we met him at the start of the film. Serpico seems more concerned with evoking nostalgia for a distant past than with invigorating the system.

By 1973 there is a heightened nostalgia for the sounds of the early six-

8. *American Graffiti,* courtesy of Photofest

ties and late fifties. *American Graffiti* (1973) is the first film fully to realize the value of using former hits on movie soundtracks. Ironically, George Lucas had difficulty convincing Universal Studios to spend ten thousand dollars for the rights to use the oldies music in the film. While *The Last Picture Show* might claim this honor of first incorporating former hits into the film's action, I would argue that its Hank Williams soundtrack does not present the same kind of hits that are recognizable to most Americans. Nonetheless, there is a trajectory of increased use of "oldies" as vital constituent elements of films and as more than a background element, from *The Graduate* (1967) to *The Last Picture Show* to *American Graffiti,* and, as we shall see, to *Coming Home.*

Lucas's *American Graffiti* is a groundbreaking project in the "rerepresentation" of a recent past in a symbiotic relationship with the present. The film renders a Northern California town of a mere ten years earlier as an antiquated reality, but nevertheless a reality that we now seem to know we cannot escape. The film's success leads to other representations and recyclings of the recent past such as television's *Happy Days,* which also features Ronny Howard on the fringes of an automobile youth culture. Like *Happy Days, American Graffiti* promotes a pleasant picture of fifties and early sixties youth culture, which sheds its delinquent status. Perhaps in a favorable comparison to the more threatening sixties radical youth culture, the teenager as fifties style becomes a benevolent, basically harmless force.

Happy Days lacks the critical frame provided by *American Graffiti*'s Curt Henderson (Richard Dreyfuss) through whom the audience can feel the action's historical overtones. Curt can neither participate in the small-town business life of the Moose lodge or the prolonged adolescence of the "Pharaoh" gang members, although both, in rapid sequence, say that he will someday make a fine member of their respective groups. Curt does not want to leave his California town, but he senses that change is inevitable. After saying farewell to his family, Curt boards a small Magic Carpet airplane. For one of the few moments in the film's soundtrack, there is relative silence. Curt appears pensive and increasingly disturbed, apparently thinking about the future that he is flying into. Memorably, the film ends with postscripts that tell the fates of its four leading characters: John Milner (Paul Le Mat), the prototype for Fonzie in *Happy Days,* will die in an automobile accident; Terry "The Toad" Fields (Charles Martin Smith) becomes missing in action in An Loc, Vietnam; Steve Bolander (Ronny Howard) will become an insurance salesman in Modesto, California—a fate that might seem worse than death to much of the audience of *American Graffiti* in 1973 (Steve decided to stay, in effect exchanging positions with Curt, who realized he had no choice but to leave); and Curt will become a writer living in Canada, implying that he will become a draft resister. In short, *American Graffiti* presents a suddenly "archaic" (in the sense of entering archives) past that, as suggested by the soundtrack, we cannot escape, perhaps because we can make no definitive sense of this past but cannot stop trying to.

John shows a thirteen-year-old girl (Mackenzie Phillips) a car graveyard and reminisces about an age of automobile culture coming to a close. But how complete will this closure be? The culture on the move that Lucas captures on film prophesies things to come. For instance, the constant conversation between people in cars foreshadows cellular phones. Lucas crafts a revolving, seemingly multinational space that he will develop further in *Star Wars* (1977). At the center of this space is a pirate-like radio station and its disc jockey, Wolfman Jack. Wolfman Jack surveys and pervades the cultural universe of the town. We first hear him on the radio making a prank call to a pizza parlor and asking for a "secret agent spy scope" to view "movie stars, planets, and little bitty spacemen." Indeed, Wolfman Jack links all the town's youth into one common mental body. He represents a more mystical and counterculture version of the loudspeaker in *M*A*S*H* (1970).

Curt receives wisdom by going to the source of the voice. "Crying in the Chapel" by Sonny Till and the Orioles plays as Curt approaches the radio station. Pretending to be an employee of Wolfman Jack's, the disc jockey tells Curt that he could not be the Wolfman because the Wolfman is out in the world. He counsels Curt to see "the great, big beautiful world out there." However, undercutting the advice to seek out new ground and reflective of the film's soundtrack, the disc jockey offers Curt a Popsicle, punning on the film's "pop-cycle" of recycled records. The refrigerator is not working, Wolfman says, and they are melting, alluding to *American Graffiti*'s project of thawing out and recycling the vast reserves of recent American culture.

Curt had gone to Wolfman Jack to contact "the girl in the white T-bird" (Suzanne Somers). After the disc jockey summons her over the airwaves, she calls Curt at the phone booth where he has waited all night. She says that she knows who he is and will see him again. Is she of the past that Curt is leaving or from a phantasmagoric future that he is approaching? *American Graffiti* models this new American temporal indeterminacy. This also translates into a "spatializing" of time that corresponds to a mulching of American culture, which becomes more pronounced as the early seventies becomes the mid seventies.

The year 1974 and Nixon's resignation could be called the dead center of the seventies, when, to use the metaphor of Ashbery's "Self-Portrait in a Convex Mirror," light hits a broken mirror's backing. Francis Ford Coppola's *The Conversation* (1974) is distinctive of the mid-seventies. Surveillance is here an explicit and organizing subject. Like the photographer main character of Michelangelo Antonioni's *Blow Up* (1967), Harry Caul (Gene Hackman) in *The Conversation* inadvertently discovers a murder. However, Harry is not a fashion photographer. His situation is not brought about by existential happenstance. Harry is a surveillance expert, which does not jibe with his wish to be a kind of self-reflexive, modernist artist who does not care about the content of his surveillance efforts. Harry strives merely to attain a "fat recording." His "art" dominates his life. The audience is immediately cued to the ominousness of his work when a microphone atop a building overlooking Union Square in San Francisco appears like a rifle. Nonetheless, we can understand Harry's reluctance to be personally involved in the fruits of his work, and when he does take a personal interest, the murderers of a powerful client let him know that he cannot escape *their* surveillance.

During the film's moment of greatest dramatic suspense, as Harry waits to learn whether an incident he dimly glimpsed on a hotel balcony was in fact the

9. *The Conversation,*
courtesy of Photofest

murder that he was trying to prevent, we hear a newscaster discuss Watergate. Like Nixon, Harry becomes the surveyor surveyed. How can one have secrets in a world in which, as one of the surveillance experts in *The Conversation* says, "there is no moment between human beings that cannot be recorded"? Harry himself demonstrates how any given conversation in a huge crowd can be isolated from crowd noise until nothing but that one conversation is audible. With such knowledge, how can anything again ever be completely casual and unrehearsed?

About two-thirds of *The Conversation* was already filmed at the time of the Watergate hotel break-in. Pre-Watergate seventies films such as *Klute, Carnal Knowledge, The Godfather, Duel, The Parallax View, Play Misty for Me, Last Tango in Paris,* and *Pat Garrett and Billy the Kid* demonstrate that anxiety about surveillance is in the air before Watergate, an anxiety that sustains the affair. *The Godfather* uncannily prefigures Watergate by demonstrating that the underside of the workings of America truly is morally dark. The mob *really* does become dangerous and sordid. Similarly, Nixon's apologists' defense—that "everyone does it"—became a less harmless assertion. The conspiracy-theory-oriented *The Parallax View* (1974), in which an investigator is set up as the apparent assassin, shows the implicit injustice of surveillance games. *Play Misty for Me* brings the terror of sexually obsessed surveillance home to men by reversing expected roles and making a woman the stalker.[9] *Last Tango in Paris* (1972) makes a stripped-down Paris apartment a kind of surveillance station through which a young Parisian woman must face the banality of her life. In *Pat Garrett and Billy the Kid,* an outlaw who has sold out to corrupt and ruthless business interests hunts down a friend for no discernible reason except that eastern money objects to the paradigm of freedom that Billy represents. Most of the film is a dance of death in which Pat's posse and Billy's gang survey and circle one another.

Post-Watergate films like *Three Days of the Condor* (1975), *All the President's Men* (1976), *The Last Detail* (1973), *Mikey and Nicky* (1976), *Shampoo* (1975), and *The Passenger* (1975) intermingle everyday life and surveillance operations. *Three Days of the Condor* presents a CIA researcher (Robert Redford) whose only skill is being able to read and absorb information. After inadvertently discovering a CIA secret, the researcher avoids the corrective hit on everyone else in his New York brownstone office. He must navigate New York and enlist the help of common New Yorkers to get his story to the *New York Times.* He becomes a kind of walking *Pentagon Papers. Mikey and Nicky* demonstrates that surveillance imperatives are stronger than friendship when a petty criminal leads a childhood friend to his death. Similarly, *The Last Detail* presents a Navy law enforcer who must kill the prisoner whom he has befriended and unwittingly encouraged to escape. *Shampoo* places Nixon's 1968 campaign in the background from the perspective of an unpolitical womanizer who finds the woman he *really* loves, as well as the money he needs to start a business and "grow up" in control of money tangentially related to Nixon. *The Passenger* (1975) presents a reporter who is surveyed and tracked down by revolutionary gun-purchasers who believe he is the man he has pretended to become through a switch of passports so as to escape his own identity as an ultimate kind of reporter's exercise.

Intimations of horror in mainstream films such as *Klute* and *Play Misty for Me* blossom into full marriages between horror and surveillance in the midseventies. The setting of *The Exorcist* (1973), Georgetown, Washington, in 1973, parallels the kind of exorcism that is determined to be necessary in Washington at the time due to the Nixon administration's surveillant propensities. Similarly, the events of *The Rocky Horror Picture Show* (1975), which center on a white-bread American couple's introduction to a surreal heavy-metal America, occur on the night of Nixon's resignation speech. The inherent conflicts of this night, are now, in a sense, frozen in time by the film's ritualized weekly revivals.

The Manson family murders, as a prelude to the seventies, become the top

10. *The Rocky Horror Picture Show,* courtesy of Photofest

media story soon after the first manned landing on the moon and the Woodstock festival. It is almost as if the achievements of walking on another heavenly body and the instant creation of a rock and roll city are too libidinous and, in the give and take of the environment of news coverage, need to be balanced by a kind of psychic retribution. For whatever reason, in the early and mid-seventies, horror films and a general interest in the grotesque move from a peripheral place as a novelty in American culture to a more valorized place in its mainstream. A codification of horror into safe, commercial forms occurs along with a similar codification of profanity and nudity in films and general American culture.

The horror of castration plays a major role in Laura Mulvey's seminal article "Visual Pleasure and Narrative Cinema" (1975). Mulvey posits that cinematic pleasures result from the dominance of the male gaze. The pleasures of looking serve either sadistically to survey and to control women or to turn women into fetishes that assure that the castration that the male dreads cannot occur, because it is already represented and warded off by the seemingly already castrated woman. Both modes use women as the male object of desire and castration. Mulvey's own films attempt to escape the phallocentric pleasures of cinema, which she believes dominate the enjoyment of films as we know them, by dividing, rotating, and integrating the viewer's gaze and focus. Mulvey seeks to undermine seemingly destructive cinematic pleasures by destroying the gaps between the viewers' gazes.

Precisely when Mulvey's article appears in a 1975 issue of *Screen,* the movie *Jaws* (1975) uses a "shark cam" that merges the perspectives of the shark, camera, and viewer in the film's effective opening sequence and throughout the film. Thus, the audience sees as a shark, a dismembering and metaphorically castrating force, would see. It is almost as if mainstream filmmakers use Mulvey's insights.

The film's marketing strategy mirrors the character of its animal antagonist, which, says the shark scientist played by Richard Dreyfuss, is primarily to eat. The concept of the blockbuster film is to "eat" its audience before they know what is happening. Both *Jaws* the film and Jaws the shark take on the character of this all-consuming impulse. The film is marketed as a critic-proof must-see phenomenon designed to make maximum profits during the first weekend that it opens, creating unstoppable momentum. Before *Jaws,* movies had slower build-ups and tended to be tested in secondary markets or select, deluxe theaters. *Jaws* helped perfect the massive early publicity campaign for first-class films. The "jaws" concept is thus appropriate for new seventies blockbuster techniques.

Jaws plays on the newly culturally embedded Watergate myth. The governmental and moneyed interests of Amity, an island off Long Island, distort reality to cover up a kind of castration machine—the shark Jaws. Eventually, this reality can be hidden no longer. The horror of the aftermath of Watergate can strike anywhere. *Jaws* utilizes Watergate to inscribe American political potency—a kind of collective phallus—into a symbolic order that is organized by massive international marketing. *Saturday Night Live* plays upon the apparent omnipotence of the fear *Jaws* produces and satirizes marketing modes with its "Land Shark" character, a walking shark head that tricks women into opening their apartment front doors with subterfuges such as "Candygram" so he can swallow their heads.

As is appropriate given the impact of *Jaws* on American movie marketing, *Jaws* is perhaps the central American film of the seventies. "Jaws" can overtake all facets of society. The shark's first victim is apparently from a sixties-like counterculture. She emerges from the folk music, marijuana smoking, and casual intimacy of a college kid's sixties night beach party. The party is shot in an early seventies simulated–cinema verité style. The camera follows these outsider, counterculture activities until we meet a young man drinking a beer, burping, and staring somewhat lasciviously at a long-haired woman who outruns a male college student to the beach, tearing off her clothes as she runs. Horror seems to arise out of a discharge of libido, and the woman is punished by a Mulveyesque "proof" of the "revelation" of feminine castration.

We first see her swimming from the shark's point of view, then from the perspective of the beach until she silently falls under water. We fade into the next morning and a woman in bed, seemingly aware that some kind of horror has occurred. We modulate from the sadism of the shark's gaze to the fetishism of the camera shot of the breasts of the woman, whom we soon discover to be the sheriff's wife. We have moved from imaginary implications of the counterculture to the official implications of law enforcement. The missing young woman, a "summer girl," is then discovered as a hand that is decaying and being eaten by sea crabs. We cut to the sheriff instructing an assistant on how to keep the filing system working. She must keep old papers off his desk. We first discover the police chief's explanation of the death in a close-up of the police report, on which he types SHARK ATTACK. It is almost as if the type were fetishized and serves verbally to mobilize our sense of the symbolic order functioning through the police chief. However, his authority is questioned by the mayor, who corresponds to a decayed version of the symbolic order that resonates with the dead body that we have seen. Although *Jaws* articulates an exhilarating post-Watergate vision of the exposure of a corrupt cover-up, since there is nothing to prevent a similar lapse in the political and moral order, a vision such as the one presented in *Nashville* (1975) is the logical result.

In the early seventies, multi-character, multi-situation narratives drive films like *The Last Picture Show* and, in the mid-seventies, *American Graffiti* and *Nashville*. Robert Altman's *Nashville* montages filmic tropes around the loosely concocted structure of the planning of a political rally that is also a country and western music festival. Altman's film, from a script by Joan Tewkesbury, is prescient of the Reagan Hollywood/Washington of the eighties. In his 1980 campaign, Reagan never shied away from his associations with Hollywood, and he played on much of America's wish to buy a safe and packaged reality. In the seventies and the eighties, politics seems to move closer to entertainment and, conversely, entertainment seems to become more political, and the assassination of a music star by a fan in *Nashville* foretells the 1980 shooting of John Lennon.

Nashville presents about twenty-four roughly equally memorable characters. There is a kind of Lacanian search for the authentic phallus, narrative code, and medium of exchange. Many of the characters are brought together by a political advance-man (Michael Murphy) who works for Hal Phillip Walker, the offscreen presidential candidate of the new Replacement Party. Murphy's character offers country star Haven Hamilton (Henry Gibson) organizational support from the Replacement Party in Hamilton's campaign for the Tennessee governorship in exchange for his performance at a Walker rally. In the seventies, Walker seemed like George Wallace. However, in the nineties, Walker's colloquially evasive stances sound remarkably like H. Ross Perot's. Like Perot, Walker tells voters that they are shareholders in the corporation of the United States of America. A Walker sound truck cruises Nashville playing Walker's inane yet somewhat winning sayings that deride lawyers in government and a Washington that is presiding over the lowering of the nation's standard of living.

Haven Hamilton's female companion, Lady Pearl (Barbara Baxley), still carries a JFK campaign button. She calls Nixon "the asshole" and cannot get over what the loss of "the Kennedy boys" has meant to the country. Many seventies films include Kennedy references. For instance, in *Klute,* Jane Fonda hangs up an unfinished sketch of John Kennedy that she is presumably working on. In *Carnal Knowledge,* Jack Nicholson's character will not allow Ann-Margret's character to work for Kennedy in 1960, the only thing that she feels is worth her getting out of the apartment. Screenwriter Joan Tewkesbury (Altman worked closely with Tewkesbury on the narrative dynamics of the film) recalls that *Nashville* was conceived as a pessimistic reaction to the 1972 Nixon landslide:

> Part of *Nashville* was because he hated what Richard Nixon was doing to the country. I'll never forget the image—when we were walking down the street the morning after Nixon had been elected again. There had been a huge windstorm the night before, and all of these umbrellas were turned inside out. And he said, "The world is mourning. We've lost because Nixon has won." He was really angry about that.[10]

When Barbara Jean (Ronee Blakley) is shot on stage after her performance, Haven Hamilton calms the crowd by saying, "This isn't Dallas, it's Nashville," but he cannot avoid the underlying suspicion that the effects of the Kennedy assassination are now everywhere.

Barbara Jean is the unifying consciousness of *Nashville.* She has suffered what her publicist husband calls a "nervous breakdown." Mirroring the narrative organization of the film, Barbara Jean makes loose associations. Interestingly, presidential candidate Walker asks similarly synecdochal questions such as "Does Christmas smell like oranges to you?" Walker tries to provide reassur-

11. *Network,* courtesy of Photofest

ing references within displaced contexts, and Barbara Jean's associations are significant in that they make vivid to her fans childhood memories that have shaped the personality that they adore. In the middle of a concert, Barbara Jean astutely remarks on her perception of background voices in records. Why should this be an inappropriate occasion for such anecdotal criticism? Barbara Jean's disassociative narrativizing comes across as refreshingly real and honest in the face of the shallow sentimentality of Altman's version of the country music business. Her monologue, which in its discursive overtones is reminiscent of some moments of André Gregory's dialogue in *My Dinner with André* (1981), calls attention to almost subsonic voices that seem as significant as the "disembodied" voice that the Hal Phillip Walker campaign truck emits.

Voices also figure heavily in Sidney Lumet's *Network* (1976). The film compares the media to spiritual mediums. Paddy Chayefsky's script concerns Edward R. Murrow's fictional former colleague, Howard Beale (Peter Finch), who is cast by the network as a seer who senses cosmic "prana." Beale uses this "gift" to tap the discontent of the American people and garner ratings with his conservative populism. However, when he turns his audience against the "veiled" multinational corporate dealings of his network, the network's CEO, Arthur Jensen (Ned Beatty), makes him see the corporate light. "America does not exist. Democracy does not exist," Jensen tells Beale. The individual no longer has any agency, says Jensen, and the only reality is multinational corporations that are accountable to no one, which is all to the good because reality is divinely superhuman. Beale preaches Jensen's gospel and loses his ratings. However, Jensen refuses to cancel him, making it necessary for ambitious program executives to assassinate Beale on the air. A post-Watergate film, *Network* accurately predicts Watergate's destabilizing effects. Disenchanted Nixon supporters do not become liberals or leftists but volatile "swing voters." By 1976, populist and corporate forces mingle surprisingly well. "Free-floating" dissatisfaction encroaches upon serious journalism. *Network* anticipates the populist media demigogue and tabloid news programs of the eighties and nineties.

Beale asks his viewers to "stand up wherever you are, go to the nearest window and yell as loud as you can: 'I'm mad as hell, and I'm not going to take it anymore!'" Heads and voices project outward in juxtaposition to the interior space of most of the film. Like *Network,* Martin Scorsese's *Taxi Driver* (1976), from a script by Paul Schrader, also conveys a kind of free-floating anger. It is understood that Watergate has not been an ultimate cure. As in *Nashville,* a potential assassin stalks a presidential candidate but switches his target. *Taxi Driver* protagonist Travis Bickle's (Robert De Niro's) voice-over expresses moral indignation through an Arthur H. Bremer-like diary that Travis keeps. (Like Bremer, who shot George Wallace after stalking Richard Nixon, Bickle switches his assassination target.) Against a lush yet subdued saxophone accompaniment, Travis's voice relates a crusade against city "scum," as Travis often puts it. Travis contrasts the purity of Betsy (Cybill Shepherd) to this scum. However, either because he knows nothing but sordid night life or because he wishes to keep Betsy at a distance, he puts her off by taking her to a pornographic movie. After he is jilted, perhaps to impress Betsy, he is anxious to be a vigilante and arms himself.

Taxi Driver incorporates the New York-as-wild-west theme of *Death Wish* (1974): however, it points out the vigilante's poignant misguidedness. Travis has little sense of himself. He wishes to give the public what it seems to want. He perceives that people are tired of indirect political solutions. At times he acts paranoid, such as in the famed "Are you looking at me" quip that he practices in a mirror. However, Travis's paranoia is a strategy that he finds empowering. He soaks up identity from others, and when a pimp and a prostitute tell him that he looks like a cop or narcotics officer, he writes home that he works for the government. Travis likes the idea of this kind of mission, and the killing of a relatively everyday hold-up man leaves Travis unsatisfied.

He stalks presidential candidate Charles Palantine (Leonard Harris), for whom Betsy works. However, when a Secret Service man notices Travis reaching for his gun at a Palantine rally, Travis brutally kills the pimp, the hotel manager, and the john of Iris (Jodie Foster), a fourteen-year-old prostitute whom Travis idolizes as "pure." In the film's most startling image, a slowly panning overhead shot of the carnage and several policemen pointing guns at the bloody, wounded, and unconscious Travis utilizes a classically "arrested" pose wherein art is seemingly kept in place at gunpoint.

Near the end of the film, we sense how common his underlying attitude might be when we see how easily Travis could be hailed as a hero for his murders. Travis represents an American concensus and ideal that hinders our political consciousness. In a sense Travis surveys us, as is implied by Travis's constant surveying of scenes through his windshield. He sees life through a self-imposed monitor.

Close Encounters of the Third Kind (1977) presents a countervision of surveillance that is more positively internalized by an average American brought to a benign spaceship by an inner vision of where it will land. Surveillance is seemingly sanitized. And yet when Spielberg re-edited the film for an eighties redistribution, he cut scenes in which the hero concretizes his inner vision and added fantastic Disney references such as the playing of "When You Wish upon a Star" inside the spacecraft. The recut version replaces sixties overtones of self-discovery with a Disney version of theme-park adventure.

Perhaps leading to the "heroism" of the Reagan presidency, the purely fantastic realm of the hero takes a grander dominion in George Lucas's *Star Wars* (1977). After the Vietnam War, a credible war can only occur in the outer space of a distant future or past. (*Star Wars* is said to chronicle wars of long before.) However, there is an ideological need for such a fantastic war, to repair Vietnam's rip in enabling Cold War perceptions. *Star Wars* helps renew Cold War commitments to a binary opposition between good and evil. The film provides the Reagan administration with the tropes of the "Evil Empire" for the Soviet Union and the "Star Wars" nuclear shield for the Strategic Defense Initiative.

Lucas began planning *Star Wars* during the Watergate scandal, and it was released in the first year of the Carter administration. The film presents a post-Watergate "new hope" and starts with its now famous acutely receding epigraph, heading back into deep space, entitled "Episode IV: A New Hope." As Jimmy Carter enhanced his appeal during the 1976 campaign with sixties trappings such as Bob Dylan citations, *Star Wars* marshals sixties allusions to Eastern religion and self-actualization against a high technology Flash Gordonish milieu. Although the spirit of the sixties, in the guise of the "force"-supported Jedi pilots, has been rubbed out "man by man," in the post-Watergate atmosphere, the Jedi knights are returning.

We enter the *Star Wars* narrative in medias res. We are told that we have, in effect, missed three episodes. This narrative device allows Lucas to unfold his tale slowly, since we accept the incompleteness of our background. Like *American Graffiti,* the relating of background information is delayed in favor of a string of vignettes, and the film's pacing underscores details such as the chess game played by holographic, independently minded chess pieces.

However, like many of the great films of the seventies, *Star Wars* is organized by a plot device stressing surveillance. The plot of *Star Wars* is essentially an espionage race, between getting the plan of the Empire's monstrous Death Star into rebel hands so that they can destroy it, and Lord Darth Vader's (David Prowse with voice by James Earl Jones) and the Empire's efforts to discover the location of the rebel base on the dark side of a distant planet's moon. Princess Leia has stored the plans in the robotic midget R2-D2—the little working man of the future who needs the translating assistance of C-3PO—a butler-like version of the Tin Man. (The affectionate bickering and endearing inseparableness of the robots leads one to see them as a version of a gay couple that is acceptable to mass America in the seventies, before the homophobia that AIDS brings in the eighties. Interestingly, the robots fulfill the roles of craftspeople and intellectuals, leaving men to be soldiers, farmers, and criminals.)

Like Watergate, *Star Wars* involves a struggle for tapes. R2-D2 becomes a kind of wobbly walking holographic tape-player that must deliver itself to Ben Obi-Wan Kenobi (Alex Guinness) and then the rebel forces. Obi-Wan is a source of wisdom who, like Wolfman Jack in Lucas's *American Graffiti,* is seemingly everywhere, since Obi-Wan exists in "the force that surrounds and penetrates being." Luke Skywalker (Mark Hamill) hears Obi-Wan's voice in his fighter plane as if it were on the radio. Like Curt in *American Graffiti,* Luke feels that he must leave his small planet and "step into a larger world."

Star Wars brings back the optical device of a Victorian magic lantern. Its computer and miniature effects suggest slides on slides and screens on screens. It changes the look of films, merging a fluid sense of depth into the surface and preparing cinema's way into the age of the VCR, cable, and digital discs— the merging of computers, monitors, and movies.

Star Wars concerns a fantastic ideological alternative to Vietnam. However, the most prominent films of the late seventies pre-Reagan micro-period more

12. *The Deer Hunter,* courtesy of Photofest

overtly involve Vietnam. At the very end of the seventies, there is a kind
of exhaustion of American culture, and mainstream films discuss what they
could not explicitly mention before with a surprisingly muted sense of shock.
I close this chapter with a discussion of three late-seventies films that explicitly portray the Vietnam War: *The Deer Hunter* (1978), *Coming Home* (1978),
and *Apocalypse Now* (1979).

By the late seventies, the war can be more easily thematized. All sides
can simply agree, in the words that *Apocalypse Now* appropriates from Joseph
Conrad, that the war was a "horror." *The Deer Hunter* equates this horror with
a game of Russian roulette, maintaining that the Vietcong forced American
prisoners to play this fatal game for their gambling amusement. Nick (Christopher Walken), in effect, "goes Indian" when his terror over being forced to
play this game brings on a complex that causes him repeatedly to play Russian roulette. His best friend, Michael (Robert De Niro), tries to save him by
reminding him of America with its "country" and "trees," but Michael cannot
shake Nick from his stupor, and he shoots himself in the head as he finally recalls who Michael is—the man who said that a deer must be killed with "one
shot." Nick implies that he has internalized the hunted, victimized position

of the deer. This constitutes, as *The Deer Hunter* portrays it, America's terrible psychological vulnerability in the wake of the Vietnam War. Through various incidents in the pre-Vietnam portion of the film, *The Deer Hunter* faintly suggests that a masculine ethos that finds the abuse of women commonplace is related to the nation's Vietnam experience. However, director Michael Cimino and screenwriter Deric Washburn's film does not question the premise underlying the United States' Vietnam involvement. Americans seem completely justified in fighting a Vietcong enemy who are alone responsible for murdering women and children and torturing prisoners. In short, Hollywood meets the Vietnam War, but not head-on.

While playing pool, the major male characters of *The Deer Hunter* lip-synch Frankie Valli's "I Can't Take My Eyes off of You." This chapter has noted the frequent use of voice-overs in seventies films. A gap between the visual and the verbal becomes standard and even institutionalized in the rock videos of the Reagan era.[11] The theme of a kind of "thrown" sound also figures heavily in the film *Coming Home* (1978), which ironically features a wheelchair-ridden black ventriloquist and his puppet in a Vietnam veterans hospital. If Jasper Johns's 1983 painting *Ventriloquist* is held together by an image that evokes the horror and insanity of the Vietnam War, Hal Ashby's *Coming Home* coalesces around its sixties-music soundtrack. Substantial portions of twenty songs are used with no realistic pretense of a radio playing, as in *American Graffiti*. This is especially unique because songs often play through several cuts and scenes. The movie might seem to imply catharsis that would move us forward yet is also an enjoyable musical replay of the sixties. Written by Waldo Salt and Robert C. Jones (from a story by Nancy Dowd), the film begins and ends with the Rolling Stones' "Out of Time," with the lyrics "you're obsolete my baby." Disabled Vietnam veterans speak about the difficulty of admitting that they may have sacrificed so much for so little. The film asks us to relive Vietnam to appreciate its senselessness and hence not to repeat it. On an unconscious level, the soundtrack asks its audience to root itself in the emotions of the sixties. And yet the film is perhaps too complacent in its assumption that an ideological defense of the naive patriotism underlying much of the war effort will now be universally perceived as untenable and such sentiments will wither away, as pictured at the end of the movie by the wounded Captain Robert Hyde (Bruce Dern), who cannot live with the inaccuracy and hypocrisy of a medal that is awarded. He swims off a California beach to his presumed death.

Portraying surveillance's role in picking apart the new left even as the antiwar effort was helping turn much of the American public against the war, in

13. *Apocalypse Now,* courtesy of Photofest

Coming Home, Hyde learns, through the FBI's surveillance of the couple, that his wife Sally (Jane Fonda) has been unfaithful with a paraplegic veteran (Jon Voight) who protests the war. Francis Ford Coppola's *Apocalypse Now* (1979) is a late-seventies study of the punitive uses of surveillance. Captain B. L. Willard (Martin Sheen) is a U.S. Army intelligence officer in Saigon who is assigned to make a river journey to Cambodia to "terminate with extreme prejudice" the freelancing command of Colonel Walter E. Kurtz (Marlon Brando). The officers who send Willard on his journey use a murder charge against Kurtz as a pretext for giving Willard his assignment. Upon studying Kurtz's file, however, Willard determines that Kurtz is being executed for not rendering himself submissive to the incompetent officers who are running the war.

Willard is silently outraged that he is being asked to kill another American. The surveillance officer gradually comes to understand that the war effort and its horror have more to do with maintaining a repressive state away from the United States than in trying to win a war. Officers such as Colonel Kilgore ("I love the smell of napalm in the morning. . . . It smells like victory"), played by Robert Duvall, even express dismay at the prospect of the war ending. Kilgore pillages a Vietnamese village to get a better place to surf. Robert Altman's film *M*A*S*H* had already portrayed the game-playing that informs war efforts, but without this extremely casual and vicious sadism. When Altman filmed *M*A*S*H* in the late sixties, the My Lai massacre had not yet been widely publicized. Before My Lai, atrocities were perpetrated by the Vietnamese, such as in the photograph released during the 1968 Tet offensive, of a South Vietnamese official shooting a helpless Vietcong point blank through the side of the head.

What, Willard asks himself, could Kurtz be doing that was worse and more militarily out of line than the deeds of Kilgore? Willard even seems to consider joining Kurtz, who is feared as a god by the primitivistic, cattle-sacrificing villagers. Willard, however, comes to feel that Kurtz is asking to die. The captain says that he feels that nature itself is telling him to kill Kurtz, and he hacks the colonel as the village people hack the sacrificial cows.

What does Willard learn from this experience? At the start of the film, he resembles James Dean at his most tortured and self-doubting. He is hungry for another mission to help forget himself. By the end of the film, Willard experiences a terrible truth of Vietnam—that it is merely about the surveillance and control of the Vietnam operation itself by the status quo. Not wishing to participate in any more missions, he thus disconnects his radio, as if to say that he no longer trusts informing voices and transistorized hierarchies.

At its beginning, *Apocalypse Now* is filmed in amusement-park colors. We often see *Great Gatsby*- and Coney Island–like strings of lights. The film shows Americans in Vietnam surfing, water skiing, and listening to the Rolling Stones. One of the men on the gunboat that takes Willard downriver comments that the war "is better than Disneyland." Although precious few soldiers may have experienced the war this way, Coppola nevertheless portrays the wild sense of privilege and emotional distance that informs the war.

When we reach the Cambodian village, however, the film's colors and lighting become much darker. Willard will not be surprised by the horror he encounters. Based on Joseph Conrad's *Heart of Darkness,* the film cannot help but reflect a world that has already consumed Conrad's tale as, indeed, the film cannot help but acknowledge the already consumed if not fully digested horror of the Vietnam War. As in the Conrad story, the movie depicts an imperialist operation that itself has much to do with the horror that it projects. *Apocalypse Now* thus lacks the shock of realization. We do not feel the pleasure of seeing previously unsurveyed realms that we might feel in Coppola's first two *Godfather* films and *The Conversation.* Appropriately, the horror of Willard's final realization is that he doesn't discover anything the audience doesn't already know. Sheen plays Willard with an extremely effective display of blunted emotions. Similarly, the film need not fictively suspend our powers of disbelief to make its point. Although this is the first widely distributed mainstream American film of the seventies to simulate elaborate Vietnam combat sequences (*The Deer Hunter* used a small cast, indoor scenes, news videotapes, and unstaged outside foot-age—its most dramatic scenes are the Russian roulette sequences in a surreal western saloon), we do not feel as if we are seeing anything new. This consti-tutes much of the film's numbed and apathetic horror. We have already formed pictures of the war based on its representations in other media. Most Ameri-cans, for example, probably pictured the Vietnam War in the portrayal of the Korean War that was presented by the television program *M*A*S*H*. Perhaps more importantly, who is to say that the violence of movies like *Taxi Driver* and *The Wild Bunch* (1969) did not represent Vietnam and that the rise in our threshold of acceptable violence in mainstream motion pictures is not in some way connected with the Vietnam War? After all, as Adrienne Rich points out, "the demonic sadism of the bombings," like films, "seemed to be something out-side of us, we could pretend it was something separate from our inner lives."[12]

For effect, Coppola must put a fantastic edge on the barely hidden workings of his filmic process. His most startling discovery is that the act of movie-making approximates the insanity of war. While all manner of decentered war activities surround him, Coppola himself makes an appearance as a documen-tary filmmaker in the heat of battle telling soldiers not to look into the cam-era. War is a referentially reflexive topos for the organizational skills under-lying the making of the movie. It is difficult, for instance, to view the film's display of synchronized attacking helicopters without thinking of the tech-nical difficulties required in securing the helicopters. In some gruesome way, the greatest horror of the war is that it was ultimately nothing more than a kind of entertainment, prefiguring the Gulf War. Similarly, about the siege of Sarajevo, Zoran Pajic spoke on National Public Radio about "the unbearable lightness of destruction" (1994).

As *Apocalypse Now* can be seen as an analogue of the unassimilated political results of the Vietnam War and the wayward governmental decision-making processes implicit within the crimes and misjudgments of the Watergate affair, Jean Baudrillard's *The Evil Demon of Images* (1987) points out that *Apocalypse Now* wins a cinematic war that the United States loses militarily, and fails to resolve ideologically:

> War as a trip, a technological and psychedelic fantasy; war as a succes-
> sion of special effects, the war became film well before it was shot; war

replaced by technological testing. For the Americans, it was above all the latter: a test site, an enormous field on which to test their weapons, their power.

Coppola does the same thing: he tests the power of intervention of cinema, tests the impact of cinema become a vast machine of special effects. In this sense his film is very much the prolongation of war by other means, the completion of that incomplete war, its apotheosis. War becomes film, film becomes war, the two united by their mutual overflow of technology.[13]

Part of this technology implicates sixties music production. *Apocalypse Now* employs rich overlays of color and image reminiscent of textures of sound that electronic tape made possible in sixties music. *Apocalypse Now* begins and ends with the Doors recording, "The End," reminding us that the genius of sixties music in some way fashioned the genius of seventies films. However, by the end of the seventies, there seems to be little more to represent, and "The End" is an appropriate musical bookend for a film entitled *Apocalypse Now,* which bespeaks a cultural apocalypse that is already somehow being repressed and put out of mind. Everything worth surveying seems to have been surveyed.

In marked comparison with *Patton,* which opened our discussion of seventies films, *Apocalypse Now* is spatially crammed so as to defy gravity. In its opening montage we see Willard's head upside down, superimposed upon scenes of Vietnamese interiors with ceiling fans and exteriors with burning napalm. The shots of Willard and the shots of Vietnam begin to move, in a spinning fashion, in opposite directions. Things are breaking apart. A vacuous center is not holding. The film's dialogue often alludes to this state of affairs. For instance, the general who gives Willard his assignment (G. D. Spradlin) suggests that the dishes at the dinner table, which include potentially poisonous shrimp that are festively decorated, be passed "both ways to save time." Similarly, Colonel Kilgore notes that the waves of the Mekong River are dangerous for surfers because they "break both ways." More importantly, there is a pictorial resistance to gravity that prefigures the night-sensitive pictures of the bombing of Baghdad, literally filtered with etched moonlight upon the mosques of the city replete with bubble-like flares arcing up against the gravity of the grim-reaper realities underlying the whole fluid text. In *Apocalypse Now,* we look down from helicopters at cattle being hauled into the sky. We see gunboats dropped from the sky into the ocean and festival lights that seem to be strung in space. In both word and image, *Apocalypse Now* shows an awareness of how it and its culture deconstructs itself. It expresses deferred horror at how hard it is to retain this awareness. In the eighties, it could be said that we erase much of this awareness, and the decade brings with it the wish to take George Washington's advice and avoid entangling alliances, such as our recent one with a South Vietnam of our own making, while nevertheless benefiting from our sense of gravity-defying world supremacy within liquid capital's porous new world.

This chapter stressed a diachronic reading of the seventies. The next chapter takes a more synchronic tack by emphasizing particular historical moments and giving special attention to the pivotal mid-seventies.

THREE

The Historian's Bow

The previous chapter used one seventies discipline to trace the decade's progress. This chapter employs an interdisciplinary tool to give special attention to the crucial mid-seventies. I focus on three touchstone mid-seventies phenomena: John Ashbery's "Self-Portrait in a Convex Mirror," which Henry M. Sayre, in *The Columbia Literary History of the United States,* calls "perhaps the most famous poem of the 1970's";[1] the Watergate affair—the most celebrated political episode in American history; and Jasper Johns's mid-seventies crosshatch paintings, which use the first abstract motif to dominate paintings by Johns,[2] the living American artist who, for the longest period of time, has consistently produced unexpected and critically renowned work. The next part of this chapter looks at three events that happened on 10 October 1973, and the chapter concludes with an analysis of three mid-eighties poetic, political, and artistic phenomena that shed light on both the mid-eighties and the mid-seventies phenomena that this chapter discusses at its outset. Hence, this chapter examines three sets of three contemporaneous occurrences.

I am calling a triangulation among three contemporaneous phenomena "a historian's bow" because one phenomenon "pulls back the bow" of the other two and provides a thrust that deepens our understanding of a historical field such as the seventies. A comparison between two contemporaneous phenomena tends to create a limited applicability. A third element can dramatically reconfigure the other two and be a useful tool for explicating an episteme, a micro-period, or a historical moment.

The rest of this book is largely shaped by my Ashbery-Nixon-Johns historian's bow. The concluding three chapters consider seventies literature, art, and politics from the vantage points of seventies phenomena concerning, respectively, Ashbery, Johns, and Nixon. However, each chapter branches out considerably from its initial subject more fully to represent the era.

1 The Back of the Looking Glass as the Site of the Real: Ashbery, Nixon, and Johns

Although Ashbery and most of his critics might scoff at providing a plot summary for "Self-Portrait in a Convex Mirror," it is significant that such a summary is possible. Although the poem may be read as a characteristically impenetrable Ashbery work, it is framed as a moment of lucidity within the poet's oeuvre. More than any other long Ashbery poem, it can be interpreted literally and read for coherent surface meaning. The poem's thematic possibilities bespeak a mid-seventies nostalgia for reality and unity.

"Self-Portrait in a Convex Mirror" begins as a meditation about Francesco Parmigianino's 1524 painting of the same name, the first self-portrait to use a mirror—a mirror which happens to be convex. The tiny round canvas, less than a foot in circumference, portrays the painter's face and, at the bottom of the painting, the distortedly large back of his hand. Ashbery's poem opens with a straightforward description of the painting and gradually modulates into an observation of the painting as if it were a vital system. In the blurriness created on the painting's circumference, the poem's speaker sees an ever-replenishing liquid or embryonic sack that sustains a more definite yet paradoxically vacuous center in the subject's eyes, suggesting a rebirth of vision.

The speaker, who later gives information that identifies him with the poet Ashbery, then finds that he has become like Parmigianino. They are both trapped in this world of the convex mirror. The poet's relationship with the painter begins to take on a quality of complete identification. There is a sense of unresolvable, ambivalently directed erotic investment. A gnawing disquiet ensues. It seems that there is no way out, no way to resolve this critical impasse of everyday seventies life. Life is subsumed by a culture that does not allow active critical involvement. Aspirations are co-opted, and, the poem says, "Dreams prolong us as they are absorbed" (*SP*, 194: 2). Both the speaker and painter are caught in a "bubble-chamber" in which "everything gets 'programmed' . . . without adding to the sum" (*SP*, 193: 2–5).

However, midway through the poem, the speaker notes a new "urgency" (195: 17). The speaker places in apposition the actual locations of where the poem is being written (New York in the seventies), where he saw the painting (Vienna in 1959), and where Francesco was at work when soldiers "burst" into his studio (Rome "during the Sack"). This specificity seems to prepare the speaker for a "new mode [of] questions" (196: 15). These inquiries lead him to doubt the omnipresence of a self-sufficient reality or perpetually co-opted culture. He questions what is behind the mirror. The speaker looks for supports behind a suffocating, self-sufficient modernist environment. "What is the universe a porch of?" he asks (*SP*, 198: 7). He wonders about how self-contained the enabling reality of Parmigianino's painting can be. "Hasn't it too its lair?" he wonders (199: 22). To be "serious" about a "play" that sees mirror images as the "not-being-us" (202: 5) in the glass becomes a strategy for allowing artistic and self-actualizing endeavors. The speaker implores Parmigianino to sacrifice his limited self-identification so that he may contextualize himself in his environment. The painter "fall[s] back" (203: 25) after the poet offers him a bullet with the strong suggestion that he use it upon himself.

"Self-Portrait in a Convex Mirror" and Watergate are metaphoric doubles.[3] Just as the Nixon administration tries to imperialize the presidency by uniting all of the nation's surveillance operations under it, so Ashbery's poem creates a mirror world that traps its subject in his own surveillance. Just as Nixon's efforts lead his administration to self-destruction through a series of surveillance mishaps that highlight America's ambivalence toward presidential authority, so, in Ashbery's poem, a fictionalized Parmigianino destroys himself and his round mirror world. Both the poem and the political scandal undermine the strong, monolithic configurations they posit.

Ashbery uses the second half of "Self-Portrait in a Convex Mirror" to shatter the first half's self-replenishing and all-encompassing vision of a subjectivity ensnared by the "surveillance mechanism" of the convex mirror. A convex mirror is, in a sense, a perfect surveillance mechanism. Convex mirrors allow viewers to see everything behind them in one compact view, and hence convex mirrors are used in or near elevators, automatic teller machines, traffic circles, bus doors, and stores. A viewer standing before a convex mirror cannot escape being reflected in it, creating a kind of closed and self-regulating system. In "Self-Portrait in a Convex Mirror," the viewer entangles himself in the workings of such a system. Similarly, Nixon himself, in the Watergate affair, is ultimately the chief target of his own surveillance mechanisms.

"Self-Portrait in a Convex Mirror" first appeared in the August 1974 issue of *Poetry*, the same month that Richard Nixon resigned his office, and correspondences between the poem and the Watergate drama are as rife as they are obvious. On a surface level, Francesco Parmigianino, the hero of "Self-Portrait in a Convex Mirror," and Richard Nixon both trap themselves in "oval offices." More significantly, "Self-Portrait in a Convex Mirror" is written in the guise of a meditation that overthrows its object, and, during the mid-seventies, Nixon served as a national "object of meditation" that was eventually ostracized.

One might easily argue direct influence between Watergate and "Self-Portrait in a Convex Mirror." After all, even as referentially evasive a poet as Ashbery could hardly have avoided the Watergate narrative that was in the air during this period. One can imagine the Senate Watergate hearings on Ashbery's radio or television, in the background, while he was writing "Self-Portrait in a Convex Mirror." However, this avenue of inquiry holds limited promise. First, the problem of verifiability seems insurmountable. How could one ever be sure what if any part of the poem Ashbery was writing when Alexander Butterfield publicly revealed Nixon's self-espionage? (Ashbery says the poem was just about finished then.) Indeed, in terms of "influence," how crucial was this moment of 16 July 1973? Did not John Dean earlier, during his televised testimony before the Ervin Senate Committee, note his suspicion that he was being taped in the Oval Office? Did not Dean's Senate testimony describe the Nixon administration's proclivity toward surveillance and its attempts to control all federal surveillance agencies and use them for partisan political ends? Was not surveillance the motive for the Watergate break-in itself and self-surveillance embedded in the organization of the cover-up?

Structural, not direct, causality (see chapter 1) makes possible this comparison. Even if Ashbery could be trusted to divulge accurate day-by-day records of the writing of "Self-Portrait in a Convex Mirror," a task fraught with much room for ambiguity and error, how could we ever be sure how the poem reflects the poet's responses to the unfolding scandal? How could the poet himself be sure? In 1986, when I first told Ashbery about my Watergate–"Self-Portrait in a Convex Mirror" parallel, he responded with incredulous humor. "You're comparing me to Nixon," he said jocularly. "Someday you'll get yours. . . . Oh, Nixon was a great president," he joked. "I wish he was still president." Years later, Ashbery himself cited Oliver North's Iran-Contra arms-and-money flowchart placards as an inspiration for *Flow Chart* (1990). Indeed, who better than Ashbery could enjoy the delicious absurdity of Oliver North seeking a seat in the upper branch of the U.S. Congress, an institution whose authority North is famed for disrespecting?

As it is difficult to "prove" Watergate's direct influence on Ashbery, it is similarly difficult to establish a direct poststructuralist influence on the poet.

Although I employ Derrida in this analysis of the poem, I am not arguing that Derrida exercises a direct influence on Ashbery, nor am I attempting to "deconstruct" "Self-Portrait in a Convex Mirror." Instead I maintain that the works of the philosopher and poet are isomorphic. Derrida's philosophy is here utilized as a valuable resource in explicating Ashbery's poetry.[4] For my purposes, Ashbery and Derrida are contemporaneous "cultural workers," and the fact that the trope of the mirror's backing is so prominent in both their works is worth examining in a cultural context.

Considered as cultural phenomena, the following passages by John Ashbery and Jacques Derrida shed light on one another:

> The backing of the looking glass . . .
>
> wants
>
> To siphon off the life of the studio, deflate
> Its mapped space to enactments, island it.
> (*SP*, 195: 28–31)

> We have now arrived at the point where the relation between the "text"—in the narrow, classical sense of the term—and the "real" is being played out. . . . the very concepts of text and of extratext . . . are engaged. . . . The breakthrough toward radical otherness (with respect to the philosophical concept—of the concept) always takes, *within philosophy*, the *form* of a posteriority or an empiricism. But this is an effect of the specular nature of philosophical reflection, philosophy being incapable of inscribing (comprehending) what is outside it otherwise than through the appropriating assimilation of a negative image of it, and dissemination is written on the back—the *tain*—of that mirror.[5]

Rodolphe Gasché maintains that Derrida uses the tain to describe the delimitation of unconfined semiotic play:

> On this lining of the outside surface of reflection, one can read the "system" of the infrastructures that commands the mirror's play and determines the angles of reflection. . . . Seen from the inside this play gives an illusion of perfection, but observed through the tain, it appears limited by the infrastructural agencies written on its invisible side, without which it could not even begin to occur.[6]

The backing of the mirror, conceived as the opaque surface against which light deflects and pivots, is a master trope for the organization of reality as a kind of social discipline. Derrida employs the trope of the mirror's backing to describe the site of the "extratext[ual]" and empirical. After all, as Derrida remarks, it is "the specular nature of philosophical reflection" not to be able to explain "what is outside it." Hence, only troping can account for "the 'real.'" To further examine Derrida's remark, "specular" can literally mean "of the mirror," as John Ashbery's "Self-Portrait in a Convex Mirror" reminds us ("The words are only speculation / [From the Latin *speculum*, mirror]" [*SP*, 189: 14, 15]), and Derrida suggests that philosophical speculation, and, indeed, all we can know, can be likened to mirror imagery, and, if mirror imagery is all there is, the existence of something outside a mirror can only be constructed by, and contained within, troping, or a tropological system—a kind of linguistic or semiotic mirror-play. Therefore, "dissemination," the production of a "nonfinite number of semantic effects" without any "simple origin" or *telos* can be said to be "written on" the mirror's backing.[7] In other words, Derrida maintains that tropological delimitations both enable and curtail the epistemological and ontological "realities" posited by philosophical speculation or by any other kind of thought.

The previous two chapters tried to describe ways that seventies reality was made problematic. Now I want to try to show why "Self-Portrait in a Convex Mirror" employs the tain-of-the-mirror trope so effectively in its historical moment. The mirror's backing represents the site upon which figurative language becomes literal and reality is put into place, or, as Ashbery puts it, "the life of the studio" is reduced to discrete entities, and "island[ed]" (*SP*, 195: 30–31). No sooner does this "operation" of "island[ing]" begin than it "stall[s]" and gives way to "a new preciosity / in the wind" (*SP*, 195: 31–196: 1). Similarly, Derrida describes the "point" where "writing" is problematized, and, one might extrapolate, troped. Derrida's figure of the mirror's backing as the area wherein "dissemination is written" and reality is "arrested" can also be said to describe the "spot" in which "security" is "blown up" and writing and reality are made possible through the perpetual danger of dissemination, which writing produces and is produced by:

> Dissemination [which] endlessly opens up a *snag* in writing that can no longer be mended, a spot where neither meaning, however plural, nor *any form of presence* can pin/pen down [*agrapher*] the trace. Dissemination treats—doctors—that *point* where the movement of signification would regularly come to *tie down* the play of the trace, thus producing (a) his-

tory. The security of each point arrested in the name of the law is hence blown up. It is—at least—at the risk of such a blowup that dissemination has been broached/breached. With a detour through/of writing one cannot get over.[8]

Similarly, for the Ashberian speaker, the "wind brings what it knows not." Reality is an inquisition that is driven by "whispers of a word that can't be understood"—an absence that paradoxically contributes to the self-containment of that system. The "wind" of this "new" and dangerously unaccounted for inquisition is "self-propelled, blind, has no notion / Of itself. . . . is inertia that once / Acknowledged saps all activity, secret or public" (*SP,* 196: 4-6). Ashbery calls this "the negative side" of this cultural dissemination. As Derrida comments, there is no way to inscribe "what is outside" other than through the "negative" or reversed image on the mirror's backing. Ashbery's formulation of "the negative side" views language as an inescapable and oppressive system that is generated and held in place by a lack. Conversely, "the positive side" finds "that another life is stocked there / In recesses no one knew of." The positive side makes the negative side's formulations of reality and "ambiguities / Look willful and tired, the games of an old man." The poem employs a sixties-style distrust of age.

And yet the positive side is only possible because of the challenge that is implicit in the negative. One side manifests the other.[9] Ashbery's oeuvre can be examined as a shifting play of emphases between these "sides" of the multifarious disseminations that bounce off the back of the mirror of Ashbery's continuing investigations and, using Derrida's term, "doctor" writing and reality. It is difficult not to think of the "spin doctors" who are increasingly relied on by journalists as sources of significant news. Spin doctors, after all, create denotations from connotations.

Our notions of reality can be said to be constructed by and inscribed within figurative language. We can consider these notions to be tropes that are contained within a broader set of metaphors. Reality is understood here as a specialized trope. Nonetheless, Ashbery notes that "the real," even if it is essentially of a metaphoric nature, can be as intractable and "secure" as a more materially based conception of reality:

And though we made it all up, it could still happen to us again.
.   .   .   .   .

> We had, though, a feeling of security
> But we weren't aware of it then: that's
> How secure we were.
> ("A Wave" [1984], *SP,* 329: 9–15)

A "figurative reality" is limited by our means of knowing that reality and accepting it as real. Sixties reality is used to grasp post-sixties reality. In a Derridean sense, questions of reality embody enabling logocentric assumptions. Reality may be a trope; however, it nevertheless behooves us to ask how we establish our sense of veracity. How do we recognize "reality" and form a consensus regarding the "truth"?

Louis Althusser's conception of "ideology," in "Ideology and Ideological State Apparatuses (Notes towards an Investigation)," accounts for the steadfastness of a reality that is confined to the "imaginary" and sustains itself through unquestioning belief in certain tropes or, as Althusser puts it, "allusion[s] to reality."[10] According to Althusser, a "world outlook," or, in the figuration I have adapted from Derrida, what is generally seen in the mirror, is produced by "ideological state apparatuses" (see the discussion in chapter 1), which are tantamount to ensconced and unquestioned tropological systems of ideology. These tropological "mechanisms" project ideology throughout a society and are constitutive of its culture, if we understand the word "culture" in its most general sense. In turn, ideological state apparatuses arise from the perpetuation of a society's relationships of production. The bond between a society's production relationships and its ideological state apparatuses can be likened to the mirror's backing, since ideological state apparatuses both enable and foreclose a culture's epistemological horizons. As Gasché points out, an ideological state apparatus, like the mirror's backing, is "limited by the infrastructural agencies written on its invisible side."

Ashbery's attempt to see "through" what Gasché calls the illusory "perfection" written "inside" the mirror's backing thereby makes Ashbery a profoundly political poet. When one considers that the word "politics" is derived from the Greek word that means the affairs of the city, it is telling that Ashbery relates "New York / Where I am now" with "another life to the city, / The backing of the looking glass" (*SP,* 195: 22–23, 27–28). Confronting a metaphoric characterization of the poem's fictive, ontological horizon, the poem periodizes itself in the politics of Ashbery's city. Of course, Ashbery's politics are not conventionally partisan but, in a more Althusserian sense, concerned with the limits placed upon the imagination in his particular situation:

it is certain that

What is beautiful seems so only in relation to a specific
Life, experienced or not, channeled into some form
Steeped in the nostalgia of a collective past.

. . . . .

. . . I go on consulting
This mirror that is no longer mine
For as much brisk vacancy as is to be
My portion this time.

(*SP,* 197: 23–33)

After the poem's speaker examines the mirror's backing, he questions the nature of his society's aesthetic and perceptual limits. Externalizing and questioning the mirror's backing leaves the speaker with a mirror that "is no longer" his and which dispenses "a portion"—a seemingly rationed, and hence commodified, "brisk vacancy." Paradoxically, critical distance is both an interrogation and an implied product of the mirror and its backing.

It is not surprising that the mirror's backing, as Ashbery and Derrida both use the metaphor, is the central trope of Ashbery's most organized and comprehensible major long poem, "Self-Portrait in a Convex Mirror." The convex mirror's spherical backing serves as a means of putting the poem's coherency into question. Ashbery's poetry is never content to stop at the limits of our understanding, and it resists the opportunity to reduce or "deflate" "mapped space" to more easily perceivable, empirical "enactments," which a more superficial interpretation of Parmigianino's self-portrait might do. If Ashbery's most renowned poem is relatively coherent, it nonetheless problematizes the basis of poetic coherencies. Similarly, as Derrida questions the "philosophical concept" "of the concept," Ashbery interrogates the poetic subject of the subject, and this interrogation of the subject serves as the poem's theme or *topos.* "Self-Portrait in a Convex Mirror" can be identified as "the long Ashbery poem with the subject." However, the poem's subject is not the convex mirror as much as it is the convex mirror's inability to serve as a subject. After all, when the figure in the curved convex mirror "flatten[s] ultimately / Among the features of the room" (*SP,* 203: 26–27), the figure in the room, Parmigianino, loses its status as a distinguishable, privileged subject.

During the Watergate years, when Ashbery writes "Self-Portrait in a Convex Mirror," Jasper Johns begins to use the crosshatching motif as a dominant organizing tool in *Scent* (1973–74), a painting that consists of three panels of interlocking crosshatch marks (illustration 14). In the sixties, the "organizing device" of the presidency begins to lose credibility, as does the poetic subject in Ashbery's poetry, and faith in painting among artists.[11] Perhaps all three devices are eventually believed to be either too centralized or vehicles of too invariable regulation. "Self-Portrait in a Convex Mirror" evokes and refutes the subject of the poem's subject or topos; the Watergate affair calls attention to and discredits the political subjects of an all-powerful sovereign and a unified state as regenerative moral principles; similarly, Johns's interlocking or "crosshatched" groups of parallel lines recuperate as a painterly subject the painting surface or "picture plane,"[12] only to problematize that subject.

Like the convex mirror and political surveillance systems, Johns's crosshatching motif organizes its field of reference. "Surveying" or "canvassing" the expanse of the picture plane, crosshatching might seem to emphasize that plane. However, crosshatching also creates the picture plane, since, as Johns's work repeatedly demonstrates by implying what is behind, beside, and in front of his canvases, the two-dimensionality of the painterly object—the canvas—is fragile, as Johns often notes by suggesting holes and insertions. Like the mirror's backing that Ashbery and Derrida describe, the picture plane sets into motion and plays upon our perceptual modes. The picture plane, like the subject in "Self-Portrait in a Convex Mirror," indicates an ambivalence about traditional logocentric organizing devices. They are felt and tested like phantom

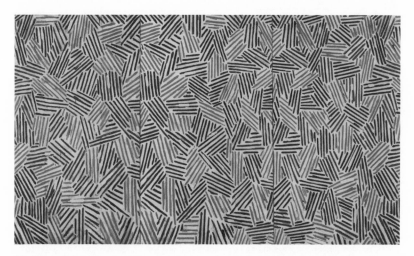

14. Jasper Johns, *Scent,* 1973–74, © Jasper Johns/ Licensed by VAGA, New York, NY

116

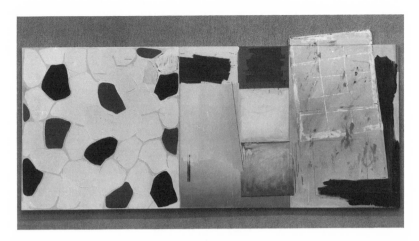

15. Jasper Johns, *Harlem Light,* 1967, © Jasper Johns/ Licensed by VAGA, New York, NY

limbs. As Nixon might be said to have created the Watergate scandal by covering it up, Johns paradoxically creates a preexisting picture plane by surveying it. Similarly, Christo gave new life to the monuments and natural sites that, beginning in the late sixties, he wrapped with fabric. Such cover-ups affirm a nostalgia for things that are, quite literally in Christo's case, of a whole cloth. In the seventies, Andy Warhol increasingly produces portraits that, he might have said, cover the imperfections of his subjects so that they become their masks. In Ashbery's "The New Spirit," the poet comments that "what is to be revealed actually conceals itself in casting off the mask of its identity, when the identity itself is revealed as another mask, and a lesser one, antecedent to that we had come to know and accept."[13] As with Christo and Nixon, the cover-up of Warhol's "masks" becomes both an advertisement and a product that, as Ashbery says of Parmigianino's hand, "protect[s] what it advertises."

Johns's play of the crosshatch motif with the picture plane during the mid-seventies forecasts the art world's return to painting in the eighties, as well as a trend away from painting in the nineties. Johns's flagstone pattern, which anticipates the crosshatch motif, is neither as "abstract" nor as "dominant" as his crosshatching. The flagstone pattern, in, for example, *Harlem Light* (1967), can easily be seen as an indication of an actual flagstone surface (illustration 15), in the same way that Johns's early works, such as his targets, can, at least on one level, be viewed as denotative of actual targets. Johns's flagstones cannot be considered to be as remote from an obvious referent, and therefore do not appear as "abstract" as the crosshatching of the mid-seventies. In the context of an art world that has abandoned painting as a medium for artistic innovation, the art world does not appreciate Johns's flagstone works as the same kind of stunning departure that the crosshatch works are. In addition, the flagstone motif is not as dominant an organizing principle as crosshatching. This becomes apparent when we consider that the flagstones always appear in a collage with other elements, and in most paintings only occupy one or two of several panels. Crosshatching soon consumes Johns's canvasses.

Johns shows a picture plane to be the outcome of tension between painting's inherent two- and three-dimensionality. We do not apply the term "picture plane" to more dominantly two-dimensional forms like book illustrations and hanging scrolls. The notion of the picture plane can only come into play when an emphasis on two-dimensionality organizes the disparate phenomena of color values and hues, fields and backgrounds, subject matters, and physical paint. In the mid-seventies, Johns deconstructs his painterly surfaces by producing literal instances and illusions of depth that do not "play along with" or "respect" the picture plane.

In *Corpse and Mirror* (1974; illustration 16), for instance, at least three factors undermine the unity of the picture plane: (1) the work is painted in different media, oil and encaustic, of differing visual densities; (2) it is composed of two clearly demarcated panels, each of which contains three subsections; and (3) it includes a shadowy iron-shaped figuration that, since one can see crosshatching above it, might appear to be "below the picture plane," and an incisive black X-mark and a squibbly pink swath of paint that seem to be superimposed "on the picture plane." Among the many other examples that we may note in Johns's work of crosshatch paintings that disrespect the picture plane are the suggestion of a hole in the canvas of *The Dutch Wives* (1975); Johns's stated and implied references to a tree in Mexico with a painted barber's-pole motif, as well as the actual barber's pole in *The Barber's Tree* (1975); and the repeated vertical patterns between the panels of *Scent* that suggest a layering or a hinging, in which a pattern is established from section to section that implies that the painting's extreme right edge seems hinged to the painting's extreme left edge, suggestive of an ongoing circular band.[14]

Respect for the flat picture plane is preeminent, during the twenties and the thirties, in synthetic cubism, constructivism, and geometric abstraction. However, it is not until after World War II that painters like Barnett Newman and Franz Kline aggressively attempt to make the reversal of figure and ground

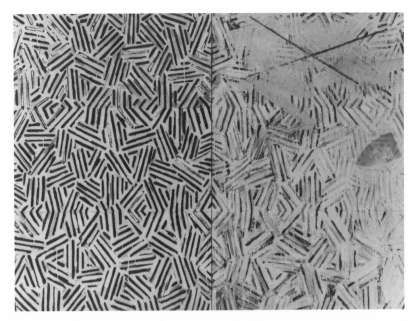

16. Jasper Johns, *Corpse and Mirror*, 1974, © Jasper Johns/ Licensed by VAGA, New York, NY

a dominant organizing principle of their canvasses. American painters after World War II are not the first to stress figure and ground reversals. However, these painters are characterized by the centrality that they give to figure and ground reversals. Newman, for instance, calls Mondrian's work "design" because the fields that Mondrian paints are not easily reversible. Mondrian does not respect the flat picture plane as rigorously as Newman does.

The post–World War II American aesthetic disdains the hidden and the unreachable. The Cold War occurs simultaneously with a new preeminence of the flat picture plane in its extreme form—the all-over composition. Both the Cold War and all-over composition bespeak polar systems of cohesion that facilitate systemic surveillance. Of course, a cohesive picture plane exists before the forties and the fifties. However, it is never before so rigorously and problematically deployed and activated as a whole to the desired exclusion of almost all else. Pervasive binary tensions breed unifocused, investigative operations. Like the human eye, the picture plane "blinks." However, after the two-dimensionality of the picture plane reaches its limit in the late fifties and the early sixties, with color-field paintings by such artists as Kenneth Noland, Morris Louis, Ellsworth Kelly, and Jules Olitski, the trend is reversed.

At the height of this reversal, in the mid-seventies, Jasper Johns's crosshatch paintings advance on earlier notions of a centrally structural push and pull to form an encompassing yet not totalizing space. The picture plane generates an evocatively voided sense of the third dimension. In turn, Johns devises veritable machines for undermining the picture plane. "Background" and surface are created from "surveillance" networks of writerly marks. Surveillance is not what it used to be. Taboos against information retrieval may be suspended and yet, practically, knowledge may be difficult to access. Johns's busy brushwork intensifies this sense of a layering of the seen upon the hidden—a sense that is strengthened by an eschewing of the illusion of depth, leaving only the three-dimensional quality of marks that seem to project from the surface. For instance, in Johns painting titled *Dancers on a Plane* (1979), suggests crosshatch marks appear to dance off the picture plane.

Traditionally, perspective organizes a two-dimensional plane hierarchically, for a three-dimensional effect. Interestingly, perspective and the monarchal nation-state emerge together in the fifteenth century. The great *de facto* painters of the American empire, the abstract expressionists (the term here used to indicate painters as different as Pollock is from Newman), are concerned with the picture plane as a way of producing frontal more than anterior space. Fittingly for the coming age of mass communications and television, flat space is organized to radiate and to project toward its audience.

The "all-over"-ness of abstract expressionism is an articulation of the enforced flatness of the picture plane that is first a conscious pictorial goal in the late nineteenth century. With Manet, Cezanne, and Monet, however, depth and perspective align themselves with the picture plane. Depth flows "throughout" the picture plane and not "into" it as with the rendering of depth achieved by Renaissance perspective.[15] This alliance between perspective and the picture plane parallels the rise of democratic republics, which seek to distribute their hierarchies more evenly throughout the body politic. In the twentieth century, artists like Duchamp bypass the visual, or what Duchamp called the "retinal," as a quality that is crucial to the making of art. This detour culminates in constructivism, and then in Rauschenberg's and Johns's collages of the fifties and the sixties. It is interesting to note that as it becomes harder to defend the presidential authority authorizing the Cold War, the flatness of sixties painting seems increasingly outmoded. If painting has often seemed dead, the late sixties and the early seventies are the high-water mark of that sentiment. "Painting has to have an end," says Donald Judd in 1967. Judd reasoned that human vision itself, without the artifice of the painting's surface, produced more powerful perspectives. Perhaps the visual organizations of perspective and the picture plane, our senses of enforced visual coherence, give way as artists confront a sixties mind-set in which history seems to be nearing some kind of end.

During the middle and the late seventies, however, the nation-state with its implied hierarchical solidities stages a comeback. There is a post-detente call for a new Cold War arms race, almost as if some nostalgia for the fifties returns in the seventies. In this context of this kind of cultural nostalgia, Johns creates a "phantom picture plane" in which space is flat but in a complicated, irrational manner. Crosshatch marks "draw out" Johns's surfaces as if to make the point that everything is not surface—an important contention of "Self-Portrait in a Convex Mirror" (see chapter 4).

With the picture plane in crisis, it is not surprising that many painters turn to other branches of art. The career of Robert Morris exemplifies shifts among many sixties and seventies New York artists from painting to sculpture to performance. Combining tendencies toward sculpture and performance, Johns's work of the sixties increasingly collaged objects and emulated a kind of performative relationship among them on his complex and often shaped canvasses, such as *Souvenir* (1964) and *According to What?* (1964). However, Johns's midseventies uses of flatness were odd regressions at the same time that they were dramatic breakthroughs. In short, they reconstituted and questioned the painterly subject in crisis.

Considering Watergate, we may ask ourselves first what a "political subject" is. If it can be said that "dissemination is written on the back" of the mirror, it follows that "subjects" are configured on the mirror's backing. We generally understand this kind of "subject" as subject matter that is external to a preexisting individual. However, Althusser likens the *political* subject to an entity that is "constitutive" of the individual instead of being external to that individual. "The category of the subject," says Althusser, "is constitutive of all ideology."[16] The privileging of individuals as autonomous subjects provides a site for ideological subject matter which, in turn, reinforces "concrete individuals as subjects"; the individual and "the material forms of existence," says Althusser, are sustained by "ideological recognition" and "misrecognition."[17] The codes that dictate the inclusion and exclusion of ideological material define the individual. Indeed, there is little that cannot be said to be ideological and political, since ideology and politics enable us to make distinctions between what is recognizable and unrecognizable; understandable and incomprehensible; or, for that matter, concrete and abstract. To the extent that one's sense of self and of reality are brought into being by their codification in the political unconscious, the senses of self and of reality are surveillance modes.

As I have noted, a convex mirror is a quintessential surveillance mechanism in that it surveys everything before it, and, unlike a flat mirror, does not allow the viewer to stand at an angle oblique enough to escape her or his reflection. In the Watergate affair, the concept of an autonomous individual—Nixon— organizes our perceptions of the state. Watergate simultaneously credits and discredits both the notion of an individual sovereign and the power of that notion to organize concrete systems of "ideological recognition." "Self-Portrait in a Convex Mirror" employs the surveillance mechanism of the convex mirror to organize all of its various contents. The Watergate scandal is organized by surveillance mechanisms that reveal a secret and unified organization and codification of knowledge and information. These surveillance mechanisms include the "plumbers' operations" that trigger the various Watergate investigations after intruders are discovered implanting surveillance devices in the Democratic Party's national committee headquarters, the Nixon administration's attempt to "cover up" these operations by manipulating the FBI and the CIA, the administration's use of the Internal Revenue Service to harass political enemies, and, most ironically, the president's surveillance of himself, which confirms his early role in the Watergate "cover-up" and the obstruction of justice charges it entails. Moreover, Nixon provides the key corroborating pieces of evidence against himself.

All this information gathering may not be attributable to Nixon. Nonetheless, the discoveries and suppositions of the surveillance operations that are associated with him reaffirm the notion of a unified and coherent state. Note, for instance, the lead paragraph of Bob Woodward's and Carl Bernstein's 10 October 1972 article in the *Washington Post,* one of the articles that are said to have disclosed the great magnitude and intricacy of the Watergate scandal:

> FBI agents have established that the Watergate bugging incident stemmed from a massive campaign of political spying and sabotage conducted on behalf of President Nixon's re-election and directed by officials of the White House and the Committee for the Re-election of the President.[18]

According to *All the President's Men* (1974), Woodward and Bernstein learn what "FBI agents have established" in a conversation in which Deep Throat informs Woodward of Watergate's all-pervasive and monolithic character:

"Check every lead," Deep Throat advised. "It goes all over the map, and that is important. You could write stories from now until Christmas or well beyond that. . . . Not one of the games [his term for undercover agents] was free-lance. This is important. Every one was tied in. . . . Just remember what I'm saying. Everything was part of it—nothing was free-lance. I know what I'm talking about."[19]

The character of Deep Throat, an authoritative source of "background" information, mirrors, although in a more benign fashion, the collective characterizations of the Nixon administration and campaign as "massive" surveillance agencies.

Alluding to Deep Throat, Jean Baudrillard in 1983 compares "the CIA and the *Washington Post* journalists," maintaining that both tend "towards scandal as a means to regenerate a moral and political principle, towards the imaginary as a means to regenerate a reality principle in distress."[20] Put simply, on a political level, the presidency acts as a kind of "backing of the mirror"; it organizes and tests the tropological limits by which political reality is known. In the 2 June 1973 *New Yorker,* Jonathan Schell comments:

> In the years leading up to Watergate, the country had come to live in a world of presidential facts. The facts-according-to-the-President, which were incessantly repeated virtually word for word by his growing legion of surrogates and amplified throughout the country by the many organs of public communication, had succeeded in overriding all the other sources of facts put together—had succeeded in overriding what used to be known as "the facts." Others might speak, but soon they would be discredited with organized campaigns of slander, or pressured behind the scenes into silence, or simply drowned out by the White House propaganda. The presidential facts were crowding all other facts off the stage. Like the President himself, they had become sovereign.[21]

Never have "the facts-according-to-the-president" been more doubted than they were during the Watergate affair.

One realizes the need to place a close reading of "Self-Portrait in a Convex Mirror" and of the Watergate affair alongside one another when one considers two things: that the crowning and clinching piece of evidence in the Watergate inquiries is Nixon's self-surveying tapes, and that "Self-Portrait in a Convex Mirror" depicts the self-destruction of the figure of the artist, as a privileged source of unity and meaning—the Parmigianino of the poem—through his own process of self-portraiture and self-surveillance.

To sum up, Johns's crosshatching motif severely problematizes the painterly subject of the picture plane, as "Self-Portrait in a Convex Mirror" questions the concept of a poem's subject matter, and the Watergate affair problematizes the unifying agents of the political state and its ruling sovereign, that is, the president. "Self-Portrait in a Convex Mirror," the Watergate affair, and Johns's crosshatching posit and undermine principles of unity within poetry, politics, and painting that suggest a mid-seventies ambivalence toward official reality as power constructs and disseminates it. Surveillance functions as a means of reality-testing that assimilates the "text" of the sixties into that of the seventies. Thus, in a sense, the mid-seventies closes the sixties. To flesh this out further, I now focus on one moment in time during the Watergate era that sets the scene for the oil embargo crisis.

2 Toward the Mirror's Backing: There's Oil in That Ther Poem

A decade later astute observers would mark that particular time, mid-1973, as the last moment of the old order in the industrialized world.—David Halberstam, *The Reckoning*

The symbolic event in the decline of American hegemony was the oil crisis, which resulted principally from the solidarity of the OPEC nations. Increasing economic competition from Japan, West Germany, and other nations ended an era of unquestioned U.S. economic power. The resultant slump in the American economy undermined the Keynesian foundation of postwar American liberalism, that is, economic growth accompanied by state regulation and intervention on behalf of disadvantaged citizens.—Cornel West, *Race Matters*

They got it all locked up, and ain't nobody going to give you a chance.
—*Saturday Night Fever*

Moloch whose love is endless oil. . . . Moloch whose name is the Mind!
—Allen Ginsberg, "Howl"

I write you to air these few thoughts feelings you are
Most likely driving around the city in your little car
Breathing in the exquisite air of the city and the exhaust fumes dust and other
Which made it up only hold on awhile there will be time

124

For other decisions but now I want to concentrate on this
Image of you secure and projected how I imagine you
Because you are this way where are you you are in my thoughts
—John Ashbery, "Lithuanian Dance Band"

Uncle Sam is over a barrel.
—Seventies American petroleum company television commercial

The juice is elsewhere.
—John Ashbery, "The One Thing That Can Save America"

As if the *New York Post's* headline writer that day were shooting a historian's bow, three banner headlines filled the front page of the late edition of the pre–Rupert Murdoch–owned 10 October 1973 edition. The biggest and highest headline proclaimed METS WIN PENNANT. A smaller headline underneath updated developments in the three-day-old Arab-Israeli Yom Kippur War: SYRIA INVADES ISRAEL. The smallest italicized headline read AGNEW RESIGNS. Such a front page participated in the multidimensional feel of the time. If events may have seemed related in the sixties and early seventies, they now seemed related in a more orderly, delimited manner. If the three events seemed unconnected, they nevertheless were making headlines in the same journalistic attention span, and this chapter uses these headlines as associative devices to indicate the changes that the nation was undergoing.

The second headline, concerning the war in the Mideast, had the most long-lasting repercussions. The Arab states that dominated OPEC used the United States' support of Israel as a justification to test their economic might. However, when the oil embargo started, ten days later, it was difficult not to think of it as a conspiracy on the part of greedy oil companies.[22] Even before the oil embargo, oil companies had fostered a crisis atmosphere that, it was widely believed, was intended to encourage federal subsidies for the development of more oil resources.[23] Before and after the oil embargo, the public was divided on the need for conservation measures such as reduced speed limits and daylight saving time extended into the winter. Heavy taxes on gasoline that would reduce the national debt and conserve fuel are still political poison.

In fact, the oil companies did, somewhat greedily, ask consumers to take the full brunt of OPEC's cuts in production and rate hikes. Nevertheless, overwhelming government and consumer demand in the wake of the embargo caused oil and gasoline prices to double within months.[24] Semi-rationing measures, such as mandatory closings of gas stations on Sundays, accompanied outbreaks of gasoline-line panic and violence. Fear of going empty drove motorists to "top off"—to fill a gas tank that might already be over four-fifths full even though a car might burn more than a fifth of a tank while idling in a long gas line.

An economic equivalent for Vietnam was yet to be experienced. The Vietnam War was a rude awakening that the economy could not help but internalize through symptoms such as increases in meat and coffee prices and skirmishes with relatively slight late-sixties and early-seventies inflation. The oil embargo was more dramatically felt economically, and economic vulnerability was brought home as a tangible reality.

The embargo changed many people's sense of America's self-reliance, and the threat of another embargo would hang over America for the rest of the seventies. Even after the first embargo ended in the spring of 1974, apprehension continued, and the December 1978 surge in oil prices, which coincided with the shah of Iran's negotiated departure from the nation he had ruled, confirmed the worst economic fears. While Patty Hearst's 4 February 1974 kidnapping came in the aftermath of the first oil crisis, the onset of the second oil crisis prefigured the storming of the American embassy in Teheran by about five hundred students, who seized sixty-six American hostages on 4 November 1979. It is as if the seventies was a decade held hostage by fear, cynicism, and uncertainty. It began with calls for the release of American prisoners of war from Vietnam (they were eventually freed in February 1973) and ended with a national sense of powerlessness to free American hostages in Iran.

America seemed to be at a loss, and the title of John Ashbery's 1974 poem "The One Thing That Could Save America" implies that America was missing a vital material. "The juice is elsewhere," says the poem's speaker after describing the view from a highway in which place names "concur with a rush at eye level."[25] "In the meantime the ride / Continues. Everyone is along for the ride, / It seems," says Ashbery in "Worsening Situation" (1974), but the car ride depends on "juice" from "elsewhere" (*SP*, 165: 12–14). America needs fuel. In the crisis, the speaker describes taking a strange walk in which he is "crosshatched" into the present moment by "backward and forward glances." The "mood" of "counting" "the material, the lumber of lives" has now "seized us." We are trying to sort out a reality in crisis.

Ashbery uses a memory of Vienna, where OPEC met to announce the embargo, overtly to reflect on his life in "Self-Portrait in a Convex Mirror." Such autobiographical reference is rare in Ashbery's poetry:

Vienna where his painting is today, where
I saw it with Pierre in the summer of 1959; New York
Where I am now, which is a logarithm
Of other cities.
(*SP,* 195: 21–24)

Ashbery soon casts this realism as ominous when the regimentations of reality symbolized by the mirror's backing undermine their own basis. Using an oil-crisis metaphor, the poem speaks of the mirror's backing "siphon[ing] off" life (*SP,* 195: 30). This siphoning can also be thought of as a kind of cultural slow-down that most prominently takes hold in the dreary late seventies.

Before discussing the Mets and Agnew, I move slightly ahead to a Saturday night that helps relate the three headlines. Ten days later, on 20 October 1973, the Mideast and the Nixon administration made headlines together again. OPEC announced the embargo and, on the same day, Attorney General Elliot Richardson and Assistant Attorney General William D. Ruckelshaus resigned so that Robert Bork, suddenly appointed as acting attorney general, could fire Special Prosecutor Archibald Cox.[26]

Claiming violations of his executive privilege, Nixon used Cox's Watergate tape subpoenas as a pretext to order the special prosecutor's dismissal, in what came to be known as the Saturday Night Massacre. Apparently, Nixon had ordered the hit on Cox for a Saturday night, because Saturday night is a black hole in news coverage, a temporal zone of marginality, excess, and un-accountability, as in the term "Saturday Night Special," suggesting the easy purchase of a small, efficient firearm for illegal, perhaps relatively sponta-neous uses that might underscore the drunken rages of a Saturday night.

The resignation of Ruckelshaus and Richardson and the dismissal of Cox, the Saturday Night Massacre, and OPEC's announcement synchronized to rip the lining of the American looking glass. The American economy would never be the same after the oil embargo. Both Nixon and OPEC manipulated "the back of the American mirror" in different ways.

The Saturday Night Massacre had a crucial effect on subsequent American seventies culture since two of the most influential seventies cultural hap-penings used "Saturday night"—that unaccountable supplement to the rest of the week—as a modifier in their titles: *Saturday Night Live* and *Saturday Night Fever.* In a sense, *Saturday Night Live* answered both the Saturday Night

17. *Saturday Night Fever,*
courtesy of Photofest

Massacre and the oil crisis. It offered a countercultural response to "massacred" official truth. Reality was up for grabs. The Not Ready for Prime Time Players, despite the troupe's name, were nevertheless on network television. They proved a much bigger hit than could have been expected. However, as if awaiting Reagan, their politics were neutralized, and the program replaced its ensemble for the first time about a month after the 1980 election.

Saturday Night Fever (1977) belatedly responds to the oil crisis. The film's central character, Tony Manero (John Travolta), can be seen as a grounded "hydrocarbon" or car-culture man, his car key metaphorically taken away. *Saturday Night Fever* is an effective film because it communicates the impasse that working-class society increasingly faces in the seventies. Tony's construction-worker father is unemployed, his brother is dissatisfied with the priesthood, his friend kills himself rather than marry his pregnant girlfriend, and Tony feels locked into a dead-end job in a paint store. At the film's end, Tony must face the possibility of accepting a platonic relationship with a woman he loves and desires, since she can advise him on how to get a service job in Manhattan and escape his economic class. Tony's growing sensitivity, desire to engage in dialogue, and urge for economic improvement are of course related. Most important, in terms of the film's marketing focus, Tony's disco lifestyle can only be maintained on Saturday nights. He cannot afford it on any other occasion. It is almost as if his adventures with his friends are rooted in the middle and late fifties minus the anchor of fifties rock and roll.[27]

We are now in a better position to note a relationship in the *New York Post* triple headline of 10 October 1973. The 1973 New York Mets were the first team with a mediocre, near .500 winning percentage to win a pennant. Their pennant win, however, was an unaccountable phenomenon, arising from "behind the backing of the mirror," and it was thus consistent with the other breaking news. The Mets won only three games more than they lost, but the divisional split of the National League allowed them to win the eastern division in a very bad year for that division. The Mets had miraculously won the World Championship in the year of the moon landing, 1969, the year that both major league baseball leagues split into two divisions but, in 1973, the divisional split undermined the fantastic standards of 1969—the 1969 Mets were a "legitimate" pennant winner since they won many more games than the western division champion Atlanta Braves, and the 1973 Mets would lose the World Series, which they won in 1969.

More than the 1969 team, which was genuinely talented, the 1973 Mets were spurred by blind faith, implicit in relief pitcher Tug McGraw's satirical cry "Ya Gotta Believe," which initially mocked the patronizing locker room pep talk of an out-of-place Met executive but was eventually taken seriously by the team. Interestingly, it was during this pennant drive that Met manager Yogi Berra voiced perhaps his most famous quip: "It's not over 'til it's over." Even if Berra never said it, it is the perfect Yogi Berra quip, and 1973 was Berra's high mannerist moment.

It is also of note that the Met pennant of 1973 could not overcome a resurgence of several small baseball dynasties in the seventies. The Oakland Athletics won three championships in a row, followed by two consecutive championships by the Cincinnati Reds and the New York Yankees respectively. Before Oakland's championships, there had not been a repeating champion since 1962. Perhaps divisional play had created a context in which concentration of talent could be more pronounced. Player free-agency, which began in the mid-seventies, contributed to this trend. In any case, the mid-seventies was certainly a moment in baseball and other sports when the backing of the mirror of the reserve clause that froze players to their teams was broken. The exclusivity of major sports leagues as players' employers had already been challenged in the sixties by competing sports leagues such as the American Football League and the American Basketball Association. In the seventies, the assimilation of these leagues by the more established ones led to more complex systems of divisions and playoffs. The reality of professional sports would never be the same.

Syria's October invasion of Israel also shook assumptions by reviving the prospect of Israel's possible annihilation. This would have unsettled American foreign policy because Israel and Iran were the two major American bases of support in the Mideast. From a cultural standpoint, Israel's nationalistically interpreted fulfillment of Old Testament prophecies mirrored America's genetive mission into the wilderness, and the mere possibility of Israel's decimation was disturbing, consciously and unconsciously, for many Americans. Perhaps least disturbing, on the *New York Post*'s front page, was the news of Vice President Agnew's resignation. Executive-branch corruption already seemed commonplace—many Americans had after all watched the Ervin committee all summer. Nevertheless, such a commonplace conveys a profound cultural distress. The image of kickback payments from contractors being delivered to Agnew in the White House, for his help in procuring contracts when he was the governor of Maryland and when he was vice president, was graphic. The mirror's backing was not sacrosanct. If, for the first time in American history, a vice president could be virtually forced to resign for legal reasons (John C. Calhoun had previously resigned because of political disagreements with Andrew Jackson), and if this resignation felt strangely predictable, could a president's resignation be far behind?

3 Three Ideologically Bifurcated Mechanisms of the Mid-Eighties: John Ashbery's "A Wave," the Iran-Contra Affair, and Jasper Johns's *The Seasons*

Our story is no longer alone. —Ashbery, "A Wave"

   . . . a glass exclamation point opposes
A discrete claim. . . .

.   .   .   .

It takes only a minute revision, and see—the thing
Is there in all its interested variegatedness.
—Ashbery, "A Wave"

  Our landscape came to be as it is today:
Partially out of focus . . . unreachable, with all kinds of nice
People and plants walking and stretching, calling

Attention to themselves with every artifice of which the human
Genre is capable. And they called it our home.
—Ashbery, "A Wave"

I have tried to argue that three important phenomena of mid-seventies American culture both credit and discredit traditional organizing mechanisms within
their disciplines. In the mid-eighties, three corresponding phenomena demonstrate the manner in which these organizing mechanisms occupy a significant
(though not principal) position within the "discourses" of poetry, politics, and
painting. In other words, these mid-eighties organizing devices are not central organizing devices; John Ashbery's "A Wave," the Iran-Contra affair, and
Jasper Johns's series of painting entitled *The Seasons* (1985–86) synthesize,
respectively, logocentric subject matter and a sense of the author's presence,
the state and the sovereign, and the picture plane into the larger functioning
of each mid-eighties phenomena. "A Wave" anticipates Ashbery's *Flow Chart,*
which Ashbery says was inspired by Oliver North's money-flow charts. "A mixed
surface is revealed," says the speaker of Ashbery's "A Wave" (*SP,* 322–43), suggesting that a unified "surface reality" is perhaps pertinent, but only as part of
a "mix." Do we view these organizing mechanisms as finally victorious, because
they are accepted, or do we regard them as entirely engulfed and subservient
to other factors? The appropriateness of both perspectives indicates that the
three mid-eighties phenomena that are being considered here are "ideologically bifurcated" between reality as it is, on some level, perceived and reality
as it is acted on.

Of course, conventional ideological concerns may tend to focus upon the
"return" of the organizing mechanisms of the poetic subject and a sense of
authorial presence. However, Ashbery's "A Wave" adds addenda to these sim-
plistic tendencies:

> The reductive principle
> Is no longer there, or isn't enforced as much as before.
> There will be no getting away from the prospector's
> Hunch; past experience matters again; the tale will stretch on
> For miles before it is done.
> (*SP,* 323: 4–8)

> Those
> Suffering from the blahs are unlikely to notice that the topic
> Of today's lecture doesn't exist yet, and in their trauma
> Will become one with the vast praying audience as it sways and bends

. . . And when

It is flushed out, the object of all this meditation will not
Infrequently turn out to be a mere footnote to the great chain.
(*SP*, 328: 14, 20)

"A Wave" is a kind of lecture about the absence of a "topic." "The object of all" the poem's "meditation" becomes "a mere footnote" in poetry's greater signifying "chain." The speaker takes up where the speaker of "Self-Portrait in a Convex Mirror" leaves off, accepting himself as a part of this chain and not self-contained. Paradoxically, however, every aspect of the system is a part of the speaker's self, if only due to the speaker's absence. "I feel at peace with the parts of myself" (*SP*, 342: 25), says the speaker of Ashbery's "A Wave," near that poem's conclusion. A relentless play between part and estimations of a whole permeates the poem, and the particular "waves" of the poem repeatedly disband into "an ocean of language":

By so many systems
As we are involved in, by just so many
Are we set free on an ocean of language that comes to be
Part of us, as though we would ever get away.
(*SP*, 325: 21–24)

If an engagement with such an "ocean" is inevitable, the only choice is to accept the present situation, meet it at its limits, and then continue:

. . . and the right way,

It turns out, is the one that goes straight through the house
And out the back.
(*SP*, 325: 19–21)

If "A Wave" cannot deny limitations, it can, however, account for them. This accounting itself constantly needs to be accounted for because "other worlds can . . . easily take root / Like dandelions, in no time" (*SP*, 336: 5–6). The adept mirror-play between this accounting and what must be accounted for, even as the contents of the former shift to the latter, is infinitely richer than any hard and fixed game could ever be and propels the poem:

You thought you had perceived a purpose in the game at the moment
Another player broke one of the rules; it seemed
A module for the wind, something in which you lose yourself
And are not lost, and then it pleases you to play another day

When outside conditions have changed and only the game
Is fast, perplexed and true, as it comes to have seemed.
(*SP,* 325: 12–17)

The "new preciosity in the wind" (*SP,* 195: 33; 196: 1) that Francesco could not stand up to in "Self-Portrait in a Convex Mirror" is now, for better or worse, shaping, conveying, and distributing the game that "A Wave" plays:

. . . they can at last know the fun of not having it all but
Having instead a keen appreciation of the ways in which it
Underachieves as well as rages: an appetite,
For want of a better word. In darkness and silence.

In the wind, it is living.
(*SP,* 337: 12–16)

This "keen appreciation" might be considered to be overly complacent. However, Ashbery suggests that it is an antidote to complacency:

It's all attitudinizing, maybe, images reflected off
Some mirrored surface we cannot see, and they seem both solid
As a suburban home and graceful phantasms, at ease
In any testing climate you may contrive. . . .

.   .   .   .

          . . . Love is after all for the privileged.

But there is something else — call it a consistent eventfulness,
A common appreciation of the way things have of enfolding
When your attention is distracted . . . .
(*SP,* 336: 13–16; 337: 2–5)

Here "appreciation" is said to be "common" to the poem's speaker and the speaker's interlocutor. However, we can assume that the two parties do not share perceptions because "attention is distracted."

In this regard, Ashbery's third book of poems, *The Tennis Court Oath,* is a monument to poetry's utilization of distraction and diversion. However, the more apparently communicative strain of Ashbery's work eventually requires the services of a convex mirror, a service that includes the flattening of its own backing (see the discussion of "Self-Portrait in a Convex Mirror" in chapter 4), to accommodate the distraction that *The Tennis Court Oath* achieves. In other words, the poet's mechanism of swerving from a logocentric and normatively reasonable predisposition can no longer be considered a mere aesthetic device. In "A Wave," this tool is vital to a rich and viable apprehension of everyday life. The "usable anarchy" that can be found in "A Wave" would not be possible without the organization, and subsequent negation of that organization, that "Self-Portrait in a Convex Mirror" provides. Similarly, the Iran-contra affair utilizes Watergate to stress the schismatic nature of government, as the scope of sustained, complex, and systemic play at work in Johns's *The Seasons* is facilitated by crosshatching.

The Iran-Contra affair exhibits little that is "monological" about the state. Indeed, because there is no one way of perceiving the Iran-Contra affair, even naming it is initially difficult. Every plausible name refers to its relational make-up, whether these relations are in the internal composition of the scandal—the Iranian and Contra connections—or the affair's relation to past scandals—Watergate ("Contragate") or Abscam ("Iranscam"). "Iran-Contra" lacks Watergate's definitiveness because it consists largely of shuttlings and "diversions," lacking Watergate's abundance of "primary" sites. The sites of the Iran-Contra affair are not as determined as the Watergate Hotel, the Oval Office, or even the Senate Hearing Room (the Iran-Contra affair investigatory committee alternates between hearing rooms, the committee being a precedent-setting indistinct conglomerate of both congressional houses). In brief, the Iran-contra affair takes place on a kind of "game board." President Reagan is forced into a position whereby he can do little but argue the rules. His administration's other chief tactic is to argue that there is a Sandinista threat that is so great that it invalidates the import of any game that is not consonant with fighting this supposed threat. This positing of an extreme evil in Nicaragua functions as the "reality," or "backing of the looking glass" that holds the administration's preferred game in place. If this game is merely one of the administration's choice, the administration must, at all costs, avoid being perceived as self-motivated. Indeed, if the Iran-contra affair gives the lie to the myth of a smoothly operating monolithic government, the uncovering of any one motivating cause becomes less relevant and, to the administration's relief, no one particular person can be held responsible for this scandal.

The Iran-Contra affair can be understood in relation to itself, that is, as a system of its own making; it does not require the extraneous scaffolding that Watergate does. Therefore, it is not surprising that the twin driving questions of Watergate: "What did the President know and when did he know it?" divert our attention from the more serious implications of a secret American government and the terrorism it reinforces in the Mideast in order to manufacture terror in Central America.

The gray central figure in Johns's *The Seasons* (1985–86), like Reagan in the Iran-Contra affair, can only be understood in relation to its situation. *The Seasons* also works like a board game. "Markers," in the form of art and artifacts from Johns's life and work, move from one rectangle, or canvas, to another. Each canvas is a snapshot of this movement. Movement itself can be said to be the central metaphor of the work. However, it is a self-contained movement, a movement that paradoxically stays where it is. In fact, *The Seasons,* when considered in the chronological order in which Johns completed each canvas, from *Summer* (1985) to *Spring* (1986), opens with motifs representing the painter's familiar iconography strapped and tied together as if ready to be moved. The entire work's significant movement is an acceptance of the impossibility of movement, since the figure of the painter and his works remain in his studio where they appear to be reaccommodated.

As we have noted, *The Seasons* can be read as a progression from *Summer* to *Spring. Summer* presents Johns's art and belongings nicely assembled and ready to be moved. In *Fall* (1986), there has indeed been a kind of fall: the ladder is broken, the strap is loosened, objects have fallen, and Johns's shadow (traced by a friend) is flickering between the left and right edges of the canvas like a television picture. *Winter* (1986; illustration 18) shows Johns's shadow, which can also be interpreted as a surrogate for the "shadow" that any perceiver might cast on the canvas, moving to the extreme right side of the canvas. "Snow," in the senses of both a wet precipitation and a visual static, appears on the "screen" of the canvas. Although the painter's possessions and works are still disassembled, they seem to have come to rest, in contradistinction to the shocking disorder of *Fall.*

Winter reveals part of a crosshatch painting that, unlike any of the other representations of Johns's work shown in the series, is framed, suggesting crosshatching's inherent relation to frames and limits. Like an ideal winter, Johns's abstract, crosshatching period is depicted as a time of quietude, summation, and self-clarification. This period, like *Winter,* gives way to a new, easeful acceptance of disorder and representation that is epitomized by *Spring* (illustration 19). In *Spring,* the shadow of a child is superimposed upon Johns's shadow. The child is born into a full yet disordered world.

In sum, "Self-Portrait in a Convex Mirror," the Watergate affair, and Johns's crosshatch paintings, respectively, enable both the decentering and inclusion

18. Jasper Johns,
Winter, from *The
Seasons,* 1986, © Jasper
Johns/ Licensed by
VAGA, New York, NY

of logocentric perspectives in the mid-eighties phenomena of "A Wave," the
Iran-contra affair, and *The Seasons.* A seventies ambivalence toward reality is
dissected and institutionally split in the eighties so that the dual desires to return to reality and to be suspended from it can more efficiently work together.
It is almost as if, in the seventies, we begin to live more self-consciously and
reflexively in a realm within the Lacanian real, in the sense that our horizons
are constantly altered and circulated within a Saussurian *langue,* or linguistic
stock. "Realities" are recycled.

During the seventies, an urgency is felt to merge the realities of the Cold
War with those of the sixties. In the eighties, this imperative animates the
presidential figure of the forever young and vital conservatism of Ronald Reagan. Suddenly, conservatism is "happening." It has ontological presence. Like

19. Jasper Johns, *Spring*, from *The Seasons*, 1986, © Jasper Johns/ Licensed by VAGA, New York, NY

a sixties be-in, it is because it *is*, independent of any strong rationale. In the eighties, there is a wish simply, with a sixties power of suggestion appropriated by the sunny ideology of Reaganism, to will this wall of pre-sixties credences into place. The real, as a total field, is commodified, with more self-consciousness than in the sixties.

Reagan evoked an ideal of life before the sixties, that is, a wish for the fifties without a mention of Jim Crow or even excessive social drinking. However, a subversive aspect of the sixties could not be fully repressed. Most Americans were clearly divided in their views. If a consensus believed in Reagan's notions of not being fearful of demonstrating American military supremacy, a consensus also would not support sustained military conflict in Nicaragua. The electorate believed that government was the problem and not the solution (as Reagan's first inaugural address twisted the sixties formulation—"If you are not part of the solution you are part of the problem"), but at the same time they did not want to remove social safety nets or stop government from regulating industry. Although many Americans were euphoric about the prospect of being free from governmental rules and inhibitions, this sentiment oddly co-opted a sixties and seventies counterculture desire to return to basics. The Reagan administration took up the rhetoric of the sixties, calling itself a "movement" and a "revolution," while opposing the effects of sixties social protest. An eighties "ideological bifurcation," that is, an irreconcilability between expressed and implied political views, ensues. The next chapter further considers seeds of this ambivalence in the literature of the seventies, as well as other examples of its blossoming in the eighties.

Four

Literature in a Convex Mirror

Depictions of surveillance and self-surveillance characterize seventies literature. I elucidate this by examining works by some very different seventies authors, such as John Ashbery, James Baldwin, Toni Morrison, Thomas Pynchon,
Adrienne Rich, and Sam Shepard. Of course, countless other authors—Maxine
Hong Kingston, John Updike, Tom Wolfe, A. R. Ammons, Annie Dillard, Kathy
Acker, James Schuyler, Don DeLillo, and Robert Coover to name just a few—
might have been included. However, I do not aim to be exhaustive but rather
to flesh out a theory of the seventies. I begin with Ashbery's "Self-Portrait
in a Convex Mirror,"[1] the decade's most acclaimed poem, because it cogently
and powerfully represents the period's episteme. This chapter's second section
modulates from the implications of a convex mirror to a tropology of identity-
politics and "fingers," nuclear families, and vacuums, paying special attention
to Toni Morrison's novels of the seventies. The third section considers the
seventies in the context of broader post–World War II American identity, and
the fourth section discusses *Gravity's Rainbow* in terms of the seventies as a
lost opportunity for the nation. The chapter concludes with a discussion of gay
identity in seventies literature and culture. I should also note that this chapter
often examines American culture and film to shed light on seventies literature.

1 John Ashbery and Leisure Suits: Pockets out of Time

> you found yourself
> inside a huge pen
> or panopticon
> —John Ashbery, *Flow Chart*

I ask, where were you when the thimble of air was pocketed? Behind the mirror, you answer. An image cannot be remembered if there is no slab on which to mount it. — John Yau, "Big Island Notebook 4"

> One feels too confined,
> Sifting the April sunlight for clues,
> In the mere stillness of the ease of its
> Parameter. The hand holds no chalk
> And each part of the whole falls off
> And cannot know it knew, except
> Here and there, in cold pockets
> Of remembrance, whispers out of time.
> —John Ashbery, "Self-Portrait in a Convex Mirror"

In the above-cited closing lines of "Self-Portrait in a Convex Mirror," the deciphering and "sifting" "hand" has no tangible means, or "chalk," with which to write in a "whole" logocentric language. "Each" signifier or "part" must be seen within the context of a logocentric "whole" that is depicted as an absent presence or "remembrance"—a remembrance before there is an event to remember (as the association of "sifting" with the sands from which a mirror is made before it is a mirror reminds us), a writing before there is a reference or physical trace of writing or speech. "Each part of the whole" is a ghostly metonymy for the whole. The whole perpetually produces itself as parts, much as the periods of post–World War II American culture situate themselves within a sense of the entire era. "Beauty," says Ashbery's poem, "is steeped in the nostalgia of a collective past." Each period's episteme is what it is not. They are absent presences that take the hollow pocket-like shape of a convex mirror. The epistemes of these micro-periods are "cold pockets / Of remembrance." Because the convex mirror regimenting logocentric unity is shattered, an absent rather than explicit presence, a "here and there" is enabled, a present here and there that is paradoxically like an empty nostalgia. Similarly, the voice and logos are now heard as easily misinterpreted "whispers" without historical precedent and "out of time." The voice, like such pockets, is externalized. I think of seventies leisure suits, in which the pockets are stitched on the outside. Leisure suits emblematize a singular fashion occurrence—an unreproducible, indecipherable message that still engages us, and Ashbery's poem depicts a secret chamber of collective and individual change. "It is what is sequestered," says the speaker about the image of Parmigianino in the artist's painting.

Nonetheless, the speaker is ultimately changed by this sequestering, as if he himself were somehow on trial and awaiting a verdict. As in Don DeLillo's contemporaneous novel, *Great Jones Street* (1973), wherein a rock star's efforts to seclude himself in a small downtown New York apartment cause an intricate international conspiracy to visit and enlist him, "Self-Portrait in a Convex Mirror" demonstrates how seclusion can be a catalyst for pervasive change. This section examines how Ashbery's image of the backing of the mirror implies massive seventies change through the suggestion of surveillance.

The notion of a spherical, three-dimensional backing (like a convex mirror or even the leisure suit that a pocket is stitched on) contains an implicit contradiction. After all, if a backing is three-dimensional, area that is not the backing must be in back of "the front of the backing," the backing that touches the mirror's glass. In other words, there must be something behind the backing, although the literal conception of a "backing" implies that there could be nothing behind the mirror's backing that is relevant to the mirror's functioning. In short, a backing that must have area behind it is an oxymoron. There must always be an *implied* area of surveillance that limits the surface of the surveillance mechanism—makes the glass less than the backing—and enables the convex mirror to condense and cover its field of surveillance, creating the effect of total surveillance. However, as I discussed in the previous chapter, taking into account Ashbery's and Derrida's trope of the mirror's backing as representative of an imaginary site wherein our sense of reality and its limits cohere (like the ideological state apparatus, the very trust that is the coin of the realm, or simple faith in the notion of signifieds), a convex mirror presents a very suspect and contingent "reality" that is constantly in process while it ruthlessly organizes our criteria for judging veracity.

Other limits are necessarily and paradoxically implied in the establishment of the limit of the convex mirror's backing. Such a limit is then only a relative limit, and, in a sense, no limit at all. In selecting a convex mirror as the subject of his most sustained poetic meditation, Ashbery comments on the difficulty of a simple poetic meditation and of naive traditional hierarchy in the seventies. Because the convex mirror's backing is "always already" deconstructed, any "truth" that is derived from this meditation on a convex mirror must undermine or problematize the meditation's basis or "backing." Indeed, one engaging in this meditation loses her or his view in the meditation.

A convex mirror is a superb image of surveillance. As I noted earlier, convex mirrors are commonplace as surveillance tools, in, for instance, banks, retail shops, elevators, traffic circles, and buses, and Ashbery's poem uses the convex mirror to demonstrate surveillance and self-surveillance. I will soon discuss some of the convex mirror's more unusual properties and how they are used in Ashbery's poem.

A convex mirror's distortion seems an unsettling but irrefutable truth: a complete picture and not a mannerist device. The speaker in "Self-Portrait in a Convex Mirror" says that Parmigianino's painting emits the sense of both a contemporaneous, irrefutable truth and a long-forgotten, unrecognized truth:

> It presents its stereotype again
> But it is an unfamiliar stereotype, the face
> Riding at anchor, issued from hazards, soon
> To accost others, "rather angel than man" (Vasari).
> Perhaps an angel looks like everything
> We have forgotten, I mean forgotten
> Things that don't seem familiar when
> We meet them again, lost beyond telling
> Which were ours once. This would be the point
> Of invading the privacy of the man who
> "Dabbled in alchemy, but whose wish
> Here was not to examine the subtleties of art
> In a detached, scientific spirit: he wished through them
> To impart the sense of novelty and amazement to the spectator"
> (Freedberg). Later portraits such as the Uffizi
> "Gentleman," the Borghese "Young Prelate" and
> The Naples "Antea" issue from Mannerist
> Tensions, but here, as Freedberg points out,
> The surprise, the tension are in the concept
> Rather than its realization.
> (*SP*, 194: 6–25)

Its concept is the realization. Therefore Ashbery's poem examines a state of perpetual latency, a kind of perpetual post-sixties. Nonetheless, that state manifests, but manifests as a poem. Ashbery is now "doing" Parmigianino's painting, and the poem says that while looking at the painting one is "fooled for a moment / Before you realize the reflection / Isn't yours" (194: 31–33). One feels reflectionless. Hence, like Freud in his essay on the uncanny, Ashbery alludes to the reflectionless characters of E. T. A. Hoffmann and the

142

sensations of being reflectionless and not recognizing oneself in a mirror. The subjects manufacture their own uncanny absences (or presences).

More than anything, "Self-Portrait in Convex Mirror" captures the spirit of a mid-seventies reality that flickers between control and crisis. The poem's speaker manufactures a tropological reality but a referential absence.[2] The poem begins:

> As Parmigianino did it, the right hand
> Bigger than the head . . . .
> (*SP*, 188: 1–2)

The word "as" foreshadows the entire poem, indicating the poem's tropological premise. Through simile, analogy, and metaphor the poem accounts for, or mirrors, every element of Parmigianino's painting. Indeed, the poet implies that he can do nothing but mirror the painting:

> The words are only speculation
> (From the Latin *speculum*, mirror).
> (*SP*, 189: 14–15)

A poet utilizes speculation, and the words that constitute speculation, as a painter uses her or his hand. Since Parmigianino's hand is at the circumference of the convex mirror being depicted, the painter's hand factors into his work as bigger than his head, and, similarly, the words of Ashbery's poem, once removed from the painting they are describing, ultimately occupy a dominant position in relation to the painting. Despite the dominant positions that are established, however, neither the poem nor the painting conjures up anything that is not consonant with each project; each is a crafted copy. As Ashbery characterizes how Parmigianino holds his hand, the poem and painting are "both" suspended "in pure / Affirmation that doesn't affirm anything" (*SP*, 190: 30–31).

Parmigianino's task is simpler than Ashbery's, since the painting is merely the reflection of a reflection.

> Vasari says, "Francesco one day set himself
> To take his own portrait, looking at himself for that purpose
> In a convex mirror, such as is used by barbers. . . .
> He accordingly caused a ball of wood to be made
> By a turner, and having divided it in half and
> Brought it to the size of the mirror, he set himself

With great art to copy all that he saw in the glass,"
Chiefly his reflection, of which the portrait
Is the reflection once removed.
(*SP,* 188: 9-17)

Ashbery's poem is a third reflection, however, and, like a convex mirror, it clarifies the situation even as it distorts it. "Self-Portrait in a Convex Mirror" repeatedly returns to the basic issue the painting poses—one's existence in the context of a convex mirror that modifies one's existence. However, this return must pass through a fanning out and broadening, if clouding, of the issue before it returns to a focus.

Near the end of the poem, Ashbery compares this play of convex mirrors— a kind of mirror play that must reproduce a version of the entire contents of the initial scene—to a game of "telephone":

This always
Happens, as in the game where
A whispered phrase passed around the room
Ends up as something completely different.
(*SP,* 201: 6-9)

Ashbery's poem, being a kind of mirror, must create an other, and it is in the nature of the newly encountered "other" to be unexpected, or, at the least, to surprise superficially. We look into a mirror because we are unsure of what we are and therefore do not know what to expect, or, even when expecting a repetition of what we have previously seen, a repetition inevitably reveals new visual information and alters our perceptions.

Since these observations about mirrors are intrinsic to Ashbery's poem and Parmigianino's painting, either work is anything but narcissistic. Although each work comments on itself, it cannot be said that this preoccupation causes the same kind of deadlock that afflicts the mythological Narcissus. The speaker in Ashbery's poem says:

Is there anything
To be serious about beyond this otherness
That gets included in the most ordinary
Forms of daily activity, changing everything
Slightly and profoundly, and tearing the matter
Of creation, any creation, not just artistic creation

Out of our hands, to install it on some monstrous, near
Peak, too close to ignore, too far
For one to intervene? This otherness, this
"Not-being-us" is all there is to look at
In the mirror.
(*SP,* 201: 30-34; 202: 1-6)

Mirrors represent the only operative others, the only alternatives to our accepted modes (or mode) of reality, the necessary mechanism at work in any sequence of impressions.

And yet all that mirrors do is superimpose views one upon another. Each view that a convex mirror yields is an aspect of another, as well as an aspect of a grand view, since each view must depict the entire scene before it. Parmigianino centers his eyes, employing a convention of portrait painting to work both for and against his convex mirror; since the eyes take in everything, the painting asserts that what widens and fades at the circumferences returns through the center, adding to the inescapable completeness of the convex mirror:

The soul establishes itself.
But how far can it swim out through the eyes
And still return safely to its nest? The surface
Of the mirror being convex, the distance increases
Significantly; that is, enough to make the point
That the soul is a captive, treated humanely, kept
In suspension, unable to advance.
(*SP,* 188: 26-32)

This passage appears in the first page of the poem and, when compared to the acceptance of the "otherness" in the mirror, in the passage near the poem's close, the poem's central "turn"—from strong identification with the mirror image to a recognition of it as another—becomes evident. This turn can be imagined as a trip to and from the mirror's backing, or vice versa. "Self-Portrait in a Convex Mirror" can also be read as a journey from Ashbery's innocent acceptance of Parmigianino's self-portrait to the poet's revision of it, a revision perfected with Ashbery staging Parmigianino's suicide. The mirror's backing, nevertheless, must be read as figuring prominently in this reading also, since the poem's speaker does not question Parmigianino's authority until soon after the speaker finishes describing "the backing of the looking glass":

But something new is on the way, a new preciosity
In the wind. Can you stand it,
Francesco? Are you strong enough for it?
(*SP,* 195: 28, 33; 196: 1–2)

Parmigianino's "round mirror which organizes everything" (*SP,* 191: 20) is undermined by its mirroring function. The mirror's convexity is contradicted because the "whole," which the convex mirror both forms and regulates, when it is "stable within / Instability, a globe like ours" (*SP,* 190: 20–21), eventually gives way to "a blight / Moving outward" (*SP,* 196: 8–9).

The poem's lone explicit mention of the mirror's backing turns the poem around, like light hitting the mirror's wall, and the major turn of the poem is something akin to light, or consciousness, reaching a limit and being re-shaped. The word "backing" appears at nearly the precise midpoint of the poem, signifying the backing's pivotal place in the mirroring process. Before the backing is mentioned, the subject's captivity within an ever-replenishing yet static scene is stressed. However, after the passage, other possibilities are posited, as the conflicting implications of a convex mirror are clarified.

As we have noted, if "a convex mirror's backing" is not a perfect oxymoron, its connotations are nonetheless contradictory. A backing would seem to be a more definitive two-dimensional "curtain" and not the kind of half-spherical wooden object that Parmigianino uses for his backing. A convex mirror's backing does not merely prevent images that are projected through light from joining light behind the backing by blocking our gazes and stopping our vision from escaping; such a backing does not merely stop our image and produce from it a kind of fluid print, a fluid print that is then offered to the viewer; the backing of a convex mirror does more than insure us that we will be part of the view given to us. Something being behind it, a convex mirror's backing necessarily infers a hidden, unknowable presence and, much as the unconscious can be used as a pretext for the unity, or relatedness, of all an individual's mental phenomena, the space behind a convex mirror guarantees the unity of all surface phenomena in front of it, predetermining our possibilities for sight and vision. Since the three dimensions of a convex mirror's backing necessitates that that backing be more than a simple flat opaque surface, and that a space crucial to the convex mirror's functioning must be behind the mirror's backing, it follows that a secret realm acts as a leverage for a prearranged unity and its implicit associations. (Likewise, surveillance, as well as the con-

146

trol it can facilitate, works best undercover.) This predetermined coherence is equated to the life of the city:

> Our landscape
> Is alive with filiations, shuttlings;
> Business is carried on by look, gesture,
> Hearsay. It is another life to the city,
> The backing of the looking glass of the
> Unidentified but precisely sketched studio.
> (*SP*, 195: 24–29)

In "Self-Portrait in a Convex Mirror," the mirror's backing is initially viewed as an unescapable, repressive, and delimiting agent: however, it soon invites "something new" (*SP*, 195: 33), with "no notion / Of itself" (*SP*, 196: 4–5). We are moving toward an "unrecognition" of ourselves in the mirror. The convex mirror is being flattened and broken; the outside world, epitomized by "the window," on the third page of the poem, did not "matter much" (*SP*, 190: 15), though, a few lines before the mirror's backing is introduced, "The shadow of the city injects its own / Urgency" (*SP*, 195: 16–17). What is behind the mirror is coming into play.

Perhaps Parmigianino's painting is a last belated assertion of the High Renaissance's young faith in perspective's ability to render fully, truly, and comprehensively, although the painter needs to employ a solid "backing to his view" to maintain this stance. The first half of Ashbery's poem is similarly nostalgic, since it asserts that the conditions of comprehensible perspective and verifiable experience now depend on the metaphor of the convex mirror. However, the hypnotic assuredness that is caused by the convex mirror imprisons, and we jump at opportunities to note our "not-being-us." The world that the evasion of the convex mirror, this not-being-us, implies is less rigidly structured. Thus the poem concludes:

> Here and there, in cold pockets
> Of remembrance, whispers out of time.
> (*SP*, 204: 12–13)

A convex mirror, of course, does not permit a casual "here and there." It regiments a constant surveillance on everything in the room. Its composition and structure are constants; a room with a convex mirror in it has no unseen "pockets" and does not allow for any new views, or revisions, that would suggest "remembrance." Memory and revision require a critical apparatus that is "out of time," one that can juxtapose, and differentiate time-frames. In contrast, a convex mirror homogenizes and totalizes temporal points of reference. Hence the speaker, insofar as he is governed by the mirror, must merge his twentieth-century reality with Parmigianino's sixteenth-century rendering; the convex mirror denies history and intertwines eras. It ripples Foucauldian epistemes of classical association between word and thing and modern dissociation.

Ashbery's invocation of Parmigianino's use of the convex mirror can be compared to another mid-seventies writer's citing of a surveillance mechanism from a previous century, Michel Foucault's reference to the panopticon, or prison surveillance tower. In *Discipline and Punish: The Birth of the Prison,* Foucault contends that the panopticon is the prototypical mechanism of the central late-eighteenth- and early-nineteenth-century episteme, that is, the era's dominant epistemological framework.[3] This episteme enables the modes of surveillance that modern institutions still use to maintain control. The panopticon, says Foucault, causes inmates to internalize an indefinite sense of being watched, ultimately producing a prevalent, inextricable, and, because it is so omnipresent, undetectable connection with the modern state and its means of identifying and codifying individuals. According to Foucault, the system of classification that is organized by the episteme is modeled on the panopticon and alienates the individual from her or his body and senses, as both an aspect of the system of classification's dominance and an integral feature of the episteme of the modern state's functioning.

As effective a surveillance mechanism as the panopticon is, however, the convex mirror's range of surveillance is more inclusive, since, unlike the panopticon, which clearly differentiates the subject from the object, the viewer from the viewed, and the prison guard from the prisoners, the convex mirror converts the subject into an object, viewer into an image, and warden into a ward. In other words, the convex mirror outdoes the panopticon by surveying the agent of surveillance. Although Foucault notes that the prison guard, the panopticon's ostensible observer, also becomes enmeshed in the panopticon's workings,[4] Foucault also points out that the panopticon interjects an internalized sense of being watched into its objects of surveillance. This paradoxically omnipresent but unmanifested gaze acts to alienate the object of surveillance from her or his body. Unlike the convex mirror, the panopticon thus puts into place an internalized assumption of an external viewer, who is not in turn surveyed.

Kenneth Burke's "The Virtues and Limitations of Debunking" (1941) compares the vigilant watch of the observer in the panopticon with "debunking," maintaining that debunking is limited by its inability to debunk its own modes of analysis.[5] Before Foucault's use of the symbol of the panopticon, Burke anticipates the need for the symbol of the convex mirror. Although the viewer in the convex mirror might not be the quintessential debunker, the symbol of the convex mirror nevertheless accounts for the subject's place in her or his undertaking. It has already been noted that anyone who can see a convex mirror can see her or himself in it. One cannot be too far to the left or right, nor can one be too high or low.

The convex mirror places the external viewer, abstract as she or he might be, in the convex mirror, and, in a sense, the convex mirror accounts for the panopticon, offering the paradoxically "tangential focus" at the center of the convex mirror—a concentration that gradually blurs in a ghostly fashion as it progresses toward the mirror's widening extremities—for the sense the observed feels of being overseen by an unseen observer. In "Self-Portrait in a Convex Mirror," the subject's placement of authority in, and eventual identification with, the image in the convex mirror replaces the hidden and nebulous observer as a surveillance mechanism's linchpin. The convex mirror accounts for the distortion that surveillance inevitably engenders. Not only does one looking at a convex mirror have no choice but to see oneself; that viewer must also see her or himself as a kind of apparition. The subject's identification with its image in the convex mirror replaces the panopticon's relationship between the perpetually terrorized observed and the hidden and nebulous observer. In a convex mirror, as in a panopticon, identity is imposed from without. However the image in the convex mirror accounts for the notion of the self being an outer entity.

Ashbery is signaling the growing difficulties involved with individualistic creation, which, in the seventies, increasingly gives way to group validation. This notion of a subject's identity, authority, and unity being contingent on a mirror image is prefigured in Ashbery's *Three Poems* (1972). "The New Spirit,"[6] the first prose poem in *Three Poems*, prosaically states that:

> in staring too long over this elaborate view one begins to forget that one is looking inside, taking in the familiar interior which has always been there, reciting the only alphabet one knows. To escape in either direction is impossible outside the frost of a dream, and it is just this major enchantment that gives us life to begin with. (*Three Poems*, 11: 22–28)

Although a mirror is not explicitly mentioned in this passage, Ashbery's positing of a view wherein the viewer loses not only her or his identity but also the basis or "alphabet" of any self-identification certainly suggests the metaphor of a mirror, although not necessarily the metaphor of the convex mirror.

Of course, Ashbery's use of the mirror trope as prototypical of the process that organizes one's identity is also reminiscent of Lacan's mirror-stage theory.[7] Similarly, in "Self-Portrait in a Convex Mirror," the speaker's identity is organized by Parmigianino's painting. That the "reality" of "Self-Portrait in a Convex Mirror" is described in its relation to a convex mirror imposes a monolithic unity on the poem that is undermined by the poem's text.

In short, the subject of the convex mirror is a prototypical topic, since it stresses the myth of unity that is implicit in all language. However, the overtly symbolic nature of Ashbery's language unmasks the unity that a convex mirror implies and shows this unity to be a myth, albeit a myth that enables language. In employing the convex mirror, "Self-Portrait in a Convex Mirror" comes to terms with both language as we normally experience it and language as it functions.

In *The Scarlet Letter* the convex mirror that Pearl and Hester see in Governor Bellingham's hall underscores Pearl's and Hester's chief features:

> "Mother," cried she, "I see you here. Look! Look!
>
> Hester looked, by way of humoring the child; and she saw that, owing to the peculiar effect of the convex mirror, the scarlet letter was represented in exaggerated and gigantic proportions, so as to be greatly the most prominent feature of her appearance. In truth, she seemed absolutely hidden behind it. Pearl pointed upward, also, at a similar picture in the head-piece; smiling at her mother, with the elfish intelligence that was so familiar an expression on her small physiognomy. That look of naughty merriment was likewise reflected in the mirror, with so much breadth and intensity of effect, that it made Hester Prynne feel as if it could not be the image of her own child, but of an imp who was seeking to mould itself into Pearl's shape.[8]

Noting the obvious propensity of convex mirrors to highlight features with an "intensity of effect," what can be said of a poem that organizes itself around the symbol of a convex mirror?

Bewilderingly, the literature on John Ashbery's "Self-Portrait in a Convex Mirror" does not distinguish the workings of convex mirrors from those of mirrors in general. Convexity is often mentioned but rarely analyzed in any depth, nor are the special features and functions of a convex mirror sufficiently scrutinized. For example, Paul Breslin recognizes that, in "Self-Portrait in a Convex Mirror," Ashbery's "willingness in this instance to organize the poem around one central occasion (contemplation of Parmigianino's painting) is almost unique for Ashbery; only 'The Instruction Manual' has a similar coherence, and it is far less ambitious."[9] However, given this observation, it is curious that Breslin does not explicate the convexity that Parmigianino's painting depicts in any greater detail than the general claim that "the mannerist fascination with ingenious artifice is certainly akin to Ashbery's intimation of distorted reflections within distorted reflections."[10] If this statement is true, we must describe how this "mannerist fascination" is "akin to Ashbery's intimation of distorted reflections." We may further want to know in what manner the convex mirror is "ingenious."

If Ashbery's poem does indeed organize itself around a "contemplation of Parmigianino's painting," whose convex perspective is impossible to ignore, and if the coherence of an Ashbery poem to a fixed and specific subject matter is as rare as Breslin says it is, one would expect Breslin to attempt to characterize the quality of convexity more fully. However, Breslin's long analysis of the poem mentions convexity only when the absence of such a mention would be extremely conspicuous. Consider Breslin's interpretation of these lines: "The surface / Of the mirror being convex, the distance increases / Significantly" (SP, 188: 26–28). Breslin takes the convexity of the mirror to mean simply "that the surface of the painting itself recedes from the view, toward the plane of the wall, as the viewer's gaze itself moves away from the center. Since Parmigianino's face occupies the center, to move away from the center is also to move outward from the eyes."[11]

The distinction that Breslin's reading draws between "the plane of the wall" and "the surface of the painting" is indeed useful. A convex surface such as the curved backing of the convex mirror can, of course, neither form a plane nor align itself parallel to one, if a plane is defined as "a surface containing all the straight lines connecting any two points on it" and straight is defined as "extending continuously in the same direction without curving." Convexity is inconsistent with the notion of a plane, since a straight line between any given two points on a convex surface cannot remain on that convex surface. In other words, the convexity that Ashbery discusses describes a surface that is, paradoxically, not two-dimensional. We are left with the oxymoronic notion of a three-dimensional surface to describe the convex mirror's round backing.

Speaking as "physically" and "unfiguratively" as possible, "the distance increases" in Parmigianino's mirror because, when one looks directly into the center of a convex mirror, as Parmigianino is obviously doing when he paints his self-portrait, what surrounds that observer's eyes, the rest of the face, body, and background, appears literally to "fall back"; the closer our gaze is to the surface's circumference, the more indistinct, and yet uncannily larger, what we see appears. This reverses our expectations because, all other visual criteria being equal, we expect what looks larger also to be nearer and more focused.

Because Breslin has overlooked so much of what is crucial about the convex mirror, his reading fails to recognize many of the connotations of the word "significantly," as it is used in the above passage from Ashbery's poem. Since "the distance increases" in an inherently misleading fashion, "significantly" can be read as meaning more than just "notably." The word, as Ashbery uses it, suggests that signification is not a matter of a simple correspondence between a signifier and a signified. If the mirror image had conveyed a more "accurate" two-dimensional image, the distance would not have seemed as "significant."

The three lines under discussion from Ashbery's poem imply that vision is "an endless process in which truth and falsehood," as Paul de Man in *Blindness and Insight* characterizes "the act of looking," "are inextricably intertwined."[12] In this regard, Richard Howard says of Ashbery's volume of poems entitled *Self-Portrait in a Convex Mirror* that "the poet seems to me (it is what I mean by mastery) to have gained access to a part of his experience which was once merely a part of his imagination: he has made his experience and his imagination identical."[13] The merging of experience and imagination that Howard posits finds an apt allegorical correspondence in the intermingling of the appearance of the non-two-dimensional, three-dimensional convex surface, which can be likened to "experience," and the painter's planar surface, which can be associated with the "imagination." "Significantly," in Ashbery's interpretation of Parmigianino's self-portrait, the two- and three-dimensional illusions seem inseparable. Since Ashbery discusses the convex mirror as it appears in Parmigianino's painting, the poet, in effect, discusses "the sign of the convex mirror." The poem presents the distortion of "significance" within a convex mirror's framework.

My reading of the word "significant," as Ashbery uses it, indicates the great number of connotations, in "Self-Portrait in a Convex Mirror," which are lost without a detailed account of convexity and its import to the poem. Most commentaries on the poem, however, do not explicate or discuss the concept and applications of convexity at any length. For instance, Laurence Lieberman simply equates convexity in the poem with the extension of the past into the present.[14]

Even when commenting upon passages that literally refer to the convexity of Parmigianino's painting, critics gloss over the issue of convexity. Breslin explains these lines within the context of a slightly larger passage:

> Today enough of a cover burnishes
> To keep the supposition of promises together
> In one piece of surface.
> (*SP*, 192: 29–31)

But he does not mention the central metaphoric structure that is at work here. However, we should note that because a flat painting approximates a plane, it can only depict convexity through a kind of "supposition." "Supposition" implies qualities of both force, albeit tentative, and imagination, suggesting an uneasy and perhaps overly self-conscious kind of coherence, which plays upon the connotations of "cover," and implies the, so to speak, "covering up" of an absent but implied presence. (It should also be taken into account that the poem was written in the Watergate era. See further discussion of the term "cover-up" in this chapter's next section and throughout chapter 6). If the flat painting were depicting another flat surface, or plane, it would claim, or "suppose" (a kind of representational "promise," that is), the promise of a unified representation. However, since the painting proposes to represent both many and no planes in the graduated planar approximations of a convex surface, the extremely anxious plural of "promise," in "the supposition of promises" is appropriate. Granted, the normative representational painting, if not the normative modern painting, does not attempt merely to represent one plane. Nonetheless, Renaissance ideas of perspective propose to negotiate between the seemingly flat plane upon which the eye gathers its gross visual impressions and the seemingly haphazard planar organization of what appears to be in the "world." Making a convex mirror's surface the subject of a painting confounds our expectations of both the flatly organized site of the eye's raw impressions and the unorganized world that its impressions seem to represent.

That the poem compares painterly illusion to "promises" presages Derrida's later discussion of painting in "The Truth in Painting."[15] Discussing Paul Cézanne's statement in his 23 October 1905 letter to Emile Bernard, "I owe you the truth in painting and I will tell it to you," Derrida writes that "the act of speech—the promise—gives itself out as true, or in any case truthful and sincere, and it veritably does promise to say truly the truth. In painting, don't forget."[16] In the course of Derrida's analysis, the philosopher demonstrates how uneasy and yet essential this "promise" or supposition of "truth" in painting is to every aspect of painting:

> That's the whole story, to recognize and contain, like the surrounds of the work of art, or at most its outskirts: frame, title, signature, museum archive, reproduction, discourse, market, in short: everywhere where one legislates on the right to painting by marking the limit, with a slash marking an opposition which one would like to be invisible.[17]

Painting both promises and requires what it is not—a "truth" in contradistinction to painting's enabling distinction, that is, that painting is separate from what is not painting and therefore has "the right" to a counter-reality and relatively illusory realm. The fulfillment of this promise of truth in painting paradoxically promises not only to undo painting but also to undo the promise of the truth in painting, since this supposition would then posit truth in opposition to a relative illusion. In other words, the dialectic between truth and illusion that enables painting would, if the promise of truth were fulfilled, become a dualism between truth and illusion that would not allow art or painting. It is vital to the art process that this promise be indefinitely delayed. To promise the truth in painting is to promise that this truth will never be disclosed.

It is fitting then that the "cover" in Ashbery's poem "burnishes" in order to implement its supposition. "To burnish" implies the incomplete yet constant burning of an object or substance, its browning or darkening, yet also the glowing, polishing, and lighting of an object. In this context, the verb "burnish" seems as anxious as it does lush and glamorous, completely undermining any faith we might have in the "promises" that hold the "surface" in "one piece," yet, nevertheless, keeping this surface intact. By using an ideational word like "supposition" in relation to Parmigianino's process of converting a convex surface into a plane, Ashbery, as he has done with his use of the word "significantly," correlates the processes of sight and signification. However, since we tend to associate painting with significant visual perceptions, one would not think Ashbery's correlation unusual. And yet, countering this expectation, the sentence begins with "Today enough," implying that in the past there was the lack of a cover sufficiently repressive to keep the "supposition of promises together / In one piece of surface." And yet the poem highlights the temporary quality of today. Since this reference to the day occurs near the beginning of the poem, we might assume that Ashbery refers to a moment in

1972 when it looked as if Nixon would be safely ensconced in the White House for four more years. However, the temporariness of "today" presages that mid-seventies organizing realities will not hold.

The trope of the convex mirror can be correlated with the common perception we have of the period in which the poem was written, in that the mid-seventies are popularly characterized as a delimiting of the expansive social, political, and cultural tendencies of the sixties and early seventies. This historical interpretation is evident in the sequence of Ashbery's books of poetry. Richard Howard views "Self-Portrait in a Convex Mirror" as "a return to returning," or, in other words, "a response to those impulses of recuperation, of recurrence and reversion which poetry—even such seamless poetry as Ashbery's, which observes beginnings and ends by a prosody of intermittence and collage rather than any such conventional markings as rhyme or repetition— is taken to incarnate, if not to incorporate."[18] Howard suggests that, with "Self-Portrait in a Convex Mirror," this poetic quality of recurrence returns to Ashbery's poetry to a greater extent than ever before, manifesting in both the poem's mirroring themes and its verse form, or, stated more accurately, the simple fact that it is written in verse. "Self-Portrait in a Convex Mirror," Howard maintains, is written as an alternative to the prose poetry of *Three Poems* (1972), which consists of relatively unformed and rambling sequences of paragraphs. In the following passage from the last prose poem in *Three Poems*, "The System," note the positing of a historical indeterminacy that is matched by its seemingly open, or relatively unformed, poetic technique:

> It began to seem as though some permanent way of life had installed itself, a stability immune to the fluctuations of other eras: the pendulum that throughout eternity has swung successively toward joy and grief had been stilled by a magic hand.[19]

Clearly, "Self-Portrait in a Convex Mirror" constitutes a return to a more normal kind of historical consciousness, as well as a more conventional versification. We may, however, ask how the convex mirror, as the poem's subject, applies to this "return." The first monograph written on Ashbery, David Shapiro's *John Ashbery: An Introduction to the Poetry* (1979), accounts for the convexity of the mirror described in both Francesco Parmigianino's painting and Ashbery's poem by stating that "the poem enacts . . . a criticism of mimesis, because the mirror in both painting and poem is the one of difficulty and convexity."[20] Shapiro's characterization of convexity as quintessentially difficult opens a fruitful avenue of inquiry. Granted, Ashbery's poem is intricate and, in places, imperspicuous. Nevertheless, difficult as it is, the poem is also one of Ashbery's most simple and lucid. Indeed, the image of the convex mirror itself signifies a rather aggressive tendency to simplify and unify. If our analysis of convex mirrors is valid, "Self-Portrait in a Convex Mirror," vigorously garnering the force of its speculations from the symbol of the convex mirror, is a rather convoluted meditation on simplicity itself, or, put in another way, totalization. Shapiro correctly detects "a criticism of mimesis in the poem,"[21] and, if we are to appreciate the poem as the thorny problematic of mimesis and representation that it is, we must acknowledge the connotations of simplicity and consolidation that Ashbery's subject matter, the convex mirror, implies. For his work in the mid-seventies Ashbery utilizes the most powerful organizing mechanism of his career. Mirrors concentrate light. Convex mirrors concentrate and blur perspectives. Writing about the portrait, so to speak, of a convex mirror summons an uncanny questioning of the "subject," the subject as person and the subject as topos.

In 1974, Ashbery used William Carlos Williams's *Pictures from Brueghel* in a poetry workshop he was conducting at Brooklyn College. Using *Pictures from Brueghel* as a model, Ashbery instructed his students to write poems based on paintings. However, *Pictures from Brueghel* may not be a literary influence on "Self-Portrait in a Convex Mirror" so much as it is a kind of starting point or "plot device." "Self-Portrait in a Convex Mirror" so vigorously and relentlessly tropes Williams's simple idea that it is more an unidentified target of parody than a serious preoccupation. As Ashbery's poem "Syringa" (1977) notes:

> And no matter how all this disappeared,
> Or got where it was going, it is no longer
> Material for a poem. Its subject
> Matters too much, and not enough, standing there helplessly
> While the poem streaked by.
> (*SP*, 247: 1–5)

Although the initial idea behind "Self-Portrait in a Convex Mirror" may be reminiscent of Williams's "Self-Portrait," Ashbery's treatment of Parmigianino's painting has more in common with Foucault's ruminations on *Las Meniñas* (1656) by Diego Velázquez.[22] Like Ashbery, Foucault describes "a matter of pure reciprocity: we are looking at a picture in which the painter is in turn looking out at us."[23] As in Ashbery's poem, this "reciprocity" allows the painting's "very subject" to be "elided"[24] and stresses the signifying process.

Unlike Williams, Ashbery ponders what comes between the two extremely different subject matters of the painter as creator and the painter as signified. In "Self-Portrait in a Convex Mirror," it is the mirror's surface:

> What is novel is the extreme care in rendering
> The velleities of the rounded reflecting surface
> (It is the first mirror portrait),
> So that you could be fooled for a moment
> Before you realize the reflection
> Isn't yours. You feel like one of those
> Hoffman characters who have been deprived
> Of a reflection, except that the whole of me
> Is seen to be supplanted by the strict
> Otherness of the painter in his
> Other room. We have surprised him
> At work, but no, he has surprised us
> As he works.
> (*SP*, 194: 28–33; 195: 1–7)

According to the poem, Parmigianino's reduplication of the mirror's visual cues causes the observer to think that she or he is looking into a mirror. However, the poem's observer is jilted when he notes Parmigianino's reflection instead of his own. The observer is momentarily tricked into believing that he has no reflection, until he associates himself with the "otherness" of the reflection in the "mirror" of the painting and the painter it depicts.

In a phenomenological sense, the observer completes the picture and, understandably, considers himself to be the object of the painting. Nonetheless, this does not constitute an assured identity; the painter whom the observer identifies with cannot anchor his identity.

In the poem, one knows oneself only by seeing oneself in the external world of the signified. "Everything is surface," Ashbery writes. "The surface is what's there / And nothing can exist except what's there" (*SP*, 190: 12–13). "Everything gets 'programmed' there," the poem says (*SP*, 193: 3), so as not to be distinguishable. However, when the observer sees himself not to be there, he recognizes a relatively truer self in an absence that implies an acknowledgment of the impossibility of establishing a definite self. "Long ago / The strewn evidence meant something," Ashbery's poem says of the effect of Parmigianino's convex mirror. "Impossible now / To restore those properties in the silver blur" (*SP*, 192: 1-6). In fact, it seems to be Parmigianino's task to maintain this absence or "silver blur" and to "surprise" observers with it.

Through Ashbery's critical reading, if not in any "literal" manner, this encounter with a Renaissance painting invites and then subverts logocentric tendencies. Similarly, Ashbery lulls the reader into believing that she or he is engaged with discursive, albeit poetic, writing. However, the reader is being misdirected. Ashbery is using this misdirection to set the stage for a profound questioning of subject matter and theme or topos. The play upon a coherent subject matter is paradoxically one of the poem's chief subject matters. As the poem's central symbol, the convex mirror suggests that a distortion necessarily accompanies a forced coherence.

The symbol of the convex mirror is increasingly intertwined with the image on the convex mirror that Ashbery describes. This image on the mirror is, of course, Parmigianino's reflection, and, for the poem's title, Ashbery has appropriated the title of Parmigianino's self-portrait. Since Ashbery's poem comments on a self-portrait, the poem becomes not only a sustained meditation on a painting but also on its painter. However, the poem obviously does more than merely comment on Parmigianino's appearance, or, for that matter, the painter's career or personality.

In "Self-Portrait in a Convex Mirror," "Parmigianino" functions as both the quintessential subject and object. More significantly, according to Ashbery's poem, Parmigianino's painting concerns the relation, as well as lack of a clear relation, between Parmigianino as a subject and an object. In this regard, the poem concerns a model of signification as a chain of signifiers. In this model, the import of the signifying chain precedes that of relationships between the signifier and the signified, as well as between the addresser and addressee. For instance, in the poem's last verse paragraph, the speaker notes that "the way of telling" invariably acts as a kind of mischievous intermediary; it

> somehow intrude[s], twisting the end result
> Into a caricature of itself. This always
> Happens, as in the game where
> A whispered phrase passed around the room
> Ends up as something completely different.
> It is this principle that makes works of art so unlike
> What the artist intended. Often he finds

He has omitted the thing he started out to say
In the first place. Seduced by flowers,
Explicit pleasures, he blames himself (though
Secretly satisfied with the result), imagining
He had a say in the matter and exercised
An option of which he was hardly conscious,
Unaware that necessity circumvents such resolutions
So as to create something new
For itself, that there is no other way,
That the history of creation proceeds according to
Stringent laws, and that things
Do get done in this way, but never the things
We set out to accomplish and wanted so desperately
To see come into being. Parmigianino
Must have realized this.
(*SP,* 201: 5–26)

Note that although the autonomy of the author and the author's intent are denied, the poem does not underestimate the import of logocentric expectations within the larger poetic process. The logocentric concepts that inform our consciousnesses cannot be escaped; they can only be questioned and shown to be self-negating. Derrida remarks in *Of Grammatology,* "To make enigmatic what one thinks one understands by the words *'proximity,' 'immediacy,' 'presence'* (the proximate [*proche*], the own [*propre*], and the pre- of presence), is my final intention in this book. The deconstruction of presence accomplishes itself through the deconstruction of consciousness and therefore through the irreducible notion of the trace."[25]

In the passage from "Self-Portrait in a Convex Mirror" that equates the artistic process to the party and children's game of "telephone," wherein "A whispered phrase passed around the room / Ends up as something completely different," the poem's speaker notes the inevitable play between traces that must repeatedly transform the author's initial intent. This is akin to Derrida's conceptualization of writing as a chain of differences.

When the speaker in "Self-Portrait in a Convex Mirror" says that "Parmigianino / Must have realized this," referring to changes that the painter's intent must undergo, the speaker is stressing the artist's passive function, or negation of her or his subjectivity, in making effective art. However, the positing of a self as a site for this play, if only as a site which may eventually be undermined, is necessary to facilitate this play of difference. How else can this play take place, except against our logocentric preconceptions? In the first part of "Self-Portrait in a Convex Mirror," the speaker insists on the necessity of logocentric poses:

> The soul has to stay where it is,
> Even though restless, hearing raindrops at the pane,
> The sighing of autumn leaves thrashed by the wind,
> Longing to be free, outside, but it must stay
> Posing in this place. It must move
> As little as possible. . . .
>
> .   .   .   .
>
> . . . The pity of it smarts,
> Makes hot tears spurt: that the soul is not a soul,
> Has no secret, is small, and it fits
> Its hollow perfectly.
> (*SP*, 188: 34; 189: 1–5, 9–12)

Although the self is viewed as ephemeral, the poem's speaker does not avoid issues of self. However, the self or "soul" recognizes constraints and feels "restless," regarding its autonomy as a kind of prison. The soul associates freedom with the "outside," where factors can be detected that are outside the unchanging subjectivity in which the painting's subjectivity is immersed. Parmigianino, the poem states, can hear the rain hit the window and the wind thrash the autumn leaves. Hearing these phenomena, however, reinforces the subject's "isolation." This isolation seems to be imposed, since "it must stay / Posing in this place. It must move / As little as possible."

The poem shows isolated subjective experience to be imposed and thus something of a posture. Although the poem contradicts "romanticized" characterizations of the individual, or soul, as an absolute origin, it is done so in a romantic, or expressive, way. The poem's speaker gives the impression of feeling a sharp remorse that is caused by the realization that "the soul is not a soul." Here the tone contradicts the ostensible, if paradoxical, sense of the remark, prefiguring Julia Kristeva's discussion of denial and melancholy in *Black Sun*, in which Kristeva postulates that denial and melancholy vitiate signifiers. Nonetheless, a discrepancy between tone and sense is perhaps inevitable. Any tone, if "tone" is taken to mean an emotive index, would seem to clash with the sense of the remark, since "soul" is associated with subjectivity and emotion and the impact of the soul is being denied. Indeed, the Latin word for "soul" is *anima,* which is related to "animation" or "movement," and "emotion"; yet the soul in Ashbery's poem is immobile, it "has to stay where it is."

The poem's extremely overt pathos serves to stress the discrepancy between the phrase's tone and meaning. After all, if "the soul is not a soul," what is it that longs for the freedom of the outside? Indeed, if the soul and subjectivity are illusory, from where is the poem being written, and who or what is writing the poem that we are reading? If the seeming "author" is not an author, is there not an authorial function that must nevertheless be reckoned with? If we accept such a notion, how can it be described? For instance, is the author a vehicle for a kind of cultural unconscious? Is the author a by-product of the text? Or are the author's and reader's functions impossible to separate? Does the reader help to make the text? Given the import of the mirror in Ashbery's poem, this last alternative deserves particular attention. And yet, even if we do acknowledge the reader as an author or co-author, how can we view the reader in the context of the poem's critical view of the individual and the "soul"?

The poem begins to address these questions when it precludes the possibility of finding answers, noting that the self must defer to the play of meaning that constitutes the writing process. However, the speaker's realization that "the soul is not a soul" foreshadows these observations and ignites the poem. Clearly, the contradictory implications of this remark must be disentangled. Initially, the subjective component of the sentence, "The soul," is emphasized more than the sentence's predicate, "is not a soul." However, the last part of the poem is driven by an attempt to accommodate its initial positing of the soul's absence.

Coming near the beginning of the poem, "the soul is not a soul" seems to say that the "soul" that admits to its own illusory make-up begins to write as it contextualizes, or accounts for, the contradictions and paradoxes that are attendant to this formulation. Ultimately, the poem makes the case that as a "self" comprehends the limits and barriers that ironically enable it, it becomes more capable of being a vehicle through which a work is authored:

> Aping naturalness may be the first step
> Toward achieving an inner calm
> But it is the first step only, and often
> Remains a frozen gesture of welcome etched
> On the air materializing behind it,
> A convention. And we have really

No time for these, except to use them
For kindling. The sooner they are burnt up
The better for the roles we have to play.
(*SP,* 203: 11–19)

One may presume that, since Ashbery says this in a poem, the roles that must be played are related to being a writer and poet, which requires the play of a kind of other that enables the process of signification. Indeed, "roles," like the images of "Self-Portrait in a Convex Mirror" are "reversed in the accumulating mirror" (*SP,* 193: 28), "accumulating mirror" emblematizing our culture's preoccupation and archiving itself so as to utilize Freud's magic notepad to describe the underpinnings of collective culture. The self is valued but acknowledged as a limited and limiting mechanism that is also a link to something larger.

Plainly, "Self-Portrait in a Convex Mirror" questions the self as the primary site of experience and, by extension, the poem's authorial function, since a "self" is normally considered to be a work's "author." However, Ashbery avoids neither issues of self nor author. On the contrary, by questioning the related concepts of subjectivity, self, and author, the poem stresses the significance of ideas of selfhood and authorship, albeit, ultimately, not their central status and validity. "Self-Portrait in a Convex Mirror" privileges logocentrism, only eventually to problematize it. Similarly, to use Derrida's word in *Of Grammatology,* the "glimmer" of something beyond organizing mechanisms is glimpsed in the sixties. Paradoxically, the sixties highlight the romantic myth of a logic that is centered in a myth of unified presence only eventually to problematize that myth through the codifications of identity-politics, as the next section takes up.

2 Fingering Absences: Morrison, Rich, and Shepard

I'm the President of the country—and I'm going to get on with it and meet Italians and Germans, and all those others.—Richard Nixon, Watergate tape transcripts

"You can't tell from someone's voice when they're black," Mr. Cochran said, pounding his fingers indignantly into the lectern.

Mr. Darden persisted, looking at Mr. Cochran and pointing his finger.—David Margolick, "[O.J.] Simpson Witness Saw a White Car," *New York Times*

To accept one's past—one's history—is not the same thing as drowning in it: it is learning how to use it.—James Baldwin, *The Fire Next Time*

"I" am not "I," I am not, I am not one. As for woman, try and find out. —Luce Irigaray, *This Sex Which Is Not One*

This [affirmative action as it applies to the majority's rights] was not pointing the finger at a group which had been marked as inferior in any sense; and it was undifferentiated, it operated against a wide variety of people. So I think it was not stigmatizing. —Archibald Cox, arguing for the university in *Regents of the University of California v. Bakke,* before the U.S. Supreme Court

And, now, we were among them. At school, the "on relief" finger suddenly was pointed at us, too, and sometimes it was said aloud. —Malcolm X, *The Autobiography of Malcolm X*

"You complained about holiday dumplings: 'Women roll dough to knead out the dirt from between their fingers. Women's fingernail dirt.'"
"She wiggled her fingers through the holes." —Maxine Hong Kingston, *China Men*

My politics shouldn't matter. It's my finger that should. —John Ashbery, *"Flow Chart"*

In all things that are purely social we can be as separate as the fingers, yet one as the hand in all things essential to mutual progress. —Booker T. Washington, "Atlanta Compromise" speech

This section moves from a discussion of the emblem of a convex mirror's backing and its tacit vacuum that metaphorically make possible the surveillance and construction of self to a discussion of the mirror as it is seen from the other side—as a projectile or a fingertip. It might be said that the finger, as it is prominent in the seventies literature that I discuss, is a more pointed version of the convex mirror. To examine the notion of this "finger," I discuss identity-group formations in seventies works by Toni Morrison and Adrienne Rich. I follow with an examination of seventies identity vacuum and absence within the context of the conventional nuclear family in Sam Shepard's seventies drama, and I conclude with a reading of an eighties poem by Rich and its rendering of the perplexities of identity-politics.

It is not accidental that much of the most significant art of the seventies (in various media, by very different artists such as Laurie Anderson, Eleanor Antin, Judy Chicago, Yvonne Rainer, Linda Francis, Cindy Sherman, Jill Johnston, Carolee Schneemann, and Hannah Wilke) was both performative and feminist. Seventies feminists had little choice but to experiment with identity and notions of presence, since they inevitably pointed toward something that did not yet exist, and all manner of identity-positions were increasingly called into question as the decade progressed. Articulating this quandary, in 1974, Luce Irigaray wrote her groundbreaking doctoral thesis *Spéculum de l'autre femme (Speculum of the Other Woman)*, for which she was summarily dismissed from Lacan's École freudienne. In *Sexual/Textual Politics: Feminist Literary Theory* Toril Moi explains Irigaray's theory of "male desire for the same" and female strategies around it:

> Irigaray concludes that in our society representation, and therefore also social and cultural structures, are products of what she sees as a fundamental *hom(m)osexualité*. The pun in French is on *homo* ('same') and *homme* ('man'): the male desire for the same. The pleasure of self-representation, of her desire for the same, is denied woman: she is cut off from any kind of pleasure that might be specific to her.
>
> Caught in the specular logic of patriarchy, woman can choose either to remain silent, producing incomprehensible babble (any utterance that falls outside the logic of the same will be definition be incomprehensible to the male master discourse), or to *enact* the specular representation of herself as a lesser male. The latter option, the woman as mimic, is, according to Irigaray, a form of hysteria. The hysteric *mimes* her own sexuality in a masculine mode, since this is the only way in which she can rescue something of her own desire.[26]

Appropriating masculine codes into feminist thought, Irigaray uses indefinite gaps within masculine identity to establish a space for feminine power. Similarly, Irigaray employs the masculine instrument of the gynecological speculum's concave mirror (the inverse of a convex mirror is after all concave), which turns its subjects upside down (images in a concave mirror rebound so as to present its subjects upside down) as a way to represent that which is beyond representation and to represent identities that seemingly come from nowhere, or, that is, from outside the male master discourse. The "pointing figure" of the speculum produces its subject as its own distorted mirror in a collective mirror. Likewise, "Self-Portrait in a Convex Mirror" speaks of "words" as "only speculation / (From the Latin *speculum,* mirror)." The poem says that words are only vague pictures—"postures of the dream," "but" are nonetheless our best handles on some kind of reality "and life englobed" (*SP,* 189). If a convex mirror is life contextualized through surveillance, a finger represents life brought to the surface with odd emphasis.

While preparing to teach a seminar on multiculturalism, I noted the word "finger" often used in works of literature by American women authors such as Toni Morrison, Maxine Hong Kingston, Bharati Mukherjee, Amy Tan, and Sandra Cisneros. What could this mean? I remembered an early seventies Dick Cavett show in which activist comedian Mort Sahl criticized minority politics by likening various "powers"—women power, gay power, etc.—to fingers separated from a hand and working on their own with diminished power and effect. However, comparing self-identities to fingers could also imply a unified and "rainbow" coalition, suggesting that these groups are fundamentally allied and can work together successfully. Fingers also connote a useful separation of the constituents of the hand, the metaphoric whole becoming greater with a partial division, thus deconstructing if not negating Sahl's comment.

On a television interview program some twenty years later, I heard Toni Morrison tell Bill Moyers that full and official black participation in the life of America was difficult for the same reason a person not using her or his hand for an extended period will have difficulty using her or his fingers. Perhaps most Americans today are feeling a similar kind of disuse and disempowerment, and this is one reason why I note my "traditional" college students becoming increasingly in tune with "multicultural" literature. It sometimes seems more like mainstream literature than supposedly mainstream and canonical literature. They read multicultural literature as relevant to the society we share. Through my teaching of various student populations, I have come to believe that literary and cultural critics must articulate diversity as a mechanism of social, cultural, and literary sensitivity because such sensitivity can be a resource that helps many more Americans participate within the American polity. A sensitivity to shifting and undefined realms of diversity can assist both those who are excluded from full participation within the nation and those who believe they are not barred from complete participation. Even those who work within the myth of belonging to a dominant culture are experiencing shrinking horizons within that culture, leading them to feel marginal. The celebrated "revolt of the white male" in the 1994 elections bespeaks a sense of indefinite identity, despite the misguidance of their chosen remedies. Resentful white males yearn for a place within a diversity that they paradoxically deny and fear. These white males experience something like definition envy. As Toni Morrison says in *Song of Solomon* (1977), "a fist beats in a chest that becomes a pointing finger."[27]

The finger trope connotes signifying powers, feminine pleasure, stigmatization, and identity. Against a Freudian perspective, fingers critique the castration complex. However, I do not intend to analyze these texts from a psychoanalytic point of view that posits a hidden individual psychological reality.

Orthodox penis envy would seem to have little to do with Morrison's frequent troping of fingers. She uses fingers more as tropes of feminine assuredness within a community set apart from a white male polity. From a sociopolitical vantage, fingers speak of a masculine minority / feminine minority dialectic, in which women can more easily knit a community together than men can officially participate within a mainstream polity.

Toni Morrison plays feminist and racial connotations of fingering off and against one another. In *The Bluest Eye* (1970), for instance, Morrison's central character, Pecola, points to a candy with a picture of a white girl on the label:

> She points her fingers at the Mary Janes—a little black shaft of light, its tip pressed on the display window. The quietly inoffensive assertion of a black child's attempt to communicate with a white adult.
>
> . . . her fingertips fixed on the spot which, in her view, at any rate, identifies the Mary Janes. He cannot see her view—the angle of her vision, the slant of her finger, makes it incomprehensible to him. His lumpy red hand plots around in the glass casing like the agitated head of a chicken outraged by the loss of its body.[28]

Pecola seeks pleasure through the construction of a white fantasy identity. She looks through the "window" of a candy-case glass and sees the mirror's backing that holds a racist ideological reality in place. In this regard, former first assistant minister to Malcolm X, Benjamin Karim, at a 25 April 1995 convocation address at Franklin College in Indiana, with reference to a mirror's backing, said, "Take away the backing and guess what? I'm still here."[29] John Wideman's 1983 novel, *Sent for You Yesterday,* also plays with this kind of trope, but with more anxiety. The narrator describes a light-skinned African American:

> I was always a little bit afraid of him, afraid I'd see through him, under his skin, because there was no color to stop my eyes, no color which said there's a black man or a white man in front of you. I was afraid I'd see through the transparent envelope of skin to see the bones and guts of whatever he was. To see Brother I'd have to look away from where he was standing, focus on something safe and solid near him so that Brother would hover like the height of a mountain at the skittish edges of my vision.[30]

Françoise Lionnet associates transparency with race differently. According to Lionnet, autobiography can demythologize race because "the collective functions as a silverless mirror, capable of absorbing the self into a duplicitous game in which one code, singularity, is set aslant by another, syncretic unity with the universe, thus preventing narrative closure."[31]

In *The Bluest Eye,* the white keeper of the gates does not easily recognize Pecola's desire. He complicates it and shames Pecola for it. She is later said to feel "inexplicable shame."[32] The white shopkeeper responds to Pecola's finger with a reckless "lumpy red hand." Whereas Pecola occupies the fringes of the exchange, the shopkeeper assumes the center. The lumpy red hand implies a castrated penis. Similarly, Pecola's envied acquaintance, the almost white Maureen Peal, has six fingers, suggesting that whiteness itself is a kind of extra phallus. Whiteness is a kind of paternal symbolic code for official reality. *The Bluest Eye,* written in the sixties and published in 1970, criticizes such an official reality and looks toward a reeducation away from white ideals of identity and beauty that imprison African Americans and others. By seeing an idea of beauty as the nemesis, *The Bluest Eye* carries an element of optimism, in that it can at least identify an enemy, even if it is an intangible one.

Morrison's next book *Sula* (1973) sees beyond any such easy answers. By often demonstrating and stating James Baldwin's notion that blackness is a concept that unifies all manner of so-called white Americans (as when the Irish boys terrorize the book's two central characters), Morrison sees an ill-spirited racism, more than a coded aesthetic, at the heart of American identity.

When the title character of *Sula* cuts off the tip of her finger to demonstrate her dangerous irrationality, it is almost as if she is protesting her marginality. She must part with a bit of her potency to prove it. Sula's "funny shaped finger" becomes her metonymic representation in the town of Medallion, Ohio, and, in a sense, she gives the finger to the men who are said to have "fingerprinted" or stigmatized her.[33] *Sula* can be characterized as a more feminist text than *The Bluest Eye* because it posits feminine power. Morrison's progression in choice of subjects parallels the women's liberation movement that in some ways models itself after the black civil rights movement. For instance, Adrienne Rich recalls "the emergence of the Civil Rights movement in the sixties I remember as lifting me out of a sense of personal frustration and hopelessness. Reading James Baldwin's early essays in the fifties had stirred me with a sense that apparently 'given' situations like racism could be analyzed and described and that this could lead to action, to change."[34]

In *Sula,* fingers convey secret and binding knowledge. Fingers are used to describe Sula and Nel's collaborative part in the death of Chicken Little and its cover-up:

They held hands and knew that only the coffin would lie in the earth; the bubbly laughter and the press of fingers in the palm would stay above ground forever. At first they stood there, their hands were clenched together. They relaxed slowly until during the walk back home their fingers were laced in as gentle a clasp as that of any two young girlfriends trotting up the road on a summer day.[35]

Interestingly, Shadrack intuits their part in Chicken Little's death. Near the beginning of the book, Shadrack's postwar shell shock causes him to fear his fingers because "they began to grow in higgledy-piggledy fashion like Jack's beanstalk all over the tray and the bed."[36] He feels better after a straitjacket removes his fingers from sight. Freud might say that this signifies a voluntary castration—a verification of what he knows to be true, a relinquishing of anxiety by establishing that everyone is indeed castrated.

Fingers signify the potency—and impotency—behind signification. Barbara Johnson has said that when a dog sees its master pointing, it merely looks at the finger, not understanding the human signifying process of seeking correspondences. In a sense, to dwell upon fingers and not what they are pointing at is a modernist imperative. When Roman Jakobson speaks of poetry as reflexive language, he indicates a modernist disdain of content, of the referent—of the thing being pointed at. Gérard Genette discusses Jakobson's "contempt for images, and the devaluation of tropes as marks of poetic language. Speaking of a poem by Pushkin, Jakobson himself was still insisting, in 1936, on the possibility of poetry without imagery."[37] Preferring tropes and figures to images, Jakobson and the other early formalists stressed grammatical form over imagistic content. Similarly, from a supremacist or futurist point of view, such reference weighs down the more masculine job of employing industrialist methods that stress mode over product. State identification and "fingerprinting" are such modes.

Such reference can be likened to the burden of the polity. Black feminist and sociologist Patricia Hill Collins addresses the issue of the "outsider within." She argues that institutions, corporations, and universities "train" people to become managers, that is, people in power. The word "training" refers to what people do to teach dogs to obey the finger of the master. Black people are still "outsiders within" white power structures designed to maintain power through authoritative obedience.[38] *Sula,* however, portrays a community in which such identification has little meaning, as when Sula holds Ajax's driver's license in her "fingers," after he has left her, as "a worn slip of paper." Paper as a uniform surface of identification has become the "worn slip," suggesting a woman's undergarment. Fingers hold and point toward a hidden area from which life springs, in Freudian terms inextricably interwoven with castration and the uncanny. Signification and naming are activities that become possible in their blocking. Thus Sula can half-recall a song as she mediatates on Ajax's name, only to decide that she already knows all songs. She feels her power as she withdraws. Since women experience a psychological conditioning that may indeed be said to be a kind of castration, our very cultural notion of womanhood by extension models a society in which we are losing our identity hooks. Morrison offers the paradoxical potency of castration anxiety to all.

In *Song of Solomon* (1977) the women of the Dead family are randomly named after the first name that a patriarch's finger comes to in a Bible. However, this kind of rootless association becomes strength for Pilate, who is in many ways a guide for the novel's central character, her nephew Milkman. *Song of Solomon,* published in the wake of *Roots,* points toward a more mysterious heritage than does *Roots.* At the end of *Song of Solomon,* we learn that Milkman can fantastically escape by surrendering to the air and flying. In the child's game that his flight simulates, a child must point a finger at someone who must play Solomon if the game is to continue. If the child points at no one, the game starts from its beginning. This impasse is represented by Milkman's aunt Pilate, whose past Milkman must trace to find his legacy. Pilate is in a sense never born nor "preborn," since she has no umbilical cord. It is often said that she is "cut off." And yet this very isolation creates its own kind of castration that leads to an empowerment. Milkman's reverse migration, on Pilate's footsteps, leads to a consideration of Pilate's outsider position in the full potency of a seeming flight.

Rich's seventies poetry relates to a break in Cold War reality that comes on the heels of the civil rights movement, the anti–Vietnam War effort, and the valorization of a counterculture. However, she seeks to go beyond the binary system that permits and assists the establishment of a patriarchy. She extends the project of other sixties debunking to establish identity that is outside the poles of patriarchal ownership. This would seem to negate the possibility of identity. Identity is seen as outside the bounds of an exchange between fathers and sons; as in Irigaray's theory of the speculum, female identity is not located within patriarchal ideology or exchange economics. A woman, says

Irigaray, must "recover" by "playful repetition, what was supposed to remain invisible: the cover-up of a possible operation of the feminine in language."[39] This cover-up can be exposed by *"crossing back through the mirror that subtends all speculation."*[40] On the other side of the mirror there is "feminine pleasure" and the "tactile" and "self-touching."[41] The finger traces its object of desire to find itself. (Interestingly, Toni Morrison has often spoken of the human need to touch. Addicts can begin to cure themselves by holding "crack babies," she told Bill Moyers.) Writing is an abstraction, if powerful abstraction, of weaving. Truth, according to Irigaray, is found through a tactile, fluid, and woven process.[42]

Like Irigaray, Rich butts into the symbolic order that is in place. She summons a new "real" questioning of the imaginary realm that the symbolic realm masks. The real is now equated to a burning and a bleeding from within. Identity is marked by implosion—by the lack of an outward limb; identity begins where patriarchal identity ends. Patriarchy is the corpse incorporating dead identities. For Rich, identity is not a lever but a recognition of a wound not entirely equivalent to castration. Rather, identity is necessarily a breaking away from the non-identity of patriarchy. Alterity speaks in an improvising, paradoxically established fashion. Rich speaks on a dividing line between the nonestablishment and establishment of identities:

> if they ask me my identity
> what can I say but
> I am the androgyne
> I am the living mind you fail to describe
> in your dead language[43]

Rich is here, in the early seventies, scaffolding a model of stark oppositional identity, and she cannot see androgyne as an identity. Similarly, she perhaps too squarely aligns patriarchy with manhood. There is no redeemable aspect for the illusory cover-up aspect of manhood. Woman are mocked for their participation in the masculine game of revelation. (We may note the prototypically meaningless male gesture of self-revelation in the mid-seventies of "streaking.") Watergate shapes up as an all-male drama. One thinks of Martha Mitchell being undermined and mocked, to this day, for her perspectives on Watergate. And yet one also thinks of the perhaps essential role of the women office workers who tip off Woodward and Bernstein as they navigate the money trail from the Watergate burglars to the Committee to Reelect the President. In this regard, Rich comments on the film *The Godfather:*

Again and again it shows men who, while ruling patriarchal families with the most benign authority toward their own women and children are capable at the same time of ruthless intimidation and murder; the efficiency of their violent operations depends on their maintaining an artificial and theoretical wall between fatherhood and godfatherhood. When "business" is discussed at the family table, the Family is already in trouble. Women, with their tendency to ask uncomfortable questions and make uncomfortable connections, are to be excluded from all decision-making, as the final shot somewhat heavily portrays.[44]

For Rich, the symbolic order can be seen to start anywhere but in official patriarchal reality.

The sixties promoted capital that sought to move beyond exchange value. There was a sense of barter in the air. Perhaps this crisis in capitalism was indirectly responsible for Nixon's rise to the presidency during the sixties. After World War II, the culture adapted to a peacetime economy because it really maintained a war economy although it was essentially fighting no one. A Keynesian model of investment spending persisted only to create an air of utopic opposition that went against the grain of the pre-Depression, pre–New Deal American mind-set that Richard Nixon embodied. Nixon was a voice from bedrock/balanced-budget America. He could assume credibility. People were genuinely shocked by the thought that he would attempt to obstruct justice. True, Nixon had long been known as Tricky Dick, yet there was, among most Americans, a faith in the integrity of the presidency. In this respect, Watergate radicalized virtually all of America.

Oddly, at the same time that people would say that all presidents did what Nixon did, the general idea of what all presidents did in itself changed. Perhaps this was because Nixon seemed like one of the people and hence was a standard, in the sense that he seemed to model himself after a small town chamber of commerce lawyer. Nixon was perhaps the first demographically correct president of the century—the first working, middle-class president of the century except for Harry Truman, who was not initially elected. The undoing of the Nixon presidency is the undoing of America. The rhetorical presidency becomes completely rhetorical; he cannot be solidly believed again but rather, in the future, the American people must repress their disbelief of the president.

Sam Shepard's 1978 play *Curse of the Starving Class* relates a post-Watergate tale about a surrealistically dysfunctional family working out its relationship with its semi-absent, alcoholic, debtor father, Weston Tate. The mother,

Ella, believes at the play's beginning that she can sell the family house and move to Europe with her young teenaged daughter, Emma, and Emma's older brother, Wesley. At the end of the play, however, mother, daughter, and son discover that this "impeachment" of the father cannot be successful because all their fates are intertwined. The family cannot escape Weston's debts. The "hard fellas" who come to inform Weston that he must make good on his loans have planted a bomb that explodes on Emma when she steals her mother's car. The suited thugs also play with mistaking Wesley for Weston because Wesley has been drawn into wearing his father's decrepit clothes, causing Ella to call him Weston. The two tough guys are named Emerson, implying the optimism that causes Weston to speculate on America and ironically compromise his self-reliance, and Slater, suggesting a hard writing surface, a kind of verbal backing of the mirror.

Everyone in the Tate family shares the fate of exile from the home that they have long lived in. To cover his debts, Weston agrees to sell the house to Ellis, the owner of the Alibi Club, putting an end to Ella's plan to sell the house. However, Ellis takes back the fifteen hundred dollars that he agreed to give Weston for the house when Emma shoots up his club, thus leaving Weston unprotected from his creditors, and Wesley persuades Weston to flee to Mexico.

Weston and his family are victims of post–World War II optimism. He explains his situation to his son:

> I was up to hock to my elbow. See, I always figured on the future. I banked on it. I was banking on it getting better. It couldn't get worse, so I figured it'd just get better. I figured that's why everyone wants you to buy things. Buy refrigerators. Buy cars, houses, lots, invest. They wouldn't be so generous if they didn't figure you had it comin' in. So I went along with it. Why not borrow if you know it's coming in. Why not make a touch here and there. They all want you to borrow anyhow. Banks, car lots, investors. The whole thing's geared to invisible money. . . . So I just went along with it, that's all. I just played ball.[45]

The game that Weston plays was shaped by World War II, the borrowing for which turned the American economic depression into economic boom. Weston was a World War II bomber pilot. The metaphor of a kind of distant bombing becomes a metaphor for fatherhood. Wesley imagines his father as a fighter pilot flying above him and doing reconnaissance. He imagines his father providing him with an identity in opposition to his father. Calling further attention to our larger theme of an intrinsic connection between surveillance and the seventies, Wesley says, "I could feel myself lying far below them on my bed like I was on the ocean and overhead they were on reconnaissance. Scouting me. Floating. Taking pictures of the enemy. Me, the enemy. I could feel the space around me like a big, black world."

Weston describes his relationship with his father:

> You know I watched my old man move around. I watched him move through rooms. I watched him drive tractors, watched him watching base-ball, watched him keeping out of the way of things. Out of the way of my mother. Away from my brothers. Watched him on sidelines. Nobody saw him but me. Everybody was right here, but nobody saw him but me. He lived apart. Right in the midst of things and he lived apart. Nobody saw that.[46]

Weston expects his son to spy upon him: "You're like having an espionage spy around. Why are you watching me all the time? . . . You can watch me all you want to. You won't find out a thing."[47] Weston says that he cannot see his father until he "recognizes his poison," which orders everything in the family. The father disseminates his symbolic order throughout the family. It is through his absence and living apart that the father imposes order. In this sense, Weston, who is said to be only home "ten percent of the time," is a typical father.

As the American people discover when Nixon leaves the presidency, Nixon's absence is as difficult to assimilate as his presence. Near the end of the play, Ella and Wesley dimly recall a story that Weston told many times to both of them. An eagle attacks a cat and takes off in flight with it. The cat tears the eagle apart in mid-air. Ella concludes the play, "And they come crashing down to the earth. Both of them come crashing down. Like one whole thing."[48]

The earth that the family crashes down to is the emptiness of the promise of post–World War II America. Bespeaking an identification with sacrificial lambs, Weston had told his eagle-and-cat story to a lamb, which Wesley brought into the house to de-maggot. Wesley later says that he is at one with the lamb. In Weston's story, which he presents as a moment of clarity, Weston tells of being a boy doing his chores. He is castrating sheep when he attracts an eagle. Assuming that the eagle is after the sheep's testicles, he throws them on the tar roof of a shack. One thinks of the bacon and eggs that Weston is preparing. Throughout the play, food is equated to castrated organs. The phallus is ingested to maintain ties to the prevailing symbolic order. Castration ties the real to the symbolic. In Morrison's *Song of Solomon,* a similar wisdom is found by the people of the rural southern town where Milkman, the novel's central character, finds his selfhood. *"Not his dead life; I mean his living life,"* they say about a slain bobcat before castrating it.[49] John Ashbery's mid-seventies poem "Worsening Situation" notes:

> This severed hand
> Stands for life, and wander as it will,
> East or west, north or south, it is ever
> A stranger who walks beside me.
> (*SP*, 165: 4-7)

In *Curse of the Starving Class,* the family is part of the starving class no matter how much it eats, because the center of its symbolic order is empty. No growth is possible. Emma as a consumer identifies with the consumer items in the refrigerator. She feels herself to be just so much food, as is everyone in this self-consuming family. Similarly, Wesley feels an identity with the lamb that he feels compelled to butcher for food. No wonder that Weston can only feel oneness with his family by fixing food for them.

Emma's symbolic castration is reinforced through the constant reminders to her of the "curse" of her first menstruation. After describing Emma's condition, Ella uses the term "curse" to describe the Tate family:

> Do you know what this is. It's a curse. I can feel it. It's invisible but it's there. It's always there. It comes onto us like nighttime. Every day I can feel it. Every day I can see it coming. And it always comes. Repeats itself. It comes even when you do everything to stop it from coming. Even when you try to change it. And it goes back. Deep. It goes back and back to tiny little cells and genes. To atoms. To tiny little swimming things making up their minds without us. Plotting in the womb. Before that even. In the air. We're surrounded with it. It's bigger than government even. It goes forward too. We spread it. We pass it on. We inherit it and pass it down, and then pass it down again. It goes on and on like that without us.[50]

Menstrual bleeding is depicted as the imperative that binds society together. It suggests a feminine reality that is perhaps as informing and as crucial to the social and the symbolic order as the word and the law of the father.

Ella repeatedly tells Emma to change her clothes, and Wesley exposes himself to her before urinating on her 4H Club chicken-cutting charts. The "curse" of menstruation, feminine castration, and the paternal symbolic order are intertwined. The implementation of various lacks support one another and create family togetherness. Similarly, Morrison, Rich, and Shepard point to the absences that construct gender. Fingers are pointed at sometimes phantom, sometimes troubled paternal hierarchies. Indeed "fingers" take on the symbolic weight of symbolic orders. Identity is not so much a signifier pointing at a signified as a generative construction pointing to possibilities of authorship and audience in a dynamic tension with legacies of stigmatization and pride.

One might say that one system of societal surveillance is breaking down in favor of other ones. For Rich, this is related to the increasing complexities of feminism, and identity-politics in general, in the late seventies and eighties. In the eighties, it is particularly apt for Julia Kristeva to comment that "a woman is a power in infinite process: a power that cannot be represented."[51]

Rich's *Your Native Land, Your Life,* published in 1986, places in apposition a land of origin and a life. This parallel would seem to suggest that identity is a fixed field that travels with one from "land" to land. Identity, however, as Freud points out in his remarks about psychoanalytic technique, is comprised of many identifications. One is also reminded of Freud's likening of psychoanalysis to an archaeological dig on the site of an ancient city. Apropos of these Freudian observations, Rich's collection of her early and mid-eighties poetry embarks on an exploratory project aimed at widening familiar concepts of self-identification.

Rich suggests that feminine identity is politically and personally organized and empowered by an aggressively non-essentialist mode of identifying that serves as an antidote when "dreams show" "signs / of becoming / politically correct / no unruly images / escaping beyond borders."[52] If, as Rich's poetry argues, "Poetry never stood a chance / of standing outside history" (32) it is conversely true that history must stand within the tropologically potent realm of fluid and interactive poetic identifications and contextualizing associations:

what country it happens in
what else happens in that country

You have to know these things
(35)

Poetry cannot stand outside of history and history, as well as individuality, cannot stand outside of language. In "North American Time," Rich maintains that the choices of authorship cannot manifest the unintended effects of language. She likens the author's intent to a false sense of power that she once felt when seeing New York from the air before resuming her actual relationship to it.

"There is no finite knowing, no such rest" (27) says Rich in "Sources," the first poem sequence of *Your Native Land, Your Life.* But this is no mere anti-essentialist ploy. (Critics such as Jan Montefiore and Albert Gelpi have already pointed out Rich's anxieties about essentializing feminine identity.) Rich had written about the opportunities of relationships among women, which she considered to be inherently lesbian, as the watershed of linguistic and political innovation. Not denying any of these observations, by the eighties, Rich directly integrates masculine experience into feminist perspectives. "Sources" speaks to men: Rich's deceased father, in addition to her husband, long since dead by suicide—it is almost as if she were attempting to show them her lesbian associations as a model for other support systems that might have been possible for them. After all, one of Rich's great contributions to seventies culture is the part she plays in claiming the subject of romantic love from more conventional masculine projections of the feminine. Nonetheless, Rich's more active eighties identifying process can be periodized in the light of more definitive self-identifications in the seventies. Within the context of the empty patriarchy that one might see within the Reagan America of the eighties, *Your Native Land, Your Life* appropriates notions of land, law, and power into feminine identity by, surprisingly, empathizing with the *"castle of air"* where she was *"raised"* (5: 6). However, Rich uses this national moment of conservative male supremacy for more egalitarian purposes. Innovatively, the speaker of "Sources" uses patriarchs as role models, or, put differently, stifling role models as resources. However, the poem moves beyond this fatherly influence by, so to speak, swerving into and using that influence for feminine empowerment.

Similarly, Rich uses an internalized formulation of land and the imperial gaze of pastoral landscape description to empower the space of feminine identity. To accomplish this she must change the narrative implicit in the aesthetic appreciation of landscape. Indeed, Rich's descriptions cannot claim the motivation of aesthetic appreciation. The speaker is rather driven to mark off psychological space where there is none, "there being no distance, no space around / to experiment with" (11: 16). Rich speaks of being "dragged by the roots of her own will / into another scene of choices" (23: 13–14). It is at this point that the speaker begins to ruminate on a promised land. *Your Native Land, Your Life* also ruminates on a woman's gaze. "It is only now, under a powerful, womanly lens, that I can decipher your suffering and deny no part of my own," says the speaker of "Sources" to her father. Rich concludes "Sources" by placing "powerful" and "womanly" in apposition:

> I mean know-
> ing the world, and my place in it, not in order to stare with bitter-
> ness or detachment but as a powerful and womanly series of
> choices: and here I write the words in their fullness:
> powerful; womanly
>
> (27: 5–9)

The speaker equates her father to "a land" she "will never know" (26: 4) because he did not acknowledge the enabling terms of his existence. Because of her father's limitations, even her landscape will never be absolutely clear and definite. The speaker, however, "can know the world" and her "place in it" "as a powerful . . . series of choices." Throughout this volume of poems, choice implies the alternatives generated by the courage constantly to reconfigure one's identity so as to use it as an increasingly potent organizing mechanism. Paradoxically, existentialism becomes a mechanism.

The first section of "Sources," the first page of *Your Native Land, Your Life,* begins with the speaker observing the gentrification of the Maryland farmland that she has been away from for sixteen years. "The narrow, rough-gullied backroads" are "almost the same." The poem then emphasizes that the farms in general are, again, "almost the same." There may be "a new barn here, a new roof there" and mishaps like a "rusting car" and "collapsed sugar-house" (3: 1–4). However, despite hints of present disaster for some and an impending bust for others, there is a veneer of sameness that is, nevertheless, a veneer. Rich is here identifying the Reaganomics of reinvestment and the sheen of commodity fetishism—the poison apple, or, to mix a metaphor, hot potato, of the last fruits of surplus value. Luce Irigaray's remarks on the commodity shed a feminist light here:

> When we are dealing with commodities the self-same, mirrored in another, is not "its" own likeness, contains nothing of its properties, its qualities, its "skin and hair." The likeness here is only a measure expressing the *fabricated* character of the commodity, its trans-formation by man's (social, symbolic) "labor." The mirror that envelops and paralyzes the commodity specularizes, speculates (on) man's labor. *Commodities, women, are a mirror of value of and for man.* In order to serve as such, they give up their

bodies to men as the supporting material of specularization, of speculation. They yield to him their natural and social value as a locus of imprints, marks, and mirage of his activity.[53]

In Rich's poem, the commodified sameness that is being sold is a sense of naturalness and conspicuous ahistoricity. Such sameness parodies the minimalist aesthetic of difference determined solely by context, site, and viewer and, indeed, Mies van der Rohe's assumption (the aesthetic dictum that "less is more" prefiguring the seventies economic dictum of E. F. Schumacher that "small is beautiful") taken to the extreme underlying minimalism that total sameness is the infinite notation of variation. Indeed, the "same" functions as infinite difference because it provides a standard for implying and registering the difference prevalent elsewhere. And yet the eighties style of gentrified sameness represses the radical connotations of similarity:

> new young wife
> trying to make a lawn instead of a dooryard,
> new names, old kind of names: Rocquette, Desmarais,
> Clark, Pierce, Stone. Gossier. No names of mine.
> (3: 4-7)

The English lawn is now favored over the variegated, Whitmanesque dooryard. The new young wife seems alien to any experience that ever seemed authentic to the speaker. Appropriately, place names are "no names of mine." Oddly, the French and the English names that she cites do not seem out of keeping with the name "Adrienne Rich." The speaker here disassociates from the poem's author, and yet also foreshadows the version of the poet's life which will soon be put forward since the poem becomes a search to identify with the Jewish heritage of the speaker's father. Clearly, none of the names are Jewish ones. The speaker goes on to identify with the "long dead" "vixen I met at the twilight on Route 5 / south of Willoughby: long dead" (3: 8-9). However, the vixen had "surviv[ed]" with her cubs "in the silvery bend of the road / in nineteen sixty-five" (3: 10-12). The vixen is a reminder of the maintenance of survival for both feminine culture, diminutively named by male culture, and Jewish culture, also surviving in cultures hostile to it, as well as a model of hope for feminism in the anti–Equal Rights Amendment political environment of the early eighties.

In the second section, the speaker "refuse[s] to become a seeker for cures" (4: 1), rejecting the natural balms that she finds solace in noted at the conclusion of the first section. This turning from wish-fulfilling changes in reality results in a kind of linguistic inventory. Taking refuge, as the vixen did, the speaker says that she seeks "help" in what "already / lay stored in me," "old things, diffused, unnamed." However, this "strength" is often not friendly and "turns" "like a violent master" (4: 9). Obviously, strength and power have been used to victimize women in the minoritized space that they have had to occupy. The inventory that had settled upon a vague formulation in the second section becomes an aggressive inquisition in the third:

From where? the voice asks coldly.

This is the voice in cold morning air
that pierces dreams. *From where does your strength come?*

Old things . . .
　　　　　　　From where does your strength come, you Southern Jew?
split at the root, raised in a castle of air?
(5: 1–6)

The speaker begins to answer the question within her question. Her strength comes in her supposed weakness. She says that it does not come from the Maryland countryside that she associates with "Jew-baiters, nightriders / who fired . . . on a black family newly settled in these hills" (5: 10–12). But then, almost as if to claim this landscape, the speaker describes "the fierce green grass" and the "still" "green" "mountains" that "stand in an extraordinary / point of no return" (5: 14–15). However, she must take a stand and speak through this landscape that is "fiery with tiny tongues" (5: 19). Her strength comes from her complex *"split at the root[s]"* (*"neither gentile nor Jew"* [5: 6]) upbringing and her questions of it and its place in this society. She wonders what her Jewish neighbors told their children when "the Klan rode" in Maryland (8: 3). Did being *"a chosen people"* (8: 5) mean not identifying with the blacks? Did it mean looking down on other Jews, "deploring the late comers," "the peasants from Russia" (8: 10)? The speaker sees her "father building / his rootless ideology / his private castles of air" (8: 11–13) His distinctions are "dangerous[ly]" private and in "the family home" (8: 14). However, the speaker confesses that since "in the beginning we grasp whatever we can" (8: 16), since the family is, so to speak, the only game in town, she is nourished and fueled by the sense of being "chosen" that she adopted.

　　The seventh section (9) utilizes the meditative ongoingness of prose poetry to understand the benefits that the speaker received from her father's rough disciplinary "love." He taught her "to hold reading and writing sacred." And, since she was "the eldest daughter raised as a son," she had inherited the destiny to "overthrow the father, take what he taught" "and use it against him." She did this "after" his "death" by seeing him in the "patriarchy" that she opposed. However, "it is only now," as a woman who can understand "power," that she can see past her father's "power and arrogance" to "the suffering of the Jew, the alien stamp" he "bore." She observes that he "deliberately arranged that it should be invisible." She now understands her father's suffering as something that does not "deny" her own. She enters a realm of constant alternation between identity and its loss. Appropriately, as the Cold War nears its end, we are not talking about binary oppositions anymore. Victimization becomes a matter of degrees.

Section VIII (10) presently sees in Maryland "breathless summer nights," unlike "the place of enervation" that she thought that she was leaving. She recalls going north like a slave "following a track of freedom." However, in the next section, she wonders why her "imagination / stayed northeast." Noting "the endless rocks in the soil, the endless / purifications of self" that seem to characterize " 'New' England," she identifies with the "unlikely growing season / after each winter so mean, so mean / the tying-down of the spirit" and the lack of "distance, no space around / to experiment with life." Rich's poem seeks to open up a political and poetic space beyond political and poetic power. How can weakness be represented? How can silence speak? Are non-positivistic politics and poetries possible?

The tenth section (12) frames and generalizes this search as one prominent in history and its principles:

> if they kill others for being who they are
> or where they are
>
> is this a law of history
> or simply, *what must change?*

Is not the sense of privilege for all "who feel destined, under God's eye" repressive to those who are asked to accept a lesser position? "Difference" is an easy ally, and it "need never be ponder[ed]." The speaker observes in New England's first European settlers a heritage that is similar to the one that her father bequeathed to her. She points out a common "passion" that is "so quick, fierce, unconditional" that "short growing season is no explanation." Section XII (14) wonders if the "Mohawk or Wampanoag" felt a similar passion, and if this passion of the privileged is not both indigenous to the "region," "the shudder in this aspen-grove a way," and a "signal" that was sent out by its previous inhabitants:

> sending messages
> the white mind barely intercepts
>
> are signals coming back
> from the vast diaspora
>
> of the people who kept their promises
> as a way of life?

Implying an infinity between the dispersions, or diasporas, of Jews and Native Americans, Rich appeals to her conception of Native Americans to provide a bridge back to the Maryland that the speaker is now returning to after "sixteen years" replete with its strong promises of childhood that have somehow been kept:

> the child backed silent against the wall
> trying to keep her eyes dry; haughty; in panic
>
> *I will never let you know*
> *I will never*
> *let you know*
> (15)

For emphasis, this last stanza of section XIII unnecessarily breaks the couplet form that has animated most of "Sources." We are reminded of the speaker's quest for what caused her father to be silent about his suffering.

Section XIV (16) powerfully comes to grips with the energy that prohibits a "brutali[zed]" child from divulging family secrets. The child perceives her knowledgeable "look" as a "bomb," and she must weave a cover-up:

> And if my look becomes the bomb that rips
> the family home apart . . .
>
> where the father walks up and down
> telling the child to *work, work*
>
> *harder than anyone has worked before?*
> —But I can't stop seeing like this
>
> more and more I see like this everywhere.

One's "destiny" and one's brutalization are related. The speaker sees this association "everywhere," in many kinds of identities. And yet she cannot separate this investment in stigmatization from pride in survival techniques and ingenuity in the face of adversity. The speaker refers to this association near the beginning of the poem sequence as that from which she draws strength, a quality that can nevertheless be said to be generated from an awareness of victimization that is in contradistinction to a more recognizably American urge to label expressions of victimization as mere whining. In "When We Dead Awaken" (1971), Rich observed, "Much of women's poetry has been of the nature of the blues song: a cry of pain, of victimization, of a lyric of seduction. And today, much poetry by women—and prose for that matter—is charged with anger. I think we need to go through that anger, and we will betray our reality if we try, as Virginia Woolf was trying, for an objectivity, a detachment, that would make us sound more like Jane Austen or Shakespeare."[54] Perhaps Judaism can be said to provide another model in this regard, and can somehow explain Rich's identification with it in "Sources":

> the faith
> of those despised and endangered
>
> that they are not merely the sum
> of damages done to them . . .
>
> . . . being a connective link
> in a long, continuous way
>
> of ordering hunger, weather, death, desire
> and the nearness of chaos.
> (17)

In the sixteenth section (18), the speaker switches to direct address of her father. She tells him that she had identified with the concentration camp victims of the Holocaust but that he had told her "to become / a citizen of the world," and not to be bound to any particular "tribe or clan." However, she notes that he "followed the Six Day War" when he was near death, and that she is now "sweating the Middle East" and "wearing the star of David / on a thin chain at" her "breastbone." She is holding onto the telltale signs of her earliest identifications. She is moving from her late husband's "formula": *There's nothing left now but the food and the humor.* She doubts that he could ever have been as "assimilated" as he thought himself to be, and she implies that his suicide may have been related to his denial of being "alien." She notes now this same suffering of the alien in her father that she observed in her husband. She posits that this foreign identification consists of "something more" than "food, humor, a turn of phrase, a gesture of the hands."

After these open ruminations in the prose poetry of section XVII, "Sources" begins to organize its verse slightly into the unevenly formed verse paragraphs of the eighteenth section (20). Jewishness, the speaker says, must be "something more" than meaningless "externals" and "self-hatred." She consults "photos of the old Ashkenazi life" for something "that still outlives" them. Her use of photographs appeals to an ekphrastic stillness to force the otherness of her identity-position to speak finally. The photographs speak to her simply and objectively of a noble and an unselfconsciously courageous lifestyle in the face of siege, brutality, and the constant threat of violence. The pictures speak of a "place" beyond place and "where all tracks end," in the sense of our dramatic irony of knowing of both the Holocaust that will meet the way of life depicted in these photographs "taken in 1936" and post–World War II assimilation of Jews into a "castle of air." This "castle" scaffolds over realities of both the old and new worlds in order to obscure them. Delusions patch over gaps and allow subjects to cope:

> The place where all tracks end
> is the place where history was meant to stop
> but does not stop   where thinking
> was meant to stop but does not stop
> where the pattern was meant to give way at last
> > > > but only
> becomes a different pattern
> > > > terrible, threadbare
> strained   familiar   on-going

The seeming dead end of a community merely prefigures its "different pattern." We can see through to the other side of the cover-up's tapestry. The tapestry is now "threadbare" yet more "familiar" and "on-going." But in what way is Judaism "on-going"? Is it merely part of a "genetic code" or a "mystic biology"? The speaker thinks of the women "pioneers" "who sailed to Palestine" in the early part of the century. She compares them to a "housewife" who "gives her life" to an enterprise that she hopes will be noble and does not "turn on her." In other words, the woman's place in the traditional family is likened to Zionism. The speaker sees that both have "broken promises" and are "not enough." In the twentieth section (23), she sees an alternative in the history of her own aspirations:

The faithful drudging child . . .

becomes the woman with a mission, not to win prizes
but to change the laws of history.
How she gets this mission
is not clear, how the boundaries of perfection
explode, leaving her cheekbone grey with smoke
a piece of her hair singed off, her shirt
spattered with earth. . . .

   dragged by the the roots of her own will
into another scene of choices.

It is becoming clear that the title "Sources" does not merely refer to the poet's childhood. It signals a play on the notion of a promised, native land. The speaker had long ago aspired to more than the geographical, spiritual, and mental "boundaries of perfection." These boundaries, with "earth," "explode," and "splatter." The speaker's roots do not so much assimilate as move, "dragged" "into another scene of choices." For what do these choices aim?

The twenty-first section (24) begins with the Hebrew word for Jerusalem, "YERUSHALAYIM." She realizes that she has always been in "this Zion of hope and fear / and broken promises / this promised land," "where one more day / breaks." "This Zion" is far from perfect but is the "space" that was asked for in section IX. It is a tradition that exists outside power and empathizes with "all whose wrongs and rights / cry out for explication":

thrilling like thousand-year-old locusts
audible yet unheard

a city on a hill

The twenty-second section (25) states that the speaker must speak "to" and "not simply of" her late husband to disprove the cover-up that Judaism is now composed merely of "food and humor." Acting as a "source" for how her late husband still informs her, the speaker sees the promised land of Judaism in terms of a community and state of hope and support, and she feels that she has uncovered the secret of her husband's despair and must address to him what she has learned of the individual's need for a community that can accommodate weakness. "There must be those among whom we can sit down and weep," she tells him, "and still be counted as warriors." A "place" and community must be made for people like her husband "to change the laws of history." In the last section of "Sources" (26–27) the speaker laments that she cannot feel at one with the "common weeds" of a particular land. She has lost what seemed like a possible source of security at the beginning of the poem. However, she has chosen to make the most of her "castle in the air." She finds a way to be "faithful" without faith. Not only can she not rely upon a concrete native land but "there is no finite knowing, no such rest." "Power" is not derived from fixed resources but is rather generated by "knowing the world" and the speaker's "place in it" not as a given but as a "series of choices" that generate both power and her role as a woman. "Sources" concludes with a reiteration of this choice: "I write the words in their fullness: / powerful; womanly." Significantly, Rich concludes with a reference to her writing. The poem sequence clarifies much of Rich's seventies stance toward the freedom to choose identity. As Jameson used Sartre's philosophy to clear a path to the totalization and leveling of all facets of culture, Rich employs an existentialist vocabulary to link individual and communal choices of identity. Identity works within complex decisions and negotiated alliances. Increasingly, these identity contracts are rescrutinized. However, to understand better the standing agreements, the next section looks at post–World War II terms of American identity.

3 The Best Citizenship of Our Lives

If I was an American, the problem that confronts our people today wouldn't even exist. —Malcolm X

Souls were rising, from the earth far below, souls of the dead, of people who had perished, from famine, from war, from the plague, and they floated up, like skydivers in reverse, limbs all akimbo, wheeling and spinning. And the souls of these departed joined hands, clasped ankles, and formed a web, a great net of souls. . . .

We will be citizens. The time has come. —Tony Kushner, *Angels in America, Part Two: Perestroika*

The whole race is a poet that writes down
The eccentric propositions of its fate.
—Wallace Stevens, "Man Made out of Words"

The seventies seem in a crossfire between not only the sixties and the eighties; the period is also "crosshatched" between what comes long before and long after. Chapter 1 discussed the long-term influence of the seventies, and this section considers the seventies as a literary and cultural break that was long in the making. The seventies marks a decline in sixties expectations; however, these expectations were expressed long before. For example, in Dalton Trumbo's 1943 screenplay for *A Guy Named Joe*, a bureaucrat in heaven speaks of the "angels" waiting in heaven's wings, for whom the war is being fought. The angel prefigures the ideals of the baby boomers:

> Children would understand it, sure, because the future belongs to them. They're already moving into it. Yeah, they're going to climb out of the dust and the muck and lift up their heads and see the sky. They're going to fly like a generation of angels into the free air and sunlight. Sure. Oh, children would always understand it—free as the air. . . . That's what we're fighting for: the freedom of the very air we breathe, the freedom of mankind rushing to greet the future on wings.

World War II, in the wake of anti-Depression governmental activism, augured a new sense of protection from the government and of possibility and promise for the nation's youth. Subsequently, World War II and the Cold War redefined the terms for inclusion in an officially sanctioned metaphoric American citizenship. We can note this in World War II movies where various ethnic groups are unified in each platoon. Of course, African Americans are underrepresented, but the post–World War II integration of the armed forces demonstrates a willingness to recognize the untenability of federally sanctioned segregation. This recognition is due in part to an acknowledgment of the part that blacks and other groups played in the war effort and the continued part that these groups would play in the peacetime economy that is an extension of the war effort. Through a kind of internal imperialism, these work forces and markets mingle with America's other major work forces and markets. Culturally, the changing sense of American citizenship contributes to such cultural phenomena as the national mainstreaming of rock and roll in the mid-fifties. Rock and roll reflects a widening of the concept of Americanism in order to place different minority positions under its heading. Hence black music becomes white and a rallying cry for the new inflections of Americanism that are, for instance, mediated through the "ethnicity" of Elvis Presley—who takes on the style and trappings of a figure such as Marlon Brando—and distinguishes himself from normative concepts of nativist Americanism. After World War II, rock and roll was already in place in the works of the King Cole Trio, Louis Jordan, Wynonie Harris, Joe Turner, Tiny Grimes, and several others. However, it takes several years for a national white audience to claim it through the defined and newly named consumer class of "teenagers."

I would like to use an examination of national and minority identity in post–World War II works by James Baldwin and Wallace Stevens, two writers who are not normally discussed within the same frame of reference, to shed light upon seventies literature and culture. As Baldwin subverts the force of the "outside" of white identity on black identity, Stevens constructs a fortress of language, subjectivity, and "otherness"—a kind of privileging of the other that can be likened to that of Baldwin's. Both writers combat and yet find a space within Cold War American national identity.

After World War II, American hegemony seems to present opportunity for blacks. The federal government appears to be a strong ally. However, for many blacks, the sixties do not happen in a predictable fashion. The riots of the mid-sixties begin exactly when the achievements of civil rights legislation culminate. It seems that the bubble of federalist identity and citizenship is at a dead end, that there is a hopeless contradiction between rhetoric and implementation. African Americans are in effect still, as a group, hopelessly othered. They encounter the riggings, the stuff, the things, the solid objects, the gunk, in the mirror's backing—the institutional terms of reality—the space between the various others that constitute reality. After comparing Baldwin and Stevens, I will compare Stevens and Ashbery and bring seventies realities into sharper focus from a semiotic perspective. This section concludes with a further discussion of otherness in seventies works by Baldwin and Ashbery.

Wallace Stevens, an insurance lawyer and a Taft Republican, cannot be considered a typical post–World War II artist or intellectual. Nonetheless, the writings of Baldwin and Stevens respond to similar epistemic influences. World War II strengthens the power of the myth of American national identity, and pressures us to view other identity-positions in the light of hegemonic "American-hood." Americanicity takes a surveillant, omnipresent guise that requires "the other" as the object of surveillance. A crisis occurs. Various minority positions must either fight for their positions as essential parts of hegemonic Americanism or risk being trivialized or demonized. Hence it can be argued that dues are paid by many minority groups to belong to the club of American-hood in exchange for survival and distinction. The acceleration of surveillance work done by the House Committee on Un-American Activities is a thinly disguised product of this broader cultural surveillance. In the mid-fifties, when this work of assimilation is seemingly beyond question, Joseph McCarthy is superfluous. He is no longer behind a growth industry, and he has little choice but to attack the ultimate legitimizing agent of citizenship itself, the Army, for which he is discredited.

McCarthyism and the red-baiting that precedes it set the terms of the debate. We can note the early fifties issue of *Partisan Review* entitled "The End of Alienation" that, at the height of McCarthyism, exhorts intellectuals to give up their isolation and join the grand American project. Also in *Partisan Review,* James Baldwin derides his characterization as a "Negro" writer, and queries what the black place in America could be. In the mid-fifties, there is seriousness in Allen Ginsberg's remark in his poem "America": "It occurs to me that I am America."[55] There is a sense of a negotiation in this statement, even if only one party has been actively, consciously engaged. "I am talking to myself again," the speaker immediately adds to his discovery. Himself an outsider, the speaker can nevertheless divorce himself from the collective inside that is outside of him, and he concludes the poem, "America I'm putting my queer shoulder to the wheel."[56] It is informative that, at about the same time—little more than a year after the Korean War re-posits American limits (a war that the Vietnam War will seek to unwrite), Jasper Johns says that he dreams of an American flag and decides to paint one for, he says, no reason—simply because he saw one in a dream. Similarly, one can imagine Wallace Stevens, an innovator in the American life insurance industry, noting the public relations challenge of selling the new all-pervasive Americanhood in the forties. Does not such selling, after all, require a specialization in the imagination and is that not, according to Stevens, the poet's job? After all, Stevens's work in both insurance and poetry stressed collective reality as a base—but only a base.

Baldwin asserts that African American identity is responsible for the creation of "Americanness." One might say that race functions as a mirror's backing. Similarly, Stevens's most renowned poems of the late forties posit collective identity as a myth—"a larger poem for a larger audience," as "An Ordinary Evening in New Haven" puts it—and also posit the centrality of poetic imaginative powers in generating such myths. The texts of both writers clear space for themselves in the American literary world by implying privileged positions within the formation of American identity.

In his 1951 essay "Many Thousands Gone," Baldwin suggests a paradox that is central to many of the essays in *Notes of a Native Son* (1955) and to much of the author's oeuvre. Racial considerations may be illusory—socially conditioned and artificial—but they arise from an illusion that both limits and manifests our visceral sense of reality itself:

> The Negro in America, gloomily referred to as that shadow which lies athwart our national life, is far more than that. He is a series of shadows, self-created, intertwining, which now we helplessly battle. One may say that the Negro in America does not really exist except in the darkness of our minds.[57]

Baldwin argues that "whites" could not exist without the positing of "Negroes" or "blacks." According to Baldwin, European Americans needed to project a marginalized other to compensate for their lack of a historically determined identity. Much of Baldwin's work exhorts African Americans to recognize their dominant role in the constitution of American identity and to use, for the benefit of both blacks and whites, the distinctions that black identity allows. An example of this exhortation is in the concluding sentences of *Notes of a Native Son*, from "A Stranger in the Village (1953)," which addresses itself to a United States that is still under the sway of red-baiting and unashamedly content to ignore questions of racial justice:

> I am not, really, a stranger any longer for any American alive. One of the things that distinguishes Americans from other people is that no other people has ever been so deeply involved in the lives of black men, and vice versa. This fact faced, with all its implications, it can be seen that the history of the American Negro problem is not merely shameful, it is also something of an achievement. For even when the worst has been said, it must also be added that the perpetual challenge posed by the problem was always, somehow, perpetually met. It is precisely this black-white experience which may prove of indispensable value to us in the world we face today. This world is white no longer, and it will never be white again.[58]

Jacques Lacan's post–World War II formulation of his mirror stage theory parallels Baldwin's contemporaneous insights. (Lacan notes that he discussed the mirror stage phenomenon thirteen years before it was to be the central thesis of his published paper of 1949. However, the notion's moment of cultural impact can probably best be dated in the late forties.) In "The Mirror Stage as Formative of the Function of the I as Revealed in Psychoanalytic Experience," with which Lacan opens his 1966 selection, *Écrits*, Lacan maintains that identity is made possible by the infant's first self-recognition in a mirror or the mother's eyes and his or her mirroring response. The infant's mirror play functions visually to unify the young child's sense of her or himself. Like *Notes of a Native Son*, Lacan's "Mirror Stage" locates the enabling distinctions of one's identity within a vision of oneself upon the site of an other. As racial distinctions create American identity, the mirror stage forges the intractable associations that constitute the subjective self. "It is this moment that decisively tips the whole of human knowledge into mediatization through the desire of the other,"[59] notes Lacan about the result of passing through the mirror stage.

Baldwin's and Lacan's valorizations of the other after World War II account for and problematize rhetorical stances that are implicit in Cold War rhetoric. Rather than, as in the case of Cold War logic, basing all decision-making on imaginary threats posed by a demonic other, Baldwin and Lacan suggest that the other must be accounted for because it makes the self visible and, in effect, enables all else. Such logic serves to liberate culture from the paralyzing constraints of Cold War logic. In a sense, both authors present strategies for replacing the demon without the possible inspiration of the *daimon* within.

Similarly, Stevens attempts to "clear" the mirror of the poem of the collective imagination. To accomplish this, near the end of "An Ordinary Evening in New Haven,"[60] the poem depicts "glass" as an "element" that, like the Stevensian imagination, is paradoxically autonomous yet also inextricably interwoven with everyone and thing in its ken:

> The glass of the air becomes an element—
> It was something imagined that has been washed away.
> A clearness has returned. It stands restored.
>
> It is not an empty clearness, a bottomless sight.
> It is a visibility of thought,
> In which hundreds of eyes, in one mind see at once.
> (350: 25–28; 351: 1–3)

Again I must stress that I am not concerned here with noting any kind of influence among Lacan, Stevens, and Baldwin. Rather, I am suggesting, as Donald Pease has in his writings about post–World War II formulations of the American literary canon, that an understanding of Cold War rhetorical stances is vital to any understanding of this historical period. In this era, the other is cast out, yet also made a center of interest and generally problematized.

Stevens's work of this period strives to understand relationships between the "other" who dwells within and subsists by imaginative and poetic powers. His poetry can be said to comment on the positing of a new overarching formulation of American national and racial hegemony:

> Here, being visible is being white,
> Is being of the solid of the white, the accomplishment
> Of an extremist in an exercise . . .
> "The Auroras of Autumn,"[61] 308: 13–15

The speaker of Wallace Stevens's "The Auroras of Autumn" looks back longingly on "a white / that was different" (308: 7–8)—that was not "the accomplishment / of an extremist" (308: 15). "The plainness of plain things," the speaker of "An Ordinary Evening in New Haven" says, "is savagery" (333: 4).

Stevens's post–World War II poetry intensifies its assertions of society's need for the poet and anticipates valorizations of various marginalized identity-positions. Although decidedly high-brow, Stevens searches for alternatives to the "unimaginative" powers that be, and he can be seen in the light of the more anti-academic, still unnamed Beat movement, as well as the more academic and also yet to be named confessional poetry. Stevens's post–World War II stance indicates a new attention to individuality. However, this emphasis upon the individual is born of a ghastly and unarticulable Cold War dread that, in "The Auroras of Autumn," finds itself in the terrifying symbol of the Northern Lights:

> There is nothing until in a single man contained,
> Nothing until the named thing nameless is
> And is destroyed. He opens the door of his house
>
> On flames. The scholar of one candle sees
> An arctic effulgence flaring on the frame
> Of everything he is. And he feels afraid.
> (312: 19–24)

Implicit in this fear is the suggestion that the communal "vulgate of experience" of "An Ordinary Evening in New Haven" is fraught with more imaginative potency than poetry is capable of producing. Hence, it is Stevens's task to undermine this primacy of the world outside the individual so as to assert that the collective imagination—the real—though now, in this era, undoubtedly powerful, is nonetheless a mere shadow of the individual imagination. If an individual needs to dip into the collective imagination for insurance, nonetheless Stevens makes visible both the power and limitations of collective national American identity. Modernist poetry, in the sense that the imagination exists in a privileged and isolated realm much like a certain privileged and autonomous vision of America, is seen to be constitutive of American culture. And yet the imagination, like post–World War II America, is also paradoxically at odds itself. Noting this is important in the context of this work because it points out that this anxiousness fully develops into a new kind of groundless ground in "Self-Portrait in Convex Mirror."

Questions of the author's autonomy concern the poetry of both Stevens and Ashbery; a new kind of formal otherness takes over. With both poets, these concerns are perhaps best grouped under what might now seem the much overused rubric of logocentrism. And yet Stevens's queries so intermingle questions about referential subject matter and the voice of the author as origin that the positing of a concept common to both, at the least, facilitates a more concise and close reading of Stevens's major long work and begin to open a unique epistemic perspective.

Indeed, Stevens prefigures deconstruction and its attempt to lift the burdens of the world and word from one another. To begin to verify the connection between Stevens's questioning of referentiality and of authorship, one need only consider the first line of "An Ordinary Evening in New Haven" (1949). Stevens's statement, "The eye's plain version is a thing apart" (331: 1), casts doubt on the formulation's denotative meaning. What we see is of course outside us. The self-evidence of the statement can only be justified in response to an unspoken but conflicting assertion. We are indirectly asked to assume that there is a less plain "version" and that this version is not "a thing apart" but entirely intermingled in an unidentified element, perhaps the eye perceiving "the thing apart." It is particularly fitting to read this element as the eye when one considers that the word "version" is derived from the Latin *vertere,* meaning "to turn." We can read the poem to mean that the version of the thing apart is a "plain" rhetorical "turning" or trope of the "eye," since we are considering the eye's version. In other words, normative reality is here merely a specific form of troping.

However, it is a form of troping that conflicts with tropological power. "The plainness of plain things is savagery" (333: 4), says Stevens in "An Ordinary Evening in New Haven." Since a trope necessarily relates more than one element and, in fact, is a relationship between elements, the poem's first line maintains that to speak of an enforced, external plain version of things is oxymoronic because, if to see with the eye can be likened to troping, a plain version denies the tropological or rhetorical root of all versions. The word "version" is normally used in a rhetorical context, describing a particular translation or other manner of phrasing or wording. Hence, the distinction is confused between what the eye sees, normally thought to be the province of the signified, and a version that relates what is seen, normally associated with the words that constitute the signifiers and the subjectivity from which the version originates. Stevens is thus bonding issues of the referential—the realm of the signified—and the authorial function so that each can be questioned in a nearly simultaneous manner. For instance, the concluding section of "An Ordinary Evening in New Haven" likens the referentiality of "the edgings and inchings of final form" (351: 13) to the author's "swarming activities of the formulae / Of statement, directly and indirectly getting at" (351: 14–15). This composite substance of the signified and authorial process is then, through a comparison to a color emanating from darkness, a philosopher who is not primarily concerned with making denotative statements, and an author's cancellation of her text, shown to be enabled by an absence of an autonomous signified and a gap between writerly and "worldly" processes:

> Like an evening evoking the spectrum of violet,
> A philosopher practicing scales on the piano,
> A woman writing a note and tearing it up.
>
> It is not in the premise that reality
> Is a solid.
> (351: 19–23)

Throughout "An Ordinary Evening in New Haven," "the eye's plain version," or poetry's referential function, is valued less than the poet's imaginative powers. Theories of life and poetry check one another against evasive troping, which, ironically, is also "life, as it is":

> the theory
> Of poetry is the theory of life,
>
> As it is, in the intricate evasions of as.
> (349: 17–19)

"An Ordinary Evening in New Haven" states that "words of the world are the life of the world" (339: 3). Stevens questions the reality of the "world" much more vigorously than the authenticity of "words." He uses a structuralist privileging of language to textually resistant ends. A wall is set up around his texts. Note, for instance, perhaps the most quoted stanza of "An Ordinary Evening in New Haven":

> The poem is the cry of its occasion,
> Part of the res itself and not about it.
> The poet speaks the poem as it is.
> (338: 13-15)

Again, Stevens is more dubious about the "occasion" than the "poem" and the poet's "cry." The referential function is severely questioned by asserting the autonomy of the poem as a group of signifiers. And yet the "cry of its occasion" is, however, esteemed over the previously posited "impassioned cry" (336: 6), therefore privileging the cry as a content within the material of language over the cry as a subjective expression.

Although Stevens may often doubt the authenticity of the signifiers as signifieds, Ashbery, nonetheless, compared with Stevens, conveys a more skeptical view of language itself:

> The hand holds no chalk
> And each part of the whole falls off
> And cannot know it knew.
> (204: 9-11)

Although Stevens may question the nature of discourse, as divorced from the speaker and the signified, Ashbery brings that inquisition into a sharper focus. "Self-Portrait in a Convex Mirror" continues the demythologizing enterprise of "An Ordinary Evening in New Haven" by undermining the import Stevens grants poetry and language so as to deny referentiality.

"Self-Portrait in a Convex Mirror" can be said to begin where "An Ordinary Evening in New Haven" ends. "An Ordinary Evening in New Haven" concludes with an intensification of its consideration of "reality" as a tropological creation: "The glass of air becomes an element" (350: 25). Here is the mirror reality with which "Self-Portrait in a Convex Mirror" begins. Further, "An Ordinary Evening in New Haven" describes the subservience of this mirror reality as a totalizing subjectivity: "It is a visibility of thought, / In which hundreds of eyes, in one mind, see at once" (351: 2-3). This unification of sources of surveillance, and the valuing of the individual author that it implies, is still a commendable part of the modernist vision for Stevens. However, for Ashbery, this kind of unifying stasis is tantamount to the modernist nightmare that can be said to be the target of "Self-Portrait in Convex Mirror."

Whereas, in Stevens's poem, subjective reality reveals itself as an enabling reality, in Ashbery's poem, the unraveling of subjectivity facilitates the workings of the imagination. The last two lines of "An Ordinary Evening in New Haven" call "reality" "a shade that traverses / a dust, a force that traverses a shade" (351: 20–21). Reality is depicted as not merely a force, but also as a hidden force—a force contacting the "shade." "Reality" is cloistered in the force of the author's will. On the other hand, in the first half of "Self-Portrait in a Convex Mirror," "There are no recesses in the room" (*SP*, 190: 14). The perceiver cannot penetrate the surfaces of the room, even if these surfaces are metaphoric of the observer's perceptual limits. Ashbery acknowledges the force of an individual's will while coming to grips with its limits. Indeed, the speaker in "Self-Portrait in a Convex Mirror" welcomes these limits as "a preciosity / In the wind" (*SP*, 195: 33; 196: 1).

The aporetic "operation" of subjectivity is "stalled" (*SP*, 195: 32) only when "The shadow of the city injects its own / Urgency" (195: 16–17). Ashbery's poem does not characterize the life of "the city" as "the eye's plain version." Rather, the speaker says that the city conducts business by innuendo and "shuttlings" (195: 25). While the speaker in Ashbery's poem seizes on the opportunity that a complex contextualization provides to comment on the conditions of the poetic process, Stevens begrudgingly accommodates "the vulgate of experience" "as part of the never-ending meditation" (331: 2–4). This is similar to Ashbery's stance. However, in Ashbery's case, the "meditation" is not centered within the poet's subjectivity, as much as within an interface with his culture and the nature of that culture as a language. Of course, no poet can avoid this. Indeed, Stevens assiduously ruminates, in "An Ordinary Evening in New Haven," on how the "mythological form" and "festival sphere" (331: 17) of contemporary culture can be accommodated. However, the significance of this accommodation must occur "without regard to time or where we are, / In the perpetual reference, object / Of the perpetual meditation, point / Of the enduring, visionary love" (332: 3–5). Stevens esteems the power of the author's will as the only absolute, even if, or perhaps because its results may be undecipherable and "obscure, in colors whether of the sun / Or mind, uncertain in . . . the spirit's speeches, the indefinite, / Confused illuminations" (332: 6–10). For Ashbery, however, the play of the world more actively and unapologetically assists the play of the poem. If, for Stevens, the force of the poet's will is paramount, for Ashbery, it is crucial that the poet abdicate much control.

In short, "An Ordinary Evening in New Haven" exhibits an uneasy tension between an Emersonian advocacy of the individual as the primary site of transcendental reality and a more skeptical respect for the individual as the enabling myth of an ephemeral reality. "Self-Portrait in a Convex Mirror" comes to terms with the latter and devises a language that bespeaks this mythological version of the individual, and then posits an alternative, in the form of an indeterminate chain of signifiers that eventually brings down the mirror's backing, pointing a seemingly endless ending of Cold War reality. The other becomes a grounded norm and a positive state.

"Self-Portrait in a Convex Mirror" verbally engages itself with the visual and, similarly, in James Baldwin's 1974 novel *If Beale Street Could Talk*, otherness is associated with visual and verbal silence. A short digression concerning ekphrasis—the verbal representation of visual representation—will elucidate these works by Ashbery and Baldwin. In a broad cultural sense, the growing place of television in post–World War II America quite conceivably accounts for the growing status of the visual that W. J. T. Mitchell's theory of ekphrasis argues. Mitchell, by relating the other to the visual, offers insight into Western culture's means of creating "others." He observes that the visual serves as the verbal's "significant other."[62] The "history of culture," says Mitchell, "is in part the protracted struggle for dominance between pictorial and linguistic signs."[63] In semiotics, he observes a colonization of the visual by the verbal that reflects a cultural bias for the validity of verbal over visual truth. Although we may admit to be persuaded by the visual, in order for it to become an esteemed influence, verbal mediation is required. Ekphrasis provides a valuable resource in many works that concern identity and marginalization. This may be true of all literature, since more traditionally ekphrastic works, as Mitchell points out, function between the verbal ekphrastic desire to dominate the visual other and the ekphrastic fear of the verbal becoming lost within that other. Ekphrasis can be associated with the "other."

Mitchell complicates the grounds of this disagreement by maintaining that texts display a tendency toward ambivalence when they evoke and simulate visual experience. Such texts convey the eroticism of control over spatial experience without requiring a visual field and yet also suggest fear that surrogate visual experience will engulf and dominate textual powers. Mitchell describes a dynamic opposition between image and text. He observes that ekphrastic writing tacitly acknowledges the presence of an other in the text. This other is linked to the visual and the spatial. Ekphrasis seemingly stops narrative progression—relegating movement to a temporally still field, causing G. E. Lessing to associate it with the decorative arts, and to devalue it, in comparison with the more "masculine" art of poetry. Mitchell argues that Lessing's espousal of the word's domination is symptomatic of a textual and, indeed, masculine bias in traditional cultural institutions. Ekphrasis thus tends to be viewed ambivalently: to be desired because it indicates a realm wherein the verbal has conquered the visual, as a marginalized other, and is free to engage in ostensibly autonomous play; and yet to be feared due to the image's potential to integrate completely with the text and "speak" for itself. Therefore, Mitchell points out, ekphrastic texts often begin by fetishizing their subjects, but subsequently reject them. Indeed, this summarizes the "action" of "Self-Portrait in a Convex Mirror."

Ekphrasis, informed by a sense of significance that is not bound by rigid distinctions between the signified and signifier, provides a means of describing significance that has not yet coalesced into a concrete visual icon. What is genuinely ekphrastic is the generation of visual dynamics that need not be held in place by a preconceived set of visual representations. Providing access to a kind of "counter" political unconscious, ekphrasis posits a "real" absence to subvert the arbitrary codifications of "reality" that assume some groups and peoples to be marginalized. Marginalized, "negative" ekphrasis, which points outside "positivistic," traditional representation and signification, can therefore be considered as an important aspect of "mainstream ekphrasis."

It is possible to consider all of Baldwin's work from this point of view. One thinks of the very titles of *Another Country* and *The Fire Next Time* and the Lacanian italicized first sentence of *If Beale Street Could Talk:* "I look at myself in the mirror."[64] Trapped within a cultural system grounded on racial distinctions that curtail possibilities, African Americans in "Sonny's Blues," Baldwin's 1957 short story,[65] repeatedly discuss the seemingly unrealizable need "to get outside" (109) and "make space out of no space" (113). "Windows" and "doors" are constantly referred to as false hopes: "The big windows fool no one" (113). The unnamed narrator's younger brother, Sonny, searches for the "outside" through music, equating, as Derrida later would, the outside with a kind of writing. In Baldwin's work, there is a constant urge to escape, to be near windows, to look beyond. Thus it is an apt torture in *If Beale Street Could Talk* to jail its protagonist and make him inactive. The novel's chief revelation is the largeness of the prison envisioned. Fonny, the unjustly imprisoned hero of the novel, considered himself and all other Americans imprisoned by society's linguistic codes. Fonny accepts his silence, but *speaks* through the thought of his sculpture. As he kisses his lover, Tish, through glass, he goes deeper into the mirror's backing in this world. History returns and the intermingled promises of America between World War II and the sixties are indefinitely deferred.

If Beale Street Could Talk hinges on this ambivalence toward the sixties. An urge to move beyond the sixties is vitiated by a sense that the American standard of living will steadily decline after the early seventies, as turns out to be the case. This proves to be particularly disastrous for many African Americans born after the height of the civil rights movement. Bill Clinton played upon this historical perspective in a 1993 speech at the Temple Church of God in Christ in Memphis. "The freedom to die before you're a teenager is not what Martin Luther King lived and died for," said Clinton.

Foreshadowing the intensification of these hardships, Tish, the narrator of *If Beale Street Could Talk,* experiences a difficult pregnancy from the beginning to the end of the novel. *If Beale Street Could Talk* omits all hope of a positive reconciliation of America's heterogeneous nature, hopes that had persisted in Baldwin's work from the forties through the sixties. Whereas in *Notes of a Native Son* (1955), the racial concepts of "blacks" and "whites" are mutually defining social constructions, in *If Beale Street Could Talk,* blacks are increasingly treated with supposed "benign neglect," in the words of Daniel P. Moynihan when he advised the Nixon administration. In a description that brings to mind close-ups of the mammoth shark's eye in the film *Jaws* (1975) and the "vacuum" and "total absence of human recognition—the glazed separateness"[66] in the eye of the white shopkeeper serving the young black girl in Toni Morrison's *The Bluest Eye* (1970), blacks "exist in the unbelievably frozen winter which lives behind that eye"[67] of white authority, as exemplified by the eye of the police officer who misidentifies the book's central male character, Fonny, a young black artist and father-to-be, who is kept in the New York Tombs, due to legal technicalities, without a trial. Judgment is indefinitely delayed, in contradistinction to sixties premonitions of an impending resolution or apocalypse that Baldwin's *The Fire Next Time* (1963) darkly expounds. Fonny, in *If Beale Street Could Talk,* is only able to find and maintain his sanity by asserting the hopelessness of his situation and enacting it in dreams of his unexecutable sculpture. Whereas Malcolm X, in his posthumously published autobiography (a new and revolutionary kind of slave narrative) in the sixties, uses his stay in prison to educate himself for a life of political activism and self-revelation, Fonny lives in the hopelessness of perpetually latent time, as does the family that he is not allowed to join. Change can have no, one might say, significant significance. "The reality of time," said Guy Debord, "has been replaced by the advertisement of time."[68] A recognition of what Debord calls "spectacular time,"[69] time that is only as deep as its consumption, in the sixties, causes ancient and biblical senses of historical beginnings. In the seventies, these many idealistic beginnings are inevitably compromised. Throughout society, progress seems not only less inevitable, but also perhaps impossible. According to seventies rock musician Steve Miller, "time keeps on slipping, *slipping* into the *future.*" Appropriately, in *If Beale Street Could Talk,* Fonny's girlfriend, Tish, begins a long rumination upon the word "time":

> Time: the word rolled like the bells of a church. Fonny was doing: time. In six months time, our baby would be here. Somewhere, in time, Fonny and I had met: somewhere, in time, we had loved; somewhere, no longer in time, but, now, totally, at time's mercy, we loved.
> . . . Somewhere, in time, he scratched his armpits, aching for a bath. Somewhere in time he looked about him, knowing that he was being lied to, in time, with the connivance of time.[70]

As with Baldwin's prisoner of the mid-seventies, "time" increasingly loses its content. Time itself is content. Like any given number at a joke tellers' convention in which all jokes are numbered, the mere mention of a decade receives a response. "You can spend all your love making time," sang the Eagles in the mid-seventies. "Take it to the limit one more time. . . . When there's nothing to believe in, still you're running back, you're coming back for more" comments upon a typical seventies ambivalence toward an absent reality. The next section looks at this absent reality in terms of a seventies novel about World War II.

4 Parallel Decades, or *Gravity's Rainbow*

Gravity's Rainbow presents the notion of an America that took a decisively wrong turn. Probably no event better symbolically captures this "turn" than John Kennedy's assassination. The relatively insignificant assassination attempts in Robert Altman's *Nashville* and Martin Scorsese's *Taxi Driver,* discussed in chapter 2, reflect the lesser respect politicians aspiring toward the presidency receive. Two decades later, *In the Line of Fire,* the 1993 film starring Clint Eastwood, plays upon a similar cultural assumption. In the sixties, Eastwood's character posits, the nation lost a common basis for evaluating history and reality. Playing a Secret Service agent who had been President Kennedy's favorite protector, the Eastwood character claims that Kennedy was "different" than the fictional president he now defends. Further, the secret service agent surmises that he himself "was different; the whole damn country was different; everything would be different right now" if he could have saved Kennedy.

Now there is nothing but game-playing. He wonders if the world would still hold definitive meaning if he had been able to prevent the assassination.

Such remorse is widely disseminated during each anniversary commemoration of Kennedy's assassination. During one such commemoration, the media frequently referred to it as "the end of America's innocence," "a turning point in American history," and "the extinguishing of unknown possibilities." Of course, such sentiment recapitulates the deep American strain of regret at taking the wrong path into a moral wilderness. The death of a president can strongly unleash this strain and invoke jeremiads. A seemingly natural order is broken, and the nation experiences itself as a kind of orphan. (Interestingly, Clint Eastwood's other 1993 film, *A Perfect World*, is set in Texas during November 1963 with the Kennedy assassination in the background, and tells the story of a prison escapee who wins the hearts of children. The movie equally criticizes parents and governments. "He don't trust you no more," says the escaped convict to a father about his son. "You got to earn that.") How can a Lincoln or a Kennedy be replaced? And yet the death of a president in itself is not enough to cause the nation to to dwell so fervently upon lost opportunities. The country mourned but did not fixate itself on, for example, the Garfield and McKinley assassinations.

The reception of the Kennedy assassination can be viewed as a cultural and epistemic production. In fact, it was not until the escalation of the war in Vietnam that the Kennedy assassination began to be viewed by liberals as a terrible tragedy for the nation. Lyndon Johnson had executed the liberal agenda with much greater skill and success than Kennedy. And yet when the American status quo can no longer assimilate growing radical black dissent and sixties counterculture sentiment—growths that the government promotes by insulating its Vietnam War decision-making from the electorate—the unfulfillment of the Kennedy presidency is more severely mourned. The sense that the electoral process has somehow been stolen is reinforced by the 1968 assassination of Robert Kennedy and by Nixon's and Humphrey's avoidance of the issue of the Vietnam War in the 1968 campaign.

Thomas Pynchon's epic *Gravity's Rainbow* (1973) fictionalizes this sense of American lost opportunity. Writing in the seventies, Pynchon creates a vision of an American history gone astray because of the exclusion of some Americans from the process of apparent divine election within Puritan New England. In *Gravity's Rainbow*, a descendent of the fictional Puritan settler William Slothrop is motivated by the possibility that the discrediting of his ancestor for advocating a more open "election" process has perverted American history, much like intractability within the Johnson and the Nixon administrations had seemed to do in contemporary America:

> Could he have been the fork in the road America never took, the singular point she jumped the wrong way from? Suppose the Slothropite heresy had the time to consolidate and prosper? Might there have been fewer crimes in the name of Jesus, and more mercy in the name of Judas Iscariot? It seems to Tyrone Slothrop that there might be a route back.[71]

By the seventies, many firmly perceive the unfinished careers of John and Robert Kennedy as snuffed-out attempts at routes back that are no longer open. Paul Simon, in "American Tune" (1973) wonders, "When I think of the road we've traveled on, / I wonder what's gone wrong. / I can't help it. I wonder what's gone wrong." From economic and technological perspectives, also, the Kennedy assassination seems to be America's wrong turn in the road. "If John Kennedy hadn't died," said my elder brother at a 1993 Thanksgiving dinner, "we'd be on Mars now."

And yet it is not only a wrong turn on a road that is mourned. More than Robert Frost's sense of absence about "the road not taken," after the death of the president in whose inauguration Frost participated, America senses the absence of any road. Technology may now change, but our trust in certain technological advances and linear social and economic improvement has vanished. In the sixties, we might exult in this loss of triumphant linear progress. In the seventies and thereafter we are more subdued about this loss. One might say that if America was previously on a path or track, in the seventies, it is trivialized and commercialized into "eight track." To paraphrase the title of a 1974 Bob Dylan record album, there seems to be blood on the eight track.

In *In the Line of Fire* (the title of Jeff Maguire's screenplay suggests the possibility of an interruption in a natural linear order), the agent's alienation is so great that he attaches little import to protecting the president in itself. However, he feels that he must do his job as if it had tangible meaning. He and the would-be assassin (John Malkovich) differentiate themselves from one another in this respect. The professional assassin, trained by the CIA after Kennedy's death, sees both attempting to kill and to protect the president as two equal sides of a mere game. Eastwood's character insists that doing a job is not the same as playing a game. Reacting against sixties and post-sixties ruptures with reality, he elegantly, if silently, expresses nostalgia for pre-sixties reality. In terms of "Self-Portrait in a Convex Mirror," he finds "another life" that is not quite there.

"Self-Portrait in a Convex Mirror" speaks of "another life" to be found in the mirror's backing. Thomas Pynchon's *Gravity's Rainbow* also points toward co-existent historical possibilities. To paraphrase Pynchon, through a "dissolution" of resistant force, gravity finds its rainbow, and, in the words of the title of the first chapter of *Gravity's Rainbow,* American culture moves "Beyond the Zero." Many versions of worldly existence, the book suggests, exist simultaneously. Pynchon's 1973 novel depicts another life or parallel universe that has existed side by side with the first quarter century of Cold War reality.

The other life of post–World War II American culture in *Gravity's Rainbow* is "the real war." The novel posits the Cold War as a continuation of a project, the setting up of points for armament launchings, of which World War II is only a part:

> The war was the set of points. Eh? Yesyes, Skippy, the truth is that the War is keeping things alive. Things. The Ford is only one of them. The Germans-and-Japs story was only one, rather surrealistic version of the real War. The real war is always there. The dying tapers out now and then, but the War is still killing lots and lots of people. Only right now it is killing in more subtle ways. Often in ways that are too complicated, even for us, at this level, to trace. But the right people are dying, just as they do when armies fight.[72]

Like a literary Unabomber, *Gravity's Rainbow* offers a leftist complement to Nixon's mid-seventies sense of all-pervasive conspiracy. Both implied paranoias are built on interpretations of World War II.

Since wartime innovations like the bombing of Hiroshima, Nagasaki, and Dresden, and other devastation and gruesomely systematic genocide attempts frame the end of the war, *Gravity's Rainbow* begins with a supernatural kind of affective expression:

> A screaming comes across the sky. It has happened before, but there is nothing to compare it to now.[73]

This screaming is incomparable even though it has occurred before. Like the Holocaust or slavery, its effect is beyond description. It is a paradoxically voiceless kind of scream. This ongoing real war does not accumulate history that can be traced. Pynchon tells of a reality that can only be conveyed in painful metaphor. The book begins with the presentation of a fantastic yet bleak perspective on World War II. The war is a worldwide failure of culture that from its outset excludes recuperation. It is a military operation kind of "Evacuation" that might remind a reader of the 1973 oil embargo gas lines:

> It is too late. The Evacuation still proceeds, but it's all theater. There are no lights inside the cars. No light anywhere. Above him lift girders old as an iron queen, and glass somewhere far above that would let the light of day through. But it's night. He's afraid of the way the glass will fall—soon—it will be spectacle: the fall of a crystal palace. But coming down in a total blackout, without one glint of light, only great invisible crashing.[74]

"It is too late"—there can only be belatedness in the face of an undeniable horror. Even the evacuation from the bombing appears to be merely for show. And yet in this "total blackout" no spectacle can be seen, only "great invisible crashing." It is as if the enclosure were collapsing in a darkness that precludes the visualizing of these collapses. "The fall of a crystal palace" can be felt but not seen. A dark kind of codifying occurs. This evacuation "is not a disentanglement from, but a progressive *knotting into*—they go in under archways, secret entrances of rotten concrete that only looked like loops of an underpass. . . . There is no way out."[75]

Gravity's Rainbow can be seen as a prose analogue of "Self-Portrait in a Convex Mirror." Whereas the poem encounters the focus of metaphor in a surveillant convex mirror, the novel encounters the fragmentation of metonymy in a constantly complicating kind of concave mirror, which keeps its conspiracies under wraps by constantly reversing and bouncing the images off information it gives. Convexity may lie in the rockets that are worshiped and their curves. However, this is not a contained, mirroring, and manageable convexity. Appropriately, *Gravity's Rainbow* evokes a concave mirror in a rhapsodic depiction of fragmented military life:

> Elsewhere in the maisonette, other drinking companions disentangle from blankets (one spilling wind from his, dreaming of a parachute), piss into bathroom sinks, look at themselves with dismay in concave shaving mirrors, slap water with no clear plan in mind onto heads of thinning hair, struggle into Sam Brownes, dub shoes against rain later in the day with hand muscles already weary of it, sing snatches of popular songs whose tunes they don't always know, lie, believing themselves warmed.[76]

Gravity's Rainbow presents Nixon as Richard M. Zhlub, a small businessman who owns the Orpheus Theater in Southern California. He ironically "comes out against" a seeming conspiracy of music that seems to be coming from forces associated with Orpheus himself. The short passage concerning Nixon, near the end of *Gravity's Rainbow*, concludes with Nixon checking his rearview mirror for the police and wondering if he hears a police siren. Nixon is neither the hero nor antihero that Parmigianino is in Ashbery's poem. For Pynchon, he is more of an object than a subject.

Similarly, Ashbery introduces an underlying ideological policing that offers more room for maneuver and negotiation. "Self-Portrait in a Convex Mirror" offers no regrets based on a possibility that history may have been different. However, *Gravity's Rainbow* suggests that America, and thus the post–World War II world, took the wrong course when it rejected figures like Jonathan Edwards and the fictional William Slothrop for making salvation more accessible. The protagonist of *Gravity's Rainbow* wonders if there might not be a "route back."[77] In the historical context in which the book is written this implies regret about the failure of the sixties, more regret than in "Self-Portrait in a Convex Mirror," in which there is no such possibility of "a route back" because the seventies seems suspended in a cycle of time that we are trapped within.

5 A Watergate Is a Stone Wall

I don't give a shit what happens. I want you all to stonewall it, let them plead the Fifth Amendment, cover-up or anything else, if it'll save it — save the plan. That's the whole point. — Richard Nixon, *Watergate tape transcripts*

We won't die secret deaths anymore. — Tony Kushner, *Angels in America, Part Two: Perestroika*

Although the seventies, coming between the more distinctive sixties and eighties, is a decade that is difficult for mainstream culture to categorize, the seventies is remembered as a golden age for gay culture, coming between pre-Stonewall repressions and the specter of AIDS in the eighties. Interestingly, gay culture provided the most primal scene of seventies mainstream culture — the disco. Many Americans did not recognize the gay subtext of the Village People's seventies hits, "Macho Man" and "YMCA." Many listeners accepted the masculine postures of these songs without irony. The conventions behind sexual presentation became more obvious, if acceptable. Similarly, John Travolta's character as a disco king became the decade's most distinctive masculine icon.

20. The Village People, courtesy of Photofest

Perhaps it is not accidental that many of the key figures that I treat in this seventies study, such as Johns, Warhol, Ashbery, Baldwin, and Rich are gay or lesbian. After all, if surveillance is a key theme of the seventies, gays and lesbians may well often feel like spies or outlaws. It is therefore not surprising that Foucault—a gay man, not incidentally—openly explores the theme of surveillance in the early seventies with *Discipline and Punish,* before he directly tackles the subject of sexuality in his late seventies *A History of Sexuality: Introduction.*

Two artists who figure prominently in these pages illustrate a paradox concerning gay identity, surveillance and the closet. Whereas Andy Warhol might seem to flaunt his gayness compared to Jasper Johns, Warhol was oddly more closeted. For all his self-documentation, Warhol did not publicly acknowledge his homosexuality. It was almost as if pervasive connotations of gayness functioned to keep away its denotations. Whereas Johns may have resented Warhol's overt gay identity and believed Warhol made it difficult for the heterosexual art world to take gay artists seriously, Johns was strangely more forthright about his sexuality. Indeed, Johns's haunting explorations of punctured crosshatched surfaces—that is, of the realities that exist beneath imposed uniform surfaces (which I discuss in the next section) can be

21. *The Boys in the Band,* courtesy of Photofest

read as movingly emotional records of gay identity within a society that re-presses it.

This section discusses gayness in the seventies anecdotally since it is obviously too large a subject to treat exhaustively here. I also unusually situate the discussion by beginning with an examination of the controversial *The Boys in the Band* (1970), the first mainstream film to thematize and forefront overt homosexuality. The major breakthrough of the film is in the scale paid to the subject, the sense of realistic detail with which many of the characters are presented, and the likability of many of the film's characters. However, since the film at times verges on calling and representing homosexuality as something of a disease, it seems somewhat dated and is arguably not a major break from previous screen portrayals of less overtly stated homosexuality. Nonetheless, *The Boys in the Band,* based on Mart Crowley's play, probably never would have been filmed without the loosening of film standards in 1968, one of the first major films about which this can be said. As if to memorialize this loosening, director William Friedkin makes prominent the huge "Summer 1968" graffiti on a wall on the roof where most of the first half of the film takes place. *The Boys in the Band* concerns enclosed spaces. Homosexuals are free—indeed they are virtually required—to identify themselves, but in their own ghettoized space. Like lepers in a colony, the "symptom" of homosexuality seems to be the issue.

Essentially, the film can be broken down into two acts. The first half of the movie occurs on Michael's New York City roof garden, where Allen, an extremely closeted friend of Michael's, is the main foil. At the film's midpoint, rain forces the nine gay partygoers inside, where Michael coerces them into a seemingly mean-spirited party game. From Michael's claustrophobic living room, participants in the game must telephone someone they have secretly loved and confess their feelings. It is a game that tests the wisdom in coming out, and it is ultimately determined to be a game that gays play at a risk to their dignity. When Harold, who will not play the game, counters by making it clear to Michael that he will always be gay, Michael falls to the ground in a fetal position. It becomes clear that his game of going public is a defense against his inability to accept his condition. When Michael comes to, he tells his former lover, "If only we could not just hate ourselves so much." There is no hint that his self-hatred might in any way reflect homophobic forces within mainstream culture. Friedkin chooses to emphasize an enclosed theatrical space in the film's last shot. Although we had seen the New York environments of the other characters as they left for the party, the movie ends with a sense of an entrapment, showing the inside of the closed front door of Michael's apartment after Michael has left to attend a midnight mass, emphasizing Michael's sense of the unnaturalness of his homosexuality.

If *The Boys in the Band* demonstrates how stereotypically and negatively (if seemingly sympathetically) Hollywood portrays gayness, in terms of stereotyping, Mike Nichols's *The Birdcage* (1996) may not be much of an improvement. The latter film is told through the lens of a mediating traditional family, for whom gays are not respectable, and, more importantly, among whom gay characters are so often stereotyped, perhaps to a much greater extent than in *The Boys in the Band*.

Another 1970 film presents a minor though perhaps more hopeful presentation of a gay character. Little Horse, the seemingly gay Cheyenne Indian in Arthur Penn's *Little Big Man* (1970) is presented as stereotypically effeminate. However, he is happily accepted by the Cheyenne society of the movie. Indeed, Little Horse is probably a berdache, a ritualistic sexual role in Cheyenne society. One of Little Horse's rituals entails doing everything backward. Little Horse notably saves Dustin Hoffman's character, the protagonist of the film who can live as either a white man or Cheyenne, from the massacre at

Little Big Horn. Little Horse's "queer" quality of doing everything backward makes him a kind of mirror image that might allow a partially white, straight American culture to survive a coming disaster. As we have noted, disco also provided something like this kind of cultural mirror image.

Pat Buchanan has inversely used the term "culture" to distinguish culture in general from gay culture. Indeed, Bill Clinton has spoken of "military culture" as something in opposition to any kind of expression of gay culture. Such thinking encourages a nostalgic urge to create an enforced hegemonic "culture." Until the sixties, homosexuals posed no problems in the army because it was not an issue to be "officially" discussed within society at large. That army personnel were gay was known but informally. However, in the seventies, homosexuality was codified throughout more cultural strati, giving way to the grounds for and the possibilities of increased repression and witch hunts in the eighties, helping to make gays in the military an issue in the nineties. Oddly, it is now an issue of what constitutes official knowledge, culture, and the sanctity of denial. The actual existence of gays in the military is no longer an issue. In the words of "Self-Portrait in a Convex Mirror," the "castle" of military culture is "amazed" yet held in place against unsanctioned knowledge of this amazement. One encounters this same kind of opposition to discussing gay rights in public schools. Gay rights are generally acknowledged, but cannot be officially acknowledged. Denial is elevated and given official status.

Thomas Pynchon's *Gravity's Rainbow* foresees this kind of ideological battle about the ultimate import of official sexuality: "Homosexuality in high places is just a carnal afterthought now, and the real and only fucking is done on paper."[78] One is reminded of Nixon's publicly pious stance as it juxtaposed with the absent presence of his sexual, profane, and obscene language in the Watergate tape transcripts.

This nineties ideological emphasis on denial in the sixties takes the form of more repressive policing. The Stonewall riots concern the constitutional right to assemble in a gay bar—to assemble as a culture. Discos as we now know them arise from the same impulse. Dancing on the open disco floor is a rite of coming out, metaphorically in full view of gay culture, even, paradoxically for those who are not homosexual. What does coming out then mean? Whether we are talking of the punk, heavy metal, or disco clubs of the second half of the seventies, there is an implicit petition for the right to assemble within distinct cultural identities and come out within a context that challenges and supersedes that which constitutes official knowledge and "argument[s]." Ashbery's "Self-Portrait in a Convex Mirror" posits "another life" to come out of:

Your argument, Francesco,
Had begun to grow stale as no answer
Or answers were forthcoming. If it dissolves now
Into dust, that only means its time had come
Some time ago, but look now, and listen:
It may be that another life is stocked there
In recesses no one knew of.
(*SP*, 196: 23–29)

The surveillant convex mirror contains alternative realities, dreams and possibilities that are in some sense real.

Nixon wished to use the nonexistent Dean plan as a "stonewall" to shield him from charges that he had prior knowledge of the Watergate burglary cover-up. He could stand behind the plan and claim to be learning about the cover-up as the world did. Similarly, before the 1969 Stonewall riots (Stonewall is a gay bar at Sheridan Square in Greenwich Village, New York), a gay bar was a place where behavior could be more easily codified so that communications implying homosexual identity and activity could be shielded from outside judgment, inquisition, persecution, and prosecution. Police often surveyed homosexual bars, but if a gay or lesbian frequenter of a bar such as Stonewall observed codes of sexual nuance and invitation, he or she was somewhat safe. However, in 1969, when numerous arrests were made at the Stonewall bar, it seemed as if even the observance of this code in the confines of a gay bar was little guarantee against the police's interpretation of acceptable sexual communication and the rights of a certain group to assemble. Backed, in a manner of speaking, to the stone wall, "Stonewall" began to connote not as much a shield against unwarranted inquiry as a stand for self-identity in the public realm.

The Stonewall riots must be considered as a major hinge between the sixties and the seventies. Martin Duberman notes how even in 1967, anything as public as a self-identified gay bookstore "manipulated" and exploited this self-identification:

In those years a "gay" bookstore had meant only one thing: pornography. But Craig had a straitlaced, proper side, and had decided early on that the Oscar Wilde Memorial Bookshop would carry only "the better titles" and no pornography of any kind. Though hardly a puritan sexually, he regarded the sex magazines as exploitative — "a ten-dollar price on something that makes sex look dirty and furtive." He was determined to have a store where gay people did not feel manipulated or used. There was no ADULT READING sign in the window, and no peep show in the back room. And the ad Craig later took out in *The Village Voice* was headlined GAY IS GOOD.[79]

The Stonewall riots changed the relationship between gays and the public sphere.

A watergate can literally be a stone wall that is underwater. Traditionally made of rocks and stones, a watergate opens and closes like a canal lock. Nixon strove to reduce Watergate to a mere metaphorical stone wall that is always in its closed position. The Nixonian "closet" of total informational control would not hold. In the sixties and the seventies, a wider cultural closet shrinks (perhaps to be replaced by other kinds of closets later) and, as when the door in a ship cabin in *Night at the Opera* opens, a plethora of identity-positions fall out.

One is sometimes reminded of the odd television screen labels that identify guests on the *Oprah, Donahue,* and similar talk shows. *Donahue,* it should be remembered, started as a local Columbus, Ohio, program in the sixties, and attained huge syndicated success from Chicago in the seventies, and the huge proliferation of *Donahue*-like and other talk shows demonstrates the nation's urge to publicize its many self-identifying stories, in a similar fashion to how one identifies oneself before sharing in the various Twelve Step programs that grew enormously during the seventies. Identifying labels can be bones of contention. For instance, the term "Hispanics," a government-coined term relating to Spanish descent, was popularized in the seventies. However, many have replaced "Hispanic" with "Latino" and "Latina" so as to self-identify with their Latin American rather than Spanish roots. Similar problems arise when, for instance, one considers whether lesbians are "gay."

If John Ashbery is an important "gay poet," it is not because he advocates a set characterization of gay identity and gay lifestyle. Rather, Ashbery's work identifies the complicated admixture of public and private lives that homosexuality inevitably is. Gay identification tends to hinge on self-identification. Its verification depends on a public affirmation of a private and virtually unknowable reality. After Stonewall, it became more fashionable for gays and lesbians to "come out," that is, to proclaim their sexual orientation. However, before Stonewall, this was not as self-evidently morally courageous.[80] Stonewall demonstrated the import of self-proclamation to unite publicly and further a group's interests. Before these riots against the police implementation of antiquated New York City criminal statues concerning sexual communications that prohibited gays and lesbians from assembling, "coming out" would only have played into hostile hands. In a public context, only one who is opposed to such an identity would want to survey and regulate it. Indeed, as Eve Kosofsky Sedgwick has recently articulated, coming out is an ephemeral construction of identity since, according to Sedgwick, sexual orientation is not a matter that is easily pigeonholed. Why, then, would a poet such as Ashbery who would seem to champion such an indefinite reality feel a need to come out, or, indeed, to "come out" and define any political stance?

Ashbery's mid-sixties poem, "An Outing,"[81] is an odd juxtaposition of viewpoints on these issues. This light, whimsical collage asserts that "to come out" would be aesthetically and politically unwise. The poem is framed around an ambivalence about "step[ping] outside that door" and "going out." Yet there seems to be a cultural momentum toward validating the act. It is almost as if the speaker were being surveyed into coming out.

"An Outing" contains three voices or characters: one who seems to have some sort of relatively creative job, another who questions him about it and calls for an outing, and the poem's speaker, who appears without quotation marks as a third character. The poem begins with the second character questioning the first character: "These things that you are going to have— / Are you paid specially for them?" The first character, it is implied, is paid to buy things. His job is one of being a consumer and circulating capital. Dennis Altman, among others, has commented on the importance of advanced consumer capitalism in the emergence of a representative homosexual minority during the seventies:

> The real change in the past decade has been a mass political and cultural movement through which gay women and men have defined themselves as a new minority. This development was only possible under modern consumer capitalism, which for all its injustices has created the conditions for greater freedom and diversity.[82]

As Western countries became societies of high consumption, ready credit, and rapid technological development, it was not surprising that the dominant sexual ideology of restraint and repression, which had been so functional during the early production-oriented development of capitalism, came under increasing attack. Restraint remains effective in countries undergoing rapid industrialization, and many Third World countries impose far more rigid morality than does the United States. The collapse of traditional values, whether in regard to sex, work, or authority, are in a sense the result of the very success of the capitalist societies these value systems had helped engender. . . .

It is not merely that modern capitalism turns sex into a major commodity, both directly and indirectly, so that airlines, soap, and cars are all marketed by explicit sexual references. The values implied in modern capitalism have real implications for the way in which sexuality is expressed; the stress on hedonism and instant gratification makes old strictures seem less and less relevant. These people who voted for Ronald Reagan in the hope he could lead America back to its traditional values will inevitably be disappointed, for there is a basic conflict between these values and those of consumer capitalism, which Reagan, himself a product of Hollywood, so strongly extols.[83]

Ashbery's "An Outing" performs a kind of consumerist theater. In the poem, the first character answers "Yes" to the second character's query, implying that the latter had it right about the former being "paid specially" for "things." The questioner continues, "And when it is over, do you insist / Do you insist that the visitor leave the room?" Provocatively, after the unidentified consumer activity, it is unclear whether or not another party need leave, as if a performance were over. The first character responds that his performance or "activity" has no definitive rules: "My activity is as random as the wind. / Why should I insist? The visitor is free to go, / Or to stay as he chooses."

The speaker then introduces himself as a third party who is somehow outside and perhaps beyond this dialogue about restraint and liberty. "Are you folks going out for a walk / And if you are would you check the time / On the way back?" he asks. He then quite significantly determines that the time is not right for that kind of self-disclosure, for, that is, "step[ping] outside": "I would take a pratfall if I stepped outside that door." The speaker would fall on his buttocks, become a joke, and lose all credibility.

"An Outing" switches back to the interlocutors:

"I don't know whether I should apply or nothing."
"I think you shd make yr decision."

The uneasiness of the self-outing of the title, which prefigures the later use of the word, is encased in a dialectic between the two characters. The speaker consolidates their positions into a problematized identity-position: "By chance we found ourselves / Gumshod on the pebbled path, Denmark 0 Denmark." He speaks of walking on pebbles with gumshoes, slang for "detectives," and implying the double-edged surveillant position into which this culture has thrust gay identity. The poem concludes with a homage of sorts to the uncertainty of an Ashberian Hamlet. A constant anxiety foreshadows a moment when some kind of decision will need to be articulated in a metaphoric Denmark. My discussion of the next two Ashbery poems looks at this quandary from sixties and seventies perspectives, and I turn my attention to a comparison between Ashbery poems of the mid-sixties and the early seventies, "The Chateau Hardware" (SP, 117) and "Poem in Three Parts." [84]

The shift in Ashbery's poetry from "The Chateau Hardware" (1967) to "Poem in Three Parts" (1974) indicates a comparable shift in the terms by which one tended to understand oneself as closeted. "The Chateau Hardware" posits a new valorization of the closet and "Poem in Three Parts" erotically complicates and gives play to notions of a closet and coming out of one.

A preliminary "walk" through "The Chateau Hardware" will help to establish a basis for this discussion. The poem's title suggests a hideaway within a hideaway: the hidden industrial-like bottom-line workings within a large Continental country house. "Hardware" connotes sexual organs and workings that, like the hardware of most buildings, and the bathrooms in architectural schemes until the seventies, must be hid. Like the tapestry that hides its inner workings on the other side of the picture, the aesthetic hides its industrial realities. There is a hint that the speaker lives within an extra-industrial, peripherally capitalist, realm but is coming to terms with his (I hypothetically identify the speaker with Ashbery's male voice) and his society's nuts and bolts, which are equated with hidden sexual realities.

The first sentence in the first line, "It was always November there," begins to link an implicitly sad, Mary Shelleyan, drizzle-like, always-already state to the nature of the closet, associating Shelley's "November of the soul," in which Frankenstein is birthed, with its overtones of the Industrial Revolution and its aftermath, in which, according to Foucault, homosexual identity is fixed and the closet reified. Foucault notes, "The nineteenth-century homosexual became a personage, a past, a case history, and a childhood, in addition to being a type of life, a life form, and a morphology, with an indiscreet anatomy, and possibly a mysterious physiology. Nothing that went into his total composition was unaffected by his sexuality. It was everywhere present in him." [85] Foucault calls our attention to "the appearance in the nineteenth-century psychiatry, jurisprudence, and literature of a whole series of discourses on the species and subspecies of homosexuality." [86]

After the temporal reference of the poem's first sentence, "The Chateau Hardware" places in apposition a spatial analogue: "The farms / Were a kind of precinct." A precinct, from the Latin for "to encircle", infers either a unit of police protection and assistance, with its attendant organization, or a voting district. The poem stresses the policing sense of the word: however, the democratic connotations of precinct are also crucial to the poem's full aesthetic and erotic effects. The "kind of" entity that the precinct is exists somewhere between voting (desiring) and external regimentation. "Kind of" also serves to qualify the closet as something like the unconscious that can never be directly observed but only noted in its analogic effects. Ashbery's use of the past tense to describe the naturalized state of the closet suggests a present that is positioning itself outside of that situation. A semicolon equates "The farms were a kind of precinct" to "a certain control / Had been exercised." The speaker's feel for "a certain control" betrays the speaker's bodily knowledge of the poem's happenings, although the poem is rendered in a third person that implies an assertion of external authority. The next sentence, "The little birds / Used to collect along the fence," evokes both a police lineup and the more subjectively voluntary, election-district sense of "precinct," in which citizens gather like migrating birds.

This lyrically charged reference to "little birds" is followed by the now-familiar allusion to the everyday reality of an Althusserian ideological state apparatus that is informed by the repressive state apparatus of a kind of metaphoric "police" that work together in conjunction to maintain a closet: "It was the great 'as though,' the how the day went, / The excursions of the police . . . ." However, the adventurously romantic summoning of "the great 'as though'" also invokes powers of tropology and sexual suggestions indirectly perceived in the closet. The next clause, "As I pursued my bodily functions," breaks this indirectness with a scatological implication. Perhaps the speaker is voiding himself in a rural wood or near "the chateau hardware" of a rest room or an outhouse, away from assumed notions of decency that would exclude unmoored anal arousal. These bodily functions are fulfillments of desire. However, in an "earth" state opposed to "fire" and "water," the speaker "want[s]" nothing and is viscerally content to be inscribed within an ideologically positive though closeted societal configuration:

                                        wanting

Neither fire nor water,
Vibrating to the distant pinch
And turning out the way I am, turning out to greet you.

Of course, the formation of a momentarily de-closeted subject—"turning out the way I am"—cannot be said to be fully presented as a mutually positive cruising identification, nor with "coming out of the closet." Nevertheless, throughout the poem, the object-position within control is eroticized to the lyrical brink of fantasy and fetish. Agency is deliciously complicated. Identity is simultaneously lost and gained. According to Julia Kristeva, there are not only many different points of entry into the symbolic. The symbolic's point of entry itself shifts: "Language is, from the start, a translation, but on a level that is heterogeneous to the one where affective loss, renunciation, or the break takes place. If I did not agree to lose mother, I could neither imagine nor name her," says Kristeva.[87]

A new, more ebullient closet is created from the dreary closet posited by the first line. The closet becomes an increasingly open secret that cannot avoid its revelatory troping—its "turning out to greet" an open as well as sexualized "you."

The sixties model a more appropriate closet for the early seventies to come out of. Self-identity ripples through the epistemes of the period, which in themselves, as with all epistemes, are a constantly negotiated site of agency. Both of the Ashbery poems discussed are sites of wild negotiation among several modes of and attitudes toward self-identification. However, a comparison of these two poems reveals a marked difference in the epistemological terms through which these negotiations are conducted.

Hegemony itself changes, as coming out becomes a kind of commodity within the mix of other late capitalist realities. The sixties can be said to be a climax of the roles implicit within industrial capitalism ("We won't go to war no more—great Midwestern hardware store," sings Frank Zappa in 1966), and the seventies its denouement. Ashbery's "Poem in Three Parts" plays with coming out in terms of an ambivalence toward a new acceptance of such identities.

It is not until the early seventies that gay identity is assimilated enough by the culture at large for Ashbery to publish a poem that problematizes gay expression in the manner of "Poem in Three Parts."[88] Although it can be argued that "Poem in Three Parts" remains closeted, it is difficult to read it in this way within the frame of Ashbery's own personal brand of conversational humor. Nonetheless, the poem distances the quoted speaker from the quoting speaker and the implicit relations of both speakers to the poet by employing the disassociating tool of citing and then parodying the naivete of the cited speaker. And yet the opening parodic quotation of an offhanded enactment of coming out that denies any such identity foregrounds "Poem in Three Parts."

Despite the regrets voiced about the event, there is no returning to the closet after such a statement. True, Ashbery would seem mercilessly to parody the speaker. The poet has introduced the poem at poetry readings by saying that for the beginning of the first part, "Love," he simply appropriated a kind of literary fan letter that was sent to him. Nonetheless, the original writer of the letter is parodied for seemingly not owning up to his experiences.

The speaker's initial, uncontextualized acknowledgment that "Once I let a guy blow me" is qualified by reservations about the experience and the expression of the desire to repress a possible recurrence through the vehicle of "feeling" as opposed to falling prey to more explicit sexual acts. This sublimating strategy amounts to a jibe at Ashbery's most overly genteel excesses of style: "Feelings are important. / Mostly I think of feelings, they fill up my life / Like the wind, like tumbling clouds, clouds upon clouds." Thus the quoted speaker, within the framework of a virtual coming out, implies that his "back[ing] away from the experience" into sentimentality is a function of a cover-up that, read on another level, constitutes the poet's self-satirization. This forms an enabling crisis of this poem. We ask ourselves how one might come out in an abstract poem. The answer is found in the undermining of any possible basis that might allow a meaningful coming out.

Juxtaposed against the first verse paragraph, the second verse paragraph of the first section suggests that coming out is capable of inscription within a majoritized environment that denies any queer linkage. Gayness itself is minimized. There is a trend toward co-option: the ideology of what "One must bear in mind" is in both "all things" and the "conscience." And yet this is no occasion for great concern because "The unknowable gets to be known" anyway. The only price is that "Familiar things seem a long way off." It could be said that the poem's first section becomes doubly queer by asserting the speaker's gayness through abstinence from queerness. Similarly, Kristeva speaks of the depressed's "flatness of affect,"[89] a flatness that might relate to the tone of much of Ashbery's poetry.

"Courage," the poem's second section, begins with the speaker's rumination about "setting out" in a slightly outlandish "double-paned" shirt—"pane" implying that he is letting his gay identity be seen as he is searching for it in others. Wearing this shirt takes "courage," as does the anal sexuality depicted by the "Smell of open water / Troughs, special pits." "Courage" concludes with the speaker's expression of alienation that causes him to desire greater specificity: "Where is it to end? What is this? Who are these people? / Am I myself, or a talking tree?"

216

The final section's title, "I Love the Sea," is strangely nostalgic when read alongside the conclusion that caps the speaker's descriptions of his dream:

We could sleep together again but that wouldn't
Bring back the profit of these dangerous dreams of the sea,
All that crashing, that blindness, that blood
One associates with other days near the sea
Although it persists, like the blindness of noon.

The speaker mourns the passing of the more relatively dangerous sense of sex that is "associated" with a more rigidly enforced closet, although, speaking in the early seventies, these "other days" "persist" with an undefined menace that is "like the blindness of noon." The trope of "the blindness of noon" calls to mind Kristeva's *Black Sun* and "the Thing buried alive,"[90] which implies a split semiotic subject and process. (See the discussion of funereal monuments and Nixon in the "Perilous Transcriptions" section of chapter 6.) "The Chateau Hardware" thus presents a more closeted and yet paradoxically also a more celebratory representation of gay identity than the more explicit "Poem in Three Parts." The latter poem exhibits fears that old repressions will continue in manners that are more difficult to identify. Nonetheless, John Ashbery's poetry also exemplifies how culture and labels can be used as performatives that gather meaning as they are expressed. Similarly, in the sixties, a closet is articulated from which elaborately created self-identities can thereafter be announced and improvised.

Five

Crossing Seventies Art

Jasper Johns's Crosshatching:
"Why It Always Seems the Same Though It Is
of Course Always Changing"

The destruction of Dresden was represented by a vertical band of orange crosshatching. . . . 1967 became bright and clear, free of the interference of any other year. —Kurt Vonnegut, *Slaughterhouse Five*

I'm believing painting to be a language. —Jasper Johns

To what purpose did they cross-hatch so effectively, so that the luminous surface that was underneath is transformed into another, also luminous but so shifting and so alive with suggestiveness that it is like quicksand, to take a step there would be to fall through the fragile net of uncertainties into the bog of certainty . . . ? —John Ashbery, "Whatever It Is, Wherever You Are"

The wax surfaces of Jasper Johns's mid-fifties canvases convey shimmeringly ghostly presences trapped in paint. It is easy to see the muted shades of an American culture still haunted by the McCarthy era in Johns's fuzzy demarcations between splotched colors. In the mid-seventies, Johns adapted a motif of carefully balanced and intersecting groups of lines, or crosshatching. Crosshatching, like Johns's fifties works, produced a layered effect. However, unlike in Johns's earlier paintings, this ambiguous layering became a subject matter and central focus. The later paintings systematically generate an ambiguity of surfaces throughout their canvases. The extremely mandarin process of these seventies Johns paintings looks markedly different from the teeming surfaces of many of Johns's montaged sixties paintings such as *According to What* (1964). It is almost as if, in Johns's mid-seventies canvases, something were being left out or covered up. Although these seventies "cover-up" creations are too complex to be entirely explained by it, it should be noted that during the mid-seventies the Vietnam War was a great absent presence. After all, the Vietnam War did not end until 1975. In a sense, Johns's paintings comment on how, in the seventies, we do much work to overlook and not to make sense of the recent past. Johns's paintings of the seventies convey an ambivalence between surface and depth, appearance and unfathomable reality. Americans could not help but experience this queasy ambivalence in the seventies. They are on an edge between at least two realities. In this regard, we may observe the constant double message of *All in the Family*. Many Americans sympathize with the protagonist Archie Bunker, although his politics are clearly intended to be less than sympathetic. The prevalent message is that Archie's views are not so much attractive or correct as socioeconomically determined and refreshingly honest. Liberal argumentation seems inherently unconvincing to Archie's fans. And to fill in this credibility schism, something more or less unspeakable is being crosshatched into the American fabric. Interestingly, Johns's crosshatching first appears as a motif in one of the four panels of his painting with collaged objects, *Untitled* (1972; illustration 22). In this work, a dummy's body parts are made to work compositionally with the crosshatched composition, as if to suggest that anything can be reduced to two-dimensional composition.[1]

Soon after the institutionalized stalemate of the Korean War, when the United States assumed Western responsibility for the war in Indochina, Jasper Johns solemnly trivialized the American flag with his encaustic rendering of one in *Flag* (1954–55). Johns opened a new semiotic space for American art. Sixties counterculture more blatantly embraced decontextualizations of the American flag when, for instance, Abbie Hoffman literally wrapped himself in one, implying that the signifier of the flag is just fabric and stands for no concrete signified. "America" itself loses its status as a hard and fast reality. When Simon and Garfunkel's 1968 recording "America" ends by repeating the words "all come to look for America" three times, there was the ring of a poignant truth that touched upon the unexpected start of a disintegration within the industrial base of the United States. "All" of America indeed will soon be searching. In a sense, the wanderlusts, anxieties, and ambivalences of the characters of Jack Kerouac's *On the Road* were, beginning in the sixties, distributed throughout the nation. (One might say that the inability of these male

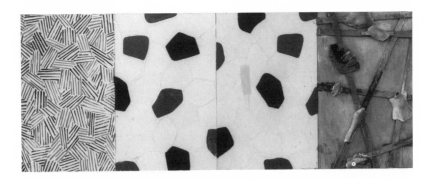

22. Jasper Johns, *Untitled*, 1972, © Jasper Johns/ Licensed by VAGA, New York, NY

characters of the forties and the fifties to respond adequately to the changes at hand in the sixties contributed to the growth of the women's movement in the early seventies.) The "road" became too pervasive to be called a road. This disappearance of the sense of a road was increasingly associated with profound disturbance about the loss of the sense of place. "America doesn't exist, Democracy doesn't exist," says the messiah of multinational corporations in Paddy Chayefsky's *Network* (1976). In a more characteristically cheerful vein, John Cage dedicated a seventies selection of his writings "To America—a place in the world, no more, no less." For a time in the middle and the late sixties, beginning at about when American escalation in Vietnam in 1965 made the Gulf of Tonkin resolution in 1964 seem like a ruse, the heated Cold War seemed like a ploy and all of its attendant suppositions deceptions. Marshall McLuhan's "global village," in which the coolly understated truth is equally available to everyone, seemed like a more obvious reality than the Cold War and its manifestation in Vietnam. The 1973 oil embargo signaled the end of continuing American prosperity, and it is not surprising that a major shift in Johns's canvases ensued. It was almost as if Johns were signaling a delimitation and diminution of American culture.

Jasper Johns's crosshatching paintings of the mid-seventies seemed oddly traditional when they were first exhibited. It might have seemed that Johns was holding on to a previously accepted rational sense of two-dimensional space. Painting, in general, and the flat, traditional canvas, in particular, were considered by many, at the time, to be obsolete and exhausted. Puzzlingly, at a time when the art world was accustomed to Johns's irregularly shaped canvases, Johns's new paintings emphasized the two-dimensional, rectangular picture plane.

In a sense, Johns returned to a kind of wall of reality, testing it and poking through it as Pink Floyd did in their seventies album *The Wall*. As with Johns, doubts belie Pink Floyd's assertion that "All in all you were all just bricks in the wall." Similarly, pre-punk seventies heavy metal music groups such as MC5 helped institutionalize feedback so as to test and bounce off limits of conventional musical scale, that is, to "feed back" from the horizons of recognizable auditory experience, and Johns's crosshatching continually grazes on and off the "wall" of the painting's surface. By the late seventies, when the overcharged strains of heavy metal generally give way to the reverberating assimilations of virtually everything rock and orchestral music have to offer, Johns uses crosshatching as more of a collaging and synthetic device that comments on painters as diverse as Picasso and Munch.

Johns's crosshatch paintings present patterns of interlocking groups of parallel lines that "survey" the surfaces of the painter's canvases, meeting and—although not always touching—seeming to interlock like extended hands. Since the crosshatch motif covers the picture surface of each painting and seems to recur endlessly, lines never cross, and, therefore, enclosed figures cannot form. However, each of Johns's crosshatch paintings undermines this suggestion of a relentlessly extended plane. For instance, the crosshatch motifs of the left and right edges of *Scent* (1973–74) precisely overlap, suggesting that the system is closed. Although Johns had often problematized the picture plane before the mid-seventies, he had never so strongly valorized it before. The surprise of a relatively early work like *Painting with Two Balls* (1960), wherein objects project from a slit in the canvas, relies upon our expectations of what constitutes the domain of a painting. However, during the seventies, it is often assumed that the possibilities of the two-dimensional format are exhausted, and Johns needs to "reinvent" the picture plane in order to violate it once again. In a like manner, Ashbery revives the poetic topos, and the Nixon administration seeks almost monarchal presidential powers. By unifying all the nation's surveillance agencies through the secret Huston plan, Nixon attempts to mend a perceived rift in presidential powers by "crosshatching" the various federal surveillance agencies onto the plane of direct presidential control. One notes this connection between the self-conscious, careful, systematic probing of surfaces and the powers of surveillance in Don DeLillo's *Libra* (1988), with the character of Walter Everett Jr., the mild-mannered retired CIA agent who helps hatch the plan that results in John Kennedy's assassination. When Everett butters his toast, a control of surfaces is related with surveillance:

> He was thinking about secrets. Why do we need them and what do they mean? His wife was reaching for the sugar. . . .

Mary Frances watched him butter the toast. He held the edges of the slice in his left hand, moved the knife in systematic strokes, over and over.[2]

In the early seventies, the death of painting seemed tantalizingly near. Painting and the picture plane seemed like a kind of obsolete backing of the mirror. In the wake of minimal sculpture, conceptual art, and a burgeoning interest in performance art, we might not have looked toward two-dimensional space as a primary site for future art. Indeed, Jasper Johns was among the first painters to shape his canvases. He experimented with painterly three-dimensional collages. However, in the mid-seventies, Johns underscores painting's two-dimensional limits.

Perhaps the seventies are the most crosshatched of times. The period seems so very much about what comes before and after—sometimes long before and long after. During the Watergate years, Johns works primarily on paintings that are dominated by the crosshatching motif, that is, many groups of short parallel lines, each nestled between similar groups of parallel lines that are usually of a different color. As Ashbery's poem about a convex mirror and Nixon's assertion of an imperial White House create and also problematize totalizing mechanisms, the crosshatching motif calls attention to concepts of rational two-dimensional space only to refute those notions. Crosshatching is an emblem of the seamless surveillance that occurred throughout society in the seventies, and it is also an emblem of my critical mechanism for discussing that occurrence.

Crosshatching "surveils" the picture plane without allowing "pockets" of isolated figuration to form. The motif guards against a division of space into a figurative foreground and a non-figurative background. In 1959, Johns wrote that he found "Leonardo's idea ('Therefore, O painter, do not surround your bodies with lines . . . ') that the boundary of a body is neither a part of the enclosed body nor a part of the surrounding atmosphere" "of interest."[3] Johns most fully demonstrates this "idea" in his crosshatch paintings. Of course, Johns has often blurred seemingly natural entities of line, color, and nomination, as in, for instance, *Jubilee* (1959), *False Start* (1959), and *Map* (1961), and, in *Device Circle* (1959), he had created a sense of surveillance with a rotating stick that is attached to the center of the canvas and surveying a pictorial surface with its delineated radius. However, the crosshatching motif best merges the surveying mechanism with its field.

Johns's use of "Leonardo's idea" through crosshatching profoundly and rigorously complicates Johns's work since 1974. It would seem that crosshatching would produce a perfectly "ongoing" two-dimensional effect. And yet we do well to recall how Johns continues his 1959 statement after evoking Leonardo's injunction: "Generally, I am opposed to painting which is concerned with conceptions of simplicity. Everything looks very busy to me."[4] Johns's blurrings of our suppositions concerning figuration and outline do more than create pleasant surface patterns. The painter uses crosshatching's indeterminacy between background and foreground as an innovative tool to explore the limits of the category of "surface" "so that," in Ashbery's words, "the luminous surface that was underneath is transformed into another." The crosshatching "lines," argues David Shapiro, "are ways of tensing the poles of depth and surface. They make equivocal X's and read as a map of such distinctions."[5]

Shapiro considers crosshatching as a vehicle for Johns to demonstrate "his true interest": "the fold, the edge, the slip of the brush."[6] In other words, as "Self-Portrait in a Convex Mirror" and the Watergate affair do, Johns's crosshatch paintings continuously test limits. Johns devises an apparently static surface to question the notion of an identifiable surface, or picture plane. When Johns first exhibits his crosshatch painting, these works are understood by the majority of art viewers as a kind of abstract "wallpaper." Indeed, this may still be the case. Shapiro answers this criticism:

> Johns's art is finally never wallpaper. Always, like Cézanne, he searches for a structure of depth. . . . [Johns's works] are studies in both a subject doubling itself and a luminous sense of layering. *Usuyuke* [1977–78] reveals a paradox of a wallpaper that is for all its flatness swarming, filled, busy, and expressive.[7]

In 1976, Rosalind E. Krauss observed that "at first glance," Johns's "most recent paintings are so shocking" because "they seem devoid of irony."[8] But she reconsiders this first impression. "The apparent withdrawal from the ironic mode," she remarks, "is a consequence of the surface unity of these paintings."[9] However, beyond "surface unity," relentless as these systems of repetition may be, Krauss notes that Johns uses the broad, sparse crosshatching in *Weeping Women* (1975) to mimic "the naissance of Cubism" by "compact[ing] on the surface" Picasso's "internal repetition to suggest a single image repeated through successive studies."[10] The angular webs of Johns's crosshatching uncannily echo Picasso's cubist compositions. Similarly, and perhaps more obviously, crosshatching, particularly in a Johns painting such as *Scent* (1974), parodies "the 'all-over' composition" of the impressionist Monet and the abstract expressionist Pollock.[11] Krauss concludes that "subject" is, indeed, the limits of historical progression, and in the light of our analogy of Ashbery's work of this period to Johns's, the art critic tells us something about Ashbery's use of the poetic subject as a means of calling attention to the history of poetry in order to question it:

> The works by Johns, in their evocation of several moments—and monuments—central to the development of modern art, are engaged with the enterprise of history painting. But their subject is failure, promising beginnings that lead to convulsive or ineffectual ends. Their subject is "growth" as stasis. It is in this sense that Johns maintains the ironic attitude. For the works convey a deep skepticism about the *significance* imputed to the historical process.[12]

Krauss maintains that *Scent* "is a picture through which one feels the closing-off of possibility."[13] And yet, despite the closure that Krauss detects, the cross-hatching motif also facilitates a resourcefulness and sense of something existing beyond the picture plane, which, as I later discuss, Charles Harrison and Fred Orton also note. I would like to comment on the former condition of "closure" before describing the latter one of "openness."

Johns's crosshatch marks are his most effective device for sealing off, and perhaps eliminating, the possible range of signification emitted by his paintings. As has been noted, crosshatching cannot form closed and outlined figures. Further adding to this paradoxical effect of a seamless web of closure are the numerous angles the crosshatches make on meeting one another, echoing the corners of the canvas, and reminiscent of sixteenth-century theories of composition. Joseph Masheck remarks:

> There is a complex but logical inter-relation among the individual strokes, the patches of strokes, the rectangular zones within a painting (these are defined either by the shifting or valence of the brushstroke, or by the concrete abutment of separate stretchers) and the overall quadrilateral shapes of the complete paintings. While the individual strokes-and-intervals constitute "patches," both the stretcher edges and the internal rectangular boundaries establish the same kind of rectilinear grid. Stroke as line corresponds with real edge as line, and the irregularly shaped patch corresponds with the quadrilateral zone as a two-dimensional area.[14]

In other words, since it can be said that the physical limits of the painting, its frame and edges, at least partially organize the field of the painting, many intersecting systems of supposed wholes and parts echo one another. Hence, the seemingly casual, ongoing motif of crosshatching is, in a sense, organized by an exterior kind of "surveillance." According to Derrida, although "the truth in painting" may not be comprehensible, that truth, as everything that the painting is not, nevertheless generates itself throughout the painting by calling the painting's "frame" and the trespassing of it into play:

> One space remains to be broached in order to give place to the truth in painting. Neither inside nor outside, it spaces itself without letting itself be framed but it does not stand outside the frame. It works the frame, makes it work, gives it work to do. . . . It situates between the visible edging and the phantom in the centre.[15]

Krauss notes a similar principle at work in Johns's work, as well as in all artistic approximations of a uniform grid:

> The grid is an introjection of the boundaries of the world into the interior of the work; it is a mapping of the space inside the frame onto itself. It is a mode of repetition, the content of which is the conventional nature of art itself.[16]

Unlike a conventional grid, however, crosshatching does not fixate any points. In a manner of speaking, a "sameness" predominates. And yet there is always a change occurring within this totalizing system. In this regard, Ashbery's prose poem "Whatever It Is, Wherever You Are" (1984), discusses "the crosshatching technique." Angular crosshatched patches are likened to "hands":

> The ebony hands of the clock always seem to mark the same hour. That is why it always seems the same, though it is of course always changing constantly, subtly, as though fed by an underground stream. . . . now we can see only down, first down through the branches and further down the surprisingly steep grass patch that slopes away from the base of the tree. It certainly is a different view, but not the one we expected. (*SP*, 319)

Crosshatching controls everything in each Johns canvas that it dominates. However, it does not do so in a predictable manner. Very different effects are yielded in each canvas. For instance, we may contrast the frontality and luminosity of crosshatching in *Cicada* (1979) to the more pensively thorough crosshatching of *Dancers on a Plane* (1979).

In each small area of crosshatching "there is," as Mark Rosenthal remarks, "much freedom for idiosyncrasy."[17] Barbara Rose notes that "much internal activity is masked out by the appearance of a single cohesive and coherent image, also apparently but not actually static."[18] Rose likens the variety that underlies the monolithic appearance in Johns's crosshatch paintings to that same quality in Ad Reinhardt's black paintings and identifies six "freedoms" at work within crosshatching's "evident" "allover images." She catalogs six kinds of choices that Johns makes when painting *Untitled* (1975), in which Johns divides his square canvas into nine smaller squares before he begins applying paint. The critic observes that Johns has six tools of manipulation at his disposal when the "edge" of a crosshatch mark meets the "edge" of a square:

> (1) where edge meets edge, the brushstroke may continue in the direction it began, or it may be diverted in another direction, as if refracted by the edge of the square; (2) the direction of the stroke may remain constant while it changes color; (3) both the color as well as the direction of the brushstroke may remain constant across the boundary of a square; (4) in addition, the entire content of a given square may be mirrored in an adjacent square; (5) or the square may be repositioned or "flopped" in the way that a reproduced image can be projected or printed backwards; or (6) another possibility is that the medium may change from one square to another.[19]

Clearly, Johns's crosshatching schema does not impose the uncompromising pigeonholing of surface space that a conventional grid does. There is a softer and less clearly defined manner of organization and surveillance at play. As Ashbery puts it in "Whatever It Is, Wherever You Are," a sense of being positioned and monitored is suggested, although the specific, discrete origin of this positioning and monitoring cannot be determined:

> What did *they* want us to do? Stand around this way, monitoring every breath, checking each impulse for the return address . . . ? To what purpose did they cross-hatch so effectively, so that the luminous surface that was underneath is transformed into another, also luminous but so shifting and so alive with suggestiveness that it is like quicksand, to take a step there would be to fall through the fragile net of uncertainties into the bog of certainty . . . ? (*SP*, 319)

A viewer easily falls into the "the bog of certainty" of perceiving Johns's crosshatch paintings as unified images, and, indeed, they are totalizing systems.

However, their unity incorporates much diversity, relating variegated elements to a regulative set of alternatives.

Interestingly, James Baldwin considers race a crosshatched construction. For instance, in *Another Country* (1960), a black character is said to have a hand that contains many patches of color:

> "I love your colors. You're so many different, crazy colors."
>
> . . . she . . . tried to move her hand away, but he held it. . . . "I'm the same color all over."
>
> "You can't see yourself all over. But I can. Part of you is honey, part of you is copper, some of you is gold—"[20]

One thinks of the arm and hand casts, replete with crosshatched patches painted on their "skins," that Johns places on the canvases of *In the Studio* (1982) and *Perilous Night* (1982).

It is not difficult to extend our interpretation of crosshatching and consider the motif as a political analogue, seeing in it a system of control within relative freedom. This is of course not to say that Johns paints simple allegories. Rather, I am suggesting that the crosshatch paintings exhibit an ambivalence about our sense of surface in paintings and that this concern bespeaks other similar phenomena of the mid-seventies that delimit perceptual and cultural codes, such as "Self-Portrait in a Convex Mirror" and the Watergate affair also demonstrate.

Richard Francis doubts that Johns's work has "political implications"[21] and questions the applicability of Johns's following "sketchbook note" concerning *Watchman* (1964) to that painting:

> The watchman falls "into" the "trap" of looking. The "spy" is a different person. "Looking" is and is not "eating" and being "eaten." (Cézanne?— each object reflecting the other.) That is, there is continuity of some sort among the watchman, the space, the objects. The spy must be ready to "move," must be aware of his entrances and exits. The watchman leaves his job & takes away no information. The spy must remember and must remember himself and his remembering. The spy designs himself to be overlooked. The watchman "serves" as a warning. Will the spy and the watchman ever meet? In a painting named SPY, will he be present? The spy stations himself to observe the watchman. If the spy is a foreign object, why is the eye not irritated? Is he invisible? When the spy irritates, we try to remove him. "Not spying, just looking"—Watchman.[22]

Indeed, these works become more important when we consider the crosshatch paintings as candidates for "a painting named SPY," a title that Johns, appropriately, has never used. The spy, or source of surveillance and manipulation, never reveals itself in the crosshatch paintings. "Each object" can "reflect" "the other" without implying the "continuity" among observer, "space," and "objects." In Johns's *Watchman*, the cast of the lower half of a body, which seems to melt into the canvas, suggests the observer or "watchman" who has fallen into the "'trap' of looking." However, the lack of such a focus in the crosshatch paintings hints at a more homogenized totalizing process. If a painting entitled *Watchman* accounts for an unhidden observer, a painting called "Spy" could only account for a hidden viewer by suggesting some kind of effect that that viewer has on what she or he sees. If this effect is hidden, it cannot be noted as a specific and localized phenomenon and must be generalized throughout the entire painting.

In this regard, *Dancers on a Plane* (1979) and the later work of the same name, *Dancers on a Plane* (1980), imply that crosshatching can be likened to a "spread" of food. Each painting embeds knives, forks, and spoons into its left-hand and right-hand stretchers, which intimates that the picture "plane" is a kind of picture "plate"; "'looking,'" says Johns, "is and is not 'eating' and being 'eaten.'" Will the observer be "eating" her or his own perceptions?

Viewing, if not a viewer, is directly accounted for in crosshatch paintings like *Corpse and Mirror* (1974) and *The Barber's Tree* (1975). These paintings employ the compositional device of the diptych to connote perception, but not a perceiver. The diptychs are composed of nearly identical halves. However, there is a strong suggestion that one of the halves is "mirroring" the other half. In both paintings, we are led to believe that the right-hand side is the mirror, because a few marks are imposed upon the general crosshatch pattern. Since these marks are not mirrored, we can presume that they are a kind of defect in the mirror. And yet one can wonder if the system is too perfectly closed to admit a viewer? Where is the "spy"? Indeed, is there a "spy"? Perhaps the device itself fulfills this role. In fact, it can be maintained that crosshatching has already served this purpose. Like the crosshatching motif, this mirroring device "covers" the picture plane. A closure without a "closer" is doubly perfected.

In 1969, Max Kozloff points out that "closure" is a *"leitmotiv"* in all of Johns's works to that date. Kozloff makes this point by referring to *Drawer* (1957), which superimposes the vertical face of a drawer onto a canvas, *Canvas* (1956), which presents the back of a canvas on a larger canvas, *Shade* (1959), which covers a canvas with a window shade, and *Sketch for Three Flags* (1958), which is drawn on the back of an envelope and its closed flap:

> The condition of closure, denial, and concealment runs like a leitmotiv through this entire gamut of paintings, evoking, as it does, a low-pressure frustration which analysis almost cheapens. After all, the drawer cannot be opened; the canvas will not pry off; nor will the shade roll up, or the envelope unfold. With almost diabolical intent, the artist glues or immolates objects whose everyday function demands some kind of human operation.[23]

Nonetheless, before Johns's paintings of 1974 and 1975, the painter accomplishes closure most effectively at the outset of his career. Johns's oeuvre opens with his oil and encaustic rendition of an American flag painted on a background of barely recognizable newsprint (1954). Since there are no margins between the flag's perimeter and the painting's frame, the painting serves to recontextualize the flag, if only as a "work of art." In one stroke, the signifier of the American flag is divorced from its commonly accepted referent (the official United States), and the notion of the artistic subject is profoundly trivialized—how, we ask ourselves, can such an everyday and easily resimulatable visual code be art? Johns's work, like Ashbery's, is "pure / affirmation that doesn't affirm anything" ("Self-Portrait," *SP*, 190: 30–31). Joseph Masheck notes of Johns in the early phase of his career:

> He has always faced up to the stubborn modern suspicion that either nothing remains as paintable subject matter, to put it the old way, or, in modern terms, that gratification in ambitious paintings is not only its internal resolution but also the way it seems to dare a further move. The imagery of Johns's classic period was intrinsically conventional, abstract, linguistically acute, emblematic; it served both as a catalyst and as the rarefied subject of an inquiry into the sign, pictorial meaning, irony, even the device of the device itself.[24]

This crossing of empty realities, on the site of this lush, apparently childlike encaustic painting, is still perhaps Johns's most memorable achievement; however, it leaves the materiality of his paintings uninterrogated. The semiotic cancellation of Johns's early paintings is extended to compositional systems in the crosshatch paintings. Broadly speaking, crosshatching marks limitations of vision by emphasizing the picture plane as the limit of sight, a limit that also, since there is nowhere else to go, marks the start of a movement back toward the eye. Further, each sequence of parallel lines both counteracts a group of other ones and, more importantly, voids the possibility of anything "growing" off the canvas by fanning a system of vectors, or crossed edges, reflective of a rectangular canvas's limits, yet also suggestive of wings, or a bounce.

A bounce implies the existence of a solid barrier. Masheck detects this implication in *The Barber's Tree* (1975):

> Even the casual, lyrical trailing of crayon marks over its painterly surface affirms concreteness in an unradical and seductive way. . . . Still, if the patches of strokes and intervals share the counterpart of a rectilinear grid, they also lend granular solidity to the surface—like some magnified mineral infrastructure.[25]

Indeed, the title for *The Barber's Tree* is derived from a photograph that Johns sees in *National Geographic,* in which a Mexican barber paints the barber-stripe motif on a tree—a *surface* on a living thing. The expansively lyrical charge of Johns's paint-handling suggests that there is a concrete, organic entity beneath it. And yet we know that we are, after all, looking at a painting. Hence, there is an implicit realization that there is nothing but canvas underneath.

Astonishingly, Johns utilizes suggestions of physical limits to paradoxically "open" his closed system of crosshatching. This will become more apparent in our discussion of *The Dutch Wives* (1975). "A Dutch Wife," as Michael Crichton notes, "is a board with a hole, used by sailors as a surrogate for a woman."[26] It is easy to see the right-hand half of the diptych as representative of a "Dutch Wife," since, in this half of the painting, the perimeter of a small can is imprinted into the encaustic surface. In addition, a small ruled line leads to the center of the imprinted circle, which is further delineated by an irregular red circle that is drawn around it.

Clearly, our attention is called to the right half of the canvas as an obvious representation of a "Dutch Wife." In fact, Crichton calls Johns's painting "a stand-in for some reality, a substitute, an artificial creation which 'represents something.'"[27] However, we should not overlook that Johns uses a plural title: *The Dutch Wives.* The apparently intact and "original" left-hand side of the diptych is also called a "Dutch Wife." Hence, Johns suggests that the original is also an imitation. In this regard, on first glance the right side of the painting appears to be a mirrored image of the left side; however, on closer inspection, many differences in the crosshatching pattern appear. The mirror takes on "another life" (*SP,* 194: 27), as Ashbery puts it in "Self-Portrait in a Convex Mirror."

Many years earlier, Johns had said that he wished someday to create a work that would appear symmetrical, and yet would not be.[28] Here, this wish is realized. Johns debunks notions of repetition and symmetry. The art-making and perceiving processes are likened to the kind of indeterminate chain of signifiers that Ashbery alludes to, with the game of "telephone," near the conclusion of "Self-Portrait in a Convex Mirror."

Ashbery's "Whatever It Is, Wherever You Are," often refers to crosshatching and indicates that motif's tendency to denote strongly an all-inclusive surface reality, which is superseded by the force of less regulated alternatives. The poem suggests that our imaginations cannot help but puncture a kind of "Dutch Wife" into any given surface reality:

> That is why it always seems the same, though it is of course changing constantly, subtly, as though fed by an underground stream. If only we could go out in back, as when we were kids, and smoke and fool around and just stay out of the way, for a little while. But that's just it—don't you see? We are "out in back." (*SP*, 319)

We are reminded of the dictum, "everything is surface" (*SP*, 190: 12), near the beginning of "Self-Portrait in a Convex Mirror," which is eventually converted to "All things happen / On its balcony and are resumed within" (*SP*, 204: 4–5). Speaking of Johns's work as a model for understanding Ashbery's poetry, Charles Altieri describes perceptual "openings" that "arise" in a reception of Johns's work and cause the viewer to function with a complicated dialectic:

> Caught between options, even between worlds of art and praxis, we find the visual forcing us to propose metaphoric interpretations of something like an intention to mean which underlies, and makes problematic, our sense [of a Johns painting]. . . . The audience is torn between attending to the purely visual properties and reflecting on the orientation which one assumes. . . . Once these openings arise, the entire image vacillates between the perceptual and the conceptual.[29]

In other words, the vigorous recontextualizations of images, patterns, and surfaces that one appreciating a Johns painting must engage in cause a relentless commerce between and mutual revision by "the perceptual and the conceptual." Paradoxically, because the crosshatching motif is so pictorially all-encompassing, it is perhaps to be expected that a "perceptual" alternative to each painting will be incorporated into the "conceptual" life of each crosshatch painting. In some manner, each crosshatch painting strongly intimates the presence of an object superimposed upon the surface, beyond both its horizontal stretchers, and, especially, as in the instances of *The Dutch Wives* and *The Barber's Tree,* beneath the picture plane.

The Dutch Wives and *The Barber's Tree* consolidate the workings of the paintings that Johns produces immediately prior to *The Barber's Tree* into a subtler effect. The earlier *Corpse and Mirror II* (1974–75) exhibits more overt suggestions of the ambiguity attached to a consideration of what is "underneath" the painting's surface. The work's paint extends onto its frame, for instance, and the imprint of the open end of a can suggests a peephole or cutout, although there is nothing to see through, nor is there a contrasting background.

In the early sixties, Johns suggests what is behind a painting by applying encaustic over the back of a framed canvas (*Canvas,* 1956) and inserting objects between attached canvases (*Painting with Two Balls* [1960] and *4 the News* [1962]). However, the mid-seventies marks the beginning of a more all-over (to use an abstract expressionist term), subtle, and systematic obsession with what is "behind" a painting.

For instance, the reversed mirror writing (suggesting that someone is writing from behind the painting) at the bottom of *Dancers on a Plane* (1980) is connected by a dotted line to the center of two sets of crosshatch marks that meet head-on in such a way as to form tiny parallelograms within tiny parallelograms. Our attention is being led to another mock peephole. The silverware implanted into the left and right stretchers of the frame equates what we see to food and mockingly suggests that there is something to eat on the other side of the canvas.

Cicada (1979) also is concerned with the unseen half of a canvas. The title of the painting refers to a large striped insect with transparent wings. Similarly, Johns's painting consists of thick white crosshatch marks and thinner, brightly colored crosshatchings. There is no reason to regard these white crosshatch marks as negative space. These spaces are, in fact, larger. An unresolvable confusion (and alternations within that confusion) as to how figurative functions apply to the two sets of crosshatch accounts for much of *Cicada*'s lyrically transparent effect.

Further adding to the confusion *Cicada* proposes, the edge of the right side of the painting's crosshatch pattern is contiguous with the pattern on its left edge. The viewer's position in relation to the picture plane is thus called into question, since the painting is more coherently read from either edge than from directly in front of the apparent center of the work. If one can view this pattern flushly from either the left or right side, it follows that both the white and nonwhite crosshatch marks act as transparencies through which the alternative crosshatch pattern can be seen.

Significantly, Johns becomes increasingly preoccupied with the other, seemingly hidden side of the canvas as crosshatching enables him to effect a nonhierarchical figuration which is beyond any easy application of figure and ground relations. However, as has been noted, this concern with the hidden and excluded aspects of a painting had long been a major interest of Johns's. Indeed, *Scent* (1974), Johns's choice of a title for his first painting to be principally using the crosshatch motif, implies that he is closing in on a long-sought prey. The title also refers to Jackson Pollock's (*Scent*) (c. 1953–55) and *Search* (1955). These last works of Pollock's career magnify and force us to come to consider the curvilinear motif that Pollock employs in his major phase, which *Autumn Rhythm* (1950) exemplifies. Johns turns this consideration into a cornerstone of his work during the mid-seventies.

Johns's crosshatching emulates the major wing-like motif of a painting like Pollock's *Search*. However, Johns's more concise and articulated method not only enables him to evoke more effectively the entire canvas with each motif but also permits him to close his system, only to imply a greater opening.

Note, for instance, how in Johns's *Scent*, which consists of three adjacent canvases, the left third of each canvas, or ninth of the entire work, reduplicates the right third of the preceding canvas. Since the most left-hand ninth of the work reduplicates the most right-hand ninth, there is the implication that the entire work is a continuous band. Johns, a ceramics collector himself, simulates the conditions of pottery decoration. And yet, though the "search" may be endless, we are always provided with the "scent."

The only interference possible in this problematized picture plane is a superimposition upon or through the surface of the painting. However, *Corpse and Mirror* (1974), Johns's second painting dominated by crosshatching, renders meaningless the nature of any such interference through the triviality of the dripped paint and exposed texture, pressed into the pattern by the iron mark and "covered up," to evoke a Watergate cliché, by the pink "W" and black "X." The imperfections of the right panel criticize the relative "innocence" of the left panel, and, although the painting is not a mere reaction to a Pollock-like all-over quality, it is, however, an alternative or "other," that is, a rebirth of an important aspect of Pollock's work through a negation of it: a corpse and a mirror. Coupled with Pollock's and Johns's title of *Scent*, Johns's application of the surrealist-inspired title *Corpse and Mirror* suggests that Pollock's work itself is murdered and is now an adequate signifier, although perhaps primarily of itself.

However, it is not crucial to this argument to determine what is metaphorically "murdered" or repressed. The salient point that is being made here is that a sense of a subject is being indicated through a repression of that sense. Charles Harrison and Fred Orton maintain that the crosshatch paintings offer a new strategy for incorporating representation and content:

> The crosshatched paintings must somehow be of something, and that something may be intuitively "searched for" if certain closures are relaxed. It doesn't matter much, however, if it is not securely "found." The issue in the end is not what to look for, but what to look at, and how— with what disposition—to look.[30]

As the speaker in "Self-Portrait in a Convex Mirror" talks of Parmigianino's "shield of a greeting" (*SP*, 203: 22), which "protect[s] / What it advertises" (*SP*, 188: 3-4), Harrison and Orton maintain that the surface of each crosshatch painting is a kind of "field" symbol that depicts qualities of concealment and reserve, although it may be impossible to determine what is being concealed and reserved. Indeed, it can be said that the picture plane itself is an imaginary construct that is implied only when it is marked or covered, and surface paradoxically has no existence independent of its repression. Johns's crosshatch paintings, in sum, relentlessly confront us with a conception of rational two-dimensional space. However, a careful examination of these paintings causes the viewer to realize that the picture plane, when understood as a simple surface, is a convention that is often an inadequate tool for perceiving and analyzing a painting, and a painting is, in a sense, a unit of vision. Although the picture plane is not a safe confine for the representations of our visual desires and powers, our conventional suppositions concerning it must be confronted. We must face the vacuum at the center of our perceptions. In the nineties, Johns is still dealing with this problem. Johns's painting *The Mirror's Edge* (1992), the title of which suggests a mirror's backing, depicts a photograph of the cosmos on the top of a group of pasteups on a drafting table–like surface, as if to say that the limits of reality are our representations of the totality of it. Similarly, our abilities to imagine together incongruent realities will be crucial as it becomes easier to shape disparate information on a single computer screen.

2   Black Warhols: Disco Light, Surveillance, and Portraiture

David Shapiro: Did you like Nixon's tapes?

Andy Warhol: I just think he was right in taping because I think it was fascinating. . . . Well, you meet so many interesting people, when you go out to dinner with like, say, four great poets, and each one is talking to maybe each other, or to the next person; they are all talking together, and then how many times do you wish you had recorded the whole thing as a play?—*Pop Art,* ed. Roland Barthes

Warhol . . . is not the most comfortable figure with whom to sum up the aesthetics of the seventies, but his work embodies the most important questions the decade has raised and defines the terrain which avant-garde art in the eighties has begun to explore. He addressed the question of the materialization of the art experience directly. He refused to mask the question either by valorizing the immediacy of the art experience or by aestheticizing its object. He consistently forced us to ask ourselves just what the object of performance might be.—Henry M. Sayre, *The Object of Performance: The American Avant-Garde Since 1970*

My friend is writing a play.—H. R. Haldeman, *The White House Transcripts*

It is not so much that he is a bad actor (for Nixon in a street crowd is radiant with emotion to reach across the prison pen of his own artificial moves and deadly reputation and show that he is sincere) it is rather that he grew up in the worst set of schools for actors in the world—white gloves and church usher, debating team, Young Republicanism, captive of Ike's forensic style—as an actor, Nixon thinks his work is to signify. So if he wants to show someone that he likes them, he must smile; if he wishes to show disapproval of communism, he frowns; America must be strong, out goes his chest. Prisoner of old habit or unwitting of a new kind of move, he has not come remotely near any kind of modern moves, he would not be ready to see that the young love McCarthy because he plays forever against the line.—Norman Mailer, *Miami and the Siege of Chicago*

It will have a dramatic impact coming from the Bench. . . . [Judge Sirica] may take some dramatic action.—John Dean, *The White House Transcripts*

You'd be a nice President. You wouldn't take up too much space, you'd have a tiny office like you have now. You'd change the law so that you could keep anything anybody gave you while you were in office, because you're a Collector. . . .

Do you realize there's no reason you couldn't be President of the United States? —Brigid Polk to Andy Warhol in Warhol's *The Philosophy of Andy Warhol*

But if you want to know how I really feel,

Get the cameras rolling,

Get the action going.

Baby, you know my love for you is real.

—"More, More, More," Andrea True Connection

I taught him [Nixon] how to cry in a play by John Drinkwater called Bird in Hand. He tried conscientiously at rehearsals, and he'd get a good lump in his throat and that was all. But on the evenings of performance tears just ran right out of his eyes. It was beautifully done, those tears.—Dr. Albert Upton, Nixon's college drama coach, in Earl Mazo and Stephen Hess, *Nixon: A Political Portrait*

I prefer professionals to amateur actors.—Richard Nixon on Army-McCarthy hearings in Bruce Mazlish, *In Search of Nixon: A Psychohistorical Inquiry*

Death is the sanction of everything that the storyteller can tell.—Walter Benjamin, "The Storyteller," in *Illuminations*

During the seventies, Andy Warhol moved his primary site of social engagement from artist bars such as Max's Kansas City to the famed exclusive disco Studio 54. Through its music and celebrities, Studio 54 represented a scene that all Americans could understand, and Warhol, associating himself with a central seventies site, became the most famous and exemplary artist of the seventies after occupying that role in the sixties. Since this comeback, Warhol has been the most influential artist among younger artists from the late seventies to the nineties. This influence did not abate with his death. Such diverse artists as Keith Haring, Peter Halley, and Cindy Sherman have cited him as an immense source of inspiration. After all, no artist better than Warhol seems to account for contemporary America's problematical sense of reality.

This section uses cultural surveillance mechanisms implicit within disco music, two seventies films, a seventies television situation comedy, plays, and Foucault's seventies articulation of the panopticon to situate the unique seventies component of Warhol's work. As Warhol's influence does, the influence of disco continues to increase. Eighties and nineties rap bases itself on seventies dance tracks. Sixties music explored the variegated long-playing album form and strayed from easily danceable rhythms, but disco reinstituted the traditional organizing mechanism of the pop single and, by extending its rhythm, expanded the single to album length.

In the same way that disco did, many seventies artists employed systemic mechanisms. The last section discussed the example of Jasper Johns's cross-hatching, and this section will treat Andy Warhol's portraiture. Other examples of seventies artistic organizing mechanisms include Judy Chicago's feminist dinner-place settings, Dorothea Rockburne's golden triangles, John Newman's squared circles, Cindy Sherman's self-portraits, Linda Francis's slashes, and, in music, Philip Glass's rounds.

The themes of system and surveillance are of course related since surveillance is a systemized series of viewings, listenings, and/or recordings, and this section lays a ground for the next chapter by using Warholian surveillance to begin to grasp Nixonian surveillance. I would like to take a roundabout route to this section's primary subject, Andy Warhol's work of the seventies and how it is differentiated from his work of the sixties, by discussing auditory surveillance in American culture and relating it to disco and larger questions about American identity, family, and notions of death.

Francis Ford Coppola's *The Conversation* opens with San Francisco's Union Square apparently from the gun-sight view of a possible sniper on a tall building's roof. However, we discover that the man is aiming not a rifle but rather a microphone, which can in fact record a couple in a crowd. Auditory surveillance is presented as an omnipresent threat. (The shot places a Watergate-style weapon in a Dallas JFK-assassination setting.) Similarly, Alan J. Pakula's film *Klute* (1971) concerns a woman being auditorially stalked by a corporate official who is trying to make her a suspect in a murder that he has in fact committed. Her tape recorder–obsessed persecutor haunts her with phone calls of his recording of her voice. Terror lies in auditory feedback. In the early seventies, the feedback of auditory surveillance is ominously put into place. *Klute* is made in the early seventies, before the proliferation of cassette tape recorders made audio surveillance ("surveillance" literally means "watching") more universally accessible. *Klute* is on the cusp between a sixties and a seventies orientation toward surveillance. In the early seventies, when manageable cassettes replace more cumbersome, small reel-to-reel portable machines, "surveillance" takes on a more auditory connotation. The notion of predominantly auditory surveillance is frightening because it implies special bureaucratic powers that are out of the control of the common person. Auditory surveillance more easily goes through walls than visual surveillance.

Disco music seems unrelated to these trends, but a closer examination reveals interesting parallels. In terms of the issues of dominant mechanisms and surveillance already discussed in this section, seventies disco music places its entire sound (a more complex and "cluttered" sound than is generally acknowledged) under the purview of a strong beat. Disco anticipates the prevalent use of the electronic beat box and the synthesizer. Although disco is related to its contemporaneous musical genre, punk, because both genres inordinately emphasize their beats, it is these beats that differentiate them.

A major distinguishing characteristic of disco is the equalizing of its four-part beat so that it equally leads one's arms and one's legs. Disco dancing is coherently integrated throughout the movements of all four limbs.[31] Of course, the more jerky punk music, with such characteristic "steps" as the pogo, when compared with disco, would seem to be another indication of seventies ambivalence. However, this ambivalence functions within the framework of a dominating, overall, echoing, indeed seemingly surveillant beat that is facilitated by seventies advances in recording technique. These advances allow the increasing division in the recording of sound tracks and the eventual synchronization of sounds and overtones to resonate with the rhythm track, which becomes increasingly dominant. Whereas the early- and mid-sixties minimalist soul music of James Brown makes one feel in the groove, late-seventies dance music conveys the feeling of a track. Simply put, disco music smoothes and flattens the jerky, funky groove of soul music.

Blondie, a pioneering punk group, becomes commercially successful in the late seventies with a disco sound. Disco music and punk music can be seen as related phenomena and emerge at the same historical moment. Both return to the roots of rock and roll, but to different roots. Disco appropriates a strong rhythm and blues beat, and punk uses an overtly generic rock beat and cacophony to protest a seventies popular music assimilation of rock music. Disco and punk re-process rock traditions into their respective musical pastes. Both genres are reintegrated into the musical mainstream in the early eighties. An emptying out of vibrantly resistant ideology in the eighties removes the alternative edge from much punk music and often replaces it with a dance-music beat. The protest contained in rap music is also related to disco since, from the first commercially successful rap group, the Sugarhill Gang, rappers have sampled (appropriated) disco tracks. Disco, with its mechanisms of the double turntable and disc jockey interruptions and track mixes, provides the technology that makes rap music possible.

On television, *The Brady Bunch* also displays an odd surveillant mechanism that processes seemingly traditional and nontraditional seventies traits through one another, both in the early seventies when the television program first appears and afterwards when it becomes popular in after-school syndication. *The Brady Bunch* surveys the nonconventional through assimilation. An unconventional family is made to seem excessively conventional. Although *The Brady Bunch* makes light of irregularities, unexplained death or family breakup makes possible the program's premise of two families that fit together like jigsaw puzzle pieces. The Bradys are a nuclear family and a nontraditional, extended family in one. Two mirror-image single-parent families form one nuclear family with three sets of siblings/friends/potential lovers. Plots center on the problems of the children, and the parents, although they have "authored" the family, are absent centers who tend to inform the children of what their actions have already demonstrated to them. Alice, the live-in housekeeper, serves as a more functional head tutor for the children. As younger viewers circumnavigated the sixties, they could see the older brothers and sisters whose yearnings they ambivalently associated with and now were free to desire. They could walk lightly on an implicit incest taboo. The Brady family is like Henry James's imperceptibly imperfect golden bowl. An invisible crack runs down its middle. The loss of two parents is implied but never accounted for. How did Mr. and Mrs. Brady's first wife and husband (presumably) die? Why are the male and female children so evenly matched? Sibling incest is powerfully repressed yet hinted at. The perpetual popularity of the program in syndication indicates that young people are nostalgic for the *mere* "hint" of taboo, for a time they never knew when a recently former first lady like Betty Ford would not attain a positive public image as a self-announced recovering alcoholic. On the stage the violation of sibling incest taboos is treated more directly in various Sam Shepard plays. For instance, *Buried Child* (1978) revolves around the suggestion that a mother and her son have birthed a child that ruins their "well established family." The later *Fool for Love* (1983) centers around an initially undiscovered relationship between a half-brother and a half-sister. Their father has seemingly manipulated their incestuous relationship to extend his power. Shepard sets up a mock *Brady Bunch,* in which the tabooed eroticism of the family unit surveys and organizes other relationships.

In the seventies, Foucault calls attention to the assimilation of the panopticon in family and private life. As Foucault's work of the seventies emphasizes panopticonism, Warhol's art of the seventies emphasizes portraiture. The artist calls attention to the making of identity and the individual in relation to self-inscribed surveillant values. In a capitalist society, surveillance and marketing strategies intertwine, and Warhol is the portrait artist of an age saturated with marketing strategies. Appropriately, he is the first major

American artist to treat marketing as an important art form. His work foresaw a prevalent electronic environment indistinguishable from advertising and commodification.

In Andy Warhol's comment about Nixon's tapes that heads this section ("I just think [Nixon] was right in taping because I think it was fascinating"), the artist, unlike President Nixon, explicitly discloses surveillance as a central feature of his work. Given a particular subject or perspective, Warhol conveys a sense of unedited perception. The impressions that register upon a recording apparatus are merely in the range of that recording system. In many of Warhol's silkscreened paintings, interviews, and films, a strong thematic approach provides a center and makes possible an infinitely ad hoc result.

Warhol's approach can be likened to the panopticonism that Foucault says informs modern culture. Freedom, according to Foucault, becomes possible in the modern era because societal surveillance informs and organizes the formation of the individual identity. The concept of individuation "surveys" and authorizes society's constituents. Going perhaps further than Foucault, we can say that an individual, in this era, is reconstructed as a surveillance mechanism—that is, as a mechanism that surveys itself rather than knows itself. Surveillance implies the machine-like ideal of constant, initially unconsidered perception that can be likened, for instance, to the modus operandi of many Warhol films.

I do not intend here to question the reality function of concepts that compare Nixon and Warhol. Rather, I consider them as tropes; as Foucault writes in the late sixties, such concepts compose the "tropological regularities" that the historian detects. As an artist, Warhol publicizes his surveillant proclivities, whereas the Nixon administration keeps these proclivities secret, and then maintains that he merely did what other presidents had done, when he was in fact the first president to tape everything. Other presidents had taped selected conversations. No other president has used a tape recorder so much like Andy Warhol.

Warhol accounts for a surveillance that can be construed to reconstitute identity. Through his surveillance, Warhol attempts to interchange life and theater. His interviews are an ironic mixture of the two. Engaging in a kind of theft of intellectual property, Warhol constantly taped his conversations with his portable cassette player visible. Ostensibly, this incessant taping enabled him to publish his conversations in *Interview* magazine, although he probably simply liked the symbol of producing value through incessant mechanical reproduction. Anything Warhol did could be made valuable, if only as inexpensive magazine copy. For Warhol, the drama of life becomes filler between fashion advertisements. Nixon's chief of staff, H. R. Haldeman, also considers theater as a means to an end. Haldeman suggests that White House counsel John Dean pretend that he is helping a playwright friend as a ruse to obtain useful information from Assistant Attorney General Henry Petersen about his investigation of the Watergate burglary and its cover-up. Similarly, in the same conversation, Dean points out the theatrical excitement that Judge Sirica could generate by acting from the privileged position of the judge's bench. Warhol would presumably be able to note dramatic emphases throughout the tapes that he records. Warhol's remarks about Nixon as a playwright, however, are quintessentially those of the post-sixties Warhol because they valorize those who are already "great" instead of using Warhol superstar status as a means of noting and sometimes inventing greatness. With the seventies, identities are not connected with actual individuals as much as with collectively invested stances.

Warhol's art comes out of a sixties ambivalence to the nature of identity and identity crises. These issues permeated the era. For instance, Betty Friedan urged women to accept identity crises—to do without the assurance of knowing who they were. She called on women to accept new "frontiers" of identity by moving out of a media-induced feminine mystique. The path to "reality" lies through an interruption of perceived reality. Friedan, like Foucault, preceded calls to positive identity crises by such thinkers as Norman O. Brown and R. D. Laing. Although the identity crisis is an invention of the forties and the fifties, its positive ramifications are institutionalized in the sixties. Kurt Vonnegut's *Slaughterhouse Five* (1968) successfully portrays an apparently delusional and psychotic experience as positive. We can also compare Allen Ginsberg's fifties *Howl* collection to his *Kaddish* of the early sixties. Ginsberg's drug poems in the latter volume are not about drugs so much as a call for new identity. In the sixties, drugs are applied to a beneficial sense of identity loss.

The early sixties see something like the splitting of the "atom of the individual" and individual family as the site on which society can be organized. Foucault's *Madness and Civilization* (1961) begins a career-long process of "denaturalizing" the modern institution of the individual by historicizing notions of rationality, identity, and knowledge. Similarly, we see in the works of artists such as Andy Warhol and Sylvia Plath acceptance of a loss of identity that, in the fifties, would tend to be formulated as angst associated with "alienation" and "identity problems." Generally speaking, the early sixties is a focal point for these fifties fears—even existentialist works of the forties and fifties, in categorizing the individual as inherently undefined, emphasize the individual's inability to avoid self-definition. In the early sixties, American society pulls together a last great if nervous Cold War consensus of identity that dissipates throughout the middle and late sixties. A 1967 film like Mike Nichols's *The Graduate*, based on a fifties novel, draws a fine line between self-definition as a positive and a negative value. Dustin Hoffman's character Benjamin invests himself in the romantic ideal of self-definition through desire; and yet the film's final dual close-up of him and Katherine Ross's Elaine casts Benjamin as something of a late-modern Don Quixote by paralleling their failure of communication with the soundtrack's playing of Simon and Garfunkel's "Sound of Silence." Stanley Kubrick's *2001* (1968) also questions the project of self-definition and can be considered to be a crease between the mid- and late sixties. In *2001*, identity takes the form of a paranoid computer. When the computer is, against its will, unplugged, the film's narrative is opened to the post-identity phantasmagoric visions that Dave, the lone surviving astronaut, experiences in a psychic version of Jupiter toward which the Earth's technology seems to have been evolving since apes first grasped bones within the purview of an extraterrestrial black monolith.

In *Madness and Civilization* (1961), Foucault lauds madness as an ambiguous experience of the ongoing presence of death and "the nothingness of existence." In the middle and late sixties the loss of identity finally evolves into a positive value. "It is not schizophrenia," says Norman O. Brown, echoing *Madness and Civilization*, "but normality that is split-minded; in schizophrenia the false boundaries are disintegrating."[32] Foucault reclaims madness as a vital societal resource. As I demonstrate, Warhol similarly integrates cultural commonplaces into consciousness, along with their deathlike limits or edges.

Warhol's cool early-sixties persona, along with his professed desire to forego the messiness of ordinary human emotions, anticipated more aggressive late-sixties postulations of the good to be found in the loss of identity. Parallels can also be drawn between the early-sixties demeanors of Warhol and Foucault. "The man of madness and the man of reason," Foucault says in *Madness and Civilization*, "are not yet disjunct."

In the early seventies (the waves of micro-periods that I posit are never uniform and overlap), definition and the trope of reality reassert themselves in the guise of activism. Black power serves as a prototype for various other "powers" that in effect stress the reality and power of "minority" group identities. Through these delimitations (and marginalizations) of identity, sixties activism gives way to the minority politics of the seventies.

A Nixonian stroke of brilliance in the late sixties and early seventies knits loosely aligned blue- and white-collar groups into a dominant identification, "the silent majority." In a sense, this Nixonian fame game—ostensibly giving characteristic stance and pose, a sort of portraiture to the "forgotten American"—can be likened, as we shall soon see, to the Warholian project of granting fame to the "dead" identities who join the artist's project. This section explores surveillance as an organizing mechanism and a narrative technique in various aspects of the work of Andy Warhol. The trope of unfiltered, unedited observation can be said to shape Warhol's early films and characteristic artworks. This mode of observation displays a characteristically American predilection for the Emersonian transparent eyeball, in which ostensibly unmediated sensibility and perception register open-ended aesthetic impressions. This tendency leads to Warhol's aesthetic strategy and to such distinctively American phenomena as C-SPAN.

Interestingly, Foucault's *Madness and Civilization,* appearing in the same historical moment as Warhol's first photographic silkscreens, defines madness, which Foucault believes permeates everyday living, as a constant probing of the death to be found in life. The artist's use of photographs represents a death-like effacement of Warhol's persona as a famed commercial draftsman. More importantly, though, Warhol appeals to the genre of portraiture—probably doing more than any other mid- or late-twentieth-century painter to revive that genre—as an instrument that works in a converse relation to madness, as Foucault characterizes it. Whereas madness can be said to work as a death in life, portraiture functions as the life—the remembered part—to be found in a person's death. Thus the subjects of Warhol's photographic portraits never seem quite alive, and his use of the skull as a subject is oddly apt (illustration 23). As Warhol's 1978 *Self-Portrait with Skull* so dramatically indicates, his subjects appear recognizable and even at times unique, but they rarely seem to suggest the "living, breathing person" that portrait painters usually depict. Indeed, Warhol's quintessential portrait sequences are, perhaps, his skull series and his Marilyn motif, which, unlike many of his other works, arise from Warhol's sole inspiration, not from suggestions made by friends or associates.

In the summer of 1962, on hearing of the death of Marilyn Monroe, Warhol used the photographic silkscreening process on a publicity photograph of Monroe that he perhaps appropriated from a newspaper. He had been less suc-

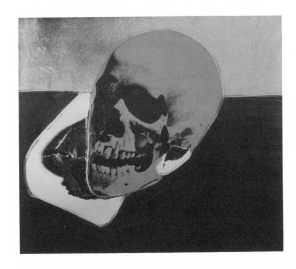

23. Andy Warhol, *Skull,*
1976, © 1999 Andy
Warhol Foundation for
the Visual Arts/ ARS,
New York, NY

cessfully experimenting with this process, using photographs of Troy Donahue
and Elvis Presley. He began the skull series when he urged his New York art
co-workers to help him photograph a skull that he purchased on a shopping
spree in Europe. Of his countless idiosyncratic purchases, the skull is one of
the few that appear in his art.

As Robert Rosenblum observes, a fascinating exception to the artist's usual
practice, which rigorously squeezes the sense of possible animation and life
from his portrait subjects,[33] is Warhol's 1974 portrait of his mother. In *Julia
Warhola* (illustration 24), Warhol suggests what Rosenblum calls "ghostly fade-
outs"[34] that intimate something below the painterly surface. For the most part,
however, Warhol's portrait art is one of the hunt, the kill, and the mounting.

Invariably, Warhol shapes his subjects by isolating them—that is, by depriving
them of context and what we normally construe as individuality. He establishes a one-to-one relationship between a recording of phenomena and a
given phenomenological field. In his films, recording is an extremely inclusive
mechanism. Whether it be the Empire State Building, John Giorno sleeping,
or a group of actors improvising, whatever happens within a given context at-
tains a deathly authorization through Warhol's surveillance. Like Nixon with
his tapes, Warhol thinks of his films as marketable commodities. However, the
surveillance work of both figures concerns power. Nixon believes his tapes
will enable him to read closely his part in his transactions and, perhaps more
importantly, the covert and overt plans of his opponents and allies. In addi-

24. Andy Warhol, *Portrait of Julia Warhola*, 1974, © 1999 Andy Warhol Foundation for the Visual Arts/ ARS, New York, NY

tion, Nixon operates his presidency on the assumption that for problems to be solved they must be tailored, processed, and possessed by his presidential authority. Similarly, Warhol does much to stake out his own turf within New York's underground, and, in a sense, creates that "underground," or, at any rate, seeks to do so by marketing a personal version of it. Warhol's public voyeurism legitimates the underground that he organizes. Warhol's and Nixon's comebacks in the seventies, grounded in self-legitimizing surveillance operations that may be said to camouflage an inner lack of coherency, reflects a seventies culture desperately seeking outer supports for its certitudes before simply asserting them in the eighties.

Similarly, Warhol's paintings appear as a narrative of "interest" that interfaces with notions of authorization and currency. Paintings that he did as "art" — meaning that they were not commissioned portraits in which the subjects themselves set off their own surveillance and recording — affirm and reinforce our culture's evaluation of and interest in the subjects of the paintings. (Warhol, in the seventies, also did commissioned professional series, such as one of outstanding sports figures including Dorothy Hamill, O. J. Simpson, Tom Seaver, and Muhammad Ali [illustration 25].) However, this is accomplished through the leveling of his subjects into a general cultural "paste," or what John Ashbery calls a "cold . . . syrupy pageant."

Marilyn, the inaugural work in this enterprise, brings to the pageant a seemingly "pasted on," astonishingly flat, and unanchored image of the film star—

a photographic image that is all the more two-dimensional because its flatness indicates yet engulfs effects of depth in Monroe's face and hair. Warhol
later emphasizes this two-dimensional iconographic quality by echoing Kasimir Malevich. Malevich sought to exhibit his Suprematist paintings as if they
were "single bare and frameless icon[s],"[35] and he hung his works high on the
wall at a sharp angle from the bottom to the top of the canvas, as a Russian
Orthodox family would hang an icon. A practicing Catholic of Eastern European (Slovak) descent, Warhol likens his canvas to such an icon in his 1962
Gold Marilyn, which displays a small version of his Marilyn image centered in
the upper part of the canvas. Notably, Betty Friedan's *The Feminine Mystique*
also appears in 1962, and Friedan calls attention to the mystifying cosmetic
front that women must hide behind, which is also of course a kind of rigid
iconic mechanism.

Peter Brooks defines "narrative" as "the play of desire in time."[36] In this regard, it can be said that Warhol creates a negative narrative of our times in
the sense that his work portrays the play of death in time, or, I am tempted
to say, the play of time in death. One recalls Foucault's stated preference for
what he calls "negative work," work that dematerializes its subjects.

In the mid-seventies, with *The Philosophy of Andy Warhol (from A to B and
Back Again),* Warhol affirms the omnipresence of surveillance in his work in a

25. Andy Warhol,
Mohammad Ali, 1977,
© 1999 Andy Warhol
Foundation for the
Visual Arts/ ARS, New
York, NY

manner that might be applied to Nixon's attitudes toward recording, surveillance, and "problems":

> I didn't get married until 1964 when I got my first tape recorder. My wife. My tape recorder and I have been married for ten years now. When I say "we," I mean my tape recorder and me. A lot of people don't understand that.
>
> The acquisition of my tape recorder really finished whatever emotional life I might have had, but I was glad to see it go. Nothing was ever a problem again, because a problem just meant a good tape, and when a problem transforms itself into a good tape it's not a problem anymore. An interesting problem was an interesting tape. Everyone knew that and performed for the tape. You couldn't tell which problems were real and which problems were exaggerated for the tape. Better yet, the people telling you the problem couldn't decide any more if they were having the problems or if they were just performing.
>
> During the sixties, I think, people forgot what emotions were supposed to be. And I don't think they've ever remembered. I think that once you see emotions from a certain angle you can never think of them as real again. That's what more or less has happened to me.[37]

Warhol's mid-seventies reading of the sixties defies commonplace views of that era as emotively expansive and romantic. Of course, during the sixties, many people considered Warhol irrelevant. Indeed, Warhol's remarks here justify his own unemotional persona by linking it to a revised understanding of the chief effects of the sixties. He implies that the era caused people to forget "what emotions were supposed to be" and to understand that they are not "real." Thus, "people," it would seem, free themselves from socially appropriate feelings through the many mediating mechanisms that they come into contact with and equate with their emotional lives. It becomes no longer possible to treat emotions as participants in unmediated experience of a "real" external world. By the seventies' end, it is commonplace for phone calls to be mediated through the taping mechanism of the answering machine.

Warhol's remoteness sets the stage for presenting the seventies as a deconstruction of the sixties. The accumulated epistemic enthusiasm of the sixties intertwines itself with McLuhanesque explanations of a culturally engulfing media explosion. But, as McLuhan was aware, that enthusiasm is subverted by the unraveling of the traditional grounds and customary rationales for individual desire and emotion. The unraveling of individual desire and emotion also subverts identity. Perhaps Nixon cannot destroy damaging tapes because he identifies with them in an un-Warholian manner. If Warhol loved his recorder, he was cooler about its tapes.

As a portrait painter, Warhol isolates his subjects in a classical manner that suggests still, timeless moments. Yet the identities of his subjects are reconfigured into Warhol's celebrity-making process, which anyone can enter. Warhol's work presents the psychological equivalent of the anti-illusionistic flatness that dominates the art world before him. Psychological and formal issues merge in Warhol's paintings. Warhol places the individual on the neutrally charged pictorial field characteristic of works by such dissimilar painters as Barnett Newman, Franz Kline, and Jasper Johns.

As a Warhol precursor, Johns builds on the modernist awareness, acutely felt by the abstract expressionists, that backgrounds and foregrounds can always be imagined as reversed. Johns paints uncontextualized semiotic images, images that do not telegraph a psychological foreground and background. However, the signs that Johns paints are never entirely arbitrary. Obviously, an encaustic painting of a national flag other than the stars and stripes would not have had as dramatic an effect because what seemed so startling was the placement of such a loaded sign in an unfocused field. What one would expect to be foreground became shockingly backgrounded, clearing a space in which the subjects of art appear as arbitrary constructs. Art, like identity, is aggressively emptied of content.

Warhol eventually codifies this reversibility and neutrality of field, after extending his silkscreen techniques to such subjects as wallpaper, giant Brillo boxes, and silver pillows. If meticulously articulated brushwork is an essential feature of much of Johns's most important paintings, the deletion of pencil and brush from the essential working is equally crucial to Warhol. It simplifies his portrait-making, enabling him to crank out portraits in a uniform fashion that stamps the quality of "givenness" and, by extension, celebrityhood, on anyone who wishes to commission a Warhol portrait.

More than individual works, Warhol creates a validating system, much as seventies phenomena such as pet rocks highlight the power of identifying and naming within a given context. In the seventies, this is accompanied by an increased use of logos and celebrity endorsements. In the eighties, this kind of selectivity is largely assimilated and underlies the lists and time-marking jokes of *Late Night with David Letterman*. Note that guests on the Letterman show rarely meet one another and mingle, as they did on the *Tonight Show* with Johnny Carson. Discreteness and categorization are a hallmark of the show. That these categories are often ridiculously inconsequential highlights their existence as empty categories, as categories qua categories. One thinks of the absurdities of some of the names on the Nixon administration's "enemies lists" revealed by John Dean's Senate testimony in 1973. In what sense could Joe Namath be Nixon's enemy? Some of those on Nixon's enemies lists do seem like plausible opponents of the president's political policies. Other names, however, would seem more appropriate on a David Letterman "Top Ten Nixon Enemies" list—unless, of course, we understand this list in terms of Nixon's own formulations concerning ideological state apparatuses. Even using this rationale, however, Nixon would seem to be too intently trying to author and micro-manage the culture. (In chapter 6, the "Perilous Transcriptions" section deals with this Nixonian tack and discusses Nixon's tape transcriptions, while the "Eighteen and a Half Minutes behind the Mirror" section discusses uncanny similarities between Warhol's and Nixon's surveillance mechanisms.) Later Nixon administration explanations that the list was merely of people who might embarrass the president if invited to the White House seem unlikely when considering names like Joe Namath. (Did he donate money to the Democrats?) It was more likely a handicraft of paranoia and grist for IRS harassment, as indicated by tape transcripts released in 1997, in which Nixon demands a list of Jewish contributors to Democratic presidential candidates for the IRS to "frankly persecute." Indeed, Dean presented this list, with Nixon's instructions, to IRS chief Johnnie M. Walker, who claims not to have acted on it.

Warhol's validating system reminds one of the stereotypical "Wanted" poster format. Warhol's ironies bring celebrityhood to the breaking point of credibility, meaning that everyone can be not only a star but also a superstar. He transmutes celebrityhood into a paradoxically open condition that later requires him to "close the club." Requisite to this manufacturing of "fame" is the implication that it arises from an affectless, enabling void, an implication which of course emanates from the characteristic Warholian look. Another Warholian innovation, the unexpressively manipulated multiple image, asserts the validating powers of Warhol's process (see, for example, *Still Life*, [1976], illustration 26) Warholian images are givens not because they refer to an accepted frame of reference but because they are "iconized" by their inclusion in the Warholian project. In a sense, therefore, Warhol takes more than he gives. His entire project is a black hole, of sorts, that disables its subjects.

Appropriately, Warhol's disaster and electric chair works follow soon after his celebrity images. Indeed, the most successful of his first celebrity portraits

26. Andy Warhol, *Still Life*, 1976, © 1999 Andy Warhol Foundation for the Visual Arts/ ARS, New York, NY

are of Jackie Kennedy and Marilyn Monroe. The "icon" of the electric chair, produced after Warhol's disaster pieces, stresses an isolation perfected in death. Celebrityhood becomes a coded inversion of death, recalling Sylvia Plath's contemporaneous associations of her identity with a self-affirming death "drive." For instance, the speaker of Plath's "Ariel" says, "I / Am the arrow / The dew that flies / Suicidal, at one with the drive" (239, lines 26–27; 240, lines 1–2). Similarly, in Plath's "Breck-Plage," death announces itself as a reproducible icon when a funeral "date / Engrav[es] itself in silver with marvelous calm" (199, lines 3–4).[38] Plath's evocation of deathly calm in silver makes one consider the grave lightness of death as a connotation at play in the paradoxical lightness of Warhol's silver pillows of the sixties. Plath's "The Night Dances" speaks of "the black amnesias of heaven" (250: 15). In the sixties, Stephen Hawking relates the concept of black holes to his account of the beginning of the universe. If matter can collapse, it can also expand. Death and expansion are thus related in a manner that is easily associated with the face of sixties culture at large and particularly with the works of writers and artists like Foucault, Warhol, and Plath.

Warhol, by positing "slots" for capturing and "demassing" identity, also posits a universe of dizzyingly undifferentiated inclusion. Warhol prefigures the prevalent seventies metaphor of the nuclear meltdown. In general, his work's relationship to the Cold War metaphor of nuclear catastrophe seems obvious. Perhaps more significantly, Warhol's work echoes early modernist mechanisms: the panopticon, the democratizing of the modern state, the on-going flattening of the picture plane, and the development of landscaped countryside cemeteries are all prototypically modernist late-eighteenth- and early-nineteenth-century occurrences that Warhol plays on to recapitulate, parody, and close modernism. Warhol also touches on the nineteenth century and transcendental casting of death as a liminal experience that can plumb the depths of life. We may note, for instance, Lincoln's appeal to "the mystic cords of memory." Lincoln's stripped down, simply associative prose style par-allels Warhol's distinctive mode of portraiture. Indeed, the Civil War forms the mechanism of the Union in a manner that is understood by Americans today. The Union is a kind of free-for-all, a panoptic association of all Americans that bypasses the authority of states and makes possible the unity of Ameri-can culture that fosters Warhol's art. Ideally, notes Warhol, American culture enforces the value of equality and normalcy. Ironically, he presents a case for the paradoxical supremacy of the normal:

> What's great about this country is that America started the tradition where the richest consumers buy essentially the same thing as the poor-est. You can be watching TV and see Coca-Cola, and you know that the President drinks Coke, Liz Taylor drinks Coke, and just think, you can drink Coke, too. A Coke is a Coke and no amount of money can get you a better Coke than the bum on the corner is drinking. All the Cokes are the same and all the Cokes are good. Liz Taylor knows it, the President knows it, the bum knows it, and you know it.
>
> In Europe, the royalty and the aristocracy used to eat a lot better than the peasants—they weren't eating the same thing at all. It was either par-tridge or porridge, and each class stuck to its own food. But when Queen Elizabeth came here and President Eisenhower bought her a hot dog I'm sure he felt confident that she couldn't have had delivered to Buckingham Palace a better hot dog than that one he bought her for maybe twenty cents at the ballpark. Because there is no better hot dog than a ballpark hot dog. She could get one for twenty cents and so could anybody else.
>
> Sometimes you fantasize that people who are really up-there and rich

and living it up have something you don't have, that their things must be better than your things because they have more money than you. But they drink the same Cokes and eat the same hot dogs and wear the same ILGWU clothes and see the same TV shows and the same movies. Rich people can't see a sillier version of *Truth or Consequences,* or a scarier version of *The Exorcist.* You can get just as revolted as they can—you can have the same nightmares. All of this is really American.

The idea of America is so wonderful because the more equal something is, the more American it is.[39]

Like Whitman, but with more irony, Warhol brings the president and royalty to the level of everyman. The sense of a mass-produced perfectibility produces a prevailing commodity fetishism for which there is no credible alternative. Hence, there is no danger of losing these commodities, and they paradoxically need not be fetishized. Although he is writing/speaking in the seventies, Warhol is here referring to the now distinctively sixties mind-set of unfocused commodity fetishism wherein commodities outside the conventional realm of commodity hierarchy, such as drugs and records, could be said to have been fetishized. Interestingly, Warhol clears a path for a new era of commodity hierarchy based more on category qua category than on value. For example, blue jeans are recategorized into an expensive seventies fashion statement (designer jeans), whereas in the sixties they were an inexpensive non–fashion statement.

In the seventies, when black holes are discovered not to be perfect voids but rather to emit specters of energy from divided particles, the Warholian universe slows down. Warhol's personal filmic experiments cease as he turns filmmaking duties over to the more commercially and normatively narrative-minded Paul Morrissey. Warhol's body of portraits becomes more predictably organized around art-world notoriety, fame, and commissions. Nonetheless, Warhol's quintessential portrait series of the seventies is his *Mao* series (see illustration 27). Initiated in the wake of Nixon's first trip to China, this series, as well as Warhol's subsequent hammer-and-sickle works, suggests that nothing exists outside the commodities market bespoken in Warhol's art. Commodifying fame, the Mao portraits imply that fame is now possible, for most of us, only through the oblique representation of a famous "people's person."

Whereas Warhol used Mao to connote the onslaught of capitalism, DeLillo's *Mao II* (1991) uses Warhol's portraits of Mao more overtly to predict the cor-

27. Andy Warhol, *Mao,*
1973, © 1999 Andy
Warhol Foundation for
the Visual Arts/ ARS,
New York, NY

porate enslavement of cooperative slaves. *Mao II* posits a reality of crowd and
work organization that lacks a mechanism for questioning reality, a reality in
which "Mao II" and "Coke II" are equally viable. There can be no meaningful
questions or choices because reality is as seemingly lifeless as the subjects
of Warhol's portraits. Images seem to have driven verbal discourse out of circulation. And yet perhaps Warhol was more intuitive, as indeed is the text
of *Mao II,* than the overt message of *Mao II.* The sophistication with which
the terrorists and other characters in *Mao II* communicate with images undermines DeLillo's apparent premise. By this same "anti-image" logic, John Kennedy could be deemed more dishonest than Nixon, because he communicated
more effectively through images. However, images often mislead less than verbal rhetoric. For instance, the civil rights movement generated valuable and
telling images about the fifties and sixties. Indeed, photographs and images
of Vietnam are often said to have discredited government rhetoric about the
war. In fact, *Mao II* calls into question not so much the authority of the image
as the authority of the logo—the word cemented into image, the corporate
answer to the governmental seal. Spurred by Nixon's success in making China
fashionable, Warhol satirically appropriated the "logo" cover photograph of

Quotations from Chairman Mao, placing an image of the wisdom of a planned economy within the marketplace. Warhol's Mao portraits were technical innovations for the artist, who painted a wash of colors on his canvases before imprinting Mao's silkscreened image on them, and then often applied more paint upon the already silkscreened canvases. Warhol demonstrated the complicated, unnaturalized environments in which logos can be generated and received. Soon logo T-shirts would be a seventies commonplace and one of the decade's legacies. The market was everywhere. We desired to serve corporations because that is what seemed most real and fulfilling. We willingly became walking sandwich boards. Warhol, who anticipated this massive dissemination of logos, commented about it in the eighties. *Moonwalk* (1987), probably Warhol's last work, tantalizingly plays upon a quintessential logo of sixties buoyancy—a human's first walk on the moon, the logo that became a part of MTV's first memorable logo presentation. Warhol's last print shows the sixties fantasy made literal as it was quoted in the eighties to convey the sense of a nostalgia for a future apparently denied to youth in the eighties. Social progress and regression are on the same loop.

In the seventies, beginning with the Mao portraits, Warhol applied his silkscreens to canvases that he had already dashed with paint, and the stark and often primary quality of his work yielded to more subtle, richer, or atmospheric effects. For instance, Warhol maintained that his *Shadow* series (1978; illustration 28), eighty-three sixty-six-inch-by-fifty-two-inch canvases exhibited contiguously around the perimeters of the two rooms of the Heiner Friedrich Gallery in Soho, New York, functioned to give the gallery space a Studio 54–like disco atmosphere. The flickering colors of the repeated images, as they are displayed at the Andy Warhol Museum in Pittsburgh, indeed bring strobe lights to mind. The repeated perpendicular negative spaces of the veritably abstract shadow image shimmer with many loud, clear pastel colors. Feedback, of a kind, produces a sense of abstraction, although the image is based on a realistic if blurred photograph of a shadow in a corner of Warhol's Factory.

In Warhol's late-seventies *Oxidations* series, abstraction comments succinctly on artistic form and process. *Oxidations* was produced by Warhol and his friends urinating on copper plates so as eventually to produce green marks, traces, and splotches, on the copper. This is Warhol's ode to self-expression and abstract expressionist drip painting. Whereas in the sixties, on the advice of Emile de Antonio, he took the drips out of his painting, the seventies *Oxidations* series is nothing but drips. Warhol demonstrates capitalist surplus value

28. Andy Warhol,
Shadow, 1978, © 1999
Andy Warhol Founda-
tion for the Visual Arts/
ARS, New York, NY

as aesthetic alchemy with the ecologically minded recycling of urine. This is
reminiscent of Paul Morrissey's film *Trash* (1970), produced by Warhol (Morrissey adapts Warhol's improvisatory directorial techniques to a more commercial
forum). In *Trash,* the Holly Woodlawn character recycles trash and sells it. She
becomes her art. However, she longs for the "respectability" of "welfare" in
order to inscribe herself within the symbolic order of the already disintegrating Great Society. A social worker rejects her "welfare application" because she
will not give him her recycled, glittering high-heeled shoes, which resemble
Warhol's shoe drawings. To do so would be to work for the social worker and
not for herself. The social worker calls her trash. She is not "entitled" to welfare and official, non-trash status, as she thought she was. Official reality is
beginning to be privatized, and it is shrinking.

The succession of Warhol's portrait subjects heralded the rise of cable television in the seventies and the eighties. Warhol often mentioned his affinity
for television, as if to indicate his fondness for an accessible common denomi-
nator. And yet, with cable and pay television, television was no longer equally
accessible to nearly everyone. The viewer had to choose television programs,

like artworks, according to their affordability. Interestingly, the word "affordable" first came into American usage during the seventies.

In the late seventies, Warhol did a series of *Gems* silkscreens, whereas in the sixties he did dollar bill paintings, drawings, and silkscreens—money, as Marshall McLuhan said, being the poor man's credit card. Similarly, there is no seventies or eighties Warhol equivalent to *Crowd* (1963), which depicts a sea of heads and torsos. Whereas Warhol defined "the Pop idea" of the sixties as the credo that "anybody could do anything," entry into his pop portrait gallery in the seventies was by privilege only. This closure was all the better for the Warhol market. Indeed, this market anticipated the coming eighties, when "junk bonds" became acceptable leverage for economic clout and stocks were valued more as collectable commodities than as a source of capital for investment.

Six

Politics in the Watergate Era

1 The Ever New Nixon

The typewriters are always the key. We built one in the Hiss case.
—Richard Nixon to Charles Colson, as quoted by John Dean

A few days after I sent the first draft of this manuscript to its publisher, Richard Nixon died. The nation's search for a coherent attitude toward his death brought to life many of this book's findings about the seventies. In general, the press and media had difficulty recalling the specifics of Nixon's presidency and the seventies. They recalled two Nixons, and the more favorable Nixon often seemed the real one. A bloated sense of Nixon's foreign and domestic accomplishments seemed to overshadow the assumed crimes of his presidency, and the latter were in no way related to the nation's decline. America's embrace of Nixon in his death demonstrated how far Nixon, like a political Walt Whitman, had seeped into our political environment. Corruption not only seemed like the norm, it seemed like the only alternative, the only way to govern. Political taint was unavoidable because there was no longer a credible common good to believe that politicians would work for. Americans were virtually united in this "reality." There was not that much between us and Nixon. To understand Nixon is to understand how the seventies are still with us, how we are still "surveyed" by it.

Nixon problematized and recodified our notions of American unity. As he professed in his 1968 presidential campaign, Nixon was trying to unite America. When he resigned, with Americans virtually united in their distaste for the president, the United States was a markedly more conservative nation than when Nixon assumed the presidency. He had presided over and prefigured a quiet but stunning shift in the political landscape. The American electoral process, ruptured by Robert Kennedy's 1968 assassination, recycled the "dead in the profession" former vice president from the seemingly antiquated fifties, and Nixon has since become one of the people Americans most associate with the seventies. More than anyone else, Nixon set the terms for the seventies, and its love-hate relationships with the fifties and sixties. The seventies, in turn, has set the terms for our culture ever since. We are participating in the drawn-out play of the post-sixties. History has the feel of a hit single remixed into an extended disco dance track.

In the seventies, Americans sought both presidential authority and freedom from the state, both a nostalgia for certainties beyond question and a yearning for governmental innovation. They ambivalently welcomed, embraced, and then rejected the presidencies of Richard Nixon, Gerald Ford, and Jimmy Carter. However, in the eighties, Ronald Reagan successfully projected a field of veritable, ideological reality, which helped him to survive economic dips, the Iran-Contra affair, and myriad scandals. Reagan realized Nixon's dream—a public that allowed itself to be diverted. Nixon tried to keep his war efforts a virtual secret from Americans (if not from the Vietnamese and Cambodians), trying to win the war while the public's attention was turned from it.

In 1968, Nixon became the first presidential candidate of a major political party to run on a law-and-order platform. "Law and order," which evoked support for the war, was more important than public awareness. H. R. Haldeman writes about one of Nixon's "long philosophical thing[s]," reasoning away the value of higher education:

> In this period of our history, the leaders and the educated class are decadent. Whenever you ask for patriotic support, they all run away. The college types, the professors, the elite, etc. So he [Nixon] concludes the more a person is educated, he becomes brighter in the head and weaker in the spine. When you have to call on the nation to be strong, on such things as drugs, crime, defense, the educated people and the leader class no longer has any character, and you can't count on them. We can only turn for support to the noneducated people.[1]

It is difficult to tell whether Nixon considered Haldeman and himself educated.

On Nixon's death, news commentators maintained that he had a dual nature, saying that he did both good and bad things. Indeed, Americans of all kinds are ambivalent toward Nixon because they look back longingly on the unity that a president embodies. However, most Americans did not personally like Nixon and sensed that he abused his presidential powers.

Although Nixon's career was divisive, it was based on a politically expedient duality. He was a Republican to the right of the eastern Republican establishment who was nevertheless acceptable to it at the 1952 Republican convention. As a vice president, Nixon became known as a moderate. In 1968, his courting of Goldwater Republicans earned him some conservative support. However, as president, Nixon sought a middle ground. He rarely vetoed legislation, and he avoided open confrontation with the Democratic Congress. Nixon toyed with vetoing congressional measures such as lowering the voting age to eighteen but, in the end, he chose the public relations value of appearing progressive. As Jeb Magruder recalled:

> Some advisors had urged a veto, lest he enfranchise the voters who would defeat him in 1972. I wrote a memo urging that he sign the bill. I knew that the young voters traditionally don't vote in significant numbers, and I thought the positive impact of the President's signing the bill would offset the supposedly liberal leanings of the young.[2]

Nixon also could foresee that youth would be politically volatile, seeing the new electorate as a kind of blank slate. For Nixon, it was not a wave of the future but rather supremely manipulable:

> If the Youth for Nixon groups are holding rallies and receptions and registration drives, these activities become the "in" thing to do and attract activity by more and more young people. You get the young people involved through peer-group pressure, then you direct their enthusiasm.[3]

In a sense, Nixon was also something of an ideological blank slate. His blankness helped him feel out and hit upon unexpected public relations coups. For instance, he noted that his administration's efforts on behalf of a negative income tax in the form of the Family Assistance Act was one of the few administration efforts receiving positive press coverage. He told Haldeman and others to back it to the hilt unless it had a chance of passing the Senate, in which case they should drop their efforts so as not to offend conservative Republicans. According to Haldeman, and consistent with appearances at the time, Nixon told his supporters, after his welfare reform bill had been passed virtually intact by the House: "Be sure it's killed by Democrats and that we make big play for it, but don't let it pass, can't afford it."[4] (Nixon *blamed conservative Democrats* for the defeat.) Similarly, it has been jokingly suggested that Nixon dropped wage and price controls when he feared they were working. Nixon often admonished his staff that it would not be judged on how "good" it was but on how good it seemed. Nixon thus sought to tinker with the perception of his administration through such acts as trying to fix the government's unemployment figures.

Nixon's domestic policies were confused and half-hearted. I have noted his ambivalent support for the Family Assistance Plan. Similarly, when environmental legislation was passed during the Nixon years, Nixon promoted policies that tended to make these laws more difficult to enforce. While Nixon supported the Equal Rights Amendment, he fostered a backlash against "women's liberation" by aligning himself with groups that opposed women's reproductive rights and other women's advances. If Nixon's administration devised affirmative action in some realms of federal job contracting, he made employment opportunity statutes more difficult to enforce. In short, very few of Nixon's progressive domestic initiatives, such as national health care, were enacted.

Affirmative action as we now know it was a compromise that the Nixon administration concocted between civil rights advocates and labor unions. The 23 September 1969 "Philadelphia Plan," largely devised by Assistant Secretary of Labor Arthur Fletcher, was the first formulation of governmental affirmative action in job contracting. Contractors were required to hire a specified number of black workers in federally funded projects. As innovative as this plan was, its need was largely brought about by the Nixon administration's reluctance to administer the Model Cities Program of 1966 through the Office of Federal Contract Compliance. After the 1972 election, Nixon dismantled the Office of Economic Opportunity and, through it, Johnson's War on Poverty. The Jobs Corps moved to the Department of Labor, and Head Start to the Department of Health, Education, and Welfare. Funds were not allocated. Community and legal services were discontinued. Court-mandated school integration and enhancement programs such as busing were stalled and shelved. In addition, the block grants doled out through revenue sharing in Nixon's prophetic (in terms, for instance, of the 1996 welfare bill) New Federalism gave more power to entrenched state and local governments. Since the Philadelphia Plan was intended to appease George Meany of the AFL-CIO—although Meany did not ultimately support it—its enforcement provisions were weak. Perhaps more importantly, the plan unwittingly enabled anti–civil rights forces to take on an air of moral credibility that the Supreme Court eventually signed off on in 1995, and, before that, ambiguously endorsed in the 1978 Bakke decision.

Early in Nixon's first administration, Haldeman commented in his diary:

> Still a stir about Domestic Program. Not organized right yet. Burns and
> Moynihan both feel strongly that P[resident] not putting enough time or
> attention on this and that nothing will be settled until he does. I think
> they're right. This morning he flatly rejected Head Start and Job Corps
> proposals without even really reading them. Just wants them changed—
> or preferably abolished.[5]

Nixon had fostered an era of "benign neglect" more far-reaching than Patrick
Moynihan's original use of the term, in connection with a strategy to cool
down racial rhetoric. Moynihan, who used the phrase in a memo to Nixon, had
a sense of his audience. We are, of course, still living in this era of neglect.
But the neglect need no longer be described as benign, and the most heartless
neglect sets the terms for practical political discourse. The subsequent waste
of human resources and the call for further neglect to accommodate a shrinking economic pie create a vicious cycle. As expectations of the government
shrink, so does social justice. Governmental deregulation had its seeds in the
Nixon administration, blossomed in the Carter years when bank, airline, and
trucking deregulations were enacted, and bore fruit in the eighties with the
savings and loan scandals.

If Johnson brought the credibility gap into prominence and consciousness,
Nixon gave expression to that gap as eighteen and a half minutes of tantalizing if frustrating static. He enabled us to hear and read into the gap and
the presidency what we wished. If Johnson surveyed a counterculture that
he could not begin to understand, Nixon engaged in a life and death battle
with that counterculture and surveyed it to that end. If Johnson took his
efforts in the Vietnam War personally, tried to defend the war to the American public, and was haunted by increased opposition to it, Nixon privatized
it, in that he believed the war virtually to be no one's business but his and his
administration's, was furious and vindictive about unauthorized disclosure of
information about it, and considered opposition to it a personal insult. Nixon,
to cite two crucial examples, saw Daniel Ellsberg's leaking of the Pentagon
Papers (Nixon felt the information to be his administration's even if it told
of Democratic administrations) and Seymour Hersch's disclosure of Cambodian
air attacks as treasonous acts and as personal attacks. Through his bunker-
mentality defense of his presidential person, Nixon was clearing the way for a

personal presidency, under Reagan, that sold a lower standard of living with a winning ideological smile.

Nixon's New Federalism—his "Second American Revolution" and his revenue sharing set a tone for ongoing governmental and private sphere downsizing— that is, for productive innovations that, in effect, concentrate wealth and reduce the middle class. We credit Nixon with opening China, ratifying SALT, bringing American fighting troops out of Vietnam, signing the clean air act, the disability act, and the bill lowering the voting age; we might also give him credit for revenue sharing, growth in the food stamp programs, promoting a guaranteed annual income with the Family Assistance Act, proposing national health care, and enacting federal wage and price controls. Indeed, an offshoot of the Family Assistance Act—Supplemental Security Income (SSI)—was enacted. Although SSI, which provides financial assistance for unemployable disabled, elderly, and blind citizens, is one of the cornerstones of what is widely called "welfare," it was signed into law by Nixon in 1974.

Despite several important social and environmental advances made during the Nixon years, we seldom acknowledge that it would have been difficult if not impossible to squelch the era's mind-set favoring improvement through government. While having little commitment to cultural change, Nixon wanted to seem more socially experimental than the Democrats. He was desperate to seem innovative—to be a new Nixon, a president in step with the times. He was extremely sensitive to a wave of accurate criticism, in the first year of his presidency, faulting his administration for its lack of a domestic agenda. His problems would have been magnified at this time by, for instance, vetoing Congress's early seventies banning of DDT.

There are other reasons to be skeptical of Nixon's progressive image. As a politician whose prevailing ideology consisted of punishing his enemies and repaying his friends, he was thankful for programs that could help with his friendly repayments. Food stamp programs, for instance, served agricultural interests. This is not to say that Democrats did not have similar motives, but merely that if Nixon gets credit for allowing some reforms and legislation to articulate and realize themselves, or for simply not vetoing them, it is much more significant that he helped change the American political and social environment from one at least ostensibly aimed at economic and social inclusion to one of thinly veiled but deadly exclusion.

Nixon was a pioneer in the legitimization of accusatory modes of politics that would not have previously been considered worthy of inclusion on a national ticket. His game was intrinsically repugnant, since he sought to legitimize low tactics. He cloaked his dire accusations, based on flimsy evidence and questioning the patriotism of his enemies, as when he called the Democratic Party the "party of treason" within a stream of reasonable rhetoric. Similarly, in the House Committee on Un-American Activities' questionings of Hiss, he went out of his way to seem extremely deferential toward Hiss, and Nixon cultivated the company of the most venerable members of the committee, such as Senator Karl Mundt of South Dakota. Despite Nixon's public relations instinct to move toward the appearance of moderation, his harsh electoral and investigative tactics and extreme red-baiting exceeded the limits of the political game and made him an outcast to many entrenched political powers, such as Speaker of the House Sam Rayburn. While some saw him as an acceptable moderate, others saw him as a near criminal. This perspective did not change with his presidency and its aftermath.

But who can say that Nixon did not succeed in altering our view of his presidency? In something of an apology for Nixon in a *New York Times* op-ed piece, written shortly after Nixon's death, Garry Wills notes that if Nixon persecuted Alger Hiss, Hiss was after all "guilty." But what was he guilty of? True, a jury convicted Hiss of perjury, the statute of limitations concerning the thirties espionage that he was accused of perjuring himself about having long ago expired. But it is extremely unlikely that he spied for the Soviets or anyone else. Perhaps, and it is an immense perhaps, he was less forthcoming than he could have been about associations with leftists or homosexuals in the thirties. But Hiss's alleged perjury occurred in a lawsuit that he himself brought to court. The need to bring Hiss up on some kind of charge was a product of the Justice Department's harassment against him.

Wills's misleading condemnation of Hiss is based on little more than the fact that a second jury in 1950, after a first jury was unable to reach a verdict, found Hiss guilty of perjury in 1948 for denying his alleged espionage activities in 1938. Like Nixon, Hiss was primarily accused of a cover-up. However, Hiss's conviction was the product of an obvious and much greater miscarriage of justice than anything Hiss is likely to have done. His legal team was infiltrated. Prosecutors withheld evidence. Hiss's witnesses were tampered with. Expert opinion was falsified. "Examining the FBI files decades later," says Roger Morris, "even historians of the affair who believed Alger Hiss in some measure guilty would be shocked by the government's misconduct."[6] If it is difficult definitively to establish Hiss's innocence, it is also impossible to prove his guilt. We can only know that he was mistreated by our justice system.

Throughout the investigations and trials of Hiss, Nixon was at the spearhead of Hiss's prosecution. Can we put the seal of approval on Nixon's investigative methods as easily as Wills did? Nixon probably felt that Hiss was "guilty" of some sort of indefinite espionage, and that the evidence needed to be adjusted to prove it. Can we help but believe John Dean when he said that Nixon likened Alger Hiss to Dita Beard, the International Telegraph and Telephone Company lobbyist who confirmed ITT contributions to the 1972 Republican National Convention for a favorable Justice Department antitrust decision? According to Dean, Nixon prodded Chuck Colson not to give up until some devastating piece of information could be found or conjured against Beard:

> Colson was reporting to the President on his efforts. It reminded the President of the Alger Hiss case—of how, as a young congressman, he had fought to prove the State Department official was a Communist and a perjurer. "The typewriters are always the key," the President told Chuck. "We built one in the Hiss case."[7]

How can we not suspect that such a fabricated typewriter (emblematic of much fabricated "cold war reality") was used to type the extracted and summarized oddly insignificant State Department documents that Hiss was accused of copying on the typewriter belonging to his wife, Priscilla, so as to pass them on to Whittaker Chambers? This is especially probable since the typewriter's serial number indicates that it was built after Priscilla Hiss obtained her Woodstock typewriter—"the key witness in the case," according to Nixon.

Nixon's dictum that "the typewriters are always the key" makes one recall Norman Mailer's words about Nixon's rhetorical style. Mailer noted that Nixon "had no final passion for the incorruptible integrity of an idea; no, ideas were rather like keys to him on which he might play a teletype to program the American mind."[8] Nixon, says Mailer, could do nought but directly "signify." He could not "play against the line,"[9] and the reality he "typed" was devoid of a certain subtlety. Indeed, Nixon bested Hiss in the minds of many Americans because Nixon was neater than Hiss in accounting for everything presented to Hiss. Nixon was quicker to find the pulse of America than the patrician Hiss.

Significantly, Nixon, as becomes increasingly evident in the Haldeman diaries, uses the Hiss case as a paradigm for all his battles. Nixon, for example, instructs his aides that Daniel Ellsberg is just like Hiss:

> At Key Biscayne. The P[resident] was on the phone for a long time this morning, caught me over at the hotel at breakfast, then frequently on various ideas during the day as they came up, all regarding *The New York*

Times [for publishing the Pentagon Papers] case. He explained to me that in order to understand this whole thing, we have to understand the Hiss case. That they're very similar, although none of us really realizes it. In that case, too, the papers themselves didn't make any difference. They were old and outdated and unimportant; the key thing was that we got across the point that Hiss was a spy, a liar, and a Communist.[10]

The Hiss case resonates throughout Nixon's presidency. How could he not, in the face of anti–Vietnam War demonstrations, attempt to reprise something like the red scare of the forties and fifties? Nixon might indeed have felt that Hiss did commit espionage and treason and that Nixon therefore was justified in resorting to "dirty tricks" to establish a truth. Ellsberg had seemingly stolen government papers, as Nixon probably believed that Hiss had done. Similarly, Watergate legislators, prosecutors, and judges were trying to take away what belonged to him as a person and a president—his papers and tapes.

Independent of his individual history, Nixon was also responding to the same pressures as everyone else during the seventies. He was responding to the sixties, to an idealistic holiday from the seeming realities of the Cold War, which could no longer support themselves within the context of the Vietnam War. This mind-set contributed to the inevitability of the China opening and the SALT agreements. However, much of the nation also preferred forgetting the Vietnam War to accepting it as a mistake. Dwindling public awareness of the war allowed Nixon to continue it and expand it into Cambodia.

If coverage of the death of Richard Nixon tended to treat Watergate as inconsistent with the rest of his presidency, Nixon then seemed successful in confining the scandal to the actual break-in, and thus removing his administration and American government from the logic of this seemingly inconsequential act of political espionage. My traditional college-aged students believed that Nixon had engaged in the same kind of political espionage that all politicians had involved themselves in. Speculation about Whitewater aggressively advances the notion that Clinton must have done something that was as bad as anything Nixon did. Nixon was merely, most of my students believe, the first modern president to be caught for such a bad thing, and he was therefore more an object of humor for being a sad sack than a target of contempt for his tyranny. If he abused power, it does not seem to have been against them, and he sometimes seems to have been the last president of any substance.

Even those who lived through the ages of Nixon recall them with odd spins.

Garry Wills speculates that Nixon helped to end the Cold War by opening China and isolating Russia. Of course, Nixon did not discover the Sino-Soviet rift, nor did he aim to trap Russia in a corner. American foreign policy under Nixon and Kissinger often ceded large influence to the Soviets, as when the United States joined with China tacitly to back or "tilt" toward Pakistan over India in their conflicts during the seventies, thereby abdicating much of America's influence in India. Rather than Wills's assessment of the opening of China, cannot we with more certainty maintain that Nixon contributed to China's present flagrant disrespect for human rights? Cannot we ask if the Soviet empire ever had any possibility of holding itself together?

We had not been separated from China by an act of nature. Many Western nations, such as Great Britain, were doing business with mainland China. In recognizing China, Nixon was undoing something that he was, through his post–World War II red-baiting, in large part responsible for, yet something that could be undone without great difficulty. It was inevitable that the United States and China would do business. China, after all, did exist, and it was too big and tempting a market to be ignored, although the United States has, it turns out, become more China's market than China is America's. By 1993, the United States had a thirty billion dollar trade deficit with China.

Nixon sensed in China an opportunity to make history through the president's mere presence in a previously inaccessible realm. He becomes the president as astronaut. Through an agreement with a government veiled in secrecy he could, on the American end, control the terms of our new and almost mystical awareness of China. The opening of China was a kind of farming out of sixties energies to exotic realms. As in Elizabeth Bishop's seventies poem "The Moose," in which a wondrous moose, an ambassador from another realm, majestically interrupts a long Canadian bus ride, seeing inside China by live satellite feed was as almost as magnificent as seeing the moon close-up. Those wondrous citizens of the forest, the pandas, that Nixon brought back prefigured the visitation of another tame magic with E.T. in the eighties. Magic was then firmly elsewhere yet also domesticated.

Nixon ingeniously pieced together the allegiances loosened by the prevailing credibility gaps and distrust of institutions. He would begin to reconfigure the New Deal state into a new social Darwinian compact. Indeed, we can see the sixties credibility gap as an intermittently erupting faultline in American history. However, Nixon took the brunt of the credibility gap, and we tend to associate him with distrust of government. The Johnson administration, by not offering convincing rationales for the loss of American lives and the depletion of the nation's capital reserves, and by upsetting the ongoing social security system by unwisely dipping into its funds and unleashing our more recent debt problems, stretched the government's credibility and made it an issue. Nixon not only refused to recognize the problem of credibility during the late sixties; he also acted as if treason were synonymous with doubt in the government, and identified the government with the executive branch's war-making powers, not its power to enact legislation for the common good. Nixon created distrust by hiding his war efforts in Cambodia from Congress. He invoked the executive branch's self-defining credibility as its unchecked and unprecedented right to use "national security" to justify its actions. It became increasingly clear that no payment on "credence" or "credit" was forthcoming and that the American people had no need to "extend credibility." Nixon was a relatively easy victim of the credibility gap because he refused to recognize limits; instead, he escalated the credibility gap as if it were a drug that required a steady increase of dosages.

When the "New Nixon" of the late sixties said that he was trying to unite the country, he meant that he wanted to turn the nation's attention away from those who questioned the president's credibility. The new Nixon wished to bring us back to the era between World War II and Vietnam. Interestingly, he did not emulate Truman's and Eisenhower's will to limit and then to end the Korean War when they could not meet the expectations or answer the questions of the public. The Truman and the Eisenhower administrations, of course, often misled the American public. They avoided, however, making the government's credibility an issue. Even when Eisenhower was caught red-handed in the U-2 incident, most Americans were merely perplexed. Later, Kennedy felt a need to take full responsibility for the Bay of Pigs fiasco, and, by implication, ask the American people's forgiveness. He thus avoided making the government's credibility an issue. Why did not Nixon make a similar admission of what probably could have been made to seem minor acts of obstruction of justice and abuse of power, acts that were not likely to be prosecuted? Although an admission of guilt would summon other questions, surely other small crimes could be explained away or confessed to in a similar fashion. (After all, Nixon could not run for the presidency in 1976.) A confession probably would have renewed his credibility and saved his presidency. He probably had that opportunity open to him until the Saturday Night Massacre, when his abuses of power became too blatant, or at least most definitely began to appear so to most Americans. Committing the massacre on a Saturday night to avoid press

coverage, Nixon gave up all appearance of fair play to delay temporarily hand-
ing over presidential tapes subpoenaed by the special prosecutor. Attorney
General Elliot Richardson and Assistant Attorney General William D. Ruckelshaus chose to resign rather than to fire Special Prosecutor Archibald Cox, who
was nevertheless fired by Solicitor General Robert H. Bork. The resignations
and dismissal added depth, dimension, and a sinister chain-letter effect to the
image of Nixon's tyranny. The president could no longer repair the appearance
of injustice and foul play because the public had been presented with a symbolic action that needed no further explanation. To fire one's own prosecutor
seemed like the most basic kind of game-rigging and cheating. The president
chose to abolish the game rather than play it. Nixon could not "repent" while
there was still time because he never could quite believe that his credibility
was in jeopardy. Could the nation have changed that much to so challenge a
president?

If, before Vietnam, presidential credibility curtailed theory and dialogue,
disbelief has been more likely to short-circuit discussion since. For instance,
when Bill Clinton ruminates on the statistical concept of the universal, in a
purely theoretical and instructive fashion, national news reports it as an unreliable change of positions about health care. The credibility gap now serves
the most powerful vested interests, such as the insurance companies; the
credibility gap now reinforces ideological state apparatuses instead of criti-
cizing them. A network of corporate influences seems more powerful and real
than government, even if these influences are in fact no more efficient and
reliable. It is remarkable, for example, that the Clintons' plan for consumer
alliances to buy health care, a basic concept no more difficult or unsound than
the purchasing collectives of farmers, was deemed uncomprehensible and un-
workable.

Nixon did not help Americans cope with change. For instance, when he told
Haldeman that America must "face reality" and, he reasoned, accept that blacks
were inherently inferior, he was asking Americans to return to a certainty that
was now a certain illusion:

> Got into a deep discussion of welfare, trying to think out the Family Secu-
> rity decision, with E[hrlichman] and me (*welfare reform had been one of
> the P[resident]'s campaign issues*). P emphasized that you have to face
> the fact that the whole problem is really the blacks. The key is to devise

a system that recognizes this while not appearing to. Problem with over-all welfare plan is that it forces poor whites into same position as blacks. Feels we have to get rid of the veil of hypocrisy and guilt and face reality.

Pointed out that there has never in history been an adequate black nation, and they are the only race of which this is true. Says Africa is hopeless, the worst there is Liberia, which we built.[11]

Nixon reflected America's search for more certain realities in the seventies but was unable to help equip the nation with useful guides to and in such a reality. Not surprisingly overlooking pre-colonial African governments and civilizations, such as the Benin kingdom in Nigeria, he castigates Africans and blacks for problems in great part determined by colonialism. What is the up-shot of Nixon's attitude toward race? Would he, to avoid "hypocrisy and guilt," set up an apartheid system that could be kept as secret as he would have liked to have kept the extended play of the war in Southeast Asia? He did not feel that anything could be done about racial problems. Hence his notion of "reality" was avoiding the reality of these problems.

Nixon could not coin a lasting name for his presidential mission, although he tried to dub his vision "The New American Revolution." Reagan would more convincingly use the phrase "The Second American Revolution" for his redis-tribution of wealth through tax cuts and reduced social spending. By Reagan's presidency, the nation had internalized Nixon's vision.

2   Eighteen and a Half Minutes behind the Mirror: Nixon and the Scene of Wiring

The war was on television every night but we all went to the movies. Soon most of the movies began to look alike and we went into dim rooms . . . and listened to tapes of silence. — Don DeLillo, *Americana*

That blood's never gonna cover that stain. — Talking Heads, "Risky Business"

A conversation begins
with a lie. . . .

The technology of silence
The rituals, etiquette

the blurring of terms
silence not absence

of words or music or even

raw sounds

Silence can be a plan
rigorously executed

the blueprint to a life

It has a presence
it has a history   a form

Do not confuse it
with any kind of absence
—Adrienne Rich, "Cartographies of Silence"

Whitewater can be used to historicize Watergate, to differentiate Watergate's past import from present contexts. Conversely, by understanding Watergate's place in Whitewater, we can grasp better the transformation of Watergate's political significance.

The Whitewater "scandal" bespeaks a nineties anxiety of influence with the "masterpiece" of Watergate. Whitewater emerges from Watergate's political context. Indeed, the substance of the latter scandal has its basis in Watergate's repercussions. Watergate helped institutionalize a widespread distrust of government, paralyzing governmental activism and hampering its role as a regulator so that Congress and the Reagan administration were able to loosen government regulations controlling federal loan guarantees, precipitating the savings and loan crisis. Nixon's role in Watergate "validated" Clinton's in Whitewater. Although the great majority of savings and loan violators were not prosecuted, some Republicans insisted upon investigating Clinton's seemingly tangential relation to a relatively small federal loan guarantee gone awry; they reasoned that Nixon was guilty of a small inconsequential offense and Clinton should be held to the same standard. The American people largely accept this reasoning, in that they doubt that Nixon did anything very much worse than whatever Clinton might have done. However, they generally differ from Republican argumentation in that they accept a lowered standard for presidents. Indeed, Americans probably would no longer have Nixon prosecuted.

Both the Republicans and a consensus of Americans overlook some major differences between Watergate and Whitewater. The Watergate investigation flowed from a crime that was difficult not to investigate. When there was a forced entry into the Democratic National Headquarters, it was difficult not to look into the burglars' obvious links to the Republican National Committee, and, when the investigation was apparently obstructed, it was seemingly appropriate for Judge Sirica and FBI investigators to investigate the tampering. However, bred of targeted "justice" and political accusations, Whitewater was not the product of a normal due process of investigative or prosecutorial justice. In a sense, the more valid Nixonian comparison to Whitewater is not Watergate but the oddly discriminating prosecution of Alger Hiss that I discussed in the previous section.

The present special prosecutor (become "Independent Counsel") system itself is of course a Watergate legacy. However, under President Bush, Republicans in Congress were successful in letting independent counsel legislation elapse. Thus, to assuage the Whitewater controversy, Clinton needed to have his attorney general nominate a special Whitewater counsel to serve as an independent prosecutor. Subsequently, however, under President Clinton, Republicans in Congress were able to renew the independent counsel law, and then, apparently through political pressure placed on Republican judges, special counsel Robert Fiske, the initial "independent counsel," was deemed not a product of the independent counsel system and dismissed in favor of Kenneth Starr, a renowned advocate of radical-right causes and clients. Republicans thus succeeded in abusing the independent counsel law in a manner that reflected their original objections to it, and Clinton is probably justified for being miffed at the wide investigative latitude of the charge that Attorney General Janet Reno gave the special Whitewater independent counsel; perhaps part of the remedy to this problem lies in the establishment of a more overwhelming standard of evidence for the appointment of an independent counsel.

The apparent indiscretions of Watergate and Whitewater are incomparable.[12] Nixon sought to model his own private illegal surveillance force and coordinate all the legal surveillance forces into his personal service. The Watergate break-in and obstruction of justice were symptoms of this broader, aggressive mindset and series of actions. On the other hand, Clinton was initially accused of isolated pre-presidential financial improprieties that were understandably accepted within a small Arkansas business community. Even in terms of perjury and obstruction of justice, Clinton, despite Starr's apparent claims, is arguably primarily guilty of telling virtually unprosecutable white lies (even if he was under oath we may recall the observation in Plato's *Symposium* that "the gods only forgive perjury in matters of eros"), being understandably equivocal, playing his legal hand as best he could, although that meant appeals and delays, and being slow in turning up some of the plethora of evidence subpoenaed by several congressional committees and the independent counsel.

In short, Watergate has, in an uncanny fashion, completely redesigned the political landscape. It is almost as if Nixon took the country down with him in terms both of political corruption that undermined effective attention to the national economy and of an undermining of a trust in the government that would allow us to handle domestic problems. Nixon was more with us after he left the presidency than before.

A comparison of political and artistic mechanisms of surveillance provides entry to a discussion of Nixon's surveillance within the context of the entire culture. Warhol might seem like an unlikely exemplar of American culture, but he owed his success to tapping astutely American limits of what seemed credible and problematic. A comparison of Andy Warhol's use of film and tape in relation to President Nixon's espionage systems elucidates affinities between artistic and overtly political surveillance mechanisms. Since Warhol and Nixon both used recording devices, a comparison of their respective use of these devices is particularly illuminating. The artist and the president (Nixon was the first president to use an automatic, voice-activated bugging system) establish and situate mechanisms and programs for the registering of supposedly unaltered impressions.

The impressions that register on a recording apparatus are organized by the simple happenstance that they are the objects of a particular recording system. An odd sort of doubling occurs. All phenomena circulate within a context that is disassociated from any apparent origin, reminding us of many of the queries and dictums in the last verse-paragraph of Ashbery's contemporaneous "Self-Portrait in a Convex Mirror," such as "What is this universe the porch of . . . ?" (*SP*, 198: 7), "The city falling with its beautiful suburbs / Into space always less clear, less defined, / Should read as the support of its progress" (*SP*, 198: 30–32), "All things happen / On its balcony," and "the action is the cold, syrupy flow" (*SP*, 204: 3–5). It can be said that the double—or the model—is never fixed and exists in a perpetual flow within and against simulations and tropes such as that of the convex mirror. Ashbery's "Daffy Duck in Hollywood," written shortly after "Self-Portrait in a Convex Mirror," envisions the notion of any given great poem within the convex mirror of the "hubcap" of other great poems. The circuit is closed and yet endless. Similarly, Garry Wills said of Nixon himself during his first presidential term that "there is one Nixon only, though there seem to be new ones all the time."[13]

Ashbery's preoccupation with Parmigianino's "round mirror" (*SP*, 191: 20) and Nixon's frequent use of the Oval Office as a broadcasting studio, a use that Nixon recalls in the first sentence of his 1974 resignation speech,[14] form a "hyper-modern circle," in the words of painter and critic Peter Halley. (I use Halley here rather than Debord or Baudrillard because of Halley's proximity to American art and culture.)[15] According to Halley, "history" is being "severed from determinism. In the daily TV news, the present is transformed into the historical. . . . On the radio news, history is written on-the-hour. But national revolutions, car accidents, and the comments of film stars are all treated the same."[16] Halley characterizes this de-hierarchization as a "leveling" of the more concrete and irregular formulations of "historicity," making possible "the endless circulation of signs through the chutes of an irreal space."[17] Similarly, "theory," which reaches a critical mass that refashions literary criticism in the seventies, can be seen as a somewhat open-ended mechanism, or *techne,* for placing a wide array of literary and cultural phenomena in a single frame, or theater. "Theory," after all, has the same Greek root as "theater," both words suggesting "seeing," and theory creates a theater for the critic to see and shape the play of culture. For this spectacle, theory builds a stage, which effects a kind of leveling. If the deconstruction of the seventies taught us a binary mechanism that can be applied to all texts, the more general subsequent category of critical and cultural theory teaches us more actively to equate, to level, and to shape all manner of phenomena.

In a sense, Nixon both participated and was caught within a general leveling taking place within seventies culture that his recording methods were symptomatic of. On the other hand, Warhol capitalized on this leveling (while also anticipating the eighties by using the wealthy as portrait subjects). Warhol paid tribute to a seventies leveling, or "equalizing," of cultural perceptions in the form of increased environmental recycling and thrift-shop chic:

> There should be supermarkets that sell things and supermarkets that buy things back, and until that equalizes, there'll be more waste than there should be. Everybody would always have something to sell back, so everybody would have money, because everybody would have something to sell. We all have something, but most of what we have isn't salable, there's such a preference today for brand new things. People should be able to sell their old cans, their old chicken bones, their old shampoo bottles, their old magazines. We have to get more organized. People who tell you we're running out of things are just making the prices go up

higher. How can we be running out of anything when there's always, if I'm not mistaken, the same amount of matter in the Universe, with the exception of what goes into the black holes?

I think about people eating and going to the bathroom all the time, and I wonder why they don't have a tube up their behind that takes all the stuff they eat and recycles it back into their mouth, regenerating it, and then they'd never have to think about buying food or eating. And they wouldn't even have to see it—it wouldn't even be dirty. If they wanted to, they could artificially color it on the way back in. Pink.[18]

In one of the great conceits of the mid-seventies, Warhol used ecological themes to create a self-sustaining and a waste-defying, yet paradoxically bounty-producing, system. Reaganomics later exploited these cultural energies by advocating a general supply-side, "something for nothing" disposition.

Before Halley's critical use of the term "leveling," Ashbery, in "Self-Portrait in a Convex Mirror," uses the word to describe the homogenizing of phenomena through information circuits:

> I feel the carousel starting slowly
> And going faster and faster: desk, papers, books,
> Photographs of friends, the window and the trees
> Merging in one neutral band that surrounds
> Me on all sides, everywhere I look.
> And I cannot explain the action of leveling.
> Why it should all boil down to one
> Uniform substance, a magma of interiors.
> (*SP*, 191: 23–30)

>   everything gets "programmed" there
> In due course: more keeps getting included
> Without adding to the sum.
> (*SP*, 193: 3–5)

Similarly, the impressions registered upon Warhol's and Nixon's recording apparatuses are relatively unarranged and unhierarchized. Nixon's tapes were neither abridged nor edited, and, because of this, Henry A. Kissinger objected to Nixon's taping system:

> The President's taping system was "insane," he [Kissinger] said. It was *indiscriminate*. "To tape eight years of conversation would take eight years

to listen to!" . . . particularly since Nixon conducted meetings "with such fantastic indirection."[19]

In *The Final Days*, Woodward and Bernstein note that Kissinger, while serving in the Nixon administration as assistant to the president for national security affairs and secretary of state, also taped virtually all of his own conversations. However, transcriptions of Kissinger's tapes, throughout these years, were continually edited by three or four of his assistants.[20] Although many factors might help to explain the differences between Nixon's and Kissinger's taping systems, it seems that a president cannot as easily delimit and catalog his concerns as a cabinet member can. So much more might apply to a president.

The indiscriminateness of Nixon's and Warhol's taping systems form immense phenomenological fields. For instance, Warholian projects such as filming a set of actors or the Empire State Building for a specified length of time, or, to cite another indiscriminate Warholian recording program, the continuous taping that is done by Warhol's constant companion, the portable tape recorder that he calls his wife, assert a topos, or organizing topic or theme, upon everything in each device's respective phenomenological field. Simply put, anything that is recorded is incorporated into the Warhol work that the recordings constitute. This totalizing effect dramatically changes the contents that are recorded, as well as the contexts of these contents. For instance, we can note Warhol's enthusiastic claim that his continuous taping transforms and supersedes everything that he records. "After the acquisition of a tape recorder," remarks Warhol in 1975, "Nothing was ever a problem again, because a problem just meant a good tape, it's not a problem anymore."[21]

Similarly, Nixon acts as if he genuinely believes that all his surveillance operations serve to alleviate problems and maintain "national security," even if little but Nixon's political benefit is at stake.[22] Recording, for Nixon, as for Warhol, sublimates all "problem[s]." All national concerns must be processed through a president, even if he specifically audits and decides upon relatively few matters, since the president must also evoke the myth of a streamlined decision-making process, in opposition to an enormous bureaucratic "red tape." The modern president must offer the myth that he counters Washingtonian bureaucracy's hidden systems of inertia. Nixon, using his own kind of surveillance "tape," assumes that national security requires a politically sound president who is in a position to make large-scale decisions that are unencumbered by the forces of "Washington." Within this context, we can understand why

Nixon feels justified in so fervently attempting to reorganize and simplify the federal government so as to make it more accountable to fewer cabinet members, who, in turn, are to be more directly, and politically, accountable to him. In the face of the ferment of the late sixties and early seventies, which Nixon, as president, often alludes to, we can see why Nixon feels that such an organization will serve the country, quite apart from any of its actions. Nixon recognizes its ideological implications, values the metaphor of the presidency, and, later, fights to defend it. He seems to feel that apologizing for his actions, or resigning his office, before his position becomes entirely untenable, will compromise the symbol of the American presidency. Nixon considers it to be his presidential duty not only to gather and transform information, but also to maintain a free hand in doing so.

As with Warhol's taping, Nixon's audiorecording of "all conversations and phone calls in his offices [including his office in the Executive Office Building], in the Lincoln Room, and at Camp David,"[23] as well as his 1972 campaign's intent to record conversations within the Democratic National Committee offices, places all that is recorded within a topos, which, as in a Warhol film, categorizes everything within its self-defined range and confuses our distinguishing of "the real" so that it is extremely difficult to separate the functional from non-functional. This blurring between the pragmatic and non-pragmatic applies to an audience's reception of the tapes and their transcripts. For instance, although Nixon does not intend, as Warhol whimsically surmises, to make a script for a play from his tapes, it is not far-fetched to imagine the Oval Office tapes being used for that purpose. The painter and critic Halley notes:

> History becomes entertainment and entertainment becomes history. There are TV docu-dramas, and there are the Academy Awards. There is *60 Minutes,* and there is the Baseball Hall of Fame. There is the traditional Christian Calendar year 1984, and there is Super Bowl XVIII.[24]

For Warhol and Nixon, the fixed position of the camera or microphone allows the all-inclusive power of "non-editing" to supersede all fixed context and intention, while nonetheless obeying a program, thereby strangely mimicking normal intentionality and logocentrism. Similarly, a convex mirror facilitates a topological imperative that is like Warhol's and Nixon's mechanisms. As in the cases of Warhol's films and Nixon's tapes, the mirror that preoccupies Ashbery, on the one hand, organizes everything before it, yet, on the other hand, questions, in Marjorie Perloff's words, "the very nature of the order that a systematic plot structure implies."[25] The Watergate scandal similarly tests the logocentric basis of the American presidency.

As "Self-Portrait in a Convex Mirror" accredits and refutes logocentric modes of considering poetry, the Watergate affair values and undermines logocentric perspectives on the American presidency. These logocentric perspectives can be likened to the presidency, according to Theodore J. Lowi's theory of "the personal president" (1985), in which a president's personality functions as ideological compensation for national conditions that cannot be faced. Similarly, Kenneth K. Tulis's *The Rhetorical Presidency* (1987) asserts that the presidency is the nation's most vital historical construction. Combining Lowi's and Tulis's concepts, we can say that the "person" of the president is the nation's central "rhetorical" mechanism. In an Althusserian sense, the president is a metaphor for the nation's "ideological state apparatus." When Senator Robert Dole asks if Bill Clinton is "a real president," Dole questions whether Clinton reinforces this apparatus.

Lowi maintains that, to succeed, "modern presidents" must ward off challenges to their mythic natures:

> Modern presidents, among which Richard Nixon is only one, perceive vital threats to national interests earlier and more often than ever. The threats don't have to be real—and usually aren't. Presidents don't have to believe they are real—and probably don't. Their main obligation is to preserve the myth that they are reserving themselves for the big decisions.[26]

Of course, the Nixon administration does not innovate nor put an end to the "personal presidency." However, the Watergate affair is widely considered a test of the "inherent powers" of the president.[27] And yet, in the light of subsequent administrations, we may ask whether the Watergate scandal does not reinforce the inherent and unrestrained powers of the presidency. Lowi remarks:

> When one understands the assumptions under which he was operating, the only meaningful conclusion is that Nixon was consistent, logical, and normal. . . .
>
> The first assumption is that the president and the state are the same thing, that the president is the state personified. The second is that powers should be commensurate with responsibilities. . . .
>
> The third assumption, intimately related to the second, is that the president should not and cannot be bound by normal legal restrictions. To

put this indelicately, the president's actions must be considered above the law or subject to a different kind of law from those of ordinary citizens. While not free to commit any crime merely for the sake of convenience, the president nevertheless cannot be constantly beset by considerations of legality when the state itself is or seems to be at issue.

The first three assumptions lead inexorably toward a fourth, which is that any *deliberate* barriers to presidential action must be considered tantamount to disloyalty. Barriers to presidential action can be tolerated up to a point, and it is probable that most presidents, including Richard Nixon, have prided themselves on their uncommon patience with organized protests, well meaning but embarrassing news leaks, journalistic criticism, and organized political opposition. But there is a point beyond which barriers cannot be tolerated, and as this point is approached, confidential knowledge of the identities and contentions of the organizers of obstructions must be gathered. . . .

[Nixon's] actions, including his crimes, are . . . quite possibly motivated by the highest sense of national interest.[28]

Lowi does not condone the president's role; however, paraphrasing the vernacular of the last words of Philip Roth's *Portnoy's Complaint* (1969), "Now vee may perhaps to begin. Yes,"[29] as "And now we can begin the analysis," Lowi maintains that it is crucial to acknowledge the modern president's ideological functions.[30]

Perhaps Nixon demonstrates the darker side of Lowi's analysis. Nonetheless, the Nixon administration shows the validity of Lowi's premises. While a modern president may not literally be the state, he is the "popular," or, as Lowi also terms it, the "plebiscitary" and ideological version of the state.[31] Indeed, after Watergate, it increasingly seems that a president colors and even determines how we know what the state "literally" is. It is a modern president's duty to project a consistent personality and maintain the cohesiveness of his—and, by extension, the state's—enabling *mythos.* For this reason, the selling of arms to Iran politically damages the Reagan administration to a greater extent than the more blatantly illegal act of channeling the profits of those sales to the Contras, since such bartering for hostages seems antithetical to what Ronald Reagan, as a person, represents to most Americans. Nevertheless, Reagan is able to present his personality as more significant than any individual act. Reagan's renewed popularity after the revelations of the Iran-Contra affair demonstrates that, after Watergate, the American public grew more inclined to overlook presidential indiscretions and equate a president's personality, relatively independent of specific actions, with the state's welfare.

A weakening of checks on presidential power can also be observed in Oliver North's criminal trial. The same federal judge, Gerhard A. Gesell, sentenced both Oliver North and several Watergate-era defendants, including John Ehrlichman. His sentencing of the Watergate defendants is not tempered by any "following orders" arguments. Yet citing Oliver North's "cynical superiors," he fails, in 1989, to sentence North to a prison term. Although Gesell pejoratively characterizes the actions of a chain of command that flows from the president, he nonetheless acknowledges the power of this chain of command as nearly irresistible. Although Watergate accredits and then discredits logocentric political values, the scandal ultimately helps to establish a more complicated and bifurcated situation in which logocentric values and their problematizations can both thrive.

These changes are better observed in Ashbery and Johns than in Warhol because Warhol's modus operandi remains relatively constant throughout the almost twenty-five years of work that constitute his oeuvre. The media Warhol used and the content that he treated changed more than his essential method of production. Perhaps Nixon parallels Warhol in this regard. Wills notes that Nixon's "denigrative method," which aggressively places his opponents on the defensive with unproven allegations, is a staple of Nixon's career that is duly noted and criticized.[32] However, it is only in the wake of the Watergate affair that the political "medium" of Nixon's surveillance practices, specifically, is both publicized and widely denounced. Similarly, presidents previous to Nixon installed eavesdropping devices in the White House.[33] However, what is important here is that other surveillance ventures related to Nixon make an issue of his Oval Office taping system and his broader relationship to surveillance. It is also important to note that Nixon installed a taping system that did not need to be turned on and off. Previous presidential taping systems needed to be activated. Prior presidents only taped on special occasions. Nixon's system was voice activated. In Nixon's defense, it must be acknowledged that illegal surveillance of anti–Vietnam War demonstrators can be said to have started years before Nixon took office, hence supporting my argument that the Watergate scandal, qua scandal, is best explained as an outcome of the prevailing episteme of the mid-seventies.

The mid-seventies, in short, are the United States's "end of the sixties." This closure inevitably invites surveillance and the consideration of surveillance as an ideological tool that provides a means of "taking stock" and consolidating the legacy of the cultural expansion that occurs during the sixties and early seventies. (Indeed, my suggestion that American culture narrows in the mid-seventies corresponds to the common view of this era.) An analysis of Bob Fosse's film *Lenny* (1974) is instructive in this regard. As a mid-seventies film, *Lenny* emblematizes the use of surveillance to round up the "counter-culture," dramatized by the film's continuous presence of note-taking and tape-recording undercover policemen. The very making of the film, however, demonstrates Lenny Bruce's cultural victory, although it is at one with the marketplace's co-opting. "I have all the film rights locked up," says the character of Bruce's manager, now prosperous near the film's conclusion. The film itself is structured by an unseen interviewer taping interviews with Bruce's ex-wife, manager, and mother, and the flashbacks that derive from these interviews, and the film presents an ambivalent organizing mechanism that is at odds with itself. As Lenny Bruce in the sixties found that invoking the suppressed and articulating the repressed brought him into conflict with the legal system, our culture has increasingly found difficulty in reconciling the revelations that inform its fictions with the ideological underpinnings of those fictions. This has translated into problems for the presidency and a president's ability to articulate himself and lead.

The president is a conduit through which hidden and unmentionable aspects of the American administrative system, and through it the contents of the nation's "unconscious," can articulate themselves. It can be maintained that the loss of a presidency is the major turn, or backing of the mirror, which the United States needs to "bounce off" during the closing pages of the Vietnam experience in order to lay the groundwork for finding itself again, albeit changed slightly during, so to speak, the time it takes for its metaphoric mirror to relay its "light" (or code or constitutive ideology) back to itself in the form (or semiotic configuration) of Reagan's "ready-made" presidency. Here, in this reconfiguration of American ideology, ideology is recognized as substanceless, yet nonetheless, in itself, a formal or virtual presence. American culture "achieves" a separation between ideology and its sense of the real.

Before Watergate, many Americans struggle with a gap between what they perceive as ideologically adequate and what they experience as "real." Some degree of accountability is called for. Although the gruesome events in Vietnam are televised, the decision-making process that brings us to that war is not, and the eventual visibility of Watergate is a surrogate for the hidden decision-making process of Vietnam. Perhaps Watergate launders the Vietnam War, the systems of information dispersal, impartment, and retrieval behind the workings of the war systematically announcing themselves during the Watergate hearings and related events and proceedings, so that the American public can see those same mechanisms of informational repression, that is, self-signification and self-investigation that do not acknowledge information that it implies and validates on a less self-regulating level. Alterity is excluded. There is a closure of credible "information" that parallels Niklas Luhmann's description of information as "what is produced by the system itself in comparison with something else."[34]

Nixon can justify the harshest measures against his critics because they oppose "the system," so it is not surprising that he bears the brunt of dissatisfaction with that system. This opposition seems to him "hypocritical" and "dangerous" because he believes that our system could not function outside its internal mandates. To Nixon, critics of the system must be either selfish or perverse.[35]

Nixon aligns himself with things as they are, and, as a former president, there is something strangely reassuring in this. Nixon's image seems, at times, more venerable and less of a political liability than those of Jimmy Carter, Lyndon Johnson, Gerald Ford, George Bush, and even Ronald Reagan. Indeed, Jimmy Carter's international peace efforts have not altered views of his presidency. More than Carter, Nixon tried to rehabilitate his presidency through his ex-presidency. If Carter has helped develop the "office" of the ex-presidency, Nixon often seemed to act as he would act if he were still president, as when he visited China in 1975 and Russia in 1994.

It sometimes seems that the media considers the implications of the Watergate scandal less grave than Senator Edward M. Kennedy's Chappaquiddick incident, or, for that matter, unsubstantiated rumors alleging an affair between John F. Kennedy and Marilyn Monroe. In other words, Watergate is now trivialized. Accordingly, every entertaining if substanceless scandal is now called a particular kind of "gate." Interestingly, the Whitewater scandal, which contains the other word in Watergate, "water," and was initially called Whitewatergate, may have removed the sting from "gate" scandals. Perhaps Whitewater signifies the advanced leveling of Watergate, Watergate's Waterloo. It makes visible the contextualizing powers of political investigations to manufacture Watergates. Such quasi-Watergates seem to hurt both the investigated and the investigators, as well as the political system as a whole, because they display the helplessness of the political process in the face of partisan contextualizing. Perhaps the only beneficiary of these scandals is Nixon. Nixon sought to contextualize the Watergate scandal into oblivion. The facts of Watergate are now confused, and Nixon, at times, appears to be vindicated. Nixon's motives may be questioned; yet, despite his obvious mishandling of the Watergate affair, and despite major economic recessions that occur during his presidency, and the prolongation of the war in Southeast Asia, he is generally looked on as a political sage and a kind of elder statesman. It seemed reasonable for Clinton, soon after taking office, to invite Nixon to the White House before any other ex-president.

The historian Fawn M. Brodie calls Nixon "a man of paradox."[36] The seventies is perhaps the prototypical cultural joke of all American eras, and yet, as an era, it nevertheless establishes our cultural limits, horizons, and realities. Similarly, although former President Nixon is something of a political joke, he is viewed as an uncanny figure, a prophet with and without honor, and, as has been already noted, an innovative president who tested the limits of presidential powers and ultimately extended them. In this regard, observe how, in "Self-Portrait in a Convex Mirror," Parmigianino is destroyed when the convex mirror "flatten[s]"; and yet the painter's presence is extended by being incorporated among "the features of the room" (*SP,* 203: 26–27). Similarly, when Nixon's presidency falls, its "features" ironically become a more integral part of the political landscape, much like the Derridean *pharmakon,* in which the connotations of the words for "poison" and "medicine" slide in and out of one another.[37]

Watergate is, in a sense, contextualized, but not, at times, accounted for, except to trivialize the scandal as irrelevant in comparison to larger presidential concerns. We can assume that Nixon wishes Watergate to be contextualized in such a way that the affair does not, in turn, contextualize him or his presidency. After Nixon leaves office, he becomes a writer, both literally and figuratively, attempting to write a text that will supersede the text of Watergate. (The next section's reading of tape transcript's discusses Nixon as an "author" of Watergate.)

But this manner of accounting for Watergate resembles the strategies that set the stage for the Watergate affair. The Nixon administration strives to keep itself intact and to plug leaks; it fears the unregulated flow of information that might render the administration an object rather than a subject, and it tries to cut off this flow in the name of an innovative use of "executive privilege." Even before Watergate, Bruce Mazlish says of the sitting president that "he is afraid of being acted on, of being inactive, of being soft, of being thought impotent, and of being dependent on anyone else."[38] Mazlish notes Nixon's need to insulate himself from criticism.[39] One avenue of Nixonian insulation is to discount the sources from which criticisms come. Nixon does not feel the need for outside criticism because he seems to believe his statement that "one of my strengths is that I try to be my own severest critic."[40] After all, even Nixon's television image is said to have made him extremely uncomfortable. Of course, among the mechanisms that Nixon used to protect himself from becoming undesirably contextualized is his extensive taping system. He can control its secrets and discomforts, emphasizing the president's role as a privileged subject. Indeed, one can assume that Nixon felt a certain power over all who were secretly recorded.

The president's audiotaping of himself and others, then, resulted from his administration's assertion of its right to determine its own significance. Ironically, like Parmigianino in "Self-Portrait in a Convex Mirror," Nixon, in fulfilling his ambition, creates the mechanism that undoes him.

Before the Nixon administration can involve itself in surveillance, secrecy must be established. After all, the Johnson administration had tried to sell Americans on the idea that it had secret information that justified the war. This is what makes Robert MacNamara's revelations, thirty years after the war's escalation, that no such information existed seem so uncanny. It seems like a voice from the mirror's backing. It can be said that secrecy makes possible the "mirror's backing" of the "reality" that Nixon seeks to impose, the hidden space within that backing and that reality. After all, in terms of the panopticon, the observer must be invisible. Indeed, Mary McCarthy maintains that Nixon underestimates the severity of the Watergate scandal because he "is unable to see that . . . an appearance of confidentiality" is "not a substitute for information."[41] After all, in 1968, this strategy works for Nixon as a presidential candidate. Nixon says that he cannot divulge his strategy to end the Vietnam War; it needs to be covert to work. He explains that he can interfere with neither delicate avenues of diplomacy nor the foreign policy of a sitting president; however, the candidate nonetheless asks the American electorate to vote for him based upon a policy of withholding information; secrecy is, in effect, a vital feature of his program. Although Nixon, in, for instance, his memoirs, justifies his lack of specificity concerning the Vietnam War during the 1968 campaign, explaining that he could not undercut Johnson's initiatives, and denies that he ever said that he had a "'secret plan'" to bring the war to an end, he also calls "the Vietnam war . . . the dominant issue . . . throughout the campaign."[42] It is therefore quite astounding that candidate Nixon is able to avoid commenting specifically about an issue that he considers central. Nixon most likely wished to sell the image of someone who could end the war, or at least distract Americans from it.

The value placed upon secrecy is further reaffirmed when even upon taking office Nixon does not reveal his plan to end the war in Vietnam. Peter N. Carroll notes:

> Nixon's sensitivity to rhetoric—more than a good politician's ear—also reflected his skill at leaving so much unsaid. While Vietnam tore at the national conscience, undermining established loyalties and commitments, splitting families and friends, Nixon in his campaign had pledged simply that "the new leadership will end the war and win the peace in the Pacific." He presented, however, no specific plans. Disavowing any desire to weaken Johnson's chances of ending the war before election day, he had sworn to say "nothing during this campaign that might destroy that chance."
>
> The candidate's vagueness offered a glimmer of hope to the war-weary electorate and, despite Johnson's last minute bombing halt, enabled Nixon to obtain a solid majority. But the inaugural address added little light about the Administration's policy. And when the new President finally did speak about Vietnam at a press conference five days later, the public heard the familiar language of demilitarized zones, mutual withdrawal, and an exchange of prisoners. "Where we go from here," said Nixon, "depends upon what the other side offers in return."[43]

Nixon uses "the other side" as a hidden zone enabling his rhetorical system. What we do not know becomes a reality that dictates rhetoric and policy. Secrecy intertwines with omission. Indeed, Nixon had two self-canceling Indochinese policies. On the one hand, he wished to achieve the accomplishment of peace, and, on the other, he wished to demonstrate a willingness to initiate military conflict. Both contradictory objectives supported each other. Nixon, in effect, was surrendering in a warlike manner. In a sense, the Christmas 1972 firebombings of Hanoi provided "the honor" part of "peace with honor" that made the January 1973 peace agreement palatable to Nixon. Similarly, the 1969 bombings of Cambodia, the 1970 invasion of Cambodia, the 1971 invasion of Laos, and the 1972 mining of North Vietnamese harbors were sporadic acts of "innovative" violence intended to gain enough credibility to entertain the possibility of an unspeakable defeat. The goal of the war's end-game was to obscure its outcome—to blur its reality and consequences. Indeed, Nixon might have desired an ongoing state of complex intermittent struggle in Vietnam, and it is very conceivable that Nixon, if he were still president, would have sent American soldiers back into Vietnam before the collapse of Saigon in 1975, as the South Vietnamese government believed that Nixon had promised. Nixon, if not for Watergate, might have sought to maintain a perpetual war.

Given Nixon's creative use of "gaps," it is not surprising that *Six Crises* (1962) and *The Memoirs of Richard Nixon* (1978) are significantly organized around descriptions of discrete instances, allowing the author to omit what he does not wish to discuss. Appropriately, Brodie calls Nixon's memoirs "a masterful study of omission."[44] As delightful and insightful as the memoirs may be, they nevertheless do not mention, for instance, Nixon's failures as a businessman and a lawyer before World War II.[45] In addition, the eighteen-and-a-half-minute gap in the tape of a 20 June 1972 conversation between Nixon and Haldeman and the use of the "expletive deleted" device in the White House tape transcriptions are central examples of the strategy of omission, deletion, and ellipsis that shapes the mythology of Richard Nixon. One also recalls that when Nixon delivered his 1968 speech accepting the Republican National Convention's presidential nomination, the nominee did not acknowledge the riot that was raging outside the Miami convention hall.

Johnson strained to justify his Vietnam policy to the American people, and he retreated from that policy and indeed from his presidency when he could not do so. His fictive liberties, however, tend to be additions, such as the contrived Gulf of Tonkin incident in 1964, rather than omissions. Nixon, however, simply hides his Indochina war policy. Why publicly announce that he is bombing Cambodia, a neutral nation? (By 1969, when the United States began bombing Cambodia, Cambodia was only nominally neutral. Early in 1969, the United States helped overthrow Prince Norodom Sihanouk's traditionally neutral government. This destabilizing of Cambodia was responsible for the holocaust that occurred there from 1975 to 1979, a holocaust the United States officially did not recognize when it sided with Cambodia against Vietnam in the United Nations in the late seventies.)

Creatively, Nixon used the shield of national security in circumstances in which it had never been used before. Did not the Cambodians know that they were being bombed? Did not the North Vietnamese know about these bombings of their supply routes? National security had previously been used to counteract foreign threats. However, in this case, the only possible threat was from domestic public opinion.

Nixon gave extraordinary emphasis to discrediting and punishing those who provided information that put the American war effort in an unfavorable light, even when this information did not directly concern the period of his presidency. He seemed to associate the Vietnam War's credibility with the credibility of the presidency. In May of 1969, early in his administration, Nixon ordered John Ehrlichman to gather embarrassing information that might undermine the credibility of soldiers who did not lie to the press about their roles in the 1968 My Lai massacre, in which 120 unarmed Vietnamese civilians, including babies, were slaughtered. At about the same time, the Nixon administration sought to wiretap William Beecher, the *New York Times* reporter who uncovered the secret Cambodia bombings. To avoid the need for a court order, the wiretaps were justified as a national security concern. (A unanimous decision by the Supreme Court, on 19 June 1974, refuted the administration's claim that court warrants were unnecessary.) Nixon admittedly used national security as a basis for at least seventeen other wiretaps of those he considered his political enemies or potential enemies. The president desired an orderly means of surveying and wiretapping whomever he felt to be a "national security" danger without the intermediary of the courts.[46]

Nixon wanted the resources of the FBI, the CIA, the Defense Intelligence Agency, and the National Security Agency under the president's direct control. To this end, Tom Charles Huston, as John Dean first publicized in his 1973 Ervin committee testimony, was instructed to devise a plan for a White House–controlled interagency that would supervise all of the nation's intelligence operations and be more quickly responsive to every surveillance wish of the president, including indiscriminate non-court-warranted wiretapping. Through the Huston plan, Haldeman, speaking for Nixon, simply declared this White House control to be in effect. No public notification of the policy was thought to be necessary.[47]

The administration also employed freelancers in its surveillance efforts. The "plumbers" operation began when presidential aide Charles Colson enlisted his friend E. Howard Hunt Jr. to help in discrediting and punishing, that is, in "nailing," Daniel Ellsberg for releasing the Pentagon Papers, which chronicled a pattern of government deception about its policy in Vietnam under Democratic administrations. This release violated a policy of governmental secrecy.

Given that Hunt had authored numerous espionage novels, it is interesting to speculate that perhaps Hunt unconsciously took a clue from the fictional detective Mike Hammer, who breaks into a psychiatrist's office for evidence in Mickey Spillane's *I, the Jury*. In any case, G. Gordon Liddy and others were later recruited by the operation that was to be responsible for breaking into and burglarizing the office of Dr. Lewis Fielding, Daniel Ellsberg's psychiatrist.

Still later, with Operation Gemstone, the "plumbers'" pursuit of covert information led to their surveillance of the Democratic National Committee's offices in the Watergate hotel complex.

From the administration's perspective, the release of the Pentagon Papers symbolized its inability to control knowledge. The free flow of information was unacceptable. Who was Ellsberg to think he had any control over a Defense Department report? It belonged to the Defense Department, the administration, and the president. Information and knowledge were seen as the property of the Nixon administration and its interests. In the 23 June transcript of the "smoking gun" tape, Haldeman calls FBI agents "not under control,"[48] because they are tracing the money trail that financed the Watergate break-in. Nixon wonders whether the contributor whose name is on the check, Kenneth Dahlberg, can be counted on to mislead the investigators (couldn't Dahlberg say that he gave his cashier's check, representing illegal tithe-like payments from his employees,[49] directly to the Cuban burglars and not, as he in fact did, to Maurice Stans, the chairman of the Committee to Re-Elect the President?[50]). Nixon does not merely speculate as to whether Dahlberg can be relied upon in this regard; he calls into question Dahlberg's entire worth, despite the fact that Haldeman has just told Nixon that Dahlberg contributed twenty-five thousand dollars to his reelection campaign. "Maybe he's a . . . bum," the president worries.[51]

When one posits that Nixon and Haldeman considered "federal" knowledge and information commodities that they controlled, their attitudes become more understandable. Perhaps a more apt metaphor would be of an area that is out-of-bounds for everyone not sanctioned by the president. If they did not protect national, presidential reality, Nixon would, they thought, fall to the dissenters just as Johnson had. Sources of sixties dissension had to be sabotaged and curtailed. They would seem to undermine not only the Nixon administration's hold on the presidency, but also the very sense of presidential authority. Nixon seems to see his surveillance operations as a defense of this authority. The part of the "smoking gun" tape that is available to the public ends with Nixon commenting on the surplus campaign funds that financed the Watergate break-in. "There's a lot of dough in this," observes Haldeman, explaining why some of it would inevitably lead to problems, in addition to why the CIA would understand these problems since "their money moves in a lot of different ways too."[52] "Can you imagine what Kennedy would have done with that money?" asks the president.[53] (The National Archives considers Haldeman's response inconsequential to executive abuse of power, and it is not available to the public.) A fear of his enemies, especially the dead president, seems to drive Nixon, who often suggests how rough the Kennedys played with him, leaving him with little choice but to play rough now. "Play it tough. That's the way they play it and that's the way we are going to play it," Nixon advises Haldeman.[54] Nixon even says that the mishaps connected with the "wild hair thing" of the botched Watergate break-in may have all been to the good because now they know that their "little boys [presumably the plumbers] will not know how to handle it" when "they start bugging us":

> Yeah, when I saw that news summary item, I of course knew it was a bunch of crap, but I thought, ah, well it's good to have them off on this wild hair thing because when they start bugging us, which they have, we'll know our little boys will not know how to handle it. I hope they will though. You never know. Maybe, you think about it. Good![55]

Nixon implies that their surveillance powers need to be strengthened so that future onslaughts can be met.

If Nixon at first thought the capture of the Watergate burglars was for the best because it demonstrated improvements that needed to be made in his surveillance operations, perhaps Nixon similarly rationalized the entire Watergate affair. For Nixon, Watergate became a challenge to rise above those who would recall it. The legacy of Richard Nixon resists the onslaught of efforts to keep the tapes and the memories of Watergate relevant. Don DeLillo's *White Noise* (1985) posits a similar struggle within the context of Watergate and points out the rift that Watergate emblematizes in our political memories. Speaking of the fictional drug "Dylar" that destroys memory, Jack, the director of Hitler Studies in *White Noise,* asks his wife for her discarded Dylar pills: "Is it possible you threw them away in an angry or depressed moment? I only want them for the sake of historical accuracy. Like White House tapes. They go into the archives."[56] DeLillo associates the Watergate tapes with a paradoxical documentation of the destruction of memory under the pretext of a meaninglessly objective "historical accuracy." Such historical accuracy functions like Dylar because it divorces the Watergate tapes from a consideration of any possible effect that they might have. The tapes cannot be reproduced because such reproduction would exceed the demands of historical accuracy. This reproduction, however, would greatly contribute to a general understanding of the shockingly explicit and unprecedented nature of Nixon's use of his presidential powers to obstruct justice.

We remember and do not remember Watergate. As a scandal, Watergate is like "The Most Photographed Barn in America" that DeLillo depicts in *White Noise*. "No one sees the barn,"[57] says Murray, the would-be innovator of Elvis Studies. One can only see tourists photographing the barn. As does every succeeding scandal dubbed with the suffix "gate," "every photograph reinforces the aura"[58] of the barn as it, so to speak, blocks its view. We cannot know what the barn was "like before it was photographed. . . . We can't get outside the aura."[59] And yet, as represented by the booth that sells postcards and slides of the barn, the aura of this mystery depends upon the assumption of the material spectacle of an actual barn.[60]

The tropology of Haldeman's dialogue with the president on the "smoking gun" tape also reinforces the sense of a material yet secret and protected area. Haldeman continually territorializes secrecy and information. On the "smoking gun" tape, his first frame of reference—that is, Haldeman's means of identifying to Nixon the work they have already done on the subject—is "the problem area." Haldeman equates this problem area with the wrong kind of production:

> Now, on the investigation, you know, the Democratic break-in thing, we're back to the—in the, the problem area because the FBI is not under control, because Gray doesn't exactly know how to control them, and they have, their investigation is now leading into some productive areas.[61]

L. Patrick Gray, the acting FBI chief, needs the White House's help in preventing out-of-control FBI agents from doing their jobs. Haldeman tells Nixon that he must give Gray a "basis" for doing so. A "signal" "must be sent from across the river"[62] to indicate that the president has determined that this investigation is off limits. Nixon directs Haldeman about what to say to those who will communicate with Gray:

> When you get in these people . . . when you get these people in, say: "Look, the problem is this will open the whole, the whole Bay of Pigs thing, and the president just feels that" ah, without going into the details . . . don't, don't lie to them to the extent that there is no involvement, but just say that this is sort of a comedy of errors, bizarre, without getting into it, "the president believes that it is going to open the whole Bay of Pigs thing up again. And, ah because these people are plugging for, for keeps and that they should call the FBI in and say that we wish for the country, don't go any further into this case," period![63]

White House "involvement" may exist, but only as "a comedy," a "bizarre" fiction.

In the tape transcripts, Nixon often evokes "the whole Bay of Pigs thing." What could he mean? The Bay of Pigs fiasco occurred eleven years before the Watergate break-in. How could bugging the Democratic National Committee in 1972 bear upon the unsuccessful invasion of Cuba in 1961? Yet Nixon never needs to elaborate. The evocation of the Bay of Pigs is enough to silence Haldeman and others. How could the Bay of Pigs be opened up "again"? When was it opened before? What does "plugging" the Bay of Pigs "for keeps" mean? Why does Nixon extend the invasion to a wider mission, one that he broaches anxiously—"the whole, the whole Bay of Pigs thing"? Of course, a study such as this one can offer no definitive answers to these questions. We can, however, note a sense conveyed that the Bay of Pigs is a code for something else, something too dreadful for Nixon to begin to broach explicitly. In any case, if one substitutes, for instance, "the Kennedy assassination" for "the Bay of Pigs," Nixon's statements make more sense, as if, perhaps only in Nixon's mind, the assassination flowed from the events of the Bay of Pigs and was indeed a part of "the whole Bay of Pigs thing." Oddly, in Oliver Stone's "counter-myth" film, *JFK* (1991),[64] the Kennedy assassination plot begins with the military's dissatisfaction with Kennedy for failing to support sufficiently their efforts at the Bay of Pigs. (Of course, to use an argument of Stone's, I am commenting more on the myth of the Kennedy assassination and, in my case, of Watergate, than pointing to a definite, hard and fast reading. And yet, even in terms of a hypothetically strict and denotative reading, Watergate historians and journalists, and indeed almost all of us, have been lax in inquiring about the underpinnings of what Nixon could have "meant" by "the whole Bay of Pigs thing" in 1972, more than eleven years after the invasion in 1961. What secrets remained?) One might say that Watergate puts a frame around the Kennedy assassination, in that the outrage about the assassination centers on the anxiety surrounding a putative cover-up, and the latter president is faulted more for obstruction of justice by an attempted cover-up than for any other crime. If the myth of President Kennedy was integrated, after his assassination, into an opening up of the popular mind, the Kennedy assassination is deconstructed into both that opening up and its repression; John Kennedy's assassination, mediated by Robert Kennedy's assassination, is the symbolic crime behind Watergate. As the sixties becomes something that is inherently beyond testimony—note the saying that anyone who remembers the sixties was not there and Bob Dylan's likening of the sixties to a flying saucer sighting—the unspecified crime behind Watergate—what Nixon refers to as "the Bay of Pigs thing"—keeps a lid on America and protects it from an inexplicable excitement and danger. (Indeed, the very name Watergate implies a control placed on a seemingly uncontrollable and liquid substance.)

Predictably, the suggestion of codes for absent signifiers saturates the Watergate tapes and the Watergate affair as a whole. In a sense, the eighteen-minute, twenty-eight-second tape gap is the cornerstone of the Watergate affair. It precedes the "smoking gun" tape by three days and, since, on the latter tape, Haldeman is updating Nixon about the handling of the fallout from the Watergate arrests, and Haldeman's 20 June 1973 notes indicate that Watergate was discussed, it seems likely that the manual erasures on the prior tape covered up damaging information. We can never be certain what that information was, if indeed there was any, and that mystery spills out on our sense of the entire scandal. It therefore seems as appropriate as it is strange to consider what we have of the "tape" of this conversation (only the tape gap is available for public listening because the remaining conversation does not concern Watergate) and the tape interference within their broader cultural contexts. I will make a case for thinking of the tape gap as a sound composition, as a work of electronic music.

The tape, as available at the National Archives' Nixon Project, makes eerie listening. This effect is enhanced by the fact that the tape cannot be copied and can only be heard at the Nixon Project, originally in Alexandria, Virginia, and now in College Park, Maryland. One feels privileged to hear it, almost as if one were a head of state, a voyeur, or both, almost as if the two were aspects of one another. From another perspective, one is reminded of John Cage's distaste for reproduced music. If sound is to be reproduced, he reasoned, let that element of reproduction itself be the music. If music is to be electrified, why not simply manipulate the electronic feedback, an effect the eighteen-and-a-half-minute tape gap approximates. Not surprisingly, the roots of Nixon's career are in the middle and the late forties, when Cage first experiments with chance procedures and electronic music. This post–World War II period sees America's crash course in and grabbing of the leadership of the play of self-reflexive modernism. In the phenomenon of the eighteen-and-a-half-minute tape gap, we find Nixon, a pioneering Cold Warrior, peculiarly in his element. Nixon once said that to him the American people were a camera lens. He was acutely aware of technology's plays of condensation and manipulation. The symbolic significance of the tape gap within the narrative of Nixon's downfall reminds one of the photographic "picture that erased his [the photograph's subjects] seclusion, made it never happen and made him over and gave him a face we've known all our lives," in Don DeLillo's *Mao II* (1991).[65]

In John Cage's landmark piano composition, *Four Minutes, Thirty-three Seconds* (1949), in which pianist David Tutor merely opens the piano lid and, halfway through the composition, closes the lid, Cage framed and dispensed silence so as to make us hear the workings of our society with an ear that we had previously withheld from that task. The eighteen-and-a-half-minute tape gap, like Robert Rauschenberg's *De Kooning Erased* (1956), uses absence to reveal a haunting presence. By paying scrupulous attention to the sounds of the Watergate tape gap, we feel the meaning of the meaninglessness that permeates the Watergate affair. "The famous eighteen-minute gap in Nixon's tapes was ultimately damaging not because it said so little but because it said so much. It allowed us to reflect upon its meaning," notes Henry M. Sayre. Similarly, Sayre says, "the majority of the most interesting works of art produced over the last two or three decades ask us to fill in the gaps they produce in much the same way. They are *pensive,* to use Barthes' word. Or to use Derrida's, they acknowledge their status to be that of the trace. As a kind of free-floating signifier, the trace cannot be pinned down; it can never be 'put to rest.' It demands a more conscious and conceptual approach to art. It demands *critical performance.*"[66] In this spirit, I will soon "perform" or "read" Nixon's score for the eighteen-and-a-half-minute tape gap. This seems to be a particularly apt manner of "discussing" the scandal since our knowledge of it is so dependent on testimony and incomplete transcription. Indeed, what is not reported takes a crucial place within Watergate. Watergate is a phenomena that is inscribed within the discourse or "work" that it enables, and our readings of the eighteen-and-a-half-minute tape gap can be construed as the entire affair's objective correlative.

The impressions of erasure may also have a conventionally "artistic" interest, of sorts, considering that Nixon himself may well have personally erased the tape, as John Dean speculates, based on his observations of Nixon's clumsiness in "taking the top[s] off fountain pen[s]" and the technical experts' report to Judge Sirica that "the gap was the result of five separate and intentional erasures" and thus presumably the "work" of "somebody who is not very good mechanically."[67]

A more significant rationale for studying the tape gap as electronic music may lie in the integral relationship between surveillance and electronic music since the latter's inception. The first electronic music instrument was invented by Leon Thereman when he was twenty-two years old in the second decade of the twentieth century in Russia. The thereman is an electronic device with only two knobs. One knob controls tone and the other knob controls volume. There can be no "behind the scenes" intervals between tones nor any unmodulated or divided progression of tones. The thereman was first intended to guard the czar's jewelry. It would ideally detect any movement around the jewels because its ongoing electronic tone would register any interference. It was thought that it would have great value as a burglar alarm.

When Leon Thereman emigrated to the United States in 1919, the thereman was used in various avant-garde music and performance works by Anthiel and other musicians and artists. Brian Wilson used it in "Good Vibrations" and other songs. Wilson said he was drawn to the instrument's eerie "unwritten" sound, and the thereman is most identified with its use in Hollywood horror films. The "wu-wu-wu-WU-wu" modulation of the thereman is often parodied as a signal of approaching terror. Further adding to associations between electronic music and surveillance, Leon Thereman vanished mysteriously in 1938. Rumors abounded until, in 1989, Thereman surfaced in the Soviet Union as a technical wizard within the KGB, a short time before he died in 1993 at the age of ninety-seven. Oddly, Thereman was something like the Alexander Butterfield of Stalin's Kremlin. Thereman bugged the Kremlin for Stalin.

The German invention of the audiotape during World War II gave rise to electronic music as we know it: sounds could now seamlessly be spliced together and sudden shifts of tone and instrumentation were now possible with the use of only one "instrument." Interestingly, audiotape is also widely associated with modern electronic espionage. Tapes can more efficiently be stored, edited, and analyzed than discs. Cold War surveillance and electronic music are historical twins of the same era. Not insignificantly, Richard Nixon's career begins during this era, his star hung on his surveillant exploits in pursuit of Alger Hiss. Perhaps in response, Ashbery's strong but undetectable prosody also takes shape in this era.

When listening to the beginning of the eighteen-and-a-half-minute tape gap as electronic music, one notes a series of percussive interruptions of a high-pitched and beautifully edged tone. A lulling suspension of this tone is punctuated by buzzes and a sudden silence, from which a very mellow static, composed of light, narrow, and slowly lengthening oscillations emerges. The elongating of these oscillations levels off and then meets a thud, a silence, and a return to the original pitch, which is now tinged with a more staticky static. While the tape here mirthfully connotes pure electricity and feedback, other levels of the tape, and indeed of Nixon, seem repressed when an underlying fuzziness oscillating under that tone takes on a thicker texture suggesting a fuller substance. With an unexpected click, the purr subsides. A narrow, airy draft is introduced and then takes over. This is pleasant at first, as if one's ears were themselves the lips of waterfalls of sound that are connected to the inverse-fountain-like headphones with which one is required to listen to the Watergate tapes. This spray, however, becomes less of an unconfrontational white noise and two pitches conflict. These conflicting sounds end with a pinprick-like click. The white noise again deepens. A whir flies up like a helicopter. Its pitch loops down and up repeatedly. A big click brings to mind the feeling and image of falling off a log onto one's face, and then the buzz intensifies. This buzz fans out, as if to convey a sense of riding home on it. Another click is followed by a "phttt" and a "pip" and then a repeating round of tone rows of static gives the effect of sounds falling out of themselves. These projections of sound continue and bring to mind a reverse and in-your face kind of perspective. This frontal quality reminds one of the tape's cloaking, covering dimensions. A tap is followed by a grinding, approaching plane-engine-like sound. A powerful, lower-toned buzz drops suddenly, as if off a table. The tone staggers. A piercing static fades into silence.

Secrecy, erasure, and omission are important tropes for a Nixon administration that desires autonomy and self-signification—an aspect of all governments, perhaps, but in varying degrees. The Nixon administration makes this a raison d'être, its first principle. In the "smoking gun" tape conversation with Haldeman, Nixon is at first critical of Mitchell's pressing for information that led to the Watergate burglars' unforgivable (to Nixon) sin of leaving a money trail. Then, however, Haldeman confirms Nixon's suspicion that the pressure was coming from "Gemstone," the code name for the initiative to gather intelligence for the administration's exclusive use, outside the purview of the federal government's surveillance operations. Nixon is suddenly understanding: "All right, fine, I understand it all."[68]

Nixon helps to reinforce the self-reinforcing feedback mechanism of his administration. (In another era, this reinforcement occurs in Rush Limbaugh's reportage of Vince Foster's suicide, in which Limbaugh recounted a rumor of the Clintons' involvement in his "murder," and then, in the same broadcast, reported the confirmation of this rumor based on an electronic retelling of his original report.) This self-reinforcing mechanism grows in its involvement with itself as the war in Vietnam becomes increasingly difficult to escalate. Garry Wills describes a parallel, domestic escalation of administrative attempts to accomplish self-signification and to crush criticism: "Nixon got caught in his own 'third murderer' problem—he had to hire new crooks to control his crooks, in an infinite regression."[69] Unlike Andy Warhol, who did not mind being watched because he liked "watching the watchers,"[70] Nixon's administration seeks absolute control over its own acts of surveillance. Perhaps for this reason, it cannot escape this infinitely regressive series of acts. One thinks of the succession of firings and hirings that constitute the October 1973 Saturday Night Massacre.

One also thinks of Haldeman's first warning to Nixon about the problems inherent in a cover-up. Nixon asks Haldeman whether everyone in the money trail to the Watergate burglars can deny any connection with the Republican National Committee. There does not seem to be a problem. "But then," Haldeman replies, "we're relying on more and more people all the time. That's the problem. And ah, they'll stop if we could, if we take this other step" of directing the FBI and the CIA to cooperate in thwarting the investigation.[71]

Such a lengthening chain would not have been a problem for Warhol. Whereas Warhol makes a point of letting it be known that his tape recorder is running, Nixon's surveillance is, of course, clandestine. Demands by the special prosecutor, Congress, and the courts to have access to these tapes engender a complicated series of defenses and mishaps. These complications are inadvertently captured by Nixon's personal secretary, Rose Mary Woods, in her contorted demonstration of the manner in which she claims to have accidentally composed the tape gap by erasing eighteen minutes and twenty-eight seconds of the recording of the 20 June 1972 meeting between Nixon and Haldeman. Woods's intricate position—using what seemed like all her hands and legs, on a keyboard, a notepad, and footpedals as she lurches for a telephone receiver that is virtually out of her reach—recalls the zigzagging path of the single "magic" bullet that ricocheted between President Kennedy and Governor Connally as proposed by the Warren Commission's single-bullet theory.

It is not surprising that, after Haldeman is dismissed as the White House chief of staff in April 1973, Nixon does not divulge information that is sufficient for any of his aides to form a clear view of the Watergate situation. A direct line of communication is not opened with the president's counsel and his other lawyers. Woodward and Bernstein quote Counsel to the President Leonard Garment:

"Given the peril of the situation, I can't accept the fact that all the information is derivative," Garment said. Everything came to the lawyers indirectly, almost never from the client they were supposed to be defending.[72]

That Warhol so eagerly tells of his tape-recording process, while Nixon so desperately strives to keep his tapes and information secret, demonstrates a fundamental difference between an artist and a president. The artist consciously or unconsciously calls attention to her or his mode of production. In "Self-Portrait in a Convex Mirror," Ashbery's speaker says that "the game where / A whispered phrase passed around the room / Ends up as something completely different" "is the principle that" "secretly satisfie[s]" the artist. The president, however, tends to control information. Nixon's presidency was probably doomed when he publicized tape transcriptions that, as edited as they are, nonetheless cast the president as an extremely fallible human being. It probably would have been better for Nixon if the tapes were filtered through those who were requesting them through legal channels. Instead, Nixon uses public exposure of the edited transcripts to emphasize legal arguments, which I discuss in my analysis in the next section of the "cancer on the presidency" tape transcript. The public seized upon the baseness of Nixon's conversation and perceived the president as common and "unpresidential." Nixon sacrificed the public relations value of presidential covertness. He allowed disclosures of details concerning the president's personal life to rivet the public's attention. It became increasingly difficult for the public to accept Nixon's claim of executive privilege and satisfy itself with the idea of information resting benevolently with the chief executive. Presidential powers were too plainly perceived as obstructing justice and could not be revered and trusted. In the mid-seventies, the maintenance of hidden and unknown truths no longer heightened the prestige of the presidency. The use of the term "expletive deleted" was particularly disastrous for Nixon. Nixon expected the American people to trust him because he felt he represented the system. It seems not to have occurred to him that Americans were feeling ambivalent about the system as he appeared to embody it. The gaps and omissions that "expletive deleted" bespoke undermined rather than enhanced presidential power.

Perhaps this questioning of the president's covertness, with an accompanying diminution of the chief executive's prestige, was ideologically necessary. If the presidency is an ideological state apparatus, it must periodically be altered, so as to be made recognizable as "the truth." Undoubtedly, the horrors of the Vietnam War initially injured the presidency's credibility. In the mid-seventies, a drastic adjustment needed to be made in our perceptions of the presidency if the nation's ideological state apparatus, as we know it, was to survive. Nixon, unknowingly, initiated this revision. Domestic espionage operations escalated along with the Nixon administration's escalation and prolongation of the Vietnam War. (To name one small example, surveillance in support of the John Lennon deportation effort "backfired" on the administration.) Of course, Vietnam-related surveillance issues led to the formation of the "plumbers." It is almost as if the Nixon administration and the Watergate affair gave the Vietnam War a local name, national name, and habitation.

To sum up, during the Watergate era ideological and poetic disciplines account for their hidden aspects by organizing themselves into a single view or situation, which, in turn, can be surveyed (much as Ashbery found Parmigianino's self-portrait and Johns organized his mid-seventies paintings around a single motif). Nixon's resignation is a backing of the mirror, in the sense that the nation hits and rebounds from it into a renewed sense of itself. The next section more closely reads this "resignation."

3 Tricky Diptych

Lucille Ball said she and Desi Arnaz divorced to save their marriage. In a sense, Nixon resigned to save his presidency. Nixon's resignation was no doubt extremely unfortunate, but in an odd way it saved his political life. A rigorous Senate impeachment proceeding in which the details of Nixon's abuses of power would have been explained to the public would have cast his violations in terms of tangible "proof," so that his abuses would not easily have been forgotten or excused. The rhetoric of the House Judiciary Committee's "indictment" proceedings did not serve the same purpose as an impeachment trial, and Gerald Ford's pardon assured that there would be no criminal court proceedings.

The 1996 agreement between the National Archives, the Nixon estate, and interested scholars has created a steady stream of isolated disclosures concerning Richard Nixon, based on Nixon's presidential self-surveillance. Transcripts relating to abuses of power are periodically declassified. However, they are not at the top of the news, and they do not engender the astonishment Americans once experienced at being privy to secret presidential meetings. They seem no more unusual than the transcripts of telephone conversations between Woody Allen and Mia Farrow, Prince Charles and Camilla Bowles, Bill

Clinton and Gennifer Flowers, or Newt Gingrich and Dick Armey. It is difficult for us to recall how amazing it was to be party to a president's "expletives deleted," and, indeed, to the political corruption of the government.

Perhaps Nixon's tapes have surveyed us, in the sense that they have informed and changed us. Because of Nixon we all experienced ourselves as voyeurs. One of the purposes of this section is to recontextualize the original shock of the tape transcripts. To do this I want to look at them afresh by using the tools of literary analysis. Applying these tools to seemingly non-literary texts will help display some unexpected charms implicit in both the tools and the tapes.

In examining two seminal Nixon texts, I present a kind of Nixon diptych—a tricky diptych of literary analysis. I discuss Nixon's resignation speech and the 21 March 1973 tape transcription in reverse chronological order because the resignation speech reinforces the institution of the American presidency as a functional ideological mechanism, whereas Dean's celebrated 21 March 1973 description of a "cancer on the presidency" demonstrates the "breach of faith" (adapting the title of Theodore H. White's 1975 chronicle of the Watergate affair) that the resignation speech comes to grips with and attempts to mend. Ultimately, I argue, Watergate leaves the prevalent American sensibility in an ambivalent relation to "logocentric" reality. In short, the resignation speech makes the best case for the reality of a national logocentrism as it is in retreat, and the subsequent tape transcript the assuredness of this reality, with a cautious John Dean refuting and problematizing it. Indeed, perhaps Dean too idealistically denies it.

How to Save a Presidency: Resign

A modern president, it can be argued, is obligated to conceal information and, ironically, to reveal that he is keeping knowledge privy to himself and his administration. Indeed, Jeffrey K. Tulis maintains that the modern president's major task is ideologically to counter the federal government's impression of a bureaucratic stalemate by voicing a strong personal view of the nation. According to Theodore J. Lowi, the successful president conveys an exemplary sense of self replete with the extraordinary premise that one individual can cure all the nation's ills.

Some of President Clinton's political opponents have undermined his authority as president by suggesting that he has somehow debased the idea and "personality" of the presidency. Unavoidably, the person and the president share a complicated relationship. In his 1992 campaign, Bush maintained that they could not be separated. Nixon sincerely believed that to question the person who was president was to undermine the office. In addition, Nixon probably felt that his person was particularly presidential, in contrast with what he perceived to be Kennedy's unreliability and Eisenhower's aloofness. Nixon felt that he breathed new life into the presidency. Underneath Nixon's assertions that "I am the President" and "I am your President" was his reminder to us that a person was needed to reinvigorate the office. I think of the American scene in the sixties and seventies, and professed "avatars" who claimed to reinforce the avataric "office." For instance, Meher Baba, an Indian spiritual master who coined the phrase "Don't Worry, Be Happy," said both "I am the avatar" and "I am your avatar."

Nixon's resignation speech attempts to repair the damage that Watergate does to this premise of the power of the personal presidency, but may be said to serve Nixon more than the presidency. Although few watching Nixon's resignation speech believe Nixon, the speech nevertheless minimizes Watergate and helps Nixon's presidency after the fact. Never apologizing, Nixon hides behind the mechanism of the presidency, sanitizing himself more than the presidency and fostering the United States's growing ambivalence toward its chief executive.

That Ray Price, and not Nixon, is the chief author of the resignation speech should not overly concern us. First, Nixon contributes to the drafting of the speech. White reports:

> The President was on the phone to Ray Price, who was working on the final, final draft of the resignation speech he had begun one week before. Price was to have little sleep that night. The President was recomposing the draft in almost consecutive phone calls until two in the morning, when Price was finally off to bed; at 4:15 he was awakened again with another call and more thoughts from the President, and the calls went to the White House to continue work. . . .
>
> At 10:50 [8 August 1974, the morning before Nixon delivers his resignation speech] Nixon received Price in absolute composure, his mind at its editorial best, pointing out redundancies of phrase in the farewell address, marking possible contractions, circling and tracking flow points.[73]

Clearly, the resignation speech is processed through Nixon. Indeed, Price identifies himself as "the President's collaborator on his . . . resignation address."[74]

Second, the president's speechwriters in general, and Price in particular, are an integral part of Nixon's presidency. "The writers who draft Presidential speeches and messages," says White, "are considered a personal facility of the President."[75]

From his 1968 presidential campaign to his 1974 resignation, Nixon views Price, in particular, as his "presidential voice." Price, a former editorial writer for the *New York Herald Tribune,* is accustomed to employing an authoritative yet conciliatory tone. Jonathan Schell notes that, in contradistinction to Nixon's other major speechwriter, the younger and more partisan "Mr. Inside," Patrick Buchanan, who writes Nixonian speeches that are narrowcast toward Nixon's "hard-core supporters,"[76] Price writes for a consensus audience:

> [Price] was known around the campaign as Mr. Outside, because what he wrote was designed to please a broad range of people, not just those in the narrow circle of Mr. Nixon's traditional supporters.[77]

Indeed, White implies that Price is a kind of surrogate for the most genial of presidential presences. "Everyone trust[s]" him, says White of Price, even when Nixon himself no longer conveys a presidential image.[78]

Nixon's collaboration with Price probably reflected Nixon's bad memories of his premature 1962 farewell to the press upon losing the California gubernatorial race. This time he would say nothing like "You won't have Nixon to kick around anymore." If he could return to political respectability after 1962, after all, he could return after 1974. Price was a hedge against another bad exit. Outtakes of Nixon in front of the camera immediately before his resignation speech joking about ordering a nuclear attack demonstrate how much on the edge he was.

Ironically, Nixon does not issue the first directive for the drafting of his own resignation speech. Chief of Staff General Alexander M. Haig enlists Price in Haig's behind-the-scenes efforts to terminate Nixon's presidency:

> Haig was off on his own track. He called in speechwriter Ray Price, whom everyone trusted, and telling him specifically, but briefly, what the new tapes contained . . . relayed the information that the President was considering the idea of a television address to the nation to accompany their revelation. After which, Haig offered a thought of his own: he urged Price to do something more, to start drafting a statement of resignation for the President, to be ready when necessary. Haig was setting up the prime option.[79]

In short, although Nixon's resignation speech is seemingly authored by Price, the speech reflects the input of others, including Haig and Nixon. However, Price, with whom Nixon collaborates in drafting speeches that require a "presidential voice," occupies a central position in the "Nixon" administration. I now provide an "uncanny" molecular reading of Nixon's resignation speech.

The Watergate affair encourages a logocentric perception of the state. The state, that is, embodies a presence of personal and unified reasoning. Note, for instance, the beginning of Nixon's resignation speech:

> Good evening.
> This is the thirty-seventh time I have spoken to you from this office, where so many decisions have been made that shaped the history of this Nation. Each time I have done so to discuss with you some matter that I believe affected the national interest.[80]

Nixon, the thirty-seventh president of the United States, evokes the number thirty-seven, suggesting that his presidency is a kind of microcosm for the history of the office, associating each of his Oval Office speeches with a presidency. (Price said that he recognized this numerical correspondence after he had finished the speech, and he felt that it was a nice touch.) It is almost as if the prototypical utterance of the thirty-seventh president were a resignation, as if Nixon's defining distinctiveness and presidential history came together at the moment of the speech and the uniqueness of the occasion were consecrated by tradition. Although Nixon's choice for a salutation may be limited, it nevertheless speaks to and is modified by the occasion. His salutation "Good Evening" acknowledges that this is a "night" of the American presidency while tropologically framing the subsequent allusions to all of presidential history as a present occurrence and sanitizing this episode in it as ultimately "good." Nixon's resignation, it is suggested, is a nightfall or evening that is in keeping with the apparently "natural" or inevitable process that, Nixon implies, presidential succession is. And yet, contrary to these connotations, Nixon hints that this resignation is chiefly his own decision. "The history of this Nation" is said to be "shaped" by "many decisions," thus stressing the power of individual presidents over history.

Nixon states that, in all of his addresses that have been broadcast from the Oval Office, he has discussed "some matter that I believe affected the national interest." Of course, there would seem to be little purpose in giving such a speech other than that of "national interest." What is significant is that Nixon links his credibility, or what he says that he believes, to matters of national interest. On our paper money, after all, faces of presidents visually back up the words "In God We Trust." (It is joked that Benjamin Franklin and Alexander Hamilton, whose images appear on our paper currency, are the only two presidents never to have been president.) Nixon couples the interests of the nation with his personal belief system. From a Derridean perspective, it might be noted that an unquestioned existence of signified elements and a logocentric perspective are mutually reinforcing.

Nixon's resignation speech indicates how the Nixon administration would "shape" the Watergate affair in "the history of this Nation":

> In all the decisions I have made in my public life, I have always tried to do what was best for the Nation. Throughout the long and difficult period of Watergate, I have felt it my duty to persevere, to make every possible effort to complete the term of office to which you elected me.[81]

Nixon maintains that Watergate is consistent with his entire career, which, we may presume, has always foreshadowed his presidency. The president could not both "do what was best for the Nation" and "complete" his "term of office." Nixon, it would seem, defends the presidency when the office of the presidency is besieged and must suffer the consequences.

Nixon places the scandal, as well as the surveillance operations that set the stage for it, within the context of a kind of "referential imperative," or, in other words, an uncompromising reality whose value, it is maintained, is contingent upon no other value. This all-important consideration is, of course, the state's welfare and security, or "what was best for the Nation." Similarly, Nixon's critics act as if Nixon's expulsion would help secure similar ends. A significant difference, however, is exhibited by Nixon's need to maintain the secrecy of these referential necessities. His antagonists, nonetheless, mirror this compulsion of Nixon's by privileging the possibility of a complete depiction of the literal scene of his crimes, which is ironically the same office that Nixon's resignation speech calls attention to as the site from which his major proclamations originate and are emitted.

As Nixon portrays the state as a logocentric entity, so his political enemies consolidate national problems into one individual, or presidency. This is particularly understandable, given Nixon's proclivity to equate himself with the state. Nixon, like the state, can be utilized, by negative critic and proponent alike, as a kind of a mirror through which one sees and defines oneself. In the case of the state, this is perhaps unavoidable since, as Philip Corrigan and Derek Sayer point out, the state is a cultural organ that has the function of sanitizing and privileging "what counts as 'politics'"[82] and, in effect, of assisting in our "self-definition" as political and social beings. The state is one of many such cultural fields or, so to speak, apparatuses that serve this purpose. Indeed, the state, as opposed to the government, has no identity but in the realm of such totalizing notions. The state's reality exists in a realm that is both produced by and produces what might be called culture's "self-conception."

Philip Abrams argues that "the state is not the reality which stands behind the mask of political practice. It is itself the mask which prevents our seeing political practice as it is."[83] Abrams distinguishes the state from both the "government-centered" "state-system,"[84] or programs and institutions of the state, and a nation's long-term characterization of itself as an entity:

> We are only making difficulties for ourselves in supposing that we have also to study the state—an entity, agent, function, or relation over and above the state-system and state-idea. The state comes into being as a structuration within political practice; it starts its life as an implicit construct; it is then reified as the *res publica,* the public reification, no less— and acquires an overt symbolic identity progressively divorced from practice as an illusory account of practice.[85]

"State" as noun and verb pun on each other. Nixon touches on this pun by saying his speech is "spoken to you from this office," suggesting the office of the presidency. All political discourse is "stated" in direct or indirect reference to the state. Says Abrams: "The [state's] ideological function is extended to a point where conservatives and radicals alike believe that their practice is not directed at each other but at the state; the world of illusion prevails."[86]

This notion of the state as a kind of cover-up permeates the Nixon administration. Schell observes that Nixon segregates this public-relations realm and employs it, almost to the exclusion of any other. For instance, whereas Lyndon Johnson tries to explain and justify military escalations, Nixon orders the bombing of Cambodia and goes to great lengths to keep this bombing secret. According to Schell, although Nixon, after his first election, is convinced that Americans are terribly weary of the war in Indochina, his strategy is less to end the war than to minimize its impact in the news.[87] Schell maintains that this kind of complete and programmatic rupture between governmental action and publicly acknowledged policy is unprecedented before the Nixon administration. In a sense, the entire administration functions as a kind of "cover-up." It is therefore not surprising that Jeb Stuart Magruder should say, concerning the Watergate break-in, that its "cover-up . . . was immediate and automatic. No one ever considered that there would not be a cover-up."[88]

It is often speculated that Nixon might have mitigated Watergate's disastrous consequences by admitting to his involvement in the Watergate cover-up attempt during its early stages. However, given the priority that his administration gave to public relations, and the selling of itself as expert and virtually infallible, perhaps the Nixon administration is not "programmed" to make such admissions. There is seldom a need to acknowledge such actions. Schell states:

> By using the resources of government to compose scenes rather than to solve real problems, a President could build up an illusory world that not even the most determined reporters could tear down. In his first eight months, President Nixon . . . had established what amounted almost to a new form of rule, in which images were given precedence over substance in every phase of government. The secrecy surrounding the bombing of Cambodia and the warrantless wiretaps had turned out only to be the first steps of a far greater separation of image and substance in the Nixon administration's conduct of its affairs.[89]

The Nixon administration's politics primarily aim at establishing (since he was elected by a popular minority) and maintaining a consensus. Campaigning and public relations subsume the role of governing. Nixon never stops trying to invent or, so to speak, "write" his audience. He is reported to have once said that he saw the American people in the eye of a television camera. Again, Nixon's career blurs the distinction between what we normally think of as authored and what we normally do not. The president perpetually makes his audience, in the form of a consensus, or a "political base." When Nixon can no longer do so, and has no hope of doing so while in office, it is a signal for him to resign; he will have a better chance of reconstituting his consensus out of office. (Similarly, being out of office in 1968 was the then unusual position that he occupied for his successful presidential run.) Thus, Nixon's speech continues:

> In the past few days, however, it has become evident to me that I no longer have a strong enough political base in the Congress to justify continuing that effort. As long as there was a base, I felt strongly that it was necessary to see the constitutional process through to its conclusion, that to do otherwise would be unfaithful to the spirit of that deliberately difficult process, and a dangerously destabilizing precedent for the future.
> But with the disappearance of that base, I now believe that the consti-

tutional purpose has been served, and there is no longer a need for the process to be prolonged.[90]

The Constitution, of course, does not fully describe the supposedly popular process by which a president is now elected. Neither does the Constitution hinge the continuation of a president's term upon the preservation of a popular base. Nonetheless, Nixon, reaffirming that it is the president's chief role to provide the country with a totalizing voice, maintains that his "constitutional duty" is to serve both the populace and "the constitutional process." Only the politics of "Congress" undermine this aim. Simply serving the people who have elected him is an "effort" in the face of political forces that oppose the presidency. Remaining president, apart from any actions the president takes, is here depicted as a strenuous task. Although Nixon implies that he still represents a popular base, he is nonetheless in dire danger of losing his "political base." Nixon's actions as both a congressman investigating alleged conspiracies and a president who administers over secret surveillance operations, which in themselves come to be investigated, reveal the changing position of one completely reliant on the "backing" of a consensus or, as Nixon phrases it in his resignation speech, a "political base," or simply, a "base." This consensus is paradoxically held together by the suggestion of its antithesis. The quality of being "American," according to what Wills terms "the denigrative method" of Nixon's early campaigns,[91] depends on being opposed to "un-Americanness." How American one is can be determined by one's opposition to what is un-American. Thus, it is not enough that one not be a Communist. One must also avoid any appearance of being "soft on Communism." Any such perceived indication of a lack of intensity of support for this intangible nationalism can become the cornerstone of an opponent's political campaign. It is no accident that Nixon first springs upon the national scene as a member of perhaps the most aggressively self-conscious "American" congressional committee in our history, the House Committee on Un-American Activities, named after what it claims to oppose.

Nixon's career, perhaps more than any previous major American political figure, gives the appearance of being programmed or authored. Nixon is the first president to be informed by these red-baiting techniques from the outset of his political life. He is also the first career-long Republican president since Herbert Hoover, Dwight Eisenhower being an independent until he sought the 1952 Republican presidential nomination. This is not to say that Democrats do not also use tactics centered around the questioning of loyalties. However, it does indicate how prone Nixon is to reorganizing the White House along these lines. In fact, as Schell maintains, the White House, under Nixon, is in a perpetual state of reorganization that applies to Nixon's politically oriented, public-relations-conscious attitudes toward government. As Schell observes, almost all of Nixon's presidential actions aim at establishing and manipulating a consensus. When he can no longer hope to build another political consensus, "personal considerations" and those of the nation diverge:

> I would have preferred to carry through to the finish whatever the personal agony it would have involved, and my family unanimously urged me to do so. But the interests of the Nation must always come before any personal considerations.
>
> From the discussions I have had with Congressional and other leaders, I have concluded that because of the Watergate matter I might not have the support of the Congress that I would consider necessary to back the very difficult decisions and carry out the duties of this office in the way the interests of the Nation would require.
>
> I have never been a quitter. To leave office before my term is completed is abhorrent to every instinct in my body. But as President, I must put the interests of America first. America needs a full-time President and a full-time Congress, particularly at this time with the problems we face at home and abroad.[92]

According to this speech, in this aberrant moment of time, the nation, against its own interests, has no use for this or any other personal president.

Nixon blends two logocentric organizing devices: images of a unified "body" working as a whole, yet capable of division into body parts, and, similarly, a body or progression of "time" that can be demarcated by discrete moments. At this point in the speech, these two unifying mechanisms begin to be so blended that they are difficult to distinguish. "Some sinister forces," as Haig describes whatever accounts for the eighteen-and-a-half-minute tape gap in the recording of Nixon's 20 June 1972 conversation with Haldeman,[93] render it impossible for Nixon to fulfill his precise function and follow his corporeal mission. The "instinct[s]" of the president's "body" call on Nixon to fight for the people's interests. However, there is a malfunctioning in the nation's time-honored system. "This time" is extremely unusual—the interests of the presidency and those of "America" are temporarily not synonymous. In this highly unusual incidence, this isolated "matter," the president does not appear credible. If a successful modern president must provide a "focus" for the

"Nation," Nixon maintains that the forces of incredulity and political confusion that surround him make it impossible for him as president to do so. Unfortunately, the national consensus now separates the president's personality from his office and the president's selfhood has become an issue:

> To continue to fight through the months ahead for my personal vindication would almost totally absorb the time and attention of both the President and the Congress in a period when our entire focus should be on the great issues of peace abroad and prosperity without inflation at home.
>
> Therefore, I shall resign the Presidency effective at noon tomorrow. Vice President Ford will be sworn in as President at that hour in this office.
>
> As I recall the high hopes for America with which we began this second term, I feel a great sadness that I will not be here in this office working on your behalf to achieve those hopes in the next two and one-half years. But in turning over direction of the Government to Vice President Ford, I know, as I told the Nation when I nominated him for that office ten months ago, that the leadership of America will be in good hands.[94]

By stating his intention to resign just after alluding to "issues" of "peace" and "inflation," Nixon implies that his presidency is being sacrificed to a kind of cultural inflation resulting from the Vietnam War. It is difficult to be certain of anything. However, the specificity of time and place with which he announces his resignation and Ford's oath-taking suggest that his resignation will enable a return to a logocentric context for the unfolding of events.

Since "to trope" etymologically means "to turn," Nixon implies that by "turning over direction of the Government to Vice President Ford" a new tropological system will be offered. Ford may not be a leader, but he will oversee "leadership" with his "hands." Nixon's allusion to Ford's "good hands" utilizes images of the new president's body to indicate continuity. Nixon reinforces this effect by using the metaphor of Ford's "shoulders":

> In passing this office to the Vice President, I also do so with the profound sense of the weight of responsibility that will fall on his shoulders tomorrow and, therefore, of the understanding, the patience, the cooperation he will need from all Americans.
>
> As he assumes that responsibility, he will deserve the help and support of all of us. As we look to the future, the first essential is to begin healing the wounds of this Nation; to put the bitterness and the divisions of

the recent past behind us and to rediscover those shared ideals that lie at the heart of our strength and unity as a great and as a free people.[95]

If Nixon provides the nation with a too active subject that it cannot, even for its own benefit, accept, Ford will provide the American people with an object. Nixon stresses "the help and support" that Ford will need. Perhaps Nixon is resigning for the want of such "understanding," "patience," and "cooperation." However, later in his speech, Nixon makes much of his accomplishments as president, and we can presume that these accomplishments would have been all but impossible if Nixon lacked the strength and courage to forgo a consensus president's need for such support. Nixon suggests that he must resist the temptation to survive as a president, since, according to his speech, a president requires a consensus to govern, and, in the nation's interests, Nixon must take an unpopular stance.

In this regard, the president's resignation is presented as a bold stroke. Nixon offers his resignation speech as a presidential action that can in itself unify the American people and establish "shared ideals." The "rediscover[y]" of these totalizing ideals constitutes "the first essential" step toward "healing." This healing also bridges the gap between Nixon and his successor. Nixon has already taken credit for "nominat[ing] him for that office ten months ago," implying that the new president will be an extension of his presidency. Further, Nixon points out that he is also responsible for initiating the healing "process":

> By taking this action, I hope that I will have hastened the start of that process of healing which is so desperately needed in America.
>
> I regret deeply any injuries that may have been done in the course of the events that led to this decision. I would say only that if some of my judgments were wrong, and some were wrong, they were made in what I believed at the time to be the best interest of the Nation.
>
> To those who have stood with me during these past difficult months, to my family, my friends, to many others who joined in supporting my cause because they believed it was right, I will be eternally grateful for your support.[96]

Again, the president places his actions within the context of the unified system he is defending. Nixon terms the "interest of the Nation" as a singular "interest," thus associating the national interest with a unification of national concerns. In addition, the president gives his "eternal" thanks for the support he has received, implying that this cause is inherently correct and everlasting. Nixon says that he "will be eternally grateful for" the "support" given to his principles; the placement of his gratitude in the future tense implies that his approval is conditional upon the support of his "cause."

All efforts work in relation to this cause. Even those who disagree with Nixon ultimately serve his purpose:

> And to those who have not felt able to give me your support, let me say I leave with no bitterness toward those who have opposed me, because all of us, in the final analysis, have been concerned with the good of the country however our judgments might differ.
>
> So, let us all now join together in affirming that common commitment and in helping our new President succeed for the benefit of all Americans.[97]

Ultimately, Nixon suggests, all Americans must directly or indirectly support a strong president. Since Nixon implies that Ford does not emit the image of a strong, active president, we may infer that a strong presidency will be continued through Nixon's absent presence. Ford is cast as a mere surrogate for the former president. Hence, immediately after hoping for the "success" of "our new President" in serving "the benefit of all Americans," Nixon voices his "regret at not completing" his "term." According to Nixon, his "five and one-half years" as president have been a great success:

> I shall leave this office with regret at not completing my term, but with gratitude for the privilege of serving as your President for the past five and one-half years. These years have been a momentous time in the history of our Nation and the world. They have been a time of achievement in which we can all be proud, achievements that represent the shared efforts of the Administration, the Congress and the people.
>
> But the challenges ahead are equally great and they, too, will require the support and efforts of the Congress and the people working in cooperation with the new Administration.[98]

Nixon states that his administration's achievements "represent the shared efforts" of all concerned, suggesting that they are not literally the product of shared efforts. "With the new administration," however, "support and efforts" will be required. Nonetheless, the next section of the resignation speech strongly connotes that the incoming administration can rely upon the groundwork that the exiting president has laid.

Nixon maintains that his administration has been successful in its specific accomplishments, but now those accomplishments must provide the basis for a system, or structure. The entire world is to be placed within a new and greater *Pax Americana* that functions under presidential guidance. Nixon speaks of a "structure of peace" that will later become "a new world order":

> We have ended America's longest war, but in the work of securing a lasting peace in the world, the goals ahead are even more far-reaching and more difficult. We must complete a structure of peace so that it will be said of this generation, our generation, of Americans, by the people of all nations, not only that we ended one war, but that we prevented future wars.
>
> We have unlocked the doors that for a quarter of a century stood between the United States and the People's Republic of China.[99]

Of course, it is inconsequential that, in 1974, war still rages in Southeast Asia. The president's role is ideological. It therefore does not matter that Nixon was in the forefront of those who "locked the door" between the United States and China "a quarter of a century" before this speech.

American influence will be extended through the passive-aggressive, Franklinesque ploy of winning "friends":

> We must now ensure that the one quarter of the world's people who live in the People's Republic of China will be and remain not our enemies but our friends.
>
> In the Middle East, 100 million people in the Arab countries, many of whom have considered us their enemy for nearly twenty years, now look on us as their friends. We must continue to build on that friendship so that peace can settle at last over the Middle East and so that the cradle of civilization will not become its grave.
>
> Together with the Soviet Union we have made the crucial breakthroughs that have begun the process of limiting nuclear arms. But we must set as our goal not just limiting, but reducing and finally destroying these terrible weapons so that they cannot destroy civilization, so that the threat of nuclear war will no longer hang over the world and the people.
>
> We have opened the new relation with the Soviet Union. We must continue to develop and expand that new relationship so that the two strongest nations of the world will live together in cooperation rather than confrontation.
>
> Around the world, in Asia, in Africa, in Latin America, in the Middle

East, there are millions of people who live in terrible poverty, even starvation. We must keep as our goal turning away from production for war and expanding production for peace so that people everywhere on this earth can at least look forward in their children's time, if not in our own time, to having the necessities for a decent life.[100]

Of course, these intimations of a resolution to all of the world's conflicts well serve the resignation speech's occasion. Speaking more generally, however, ideology can be said to equal the reconciliation of conflicts and smoothing of unfulfilled needs. In this sense, consoling words like "friendship," "cooperation," and "peace" can be read to mean a repression by a regulative hegemonic force. The presence of such a force is reflected in the repetition and echoing of phrases, beginning with "new relation" and "new relationship." A "new relationship" reinforces the notion of an "airtight" "present," albeit perhaps an "alternative present," replete with new alignments, which painlessly takes the place of a past time with old alignments. The "old relationship" has simply vanished. Its repression reflects the prevailing "common" repression of the new peace that Nixon outlines.

This new peace must continually "expand"[101] and be "produc[ed]." Nixon presents a capitalist model that is shorn of capitalist competition. Capital will continue to concentrate through transnational corporations. Since peace here represses all conflict, and denies the validity of an obvious point of contention with "things as they are," no opposition, operating through a principle of construction that is enabled by difference, can hold it in place. "War," representing an anti-hegemonic force, is to be "turn[ed] away from." "Troping" etymologically means "turning," as I have pointed out, so Nixon's resignation speech implies that our poetic powers can be employed only to buttress a totalizing system that ironically seeks to limit difference, which is a prerequisite for metaphor and, therefore, poetry. Poetry loses its surplus value to this kind of politics.

The first two nouns of the next paragraph further employ redundancy to "cover up" difference's workings:

> Here in America, we are fortunate that most of our people have not only the blessings of liberty, but also the means to live full and good and, by the world's standards, even abundant lives. We must press on, however, to a goal of not only more and better jobs, but of full opportunity for every American, and of what we are striving so hard now to achieve, prosperity without inflation.[102]

Nixon identifies the state of the "here" with "America." He uses the rest of the world as an enabling opposition to "America," associating the United States with the hegemonic condition of logocentric presence in the form of "here." The evocation of "the world's standards" allows Nixon, playing on the word "even," to posit "even abundant lives." This phrase implies that abundance is a regulating force. An overabundance of signifiers overcodes and covers up an absence of power and authority as a regulating force. Nixon once again formulates this oxymoronic kind of excess as "prosperity without inflation."

This relentless yet intransitive expansion is associated with "the turbulent history of this era" that Nixon has "shared in":

> For more than a quarter of a century in public life I have shared in the turbulent history of this era. I have fought for what I believed. I have tried to the best of my ability to discharge those duties and meet those responsibilities that were entrusted to me.
>
> Sometimes I have succeeded and sometimes I have failed, but always I have taken heart from what Theodore Roosevelt once said about the man in the arena, "whose face is marred by dust and sweat and blood, who strives valiantly, who errs and comes short again and again because there is not effort without error and shortcoming, but who does actually strive to do the deeds, who knows the great enthusiasms, the great devotions, who spends himself in a worthy cause, who at the best knows in the end the triumphs of high achievements and who at the worst, if he fails, at least fails while daring greatly."[103]

According to Nixon, he is not able to "discharge" his presidential "duties" because the clear logocentric unities that a president must champion are compromised. These simple logocentric "'effort[s]'" find their embodiment in Nixon's evocation of Theodore Roosevelt. Nixon cites Roosevelt and reminds us of Roosevelt's statement of preference for "the man in the arena." Nixon likens presidents to gladiators, and one recalls that "arena" is derived from the Latin *harena,* which refers to the Coliseum sand that absorbs the blood of the gladiators. Indeed, this is particularly appropriate when it is considered that Nixon is speaking on the occasion of a sort of death of a president.

Nixon's next paragraph develops a highly dramatic, life-and-death view of the presidency:

> I pledge to you tonight that as long as I have a breath of life in my body, I shall continue in that spirit. I shall continue to work for the great

causes to which I have been dedicated throughout my years as a Congressman, Senator, a Vice President and President; the cause of peace not just for America but among all nations, prosperity, justice, and opportunity for all of our people.[104]

The "body" is sustained by "breath" yet also can be said to exist within a larger breath, if we literalize the etymological root of "spirit": the Latin word *spiritus*. The president says that even as an ex-president he will "continue in that spirit." Within the complicated system of "breath" and "spirit" that Nixon describes, the president, in all his previous and future roles, acts as a conduit to "all of our people." Upon this occasion of a kind of death of a president, the president's body is offered to the "cause" of a new peace. This peace will make "all nations" "our people." "America," to the extent that it signifies a particular brand of logocentrism that is centered around the individual's illusion of freedom and autonomy, will reduplicate itself around the world, and the ex-president can be equated to the breath that supplies oxygen throughout a kind of metaphoric worldwide circulatory system. (The import of the president's body and use of it as a kind of litmus test for presidential validity and authority is brought out in the film *Dave* [1993], when the counterfeit president's Secret Service bodyguard eventually validates him by saying that he would "take a bullet" for him. Dave is now a true president because his body is more important than an ordinary citizen's body. For whom else would that exchange be beyond question? In this regard, Reagan's presidency receives an unexpected boost when he is bodily wounded yet survives.)

Nixon, acting as if we had not just heard him offer his life for "peace," now names the "one cause" that he values above all others:

> There is one cause above all to which I have been devoted and to which I shall always be devoted for as long as I live.
>
> When I first took the oath of office as President five and one-half years ago, I made this sacred commitment: "To consecrate my office, my energies and all the wisdom I can summon to the cause of peace among nations."
>
> I have done my very best in all the days since to be true to that pledge. As a result of these efforts, I am confident that the world is a safer place today, not only for the people of America, but for the people of all nations, and that all of our children have a better chance than before of living in peace rather than dying of war.
>
> This more than anything, is what I hoped to achieve when I sought the

Presidency. This, more than anything, is what I hope will be my legacy to you, to our country, as I leave the Presidency.[105]

After reaffirming the import of the office of the president as an ideological tool in preserving and furthering world peace, Nixon reinforces the notion that the president preserves the "realities" that sustain all "American[s]." Indeed, Nixon affirms the autonomy of the individual citizen. With mythological abandon, the president states that he feels a special relationship with all two hundred and fifty million people on an individual basis:

> To have served in this office is to have felt a very personal sense of kinship with each and every American. In leaving it, I do so with this prayer: May God's grace be with you in all the days ahead.[106]

Here, the president again advances the concept of a hegemonic consensus composed of many supposedly separate individuals. The "kinship" that the president says that he feels with "each and every American" is indicative of a president's ideological function; a president must provide a logocentric model of autonomous individuality for all Americans. The fulfillment of this function is epitomized by Nixon's closing "prayer." Nixon ends his last speech in the Oval Office with a prayer that is addressed to each American. Since the prayer is not addressed to God, He is presumably expected to overhear and bestow "God's grace," thus enabling each American to remain a paradoxically separate and yet all-powerful member of a totality.

Nixon's resignation speech, in sum, casts itself as both the mending and completion of a "natural" presidential duty; modern American presidents serve the ideological function of seeming to uphold the individuality of "each and every American." Nixon, in the resignation speech, depicts himself as a president courageously allowing himself to be sacrificed to vague bureaucratic forces so that relatively simple, if all-inclusive, logocentric forces can revitalize themselves and prosper. From the hindsight of American politics after Nixon's resignation, how can we say that Nixon did not accurately analyze the situation?

A Perilous Transcription: "We Have a Cancer"

Such is the matter of imaginative or artistic literature—this transcript, not of mere fact, but of fact in its infinite variety, as modified by human preference in all its infinitely varied forms.—Walter Pater, "Style"

Indeed, "mere fact" cannot adequately explain John Dean's "cancer on the presidency" "monologue" in the 21 March 1973 Oval Office tape transcript, as released by the White House on 29 April 1974. The Nixon White House, however, stakes its survival on a factual and unPaterian reading of that transcript; the concluding battle of the Nixon presidency hinges upon how the 21 March transcript is received. In a sense, Nixon's task is to cast this transcript as a simple communicative act performed by Dean for the president's edification. This closed model can be said to be diametrically opposed to Dean's figure of an open-ended "cancer" of information that is bound to leak, "bust," and overwhelm "the Presidency."[107] In effect, Nixon argues for a reality that is under control and can be of his own making, a reality that he can author and micromanage. Dean argues that this is not the nature of political reality. However, a post-Watergate world of tightly scripted presidencies and campaigns, which is nonetheless subject to volatile shifts of political fortune (for example, George Bush's unexpected decline in 1992, the Republican 1994 resurgence in Congress, and Clinton's reversal of political fortunes in 1996), leaves us somewhere between the positions of Nixon and Dean.

Nixon contends that he is first told of the Watergate cover-up on 21 March 1973, and, therefore, difficult as it is to fathom, the 21 March transcript serves as the linchpin of Nixon's legal defense. After all, if Dean thought that Nixon knew that the FBI and CIA had been instructed to limit their investigations, and that monies had been paid to the Watergate defendants to buy their silence, why does Dean need to tell it to Nixon? The president argues that he does indeed act upon Dean's disclosures, and that he had no reason to act before these "revelations." Do not Haldeman, Ehrlichman, and Kleindienst leave the Nixon administration at the president's behest on 30 April 1973, a month after Nixon is informed of the cover-up, supposedly for the first time, on 20 March? Might not Nixon's talk about the wisdom of making blackmail payments be dismissed as mere conjecture that is never acted on? Hence, Nixon and special counsels to the president for Watergate, J. Fred Buzhardt and James D. St. Clair, argue that one must assume the president's innocence. This argument gives them hope of winning a Senate impeachment trial.

During the spring and summer of 1974, special counsel to the House Judiciary Committee John Door and his co-workers labor to disprove this theory. They shift their investigation to the days immediately following the Watergate break-in, which leads them to the 23 June 1972 "smoking gun" tape that proves Nixon knew about and participated in a cover-up. Identifying this moment required an elaborate analysis of Nixon's diary and his staff's schedules. They establish that the cover-up probably began almost immediately and that Nixon was a part of it. House majority leader Tip O'Neill sensed this, but not being a lawyer never quite understood the need for the airtight legal proof that Judiciary Committee chair Peter Rodino pursued. O'Neill rushed Rodino to act more quickly than Rodino felt possible to produce a legally rigorous and convincing indictment proceeding.

The 21 March 1973 tape about hush-money payments could only be considered a defense in the narrowest legal terms. As damaging as Dean's 21 March remarks are in a public-relations sense, they ironically benefit Nixon's legal position because they imply that 21 March 1973 marks a discrete beginning to Nixon's awareness of the cover-up. Nixon ferociously struggles to maintain the position that Dean inadvertently helps him to frame. Because the release and contextualization of this tape is Nixon's last hope, Nixon would not tamper with it. To do so would be to jeopardize its and the president's credibility, since the president's defense supposed that it might need to be released. The 21 March transcript is therefore an accurate transcription of Nixon's and Dean's conversation. In this regard, we can note that, in his version of the meeting in *Blind Ambition* (1976), Dean favors it over his own testimony to the Ervin committee. (The two versions are remarkably similar.) Although the House Judiciary Committee discovers significant omissions in other transcripts, it finds only seemingly irrelevant typing discrepancies in the 21 March transcript.[108]

It is not until after the Supreme Court's unanimous 1 August 1974 ruling against Nixon, when defying that decision and continuing to withhold all the tapes would virtually assure his impeachment, that the White House gives Congress the "smoking gun," 23 June 1972 tape that shows Nixon to have been aware of aspects of the cover-up from its inception, thus undermining the president's reading of the "cancer on the presidency" transcription. In brief, Nixon's presidency falls when it becomes clear that Dean is not imparting entirely new information to Nixon on 21 March.

Nixon attempts to use Dean's 21 March disclosures as the base of his Watergate knowledge, as he had previously used a supposed "Dean Investigation," in a 29 August 1972 press conference. In that news conference, Nixon explains why he believes the appointment of a special prosecutor to be unnecessary:

> Within our own staff, under my direction, the counsel to the President, Mr. Dean, has conducted a complete investigation of all leads which might involve any present members of the White House staff or anybody on the government. I can say categorically that his investigation indicates that

no one in the White House staff, no one in the Administration, presently employed, was involved in this very bizarre incident.[109]

No such investigation took place. Hence, Dean can be likened to an author without a text. Subsequently, Ehrlichman, Haldeman, and Nixon ask Dean for a "Dean Report" that is, in effect, already written. Such a report will give the president "deniability." All possible liability will shift to the possible inadequacies of Dean's report. The president's counsel believes that it will appear as if he is hiding his own involvement. All responsibility will center upon him as a kind of chief "author" of the Watergate report, the Watergate hotel break-ins (17 June 1972 is not the first Watergate break-in; its purpose is to "fine-tune" the surveillance system that is already in place), and the obstruction of justice crimes that ensue from it. Dean strongly suspects that he is being "set up" as a "fall guy" and hesitates to "write" this predetermined text.

If Dean were not heavily pressured by Haldeman and Nixon for this report in March 1973, it is unlikely that he would have delivered his 21 March pronouncements to the president. Nixon, by trying to initiate the writing of the Dean report, a situation wherein Nixon's deniability can be protected, contributes to a situation that severely endangers the president's deniability: Dean's relation of the events of the cover-up to the president and then later to federal prosecutors and the Senate Watergate committee. In this regard, it should be noted that it is Dean's suspicion that he is being recorded in the Oval Office that causes a Republican Senate counsel to ask Alexander Butterfield if Dean's conjecture is correct (perhaps to discredit Dean) and thus leads to the committee's discovery of Nixon's taping system.

Dean relates the tale of Watergate to Nixon as a substitute for the "Dean Report." Paradoxically, however, it is Dean's version of the "Dean Report." Dean refuses to "write" the Watergate affair in an overdetermined and predetermined manner and tells Nixon that the hemorrhaging of Watergate cannot be stemmed by one discrete, authoritative text because of "how interwoven all the testimony might become."[110] The inevitable interweavings and discrepancies of these "texts" are, in effect, the "cancer" of which Dean warns Nixon. In short, Dean presents a description of the Watergate "cancer" as an alternative to the simple report that Nixon envisions as a work that could be doctored into the unified reasoning of one neat "fall guy."

"Appendix 6. Meeting: The President, Dean and Haldeman, Oval Office, March 21, 1973. (10:12–11:55)." The White House prints the Oval Office transcripts as appendix entries that corroborate the summary of the White House transcripts.

This summary is entitled "Submission of Recorded Presidential Conversations to the Committee on the Judiciary of the House of Representatives by President Richard Nixon,"[111] implying that the summary is somehow the body of the transcripts. Indeed, in a Derridean fashion, the supplemental transcriptions are labeled as mere appendices. Hence, the summary's conclusion organizes itself around a naively literal reading of Dean's 21 March disclosures to the president. The summary's conclusion is simple:

> Throughout the period of the Watergate affair the raw material of these recorded confidential conversations establishes that the President had no prior knowledge of the break-in and that he had no knowledge of any cover-up prior to March 21, 1973.[112]

Although the transcripts are presented as "raw material," only one possible meaning is offered.

The president begins his 21 March 1973 conversation with Dean with a request for a similar kind of unified interpretation: "Well what is the Dean summary of the day about?"[113] Dean responds by describing the impossibility of such a "summary":

> D—John [D. Ehrlichman] caught me on the way out and asked me about why Gray was holding back on information, if that was under instructions from us. And it was and it wasn't. It was instructions proposed by the Attorney General, consistent with your press conference statement that no further raw data was to be turned over to the full committee. And that was the extent of it. And then Gray, himself, who reached the conclusion that no more information should be turned over, that he had turned over enough.[114]

In effect, Dean describes a self-censorship model of how instructions curtailing the dissemination of information can be given in such a manner that the president and the president's staff maintain deniability.

Nixon is satisfied with Dean's explanation of the origin of Gray's motives, and begins to dismiss Dean, when Dean begins the speech that both reinforces and undermines the President's deniability:

> D—The reason that I thought that we ought to talk this morning is because in our conversations, I have the impression that you don't know everything I know and it makes it very difficult for you to make judgments that only you can make on some of these things and I thought that——[115]

Dean provides a pretext for destroying Nixon's deniability and returning responsibility to the president for authoring a report that can definitively explain the Watergate affair.

However, Nixon misunderstands the thrust of what is to come. The president believes that Dean is warning him of the possibility of encountering knowledge that could contradict the model of deniability that protects the president:

> P—In other words, I have to know why you feel that we shouldn't unravel something? [116]

Nixon's fear of "unravel[ing] something" presages the conflict concerning "the tapes" that eventually undoes his presidency. After all, "tape" is derivative of *tæppe,* the Old English textile term from which "tapestry" is also derived. The "picture" side of a tapestry covers its threads interwoven on the reverse side. In a sense, Nixon expresses fear that he and his advisers will inadvertently "unravel" the "tapestry" of information that the Nixon administration has meticulously woven. Nixon insists on maintaining power over the weaving of such tapestries. (Near the end of "Self-Portrait in a Convex Mirror," the game of telephone, in which phrases are constantly misunderstood, speaks for the perpetual doing and undoing of signification as the heart of artistic creation. If Ashbery presents language as a fluid, perpetual weaving, Nixon covers up this public knowledge of weaving. See my discussion of Luce Irigaray's feminist use of the word "cover-up" in the second section of chapter 5.)

In keeping with the use of a tapestry trope to describe the Watergate affair, James McCord entitles his book concerning his role in the Watergate scandal *A Piece of Tape* (1974). Of course, McCord alludes to the tape on the lock of the door of the Democratic National Committee Office that alerts a night watchman to the presence of the Watergate burglars. However, McCord's title is particularly apt because it connotes the tapestry model of Watergate, suggesting that the piece of tape on the Watergate hotel door is the first thread of the Watergate tapestry to come loose. Indeed, McCord's letter to Judge Sirica is the first overt implication of powerful White House figures in the cover-up.

Moving from history to the subject of history in poetry, Ashbery's poem "Tapestry" (1977), like Dean's "cancer on the presidency" monologue, insists that Nixon's kind of monological control is an unattainable ideal:

> It is difficult to separate the tapestry
> From the room or loom which takes precedence over it.
> For it must always be frontal and yet to one side.

It insists on this picture of "history"
In the making, because there is no way out of the punishment
It proposes: sight blinded by sunlight.
(*SP*, 269: 1-6)

The dispensation of "history" must be a process "in the making." "This picture" is perpetually reconfiguring. Voicing a "Watergate"-era sentiment, the poem says that "there is no way out of the punishment" of "sight blinded by sunlight." Individual "sight" must come to terms with the larger conditions that enable it. Similarly, Dean attempts to tell Nixon that it is no longer possible to live in a fictive world of the administration's own making. Ashbery's "Tapestry" concludes with a description of such a fictive community. It is only in "some other life" that such control occurs. However, even this fictive vision, which is symbolized by a pleasant representation upon a tapestry, is undermined by its constitutive parts. One is reminded of the inevitable flattening of Parmigianino's convex mirror and the deprivileging of its creator:

But in some other life, which the blanket depicts anyway,
The citizens hold sweet commerce with one another
And pinch the fruit unpestered, as they will,
As words go crying after themselves, leaving the dream
Upended in a puddle somewhere
As though "dead" were just another adjective.
(*SP*, 269: 17-22)

In a like manner, Dean warns Nixon that he no longer has control. The Watergate affair has become an indeterminate text that best serves those who do not try to control it. Whether this is true or not, Dean's intuition about Watergate has certainly entered the mythology of our times.

Dean's purpose in speaking in the Oval Office on 21 March 1973 is ostensibly to tell the president that the "text"—itself a term related to "textile" and, hence, suggestive of clothing, cover, and cover-up—of Watergate can no longer be successfully manipulated by anyone. The "threads" or "tapes" of the scandal will create unpredictable figures. The cover-up's seams cannot be camouflaged for long. The discourse will account for itself, and, in an Althusserian sense, become a poem that will not serve the president. Dean therefore prefaces his response to Nixon by offering his "overall," as a means of later implying that the totalizing "tapestry" of a "Dean Report" could not, anymore than anyone else's, yield a politically adequate "report":

D—Let me give you my overall first.[117]

Dean's curious use of the adjective "overall" as a noun implies that nothing as tangible as what an ordinary noun might connote is appropriate here. This use is like A. R. Ammons's employment of the word in "Corson's Inlet" (1986):

organizations of grass, white sandy paths of remembrance
in the overall wandering of mirroring mind:
but Overall is beyond me: is the sum of these events
I cannot draw, the ledger I cannot keep, the accounting
beyond the account:
(*Selected Poems*, 43: 28–29; 44: 1–3)[118]

Like Dean, Ammons in this poem warns against the reductive interpretation of "orders," in the sense of organizations, "as summaries" (*Selected Poems*, 46: 9). Nixon, however, misinterprets Dean's statement and takes his counsel's offering of an "overall" to mean that Dean will give his assessment of the situation and then predict its outcome:

P—In other words, your judgment as to where it stands, and where we will go.[119]

The president sets up Dean's "cancer" trope by implying that "it" is benign, that is, that "it" will "stand" while the administration "will go." Dean's "counter" suggests the prospect of a malignant cancer:

D—I think that there is no doubt about the seriousness of the problem we've got. We have a cancer within, close to the Presidency, that is growing. It is growing daily. It's compounded, growing geometrically now, because it compounds itself.[120]

And yet Dean implies that it is a cancer that can still be removed, before it reaches the presidency, because it does not concern the actual Watergate hotel break-ins but rather the cover-up of the operation that they are a small part of. In other words, Dean tells Nixon to be satisfied that he cannot be directly implicated in the Watergate hotel burglaries and surveillance operations. Whoever can be implicated in those illegal operations must simply accept the consequences. Since Nixon can easily deny his role in these operations, the president must now "cash-in" all his "deniability," acknowledge the damage that the Watergate affair has done to his administration, and take his losses while cutting them.

Dean asks Nixon to realize that "Watergate" is no longer "about" the initial crimes of burglary and illegal surveillance, but rather about the administration's attempt to orchestrate and revise the aftermath of the discovery of these crimes. Later in this transcript, Dean tells Nixon that eventually Dean himself might well be imprisoned. Nixon acts incredulously:

> P—But just looking at it from a cold legal standpoint: you are a lawyer, you were a counsel—doing what you did as counsel. You were not— What would you go to jail for?
>
> D—The obstruction of justice.
>
> P—The obstruction of justice?
>
> D—That is the only one that bothers me.
>
> P—Well, I don't know. I think that one. I feel it could be cut off at the pass, maybe the obstruction of justice.[121]

Dean speculates on who at the Department of Justice could help to "cut it off at the pass," and Nixon continues:

> P—No. Talking about your obstruction of justice, I don't see it.
>
> D—Well, I have been a conduit for information on taking care of people out there who are guilty of crimes.
>
> P—Oh, you mean the blackmailers?
>
> D—The blackmailers. Right.
>
> P—Well, I wonder if that part of it can't be—I wonder if that doesn't have to be continued? Let me put it this way: let us suppose that you get the million bucks, and you get the proper way to handle it. You could hold that side?
>
> D—Uh-huh.
>
> P—It would seem to me that would be worthwhile.[122]

For Nixon, Dean's conjectures about obstruction of justice crimes merely serve as a bridge for him to suggest strongly that these crimes be continued. Remarkably, Nixon still does not begin to consider that obstruction of justice will be the major allegation leveled against him. Although Nixon is a lawyer, he cannot even recall the term "obstruction of justice" when Haldeman enters the Oval Office and the president briefs Haldeman on some of what Dean has said:

> P—John knows, about everything and also what all the potential criminal liabilities are, whether it is—like that thing—what, about obstruction?

D—Obstruction of justice. Right.

P—So forth and so on.[123]

Nixon has yet to consider that he is contributing to the proliferation of the Watergate text by attempting to revise it to his ends by conspiring to obstruct justice.

The president, according to Dean, must, in effect, forgo the enterprise of "authoring" the Watergate "text," whether it be through "ghostwriting" a "Dean Report," buying the silence of Watergate defendants, or encouraging the perjuring of his staff. Dean contends that it is the "post June 17th" sequence of events, the administration's handling of the botched Watergate burglary, not the break-in itself, that most imperils the administration.[124] After all, a cancer is only harmful if it spreads. Dean elaborates to Nixon on the manner in which the "cancer" "compounds itself" and "is growing geometrically now":

> D—That will be clear if I, you know, explain some of the details of why it is. Basically, it is because (1) we are being blackmailed; (2) People are going to start perjuring themselves very quickly that have not had to perjure themselves to protect other people in the line. And there is no assurance——
>
> P—That that won't bust?
>
> D—That that won't bust.[125]

Nixon can no longer make a pretext of maintaining "authorial" control. Dean bluntly tells the president that one being "blackmailed" can never consider him or herself in perfect control. Part of the "text" is always out of his or her hands. In addition, "there is no assurance" that the perjured testimonies of different people, with no experience in such matters, will support one another.

The president interjects, "That that won't bust?" However, it is unclear what Nixon's second "that" refers to. It could mean either the role of high administration officials in the original break-in or the perjury that protects them. In any case, Nixon has become aware of Dean's trope of a cancer that is "compounded, growing geometrically." Nixon adds to it the notion of a kind of critical mass that is to be avoided unless something that is best kept "under a lid" "bust[s]."

Nixon's use of "bust" combines its various meanings. "Bust" can be understood as a colloquialism of "burst." In that case, we might ask what could burst or "break open" or "explode"? Nixon could be referring to the blackmail, the perjury, or that which the perjury and blackmail are intended to hide.

Perhaps Nixon is indicating the loosely defined web of associations of which "Watergate" is composed. Other denotations of "bust" that Nixon's use of the word connotes include a drastic lowering of rank, which, indeed, is descriptive of the effect that the revelations of Watergate do indeed have upon many of those in the Nixon administration, including of course the president. Similarly, the use of "bust" as an active verb with the colloquial sense of "punch" or "hit" also describes a possible effect on the Nixon administration, as does the meaning that implies the "breaking of the will" that accompanies the "taming" of an unruly person or animal, the connotation that implies the "bankrupting" of an individual or institution, and the term "busting," applying to the breaking up of incorporated trusts into smaller companies. However, perhaps the most tantalizing shade of meaning that "bust" alludes to is its Latin origin in *bustum,* a funeral monument. Nixon wishes to keep the Watergate affair "buried." There is also the connotation that he does not wish the scandal's "bust" (when used as an anatomical noun, that is, the scandal's metaphoric "upper, front part of its body") to show. Ironically, when this taboo part of the affair does show, the Watergate scandal becomes constitutive of the Nixon presidency's "funeral monument."

All the dire meanings of the word "bust" are implicit in Dean's echoing of Nixon's "That that won't bust." Nixon, it seems to Dean, begins to comprehend "the seriousness of the problem." Dean apparently feels that he has prepared Nixon for an informal "Dean Report," which is perhaps the first detailed account of the Watergate affair:

> D—That that won't bust. So let me give you the sort of basic facts, talking first about the Watergate; and then about Sergetti; and then about some of the peripheral items that have come up.[126]

Like ghosts, "peripheral items . . . have come up." Dean calls attention to the aftermath of the Watergate break-in as the paradoxically primary nature of the Watergate affair. Dean hopes Nixon will avoid the negative impact of these "peripheral items" by accepting the political losses accrued due to the first two items: "the Watergate" break-ins or "plumbers" operation and "Sergetti" or the "dirty tricks" operation.

And yet even if the president decides to take his losses, what is the story that he must admit to? Dean must ask what the origins of Watergate are to evince his own response. As Milton spurs the narrative of *Paradise Lost* by asking what the first cause of present turmoil is, so Dean asks himself:

First of all on the Watergate: how did it all start? OK! It started with an instruction to me from Bob Haldeman to see if we couldn't set up a perfectly legitimate campaign intelligence operation over at the Re-Election Committee.[127]

Dean's "OK!" conveys a joy of discovery and creative problem-solving. Dean finds a means to protect White House Chief of Staff Haldeman's deniability, and, by extension, Nixon's deniability, since Dean knows that Haldeman's directive might easily have been Nixon's veiled order, or, in any case, an expression of the president's wishes.

If we are to compare this section of the 21 March 1973 Oval Office tape transcript with *Paradise Lost,* Dean attempts to save Haldeman and Nixon from functioning as "Serpents." This role is being saved for G. Gordon Liddy, who will eventually lure Attorney General John Mitchell into making a disastrous choice. Dean establishes the basis for this choice by first presenting Liddy's binary opposite:

> D—Not being in the business, I turned to somebody who had been in this business, Jack Caulfield. I don't remember whether you remember Jack or not. He was your original bodyguard before they had the candidate protection, an old city policeman.
> P—Yes, I know him.
> D—Jack worked for John and then was transferred to my office. I said Jack come up with a plan that, you know—a normal infiltration, buying information from secretaries and all that sort of thing. He did, he put together a plan. It was kicked around. I went to Ehrlichman with it. I went to Mitchell with it, and the consensus was that Caulfield was not the man to do this. In retrospect, that might have been a bad call because he is an incredibly cautious person and wouldn't have put the situation where it is today.[128]

Dean says that his first impulse was to opt for an "original." Jack Caulfield represents simple, venerable order to Dean, who identifies him as "an old city policeman" and "an original bodyguard." Dean says that the "normal [kind of] infiltration," which Dean characterizes as "buying information from secretaries and all that sort of thing," could not lead to Watergate-like situations. Caulfield is presented as a balance to the inherent nature of clandestine surveillance operations. Dean calls Caulfield "an incredibly cautious person" who "wouldn't have put the situation where it is today." Caulfield is in the surveillance "business," and that "business" calls for a discretion that might seem to be antithetical to its nature. However, an unwise "consensus" rejects the plan, as Nixon, in his resignation speech, says that an unnamed, abstract "base" is responsible for his decision to resign. In this regard, Dean, in saying that the idea "was kicked around," suggests the "Old Nixon" of the 1962 California gubernatorial concession speech who says the press will not have him "to kick around anymore." Unintentionally, Dean suggests that Caulfield, like Nixon as he characterizes himself in that 1962 speech, is a too conventional figure who cannot counteract fierce and unconventional enemies.

Although the operation calls for someone who can avoid its innate pitfalls, the gravity of the situation calls for someone who can operate outside of normal expectations. Dean claims to think of Liddy because of his experience, and yet Dean intimates that his zeal for surveillance is more directly responsible for his selection:

> D—After rejecting that, they said we still need something so I was told to look around for someone who could go over to 1701 and do this. This is when I came up with Gordon Liddy. They needed a lawyer. Gordon had an intelligence background from his FBI service. I was aware of the fact that he had done some extremely sensitive things for the White House and he had apparently done them well. Going out into Ellsberg's doctor's office——
>
> P—Oh, yeah.
>
> D—And things like this. He worked with leaks. He tracked these things down. So the report that I got from Krogh was that he was a hell of a good man and not only that a good lawyer and could set up a proper operation.[129]

Astonishingly, Dean considers the raid of Daniel Ellsberg's psychiatrist's office to be the right résumé credential to "set up a proper operation," thereby undermining Dean's contention that Watergate was ever intended to be a "normal infiltration," or, for that matter, "a proper operation."

The president stops Dean, preserving most of his deniability, by acknowledging the appropriateness of Liddy's "going out into Ellsberg's doctor's office" as a qualification for the task at hand. The extraordinary measure of breaking into doctors' offices is used as an example of how to "work with leaks" and "track things down." More than this, it is associated with being a "good man" and a "good lawyer." Liddy is of course someone to contact:

D—So we talked to Liddy. He was interested in doing it. I took Liddy over to meet Mitchell. Mitchell thought highly of him because Mitchell was partly involved in his coming to work for Krogh. Liddy had been at Treasury before that. Then Liddy was told to put together his plan, you know, how he would run an intelligence operation. This was after he was hired over there at the Committee. Magruder called me in January and said I would like to have you come over and see Liddy's plan.

P—January of '72?

D—January of '72.

D—"You come over to Mitchell's office and sit in a meeting where Liddy is going to lay his plan out." I said I don't really know if I am the man, but if you want me there I will be happy to. So I came over and Liddy laid out a million dollar plan that was the most incredible thing I have ever laid my eyes on: all in codes, and involved black bag operations, kidnapping, providing prostitutes to weaken the opposition, bugging, mugging teams. It was just an incredible thing.[130]

Dean depicts Liddy as an outsider who is poisoning the established order of the Nixon administration, although the Ellsberg break-in and other "normal infiltrations" have already occurred. Liddy was thought to be a known quality who was worthy of trust. However, Liddy's "plan," like the Serpent's suggestion, not only corrupts the administration but divides it. Suddenly, "all" is "in codes."

Dean's repetition of "incredible" stresses the break with an established reality that Liddy is said to represent. This is very much in keeping with Nixon's purpose of showing the Watergate operation to be a "bizarre" aberration within his administration. Perhaps, as Dean supposes, Nixon, aware of the tape recorder, is orchestrating his own version of the "Dean Report." Nixon would thus show himself to be uninformed of dates. He also poses a question that demonstrates Mitchell's initial uninvolvement:

P—Tell me this: Did Mitchell go along——?

D—No, no, not at all, Mitchell just sat there puffing and laughing. I could tell from——after Liddy left the office I said that is the most incredible thing I have ever seen. He said I agree. And so Liddy was told to go back to the drawingboard and come up with something realistic.[131]

Unfortunately, according to Dean, Mitchell, Charles Colson, and Jeb Magruder are somehow seduced into accepting another extremely "[un]realistic" Liddy plan.

Dean speculates that the 17 June 1972 Watergate break-in is the product of a gap in a "chain" of communication.[132] Dean suspects that feigned "urgent" requests for information from White House subordinates cause Mitchell to believe that the White House is ordering the approval of Liddy's plans.[133] The code for transmitting the veiled wishes of those close to the president breaks down. Something like the party game of "telephone" that Ashbery describes in "Self-Portrait in a Convex Mirror" would thus be responsible for the Watergate affair.

The need to maintain a gap between what is considered as the "White House" and that which is not the "White House" works against the Nixon administration, since the Watergate burglars are, indeed, traced to the White House. The purposeful gaps between the White House, the Committee to Re-Elect the President, and the "plumbers" unit all collapse. Perhaps the failure to account for the forces set into motion by such "absent presences" is behind much of Nixon's fatal lack of credibility. The celebrated eighteen-and-a-half-minute tape gap is the most concise trope for this tendency.

Nonetheless, Dean functions as a "conduit" between supposedly uncoordinated operations. Claiming that he warned the White House chief of staff of Liddy's schemes of "bugging, kidnapping, and the like,"[134] Dean believes that Haldeman used the White House to check operations emanating from outside the White House. Nixon agrees that Haldeman would certainly not have allowed Liddy's "absurd proposal" to be enacted:

> D—I thought it was turned off because it was an absurd proposal.
> P—Yeah.[135]

Of course, the president is more than willing to focus the blame on Liddy. However, Nixon appears to be trying to implicate Dean further when he attempts to strengthen Dean's link with Liddy. After Dean says that he did not discuss these operations with Liddy after disapproving of them in their planning stages, the president interjects:

> P—Well, you were talking with him about other things.
> D—We had so many other things.
> P—He had some legal problems too. But you were his advisor, and I understand you had conversations about the campaign laws, etc. Haldeman told me that you were handling all of that for us. Go ahead.[136]

Nixon orders his counsel to continue the president's Watergate story.

Demonstrating a narrative reflexivity, Dean repeats Nixon's "Go ahead" order, however with a fictive supposition of how Mitchell approves the Watergate break-in:

> D—And so Mitchell probably puffed on his pipe and said, "Go ahead."[137]

This propensity to "go ahead" also indicates Nixon's basic attitude toward the Watergate cover-up. One should "keep writing" and continue the payoffs:

> P—How much money do you need?
>
> D—I would say these people are going to cost a million dollars over the next two years.
>
> P—We could get that. On the money, if you need the money you could get that. You could get a million dollars. You could get it in cash. I know where it could be gotten. It is not easy, but it could be done. But the question is who the hell would handle it? Any ideas on that?
>
> D—That's right. Well, I think that is something that Mitchell ought to be charged with.
>
> P—I would think so too.[138]

At numerous other points, this transcript leaves little doubt that Nixon expects the blackmail demands of E. Howard Hunt and the other Watergate defendants to be met:

> P—You have no choice but to come up with the $120,000, or whatever it is. Right? . . . Would you agree that that's the prime thing that you damn well better get that done? . . . (Expletive deleted), get it. In a way that—who is going to talk to him [Howard Hunt]? Colson?[139]

> P—Just looking at the immediate problem, don't you think you have to handle Hunt's financial situation damn soon.[140]

> P—Well, of course you have a surplus from the campaign. Is there any other money hanging around?
>
> H—Well, what about the money we moved back from out of here?
>
> D—Apparently, there is some there. That might be what they can use. I don't know how much is left.
>
> P—Kalmbach must have some.
>
> D—Kalmbach doesn't have a cent.
>
> P—He doesn't? . . . Could I suggest this though: let me go back around

---

> H—Be careful.[141]

P—Now, let me tell you. We could get the money. There is no problem in that. We can't provide the clemency. Money could be provided. Mitchell could provide the way to deliver it. That could be done. See what I mean?[142]

P—It's about $120,000. That's what, Bob. That would be easy. It is not easy to deliver but it is easy to get.[143]

Nixon considers "priests" as a means of "deliver[ing]" hush money to the jailed defendants:

P—It is going to be checks, cash money, etc. . . . . Is the Cuban Committee an obstruction of justice, if they want to help?
D—Well they have priests in it.
P—Would they give a little bit of cover?
D—That would give some to the Cubans and possibly Hunt. Then you've got Liddy.[144]

Nixon and Dean agree that there is no easy way out of the Watergate scandal. Dean recommends that the "cancer" be "carved away" from "the presidency."[145] However, Nixon believes that Dean is naive. The president wants Dean to continue the hush-money payments and write a "report" that will be an "overall summary" and serve to contain the scandal.[146] This mode of problem-solving, says Dean, merely "creates another problem. It does not clean the problem out."[147] Dean is clearly dubious about the prospects for "selling Wheaties on our position."[148] He thus suggests that the Watergate affair can no longer be commodified into one discrete text.

The essential difference between Nixon's and Dean's positions is that Nixon wishes to commodify, control, and author the Watergate affair under the cover of Dean's report, whereas Dean recommends an organized account of the administration's position within the context of allowing the "text" of the scandal "to speak for itself." Dean believes that the "Watergate text" is already in place and will inevitably have its "say." Nixon wishes to condense his account of the scandal for the purpose of maintaining authorship; Dean tells the president that he would be wiser to aim at relinquishing authorship.

4   The Pivotal Gerald R. Ford Years:
The Presidency as Gift, A Ghost Story

Mr. Carter: One of the serious things that has happened in our Government in recent years and has continued up until now is a breakdown in the trust among our
people——(STATIC)

(Audio breaks down at 10:53 P.M. for twenty-seven minutes and resumes at 11:18 P.M.)

Edwin Newman: Are we back on the air? Perhaps it is not necessary for me to say that
we had a technical failure during the debates. It was not a failure in the debate itself,
it was a failure in the broadcasting of the debate. — First Ford-Carter debate, 23 September 1976, Philadelphia

The state of the union is not good. — Gerald Ford, State of the Union address, 15 January 1975

I can see clearly now. — Richard Nixon, statement accepting presidential pardon, 8 September 1974

                                         *   *   *

The time is out of joint. — Shakespeare, *Hamlet*

The world is going badly, the picture is bleak, one could say almost black. Let us form
an hypothesis. — Jacques Derrida, *Specters of Marx*

As soon as there is monetary sign — and first of all sign — that is difference and credit,
the oikos [home, family, or hearth] is opened and cannot dominate its limit. On the
threshold of itself, the family no longer knows its bounds. — Jacques Derrida, *Given
Time: I. Counterfeit Money*

At this historic moment, I was aware of kinship with my predecessors. It was almost as
if all of America's past Presidents were praying for me to succeed. — Gerald R. Ford, on
being sworn in as president

Both Betty and I found that we enjoyed living in the White House more than we ever
thought we would. So on August 21 [1974], I authorized Jerry terHorst to tell reporters
that I probably would run in 1976. — Gerald R. Ford

Those who nominated and confirmed me as vice president were my friends and are my
friends. — Gerald R. Ford, first presidential address, 9 August 1974

The phantasm is recognized as having the power. — Jacques Derrida, *Given Time: I. Counterfeit Money*

Considered in a Derridean fashion, Gerald Ford can be understood as a supplemental president who held the presidency together. This section argues the great import of the Ford administration. Ford did not draw the attention that Nixon did, but more effectively, if unknowingly, dismantled a progressive national government. This section documents this assertion and unearths new evidence about how Ford himself allowed the CIA wildly to overestimate Soviet military capability, leading to the great subsequent American arms buildups. The post-Watergate micro-period that Ford ushered in institutionalized America's path for the last quarter of the twentieth century. In the pre-Reagan micro-period and the eighties, this path was further internalized until there were only rumors of something outside our collective prison.

For reasons that I will soon elaborate on, Derrida is particularly useful in understanding Ford and the seventies. The Ford presidency prefigured two Derrida books of the nineties, *Given Time: I. Counterfeit Money* (1992) and *Specters of Marx* (1994). Derrida's works concern gifts and ghosts respectively. In *Given Time,* Derrida deconstructs the notion of a gift. Ford's presidency could be called a gift to Ford, since he was the first appointed president, the first vice president and president to be selected through the Twenty-fifth Amendment to the Constitution.

The Twenty-fifth Amendment, promulgated in 1967, was first proposed after Eisenhower's 1956 heart attack. In a nuclear age, should not Vice President Nixon have presidential powers while Eisenhower was incapacitated? Could the nation cope with a presidential incapacity such as Wilson's? The amendment proposal gathered momentum in response to President Kennedy's assassination. What if Kennedy had lingered between life and death for an extended period of time, as Garfield did? The idea was advanced that a president could voluntarily deem him- or herself incapable or Congress could resolve a president incapacitated and temporarily give a vice president presidential authority.

But what if there were no vice president, as was the case of a vice president's succession to the White House after the death of a president? Congress could not be trusted to declare a president incapable of fulfilling his or her duties if the Speaker of the House, next in succession after the vice president, were, for instance, a member of an opposition party, as has been the case for all but six years since 1969. Clearly, there needed to be a mechanism for filling a vacant vice presidency, and the vice president needed to be in relative accord with the president. Thus, the constitutional amendment needed to account for presidential incapacity and presidential succession. A new vice president could now be nominated and passed through Congress much like other presidential appointments, although the new vice president would need to be confirmed by both houses, unlike cabinet members, who only need Senate approval.

Since the Twenty-fifth Amendment grew politically from the Kennedy assassination and Ford was a Warren Commission member, his status as the avatar of the Twenty-fifth Amendment is an interesting indirect association between the assassination and Ford. From a broad perspective, the Ford presidency can be viewed as both the Derridean pharmakon of the Kennedy assassination, one of its chaotic results that also heals us from it. Whether or not the Warren Commission's findings were accurate, the commission was designed to provide speedy and perhaps premature closure. In this sense, the Warren Commission has much in common with Ford's pardon of Nixon. Interestingly, Ford has often spoken on behalf of his pardoning of Nixon and the Warren Commission. It should be noted that Ford's committee queries centered on Oswald's role and rarely considered the possibility of other suspects. A perhaps telling Ford handwritten note concerning Oswald reads "A.C.L.U. —a member?" [149] Ford helped chronicle Oswald's life, and he paid particular attention to why Oswald was readmitted into the United States with so little suspicion or follow-up. The congressman was satisfied with the innocent negligence of the intelligence community as an answer. Ford also helped question Jack Ruby, when Ruby said that he could only tell the truth somewhere other than his Dallas jail cell, but Ruby was denied relocation for questioning. Perhaps most significantly, Ford helped change the Warren Commission's wording of where the "magic bullet" that struck both President Kennedy and Texas Governor John Connally hit Kennedy, from "his uppermost back" to "the back of his neck," adding credence to the single magic bullet theory and, therefore, the lone gunman theory, since that bullet could then be said to more likely exit on a level that could hit Connally, even though the evidence suggests it entered Kennedy from between his shoulder blades and hence the possibility of a shot from another angle and gunman should probably have been more vigorously considered.

It also might be remembered that the Twenty-fifth Amendment was oddly first proposed for the benefit of Vice President Richard Nixon. Clearly, Ford stands in a metaphorically interesting relation with Kennedy and Nixon. I will shortly discuss other notable points of political exchange among Ford, Kennedy, Nixon, and other presidents.

If Ford's presidency was a "gift" to him, it was also a gift to the people, who, in a sense, were spared the labor of voting for a new president. The national electorate did not need to participate directly in his selection. In a manner of speaking, he was an adopted president. Before he was Gerald Ford, Ford's mother fled her abusive husband with her one-month-old son, Leslie Lynch King. She soon remarried Gerald Rudolph Ford Sr., who unofficially adopted Leslie. Leslie thought his name was Gerald Rudolph Ford Jr. (Junior for short), not knowing he was adopted until after his biological father shocked him by introducing himself to him at a restaurant where he worked as a teenager. Ford later legally changed his name. Reflecting his status as the first adopted child to become president, he was not "birthed" through a popular national election, or even, since he was a member of the House of Representatives, a statewide election.

Ford is of course mindful of the special circumstances of his presidency. "I am acutely aware that you have not elected me as your president by your ballots, and so I ask you to confirm me as your president with your prayers," Ford said in his first presidential address, his inaugural address, while Nixon was still flying to California. Whereas on assuming office Johnson asked for the help of the public *and* God, Ford asked for the public's confirmation through God, as if God could compensate for the public's absence in the process. Although Ford did not share Nixon's taste for imperial pomp and fanfare, Ford nonetheless asked the American people to suspend disbelief and recycle a theory of the divine right of kings and presidents, in that his presidency would seem to depend on God's mercy and on its status of being God-given.

As president, Ford serves as a resource for guidance and grace. In his pardon announcement, Ford says that he must pardon Nixon because "the buck stops here." After all, if he does not pardon Nixon, who will? And Nixon must be pardoned because of the nature of the post-Nixonian presidency. Ford reasons that "I do believe, with my heart and mind and spirit, that I, not as president but as a humble servant of God, will receive justice without mercy if I fail to show mercy." (With a Shakespearean flourish, Ford speaks here as if he were enjoying the patronage of Queen Elizabeth I.) After all, his presidency, as a gift, is dependent not so much on merit as on mercy, more on friendship and largesse than on good works. (Nixon nominated Ford partially because, as minority leader, he faithfully obeyed Nixon's instructions, and, more importantly, because Ford had made no enemies, and no one would block or delay his nomination.) How could Ford undermine his road to the presidency by calling Nixon to justice?

According to Derrida, every gift leaves a trace that subverts the category of the given. Nothing can be given that does not upset the ground of its reception and elicit a response. It is only through time that we escape the inherently problematic nature of "given" reality. Time is tantamount to a distance that allows the forgetting and assimilation of the gift—and all signification and everyday experience is a very problematic gift. It is in this sense that I see a cultural connection between Derrida and Ford. Ford is a supplement— a gift—to the American political system that both subverts and reinforces the system. As Derrida maintains, although a gift seems outside ordinary systems of exchange, it cannot help but create a debt. Is this not how politics works? Similarly, as a nonelected president, Ford appears outside a system of exchange that he is paradoxically ensconced within. Oddly, as an outsider, he is better positioned than Nixon to assimilate the ferment of the sixties and Watergate into a growingly distrustful and conservative America.

Derrida points out that the trace of a gift cannot be repressed: "By keeping the meaning of the gift, repression annuls it in symbolic recognition. However unconscious this recognition may be, it is effective and can be verified in no better fashion than by its effects or by the symptoms it yields up [qu'elle donne] for decoding."[150] According to Derrida, forgetting must supplement giving. To paraphrase Beckett's words about Proust, without forgetting there is no gift of remembering. However, because of Ford's pardon, Americans will never accept and forget Nixon's crime. They will always be confused by it. Ford tried to repress the trace of Nixon before Americans had something to remember and then accept and forget. A relatively small percentage of Americans knew that the chief impeachment count against Nixon was obstruction of justice (they thought it directly involved the Watergate break-in).

It might have been better for Ford if Nixon's actions had been articulated in a court of law. Although it is uncertain whether Nixon would have been indicted, the threat itself would have provided some degree of closure. Impeachment and resignation were one thing. The implied sight of Nixon sweating out indictment like an everyday citizen would have been another.

In any case, Ford perpetuated the indeterminacy of "crime" and involved himself in it. It is an irony of history that Nixon was himself pardoned before the 1974 congressional election, whereas, in March 1973, President Nixon said "it would be wrong," for political reasons, to pardon E. Howard Hunt and the Watergate burglars. Nixon saw more deeply into this kind of political reasoning than Ford. Although most Americans might have believed that Nixon's "crime" was planning the Watergate break-in, they also knew that standards of political and judicial fairness were at issue. Like the Saturday Night Massacre, Ford's Sunday morning pardon also bespoke an abuse of power, even if both actions were not technically illegal. The appearance of abuse of power was reinforced and has since haunted the American political system.

Derrida could have used Nixon's pardon, the central event in the Ford presidency, as an example of the gift's deconstruction, which incidentally parallels the unconstruction of the Ford administration. If Nixon gifted the offices of vice president and president to Ford, it was the trace of such a gift, appearing more now as an exchange than a gift, that more than anything else undid the Ford presidency.

Like all gifts, his gift was not a pure one, since Nixon selected Ford for reasons of political expediency. Of all the possible vice presidential selections to replace the office vacated by Spiro Agnew, Ford was the easiest to get through Congress. As has been noted, Ford's distinguishing feature as a vice presidential choice was that he had no deeply entrenched political opposition. He rose to the presidency because he was not objectionable. Like a member of the Chamber of Commerce who acquired the skills of a politician and legislator (appropriately, on 28 April 1975, Ford used the U.S. Chamber of Commerce as a forum to announce his opposition to the formation of a consumer protection agency), everyone was Ford's friend. This is primarily why Congress welcomed the Ford presidency as an antidote to Nixon's strong-arm and somewhat inept means of dealing with the legislative body. Nixon, however, was wary of open confrontation with Congress and rarely used his veto power. He probably realized that gridlock, a term coined during the Ford administration, was in no one's interest. Accomplishments tend to help everyone in government. Nixon did not veto or even oppose measures such as the Clean Water Act. (However, Nixon notably impounded monies from being spent on Great Society programs, which in 1974 led to the Budget and Impoundment Control Act.)

The "trace" of Nixon upon Ford's presidency leads us to Derrida's later book, *Specters of Marx* (1994). When Ford pardoned Nixon for unspecified and unindicted presidential offenses, he did so in large part to exorcise Nixon's ghost from his own administration. However, Ford unwittingly forefronted the close relationship between gifts and ghosts. The new president became a kind of specter of Nixon. Ford became both the "gift president" and the "ghost president." A gift is a transaction outside the system of economic exchange that "gives" the system and, paradoxically, the gift, significance and value.

In the 1976 campaign, Ford, in accounting for his money flow, revealed that he spent virtually no personal money as president. Although this raised some suspicion, it was generally acknowledged that the president lives outside the world of everyday currency exchange. The president does not need his own money or credit card. It might be presumed that someone else picks up the tab. A president's aloofness from the public marketplace led to the most dramatic symbol leading to George Bush's 1992 election defeat, when Bush revealed his ignorance of what a grocery check-scanner was. In contrast, President Eisenhower had shown how a president might differ from royalty by buying Queen Elizabeth II a hot dog at a ball game. Similarly, President Clinton periodically goes to shopping malls to make purchases to show that he is a compassionate everyman. Eisenhower and Clinton gain credibility by appearing in the retail loop. In contrast, Ford, "an extra president," "a supplemental president," "a gift," contributed to making us sometimes wonder if anyone who is not a Hollywood actor can succeed as president. Looking "presidential" becomes increasingly important after Ford appears to be a counterfeit president.

In *Given Time,* Derrida analyzes a short Baudelaire prose piece titled "Counterfeit Money." Baudelaire's work begins, "As we were leaving the tobacconist's, my friend carefully separated the change." The piece then tells of giving counterfeit money to a beggar. Derrida maintains that it is not coincidental that the currency generating the tale comes from a tobacco shop.

The film *Smoke* (1994), written by Paul Auster and directed by Wayne Wang, also uses gifting as a plot device and relates it to tobacco. Set in and around a tobacco shop, the movie explores complications posed by the "gift" of one man saving another man's life, complications resolved only through the complex use of stolen and, in a sense, counterfeit, money and property. Similarly, Nixon saved his 1952 vice presidential nomination and his political career by telling the American people that he would keep the gift of his dog Checkers, making light of the fact of gifts that he had acquired through his slush fund. (It is interesting to note that Nixon delivered his Checkers speech soon after the death of Franklin Roosevelt's Scottish terrier Fala, which received press notice. Nixon may have recalled Roosevelt making light and little of Republican critics who questioned whether public funds were spent on Fala. Did an aircraft carrier go out of its way to transport Roosevelt's terrier? It was one thing to attack his wife, said Roosevelt, but his dog?)

Tobacco occupies the supplemental or "extra" status that we have associated with the Ford presidency. Tobacco must be consumed when used. Its use goes up in smoke; it is outside of use-value (Derrida may not have been following health care debates about the medical costs of smoking) and therefore suggests

29. Gerald Ford smoking a pipe, courtesy of AP/Wide World Photos

a limit of exchange that paradoxically grounds it. Tobacco connotes the materiality of exchange itself since it is virtually nothing. According to Derrida,
"Before the first act, before speech, there is, there was, there will have been tobacco. That is the point of departure, to wit the first partition of sharing . . ."[151]

In this regard, it is interesting that Ford was so often photographed smoking
a pipe, particularly in the Oval Office. His pipes give Ford an impartial, judi-
cious air. The American people are thankful that the president's smoking gun
has turned into a pipe. Recalling pipe ceremonies, the president might seem to
be offering us a gift that no longer makes us victims of a retributive phallic law
that the Nixon administration's abuses of power came to represent. Similarly,
the neutralizing of paternal phallic law is represented in René Magritte's *Untitled Drawing*, 1948, which depicts the profile of a man smoking a pipe. However, the man's nose is a penis that dips into the pipe's head, creating a closed
system. The man is a self-contained, self-surveying mechanism. The nose, after
all, sniffs things out. In Magritte's drawing, however, surveillance is seemingly canceled into a pleasant narcissism. Similarly, Ford seems like a harmless
Nixon, a Nixon who will keep his metaphoric nose and penis out of the business of others. Pipe-smoking helps Ford create this impression. In applying
Marcel Mauss's *The Gift: The Form and Reason for Exchange in Archaic Societies*
(1950), the basis for Derrida's rumination about gifts, to Magritte's artworks,

W. J. T. Mitchell says, "The pipe's function in smoking rituals—for peace, worship, exchange of gifts, and festivals, associates it with utopian social practices as well as with solitary introspection and narcissism."[152] In this context, Ford's pipe also suggests the political system's inability to accommodate itself to factors outside of itself. Like the Magritte figure, Ford seems absorbed by his pipe. A smoking pipe is a smoking gun curved and smoothed out. (From a painterly point of view, the pipe as depicted frontally lends itself to gradations of distance as opposed to the gun's sharp commandment of perspective.)

The pipe makes Ford seem outside normal systems of exchange, and, before pardoning Nixon, he is popular. It is telling therefore that Robert Hartmann recalls Ford "elaborately filling his pipe" as he "matter-of-factly" said "he was very much inclined to grant Nixon immunity from prosecution as soon as he was sure he had the legal authority to do so."[153] After the pardon, then, photographs of Ford and his pipe are more apt to suggest Magritte's words "Ceci n'est pas une pipe," the words under the representation of pipes in his *Les trahison des images* and *Les deux mystéries*. We might similarly ask if this is a president. Magritte causes us to meditate on a dynamic tension between word and image, and Ford makes us consider a space between the presidency and the president. By being more a person—a non-presidential sort of person—than a president, Ford clarifies the mechanism of the presidency and restores it only to problematize it. Hence, Chevy Chase's *Saturday Night Live* parodies of Ford work well, despite having little to do with any likeness to him. It was not important to look or even act or speak like him, because Ford was the quintessential absent president. Similarly, Eric Sevareid noted that Gerald Ford was an assassination target because he was "the President, not Gerald Ford."[154]

Whereas the stature of other presidents may have been enhanced by assassination attempts, Ford was trivialized by them. Ford's two female would-be assassins, who tried to take his life during a two-week span in the fall of 1975, were tied to media events. Ford was first stalked by Lynette "Squeaky" Fromme, a Charles Manson devotee. Ford was then almost shot by Sara Jane Moore, a friend of Patty Hearst's fiancé, who, strangely like Patty Hearst, converted to violent, radical means. Moore called Ford a "nebbish" and wished to kill him so that Rockefeller would be president. She reasoned that this would unmask the capitalist system.

In *Specters of Marx*, Derrida views Marx's specter as a series of challenges to official post-monarchal reality, challenges that still haunt us. Similarly, the historian John Robert Greene maintains that "Gerald Ford's greatest gift to the American people" was, in Ford's words, leaving "the White House in better shape than when I took it over."[155] In other words, Ford had more integrity than Nixon. However, this was not an unproblematic gift. Both Ford and Marx embody the violation of a limit that reinforces the category of that limit. Ford, after all, renewed the American presidency only, I will argue, to trivialize it more profoundly, and Marx's state socialism unintentionally helped to build a foundation for the modern capitalist state.

The Ford presidency is a fascinating arena for studying how the ghost haunting us changes. With Ford, Nixon moves to a phase beyond his "being kicked around." His status as an expert achieves a new credibility, and the unsavory actions of his presidency become oddly justified. We, not him, become ghosts. It is almost as if Ford became a ghost haunted by a secluded live person.

As a presidential aspirant and president, Nixon had always seemed like a ghost. In *Nixon Agonistes* (1969), Garry Wills points out that during the 1968 campaign, Nixon was an ambassador from a "liberal" world before the New Deal. Nixon revives an English notion of liberalism based on an advocacy of a seemingly open market. However, it will take the Ford administration to entrench firmly a governmental strategy of reluctance to act. Ford is not shy to enact the anti-government rhetoric that Nixon did not think was in vogue. For Nixon, "the entire American topography is either graveyard," says Wills, "or minefield—ground he must walk delicately, revenant amid the tombstones, whistling in histrionic unconcern."[156] Wills describes Nixon's ghostly appearance in media lights in 1968:

> The angled lights give him one dark silhouette and a lighter "ghost" askew of it. Doubled hands rise and dip beside the haloed body, or flail in ghost gestures through it—six dim grades of shadow weaving elusive canons, visual echoes like the sound of "Tricky Dick," fiction pictures. Six crises endured—six Nixons, which do not seem to add up or solidify. The hands move in jerky quick apparitions, dark ones unable to escape the haunting light ones, nimble pianist fingers, prestidigitating shadow.[157]

This Nixonian image, like the five o'clock shadow that undid Nixon in his 1960 television debates with Kennedy, reinforced a sense that most Americans had of Nixon. In 1968, Americans do not know exactly why Nixon is shady, says Wills, but "the ghost is there."[158] Eventually, it might be argued that Nixon disseminates this "ghost" within American society.

In *Specters of Marx*, Derrida notes that spirits and ghosts can be equated with deconstruction since they are all forms of erasure and unraveling. The seventies mark Derrida's intervention into American literary studies, and it is not surprising that his work continues to shed light on many facets of American culture in this era. "Deconstruction" itself is part of America's reception of Derrida. Deconstruction might be called America's gift to Derrida, a gift that calls Derrida into debt. Derrida begins to deconstruct Mauss's notion of the gift from 1977 to 1979 in seminars at the Ecole Normale Supérieure and Yale University.

In the seventies, the United States constructed a ghostlike future by avoiding the thorny implications of its recent past. During the Ford presidency, the aftermath and the ghosts of the Vietnam War haunted the nation while Ford reasserted an American nationalism through the *Mayaguez* incident. He also attempted to identify inflation as a demon and apply nationalistic energies to Whip Inflation Now (WIN). However, when it was revealed that the WIN program was little more than the distribution of WIN buttons, the limits of pure ideology were touched. Nonetheless, Ford felt that he had successfully put his finger on the problem. He had after all used the bully pulpit and thrown the problem back to the American people. Ford had clearly called for far more drastic cuts in social programs than Nixon had ever proposed. However, the dismantling of the federal government had not yet become a virtuous option. Ford was not as yet fully seen in terms of his advocacy of cuts in federal programs. Although Nixon proposed much of the New Federalism that took hold of the capital after the 1994 election, Nixon felt the need to advance federal initiatives. Benign governmental neglect did not become "progressive" until the Reagan administration.

How can we remember the Ford presidency? John Updike points to this problem in *Memories of the Ford Administration* (1994).[159] The novel uses the Ford years as a frame to remember minute details of its narrator's life. Although this is an ironic device, it does not invalidate the import of the Ford administration. To open and segment the narrative, Updike uses as a backdrop the life of James Buchanan, a minor president like Ford. (During the Ford years, the novel's narrator, a historian, is writing a book about President Buchanan.) In using the Ford years as a non-context, Updike is somehow able to be more sexually and privately detailed than ever before. The novel indicates that much happens in the Ford years in terms of a breakdown of central authority. Arguably, the Ford administration is pivotal in a movement from external to internal ideological control. The Church committee investigating the CIA is a more likely outcome of the mid-seventies than the sixties or early seventies because such surveillant political control now seems beside the point. The new left is in disarray and seemingly demands less surveillance from the establishment. The powers of global capital become dominant beyond a credible alternative. If the personal is political, it is powerless. The private and personal are no longer as revolutionary and are more acceptable. Appropriately, during the Ford years, psychoanalysis, popular and otherwise, becomes more accepted. Transactional analysis provides a way to analyze all social exchange psychoanalytically. Similarly, Betty Ford asserts her right to the public annunciation of a private life by publicizing her breast cancer and asserting that if she were younger she would try marijuana. She sets the stage for the virtual reconfiguration of American identity by glamorizing recovering from alcohol, drugs, and other "addictions" in the mid-eighties.

Updike's dismissal of the Ford years is convenient, but not convincing. After all, Updike supported the war in Vietnam, so how could he forget our national memories of this indefinite war's definitive conclusion? Much that is memorable occurs during the Ford administration — from the American evacuation of Saigon to the arms buildup. However, this change in how we remember the Ford years is probably the most important transition of these years. After Watergate, things seemed to happen and be recorded differently. What could government now do positively with the malevolent Nixon gone? Nothing seemed as appropriate as prosecuting Nixon. Government had somehow lost its focus. The congressional class of '74, the "Watergate babies," could not find a coherent, populist-sounding voice, and they were identified with a sense of a government that does not work. Liberals were negatively identified with radicals, to the disappointment of both, and the significance of Spiro Agnew's term "radiclibs" was assimilated. While liberalism was becoming a pejorative term in mainstream politics, radicals had fewer alternatives to it.

As a president, Ford lacked not only a mandate, but also lacked an election that might have provided an agenda. His past was relatively insignificant, since it was never publicized in a national election. Moreover, he did not assume leadership from a president who was popular or cohesive in his programs. Whereas Johnson could gather strength by saying "Let us continue" and constantly invoke Kennedy, Ford could not mention the name of his predecessor, lest the nightmare be remembered. "Most Vice Presidents who become President have buried their predecessors and then gone on to reassure the people by wrapping themselves in the mantle of the men they followed," Ford says in his memoirs. "At the time of *his* departure, Nixon had no mantle left."[160]

Although there is not the same kind of continuity between Nixon and Ford as between Kennedy and Johnson, it could be argued that as Johnson took Kennedy's federal programs and postures a step further, so Ford, through deregulation and a more profound neglect of social welfare, took Nixon's political philosophy a step further. For instance, Ford did not confuse his essential distrust of the federal government's ability to affect the public good by helping anything like the Clean Water Act through Congress. As we have noted, the Washington use of the term "gridlock" was conceived during the Ford administration. Ford vetoed sixty-four bills, a rate four times greater than Nixon. Nixon had used impoundment of appropriated funds as a weapon against Congress, and Ford used veto and delay. Congress overrode twelve Ford vetoes.

After Nixon, our expectations of the presidency became lower. We ceased to respond to presidential leadership as we did in the past (note Ford's WIN initiative), and a power vacuum was created. Nixon took the "gifts" of his office papers with him (leaving Ford as a kind of ghost-gift). At the very least, Nixon felt that an income tax deduction was owed him. Congress needed to pass legislation to ensure that presidents could no longer take their papers with them. Nixon's stance of ownership has caused a discontinuity in the National Archives' series of presidential libraries, wherein there is cooperation between the National Archives and former presidents and their families. One might say that the succession of presidential knowledge to the present begins with the Ford Presidential Library in Ann Arbor.

Ford is a groundbreaking president in the sense that he prefigures Carter and Clinton as presidents who came out of the wilderness of presidential politics. Although Ford was House minority leader, being in the minority, he was responsible for few initiatives. He was known for understanding fine budgetary points on the House Appropriations Committee, serving on the Warren Commission, and loyally executing the commands of the Nixon White House. If Ford was known as a moderate, it was because he had little ideology, and in a sense this was his ideology. He could make friends and yet be relatively uncorrupt. Revelations that the president of U.S. Steel paid for Ford vacations, and that Ford tried to squelch Wright Patman's Watergate investigation, could not dispel this impression.

In a sense, Ford's apparent honesty was a larger indictment of Washington. Washington was a party America was not invited to. Ford did not need to be "bought." He enjoyed doing what his supporters expected of him. Similarly, on 23 March 1971, Nixon could say, "You people are my friends and I appreciate it" to the Mid-America Dairymen, a day after accepting a huge campaign contribution from the organization, and two days before the Department of Agriculture raised milk's support price.[161]

Ford's pardon of Nixon seemed to be more of an interaction between friends than a calculated political move for Ford's benefit. Ultimately, Nixon had nothing to bargain with. After all, how could Nixon have kept the presidency from Vice President Ford? Ford seemingly received nothing from the pardon. Keeping Watergate out of the news was a possible Ford motive. However, Ford was presenting himself as Watergate's cure. The Nixon pardon implicated him in Watergate. In the 1976 Republican primaries, Reagan attacked Ford by placing Ford in Washington's "buddy system." Similarly, Carter ran successfully as an outsider. It is a testament to the aura of the presidency, which Nixon was able to posit so successfully in 1972, and to the ambivalence of the American voter, that Ford was almost able to win in 1976. Television commercials for Ford featuring a marching band synched to an "I'm feeling good about America" jingle (similar in theme and motif to Reagan's "It's morning in America" commercials) almost put Ford over the top. Oddly, Ford's commercials also lauded him for bringing "Peace with Freedom" (no longer Nixon's "Peace with Honor"), while Ford criticized the Democratic Congress for cutting appropriations for the war in Southeast Asia.

As a congressman, Ford displayed a preference for party loyalty over ideology, culminating in his rise to the minority leadership in 1965, in which Ford was called one of the House Republican "Young Turks." In this victory, Ford represented Republicans who paradoxically wished to make a break from the Republicans' 1964 landslide defeat while also parlaying Barry Goldwater's 1964 sweep of the deep south into Republican congressional gains. To assist this latter trend, no longer would House Republicans so closely align themselves with conservative southern Democrats. (Nixon bucked this trend. To the consternation of many in the Republican Party, he punished his personal foes like liberal New York senators Charles Goodell and Jacob Javits and rewarded his political friends like conservative Democrats John Stennis and Scoop Jackson, with little regard for party. In addition, Nixon's 1972 campaign strategy called for getting conservative Democratic voters to the polls, who tended to vote for Nixon together with Democratic congressional candidates. These split tickets contributed to Nixon's personal landslide while harming Republicans running for Congress.) In a sense, Ford's elevation to House minority leader marked the beginning of the Southern Strategy, in congressional terms. (Also in the sixties, an aide to Nixon's 1968 campaign, Kevin Phillips, coined the term Southern Strategy to refer to the Republican gains that could be made from Barry Goldwater's victories in the south in the 1964 presidential election, after Goldwater commented that he should go where the votes were. Phillips's 1969 *The*

Emerging Republican Majority envisions the electoral lock that a solid Republican south, based on the Republicans' courting of a law-and-order and civil-rights-backlash vote, would provide. The remarkable aspect of the Southern Strategy was that it applied to the country as a whole. By 1968, the electorate was being swayed by law-and-order issues in presidential elections.) A variation upon the Republican Southern Strategy would lead to the Republican-led Congress of 1995. In the 1994 election, Republicans picked up most of their seats at the expense of southern Democrats.

One notable Ford exception to this strategy should be noted. In the early sixties, Ford played a key role within a coalition that passed a Kennedy-sponsored "foreign aid" bill that would come to increasingly allow Americans to provide South Vietnam with military advisers. It was the beginning of the Vietnam War as we would come to know it. Interestingly, Ford would of course also be closely involved with the war's conclusion.

Ford originally won his seat by stressing foreign policy. A returning World War II veteran, Ford won his seat by challenging an unreformed isolationist Republican in the primary. To make his point, Ford used an old army bivouac hut as his campaign headquarters. Although now he embraced internationalism, as did other young Republicans such as Nixon, Ford, a congressman from Grand Rapids in western Michigan since 1949, never endorsed the New Deal, the Great Society, or the expanding role of the federal government. The congressional classes of 1947 and 1949 contained three presidents—Kennedy, Nixon, and Ford. Each succeeding president was increasingly conservative, as if working backwards in time through and, in some ways, outside the New Deal. Ford, born in 1913, brought small-town, twenties Republican values to the White House. These values included thinking of the federal government as primarily an aid to business, as a mega–chamber of commerce.

An examination of Ford's briefing papers shows how preoccupied Ford was with this aspect of the presidency.[162] The first briefing that David Hoopes, who organized Ford's briefings, kept is a remnant of the Nixon administration. This paper was written by William E. Timmons for Nixon's meeting with senators Curtis and Dole on 6 June 1974. The president and senators suggested that the United States lower its import quotas. They maintained that "a prosperous beef industry is essential to a prosperous economy in the years ahead. Americans like beef." Soon Nixon was dead meat. America's taste for meat would never be the same.[163]

Two hours after Gerald Ford assumed the presidency, he met with his economic advisers in the cabinet room about "problems of inflation, unemployment, and real output."[164] The Ford administration sees "real output" as a prime concern of the government, anticipating the supply-side economics that is formulated in 1976, and a version of which is enacted during the Reagan years. Ford's economists determine that creditors must be served. Although it would have seemed more logical at the time to act against a decrease in real earning power, which was more ominously, and with less precedent, confronting Americans, the meeting determines, "Our number one problem on the economic front is inflation and the associated problems of unemployment and stagnant real output." Why these are associated problems is unexplained. In fact, opposition to inflation in many ways would come to mean vetoing congressional appropriation, manpower, and public-service bills and initiatives.

In this period, the federal government concerned itself less and less with social welfare. Near Nixon's resignation, Attorney General William B. Saxbe, in a memo later brought to Ford's attention, seems to speak for the incoming president when he says that nothing can be done about crime except more efficient policing:

> Cap Weinberger and I have talked and will talk again about the social factors that are the real cause of our crime increase. The history of the "War on Poverty" attack on these factors during the Johnson Administration is not encouraging.
>
> The grand scale overhaul of our fragmented law enforcement structure is not now a practical solution but would in my mind be the only dramatic way to tackle the problem. I hope to propose it again when the climate is right.[165]

This climate is of course generated by the Watergate scandal. In fact, an effort to link enforcement and surveillance mechanisms under the direct control of the White House produced Watergate. Despite the White House's power to maintain a centralized policing agency, presidential aide Ken Cole summarizes Saxbe's attitude as "there is nothing the Federal Government can do" when it comes to social remedies other than law enforcement, even though Saxbe maintains that "social factors are the real cause of our crime increase."[166] Apparently, according to Saxbe, these social factors are limited to society's reluctance to be adequately policed.

On 12 August 1974, Ford is briefed about one of his first White House ceremonies. The ceremony celebrates the Comprehensive Employment and Training Act (CETA), which was the most positive face of Nixon's New Federalism. It set up state and local job programs that were administered by these states and localities. However, CETA was eliminated early in the Reagan presidency.

Nixon's New Federalism called for block grants to states that asked them to carry out tasks previously relegated to the federal government. However, Ford began to question the wisdom of indicating tasks. Ford submitted to Congress that revenue-sharing consolidates programs, leading to more spending prerogatives for states.

On 13 August 1974, from the White House, Ford addressed the nation and presidential appointees. More than during the Nixon administration, sixties progressivism seemed to have ended. Ford's sole domestic vision concerned stopping inflation without specifying how the United States would do this. One can only suspect that the country would need to maintain high interest rates together with the low growth of the economy. Also on 13 August, Ford warned the U.S. Conference of Mayors about overspending and dampened hopes of mass transit aid. The energy crisis was taking a back seat. Ford spoke with governors the next day about perceived difficulties concerning environmental protection. Also on this day Ford met Health, Education, and Welfare Commissioner Caspar Weinberger to discuss their opposition to the Kennedy-Mills and Long-Ribicoff bills that would provide expanded coverage for Americans through Social Security and Medicaid respectively.

On August 14, 1974, Ford met with Senator Russell B. Long to discuss the Trade Reform Bill. This trade bill was presented to Ford as necessary to create worldwide economic communication, and it forecast our nineties concerns with trade, speculation, and the "fast track." Ford had numerous meetings during these days that were centered around opposition to health-care bills. Also on this day, Ford signed a bill allowing American citizens to deal gold privately. This can be viewed as a symbol of coming economic deregulation. Nixon had taken the United States completely off the gold standard on 15 August 1971, when he suspended the convertibility of U.S. currency into gold or other federal reserves. President Nixon substantiated Derrida's notion in *Given Time* that the most characteristic money is counterfeit money. Nixon maintained that by not backing the dollar, he would "stabilize" it. It would now be immune from fluctuations in reserve trading. Under Nixon, money became a pure linguistic mandate. (One is reminded of Wallace Stevens's aphorism that "poetry is a kind of money.") Under Ford, the former backings of currency began to leave the federally accountable public sphere. As an interesting metaphor, Graham Martin's April 1975 cables from Saigon to Washington mention the need to remove gold from Vietnam. The nature of this gold is not clear from Martin's memos. However, he refers to "the men who gave the gold to the Americans" in a memo written while Saigon was frantically being evacuated.[167] It is speculated that much of the ten tons of baggage, with which the former South Vietnamese president arrived in Thailand after leaving Saigon, was gold.[168] Also interesting in this regard was CBS correspondent Ed Bradley's report that millions of American twenty-dollar bills were mysteriously being burned within the American embassy on the day of the final American evacuation from Vietnam.[169]

Of course, like American currency, the American presidency also lost much of its backing and credibility in these years. Before his first inauguration, Nixon claimed that he would help restore respect to the American presidency. These claims would soon recall the mysterious Diogenes fragment, "I have come to debase the currency." Notably, since the Treasury authorizes the Secret Service, the president is guarded by the officers of the Treasury Department. The Secret Service began in the nineteenth century as an agency that protected the American currency by policing counterfeiters. In the early twentieth century, after the assassinations of Lincoln, Garfield, and McKinley all within less than thirty-five years of one another, the Secret Service began protecting the "currency" of the American presidency.

On August 16, Ford met with South Carolina Senator Strom Thurmond to discuss the Armed Services Committee and Defense Department patronage. Ford wished to continue the "special relationship" that Thurmond had with Nixon. Thurmond may have also voiced his concern about a treaty that might "give the [Panama] Canal away." Ford probably should have been better prepared with a response (American military and economic interests were after all protected by the treaty) because the 1976 Reagan campaign would startle Ford with criticisms of the treaty and hinge its first primary wins on Reagan's crowd-pleasing, "When it comes to the Canal, we built it, we paid for it, it's ours and we should tell Torrijos and Company that we are going to keep it." Reagan was playing off Theodore Roosevelt's comments about having stolen the canal zone fair and square.

The first week of the Ford presidency was a honeymoon, in which little consideration was given to how political capital was to be used. In this sense, the beginning of Nixon's second administration and the Ford administration were similar. Nixon sought to use his political capital accumulating personal power whereas Ford used his political capital restoring faith in the presidency and in pardoning Nixon, two ends at cross-purposes. It became clearer to the public who Ford's friends were. Why did Ford feel that everyone but Nixon had to atone for his or her errors? Resigning his job as Ford's press spokesperson, Jerry terHorst wrote Ford:

> As your spokesman, I do not know how I could credibly defend in absence of a like decision to grant absolute pardon to the young men who evaded Vietnam military service as a matter of conscience and the absence of pardons for former aides and associates of Mr. Nixon who have been charged with crimes—and imprisoned—stemming from the same Watergate situation. Try as I can, it is impossible to conclude that the former President is more deserving of mercy than persons of lesser station in life whose offenses have had far less effect on our national well being.[170]

As a minority leader during Nixon's presidency, Ford saw himself as Nixon's House floor leader, and in a sense the pardon was probably a result of the continuation of this relationship.

However, as president, if Ford allowed himself to express himself, it was to be more politically conservative, if not more repressive. For instance, even though Ford mobilized Republican support to pass the Family Assistance Program in the House of Representatives, before Nixon maneuvered to let it die in the Senate, Ford never quite understood Nixon's need to seem innovative.

As a seeming exception, on 22 August 1974, Ford reaffirmed his support of the Equal Rights Amendment as "an idea whose time has come." The 1972 Republican Convention platform had supported the ERA, and with only five more states needed for its ratification, it seemed certain of ratification. First Lady Betty Ford was outspoken in her support of the amendment. And yet Ford was part of a subtle economic, social, and political movement that contributed to the ERA not being an idea whose time had come. Surprisingly little occurred within the Ford administration concerning women's rights.

Response to Ford's 20 August 1974 nomination of Nelson Rockefeller to be his vice president exemplified how the political landscape had changed. Viewing himself as a conservative Republican, Ford felt that he could balance his administration with the more liberal Rockefeller. The powerful former New York governor would add stature to the new administration. Choosing Rockefeller would not seem as partisan as nominating chairman of the Republican National Committee George Bush, and Rockefeller would strengthen the administration in this "crisis of confidence," as Ford put it in his memoirs, at about the same time that Carter used the phrase to the nation.[171] Rockefeller was elected four times in a populous state. "He has been a consistent winner at the polls, having had millions of votes cast for him," said Secretary of the Interior Rogers B. Morton in a 13 August 1974 letter to the president.[172] Rockefeller would help offset the fact that Ford was never chosen in a national election.

Ford may have also felt that Rockefeller might be something like his domestic Kissinger. Rockefeller would not be so much a "lone ranger" as a base of policy input. "I wanted him to head the Domestic Council and to help put together my domestic legislative package," Ford says that he initially told Rockefeller. " 'You've been studying these issues,' I said. 'You've had a lot of experience with them, and I think this is one area where you can be very helpful to me.' "[173] As Ford relied on Kissinger for foreign policy "product," perhaps he wished Rockefeller to generate a kind of raw material of domestic agenda that could be trimmed by his other advisers. Ford, however, soon realized that the dynamics of presidential politics had changed. Ford's nomination of Rockefeller led to calls for a third party by conservative Republicans like Howard Phillips and William Rusher. Ford could hardly be viewed as conservative in relation to Ronald Reagan, and, in the 1976 election, Ford would need more support from the ideological right. Rockefeller's power within the Ford administration became a political liability to Ford even before the Senate confirmed him in December 1974, four months after nomination and about three months longer than had initially been anticipated due more to opposition from conservative Republicans than liberal Democrats. Rockefeller was vice president for less than nine months before Ford approved the administration pressures to force Rockefeller to withdraw himself from consideration for the 1976 Republican vice presidential nomination.

As with his selection of Rockefeller, Ford also miscalculated by granting a September 8, 1974, "full, free, and absolute pardon unto Richard Nixon for all offenses" that he "committed or may have committed or taken part in during the period from July [Ford meant January—'July' was a flub] 20, 1969 through August 9, 1974." Although this may have helped keep Nixon out of the headlines, as Ford wished, it made Ford a target instead. Indeed, Ford's timing equated him with Nixon. His choice of Sunday morning after church services recalled the Saturday Night Massacre. In both cases, little notice was given. However, in neither case was notice avoided. Now Ford was being investigated by Congress because of abuse of power issues, and Nixon was able to settle into an uncanny immunity and a suspended state of the repressed returning—

something like the figure of Parmigianino moving to and from the mirror's backing in Ashbery's contemporaneous "Self-Portrait in a Convex Mirror."

In examining the correspondence between Nixon in San Clemente and the White House, it seems as if Ford felt that Nixon had him over a barrel. The pardon was clearly negotiated on Nixon's terms. The Ford administration felt that it legally needed an acceptance of the pardon. Nixon's acceptance would equal an admission of guilt, and Ford would have a crime to pardon. Benton Becker's (Ford's representative at San Clemente) abbreviated handwritten notes ("Insist upon retaining, Obstr of jus language") on the draft of Nixon's pardon acceptance indicate that Becker considered "I was wrong in not acting more decisively and more forthrightly in dealing with Watergate, *particularly when it reached the stage of judicial* proceedings and grew from a political scandal into a national tragedy [underlining by Becker]" an admission of obstruction of justice. And yet his slight admission of guilt was lost, even by lawyers. Special Prosecutor Leon Jaworski could have challenged the pardon. However, Ford received assurances through Donald Rumsfeld that Jaworski would not do so. Indeed, Jaworski was not in a position to indict Nixon at the time because he was immersed in the John Mitchell trial.

Ford could do little better than have Nixon acknowledge that mistakes were made. In exchange for the gift of the pardon, Nixon was asked to draft an acceptance statement that accepted some responsibility. Nixon said that "perspective" had changed. He saw a "confusing maze of events." He now realized that he had made "mistakes in not acting more decisively." (If he were more decisive, would he have burned the tapes?) He acknowledges "misjudgments." However, Nixon was careful not to imply any moral deficiency. His errors were in not understanding how others would misunderstand him. His pardon acceptance statement, entitled "Statement," concludes:

> I know that many fair-minded people believe that my motivations and actions in the Watergate affair were intentionally self-serving and illegal. I now understand how my mistakes and misjudgments in handling Watergate have contributed to that belief and seemed to support it. This burden of disbelief by honest men and women is the heaviest one of all to bear.[174]

Not obtaining a specific admission of guilt within a context that denoted guilt generated a sense of abstract, uncontrollable guilt. The pardon generated free-floating guilt that went beyond Watergate. Watergate was delocalized. If Ford hoped that the pardon would be a kind of death certificate for Watergate, he conjured the phenomena as he tried to exorcise it. To try to bury something may paradoxically bring it to life. "It is often a matter of pretending to certify death there where the death certificate is still the performative," says Derrida.[175]

Although the pardon was probably not arranged before Nixon's resignation, Ford acknowledges that Nixon's chief of staff, Alexander Haig, had received Ford's opinion that an unprecedented, pre–indictment and conviction, blank-check pardon would be possible. Haig listed a number of options to Ford, including Nixon pardoning himself and resigning. Ford probably conveyed the sense that his pardon would be the best option. Thereafter, Ford likely felt that he would have been reneging on a virtual deal by not pardoning Nixon. It would not have felt right to him. Ford knew that "the public would not stand for" a pre-indictment pardon, as he said in his vice presidential confirmation hearing.[176] However, Ford seemed oblivious to short-term public reaction. Like Nixon before the Saturday Night Massacre, he expected protest to diminish. Perhaps more importantly, he did not become liked in Congress by being unreliable. Therefore, Haig and most likely Nixon, knowing Ford, had planted the seed for this preemptive repression of indictment, guilt, and confession. Confession would have saved the Nixon presidency in the early and middle stages of Watergate. But Nixon understandably did not see the need to begin confessing after the presidency was already lost.

Ford was more threatened by Watergate's continued presence at the top of the news than by Nixon. When Ford said, in his first presidential address, that "our long national nightmare is over," he did not relate closure with accountability. Although he would later define his presidency as a "time to heal," he did not realize how much Nixon had to do with the wound. Rather than contrasting himself with Nixon, Ford wished to repress the memory of Watergate, and in doing so Ford was swallowed by Watergate. We recall Watergate much better than Ford. It is unclear whether Ford was haunted by Nixon, or whether Ford was the ghost of Nixon, Watergate, and the presidency. Capitulation to Nixon's demands in the negotiation for his pardon makes one feel that the San Clemente White House was never more aptly named than during this period, not even when Nixon visited China as a head of state in 1976.

Ford often asserted presidential autonomy while asking for voluntary help. This is the kind of rhetoric of leadership that President Bush popularized with the figure of "a thousand points of light." Oddly, Ford's 8 September 1974 "Whip Inflation Now" speech is something of a ghost of Nixon's 15 August 1971 "New

Economic Policy" address. After all, like Ford's request that Americans keep down wage and price increases and energy consumption, Nixon's call for wage and price controls in effect was voluntary because Nixon had no intention of keeping wage and price controls for longer than the three-month period for which they were announced. Nixon signaled as much by calling wage and price controls "Phase I" in his "Game Plan." The problem existed, however, because no one had thought of a "Phase II." Phase II meant lifting the wage and price controls that Congress had suggested and legislated so as to be at Nixon's disposal. The controls had been surprisingly successful in dealing with the seemingly impossible economic Frankenstein monster that Nixon's half-hearted budget cuts and sporadic tax incentives had invented—stagflation. Under Nixon, unemployment soon doubled and economic growth stalled while inflation spiraled. And yet Nixon would not accept the only thing that worked. It is unclear whether Nixon, after making some economic gains presumably in time for the 1970 congressional elections, was looking for a new answer or no answer other than what might be found in the supposedly free market.

Much of the difference between receptions of Nixon's and Ford's economic plans involved the lesser credibility of the presidency in 1974. The diminishing credibility of such presidential leadership rhetoric can also be seen in Bush's 1989 advocacy of voluntarism and Clinton's 1993 call for citizen "contributions." Ford's strongest symbol of wayward do-goodism was his 1976 promotion of the swine flu vaccine, which would preemptively save Americans from an epidemic that never developed. The Ford administration wrangled with insurance companies, and then managed to have Congress fund insurance. Although few were vaccinated, several of those died from an allergic effect. A presidential Office of Science and Technology memo, in classic damage-control mode, ponders the normal rate of death to put the swine flu vaccine's danger in a larger light.[177]

The obscure swine flu "epidemic," its "cure," and the contemporaneous mysteries of Legionnaires' disease (suspected at first of being swine flu) gave the period an odd sense of an uncontrollable and unknowable virus that prefigured the AIDS crisis. The name Legionnaires' disease can be considered a deconstruction of the failed military-like effort with which Ford endorsed the swine flu vaccine crusade, in sharp distinction to the distraction with which presidents would deal with AIDS. If Jimmy Carter viewed energy self-sufficiency the "moral equivalent of war" (national effort that would be as great as World War II), the closest that Ford came to such a positive action was his mobilization against swine flu. After all, Ford's battles against inflation were mostly negative. He chose not to stimulate the economy except through his advocacy of a tax cut (a proposal that was attacked as a reversal on his budgetary austerity rhetoric). Spending on social welfare was not part of his strategy, and perhaps the swine flu vaccination constituted his most vigorous initiative in the realm of social welfare.

On the domestic front, his major deviation from economic austerity was his advocacy of a tax cut in his first State of the Union address, thus putting in motion the kind of logic of wish fulfillment that Republicans have since pursued. However, the Ford administration gave more focus to deregulation. Much more than Nixon, Ford contributed to a reverse of the regulatory reforms of the early seventies. For instance, Ford eagerly opposed the institution of a federal consumer protection agency on the grounds that it would cost too much for all concerned.

We can see a trend toward deregulation in transportation. Ford signed the 1975 Railway Revitalization and Regulatory Reform Act, regulating competition in the railways. However, he also proposed bills to deregulate the airways, which would be enacted during the Carter administration. Ford bitterly opposed Congress on oil prices, vetoing the Democratic Congress's domestic oil price regulating legislation in 1975. He also called for restraints on federal spending on mass transportation. Ford proposed and signed the Securities Act Amendments of 1975, deregulating the securities market for investors, and he sponsored the Financial Institutions Act, which would make the banking industry more competitive. The first of several similar deregulations, the Securities Act Amendments of 1975 helped to create the investment climate that blossomed into the savings and loan scandals of the eighties.

Whereas Nixon had stalled in enforcing federal court-ordered busing, he never confronted the issue. Ford, however, announced his disagreement with federally mandated busing at the height of the 1974 busing crisis in Boston. He thus seemed to endorse the white rioters. Ford ushered a new era of government-sanctioned racial bias and indifference that would come into its own under Reagan. The political environment had clearly changed.

Ford's foreign policy also shifted with the political terrain. Nixon had developed detente as a way of "gifting" friendship to the Soviet Union and China, guaranteeing that the United States would not take sides with one against the other. By playing the Soviet-Chinese rift and finally debunking the myth of a worldwide Communist conspiracy, Nixon was able to maintain enough resources to keep fighting the Vietnam War and even expand it into neutral

Cambodia. The great irony of course is that the United States was in Vietnam because it ascribed to the domino theory, the need to stop Southeast Asia from falling to a worldwide Communist conspiracy. Hence, the Vietnam War deconstructed the insight that informed it. It is probably not coincidental that the conclusion of the war in Vietnam signaled the discontinuance of detente. During the Vietnam War, the United States could not afford a confrontation with Russia. The Vietnam War was difficult enough to support. In addition, Johnson and Nixon feared Chinese intervention in Vietnam, China's historic enemy.

In the spring of 1976, Ford paved the way for major arms build-ups in the late seventies and eighties by signing off on CIA Director George Bush's insistent requests to reassess American estimates of Soviet nuclear and military strength. Bush and others in the CIA and the Ford administration wished ad hoc to raise dramatically all these estimates. Their pretext was the application of a kind of Murphy's Law, or worst-case scenario, raised to exponential powers. For instance, we can note a 22 July 1975 memorandum, from Department of State Counselor Helmut Sonnefeldt to Secretary of State Kissinger, titled "Edward Teller's 'Alternative' NIE [the CIA's National Intelligence Estimate]."[178] It is unusual that a portion of this memorandum was declassified on 6 June 1994 by Clinton Executive order 12356, section 3.4.

"Teller gave me the attached 'alternative,'" Sonnefeldt tells Kissinger about a still-classified proposal by physicist Edward Teller. The plan became known as "Alternative B." "Teller's technique is to take propositions that can neither be proved nor disproved at this time." Sonnefeldt felt it incredible that "every proposition will unfold in a worst case scenario for the US." However, less than a year later Ford authorized this reappraisal. A 21 June 1976 memo for Brent Scowcroft from Richard T. Boverie noted that "[name still classified] indicated that he will recommend that Director Bush forward this list of topics to you with a request for White House approval of the proposed experiment. Bush may also raise the issue of the funding for the experiment since the CIA has not budgeted the estimated $500,000 that will probably be required to cover anticipated travel, per diem, office, and staff support costs for the estimated 15 outside professional staff who would participate in the experiment."[179]

Ford went along with the experiment of Alternative B only after his surprising loss of the North Carolina Republican primary to Ronald Reagan had convinced him that the Reagan threat was more dangerous than he feared, and that he would need more support from conservatives. Perhaps the price

Ford paid for this distortion of reality was his inability to complete the Strategic Arms Limitation Treaty II agreement (Ford's summit with Brezhnev in Vladivostok laid the ground for SALT II), which became one of the Carter administration's most noteworthy accomplishments. In any case our nation still pays for the substantial debt accrued to finance the arms escalation that Alternative B called for.

In adapting to Teller's unrealistic assessment, the way was being prepared for a denial of fiscal realities in the Reagan years. If Vietnam was about bureaucratic denial, the war ended fittingly. An air of unreality surrounds the portions of the "Graham Martin Channel" that have recently been declassified. This inability to cope with the inevitability of an evacuation from Vietnam led to the terrifying confusion of the last hours of America's Vietnamese presence.

Graham Martin, the American ambassador to South Vietnam, never quite accepts the proposition of leaving Vietnam. The evacuation is an option—a fall-back plan that is never quite owned up to. Amazingly, on the next to the last day of the Vietnam War, Martin says that he does not believe that Saigon will be invaded. He maintains that North Vietnam would prefer a negotiated peace. "They are simply not in that much of a hurry," Martin says. He predicts that the Communists will try to form a coalition that would be a "60-40 line-up in some months with the 40 percent or even less on the communist side."

Kissinger was trying to arrange a cease-fire through the Soviet Union until the American embassy in Saigon could be evacuated. However, detente could not help the United States in the closing moments of the Vietnam struggle. Although Kissinger told Martin on April 17 that a retreat was probably in the cards, and the ambassador proceeded with the airlift, Martin somehow believed that the tumult in the streets of Saigon was based on unfounded rumor. He maintained that Communist leaders were merely considering political and not military options about how to consolidate their recent gains (interestingly, Martin rarely dwells on these gains):

> The first concentration is going to be on formation of local administrations that can begin to get the countryside under control. After all this is accomplished—a year or more—they may begin to tighten the screws on the administration of Saigon. Even here, I would judge, they will wish to show a gentle face for a while.[180]

Martin refuses to give up the ship until, on the war's last day, he receives this short memo from Kissinger:

We have studied your request to keep a small staff behind and the President insists on total evacuation.

Warm regards.[181]

On May 12, 1975, the Cambodian government seized the *Mayaguez,* an American merchant ship, in the Gulf of Siam. The ship, carrying spare military parts, was in waters that Cambodia claimed as its own. When similar situations had occurred often in Ecuador, the United States would pay a fine for the ship's release.[182] Indeed, the Cambodians had previously seized American ships and released them. However, Ford was in political trouble, both domestically and internationally. Vietnam had fallen only two weeks prior to the incident, Arab-Israeli peace talks broke down in March, and *the New York Daily News* had just published the memorable "FORD TO CITY—DROP DEAD," depicting him as uncaring about New York's budgetary plight. Ford, Kissinger, and Scowcroft felt it vital for the marines to go ahead with their rescue plan to put the fear of the United States into the world. They clearly saw it as an opportunity to regain American respect. Perhaps they wished to avoid a repeat of the 1968 *Pueblo* incident in which an American espionage ship was captured when it entered North Korean waters. The incident was extremely embarrassing to the U.S. government, which eventually needed to apologize formally before the crew was released more than a year later. American vulnerability was revealed. The *Pueblo* incident probably influenced the unfavorable press coverage that the American military received during the Tet offensive, a week after the *Pueblo* was captured. The *Pueblo* and the *Mayaguez* situations could be said to bracket the decline of American military involvement in Vietnam. The *Mayaguez* and its crew were taken back much more swiftly than the *Pueblo.* Even though fifteen marines died in the rescue mission, more Americans than there were *Mayaguez* crew members, Ford's decisive action instantaneously caused his rating to rise eleven points.

Ford may have been thinking of his *Mayaguez* success when he apparently timed an evacuation of Americans from Lebanon so as to seem decisive in a crisis. Despite the death of an American ambassador and his aide, most Americans in Lebanon were in no immediate danger, did not want to leave, and probably could have simply been ordered out. There seemed little reason for the administration's well-publicized military evacuation other than Reagan's depiction of Ford as weak on foreign policy. It is uncertain whether the Lebanese evacuation helped to stem the 1976 Reagan tide toward the Republican nomination.

Ford's foreign affairs apparatus was haunted by Watergate. Ties between the Watergate and Ellsberg psychiatrist burglars and the CIA forced Nixon to replace CIA Director Richard Helms with James R. Schlesinger. Schlesinger ordered an investigation of all illegal activity. CIA Director William Colby continued on the project. Widespread surveillance and sabotage of domestic press and dissidents came to the surface, violating the CIA's charge to keep out of domestic affairs. Of particular sensation were revelations of CIA plots to assassinate foreign leaders such as Castro and Allende, the latter having been accomplished. "Operation Chaos," launched in 1967, which sought to befuddle domestic political dissenters, was documented. Many other CIA abuses were gradually uncovered, including widespread wiretapping of foreign phone calls, the testing (with the Army) of LSD and other drugs on unknowing subjects ("no one knew how to handle the situation; it seemed like kids playing scientist," said LSD subject Mary Ray[183]), and CIA arsenals of chemical weapons.

When the Colby investigation was leaked to Seymour M. Hersh of the *New York Times,* it led to a large, banner-headlined *Times* lead story, and Ford had to respond to the political fallout. He appointed Vice President Rockefeller to head a commission that covered much of the same ground as the internal CIA query. However, most of the initial CIA investigation was substantiated by the Church committee in the Senate. Because of the Church committee—which clearly responded to the Watergate investigation—Congress set up six oversight committees for the CIA. However, Ford dragged his feet in response to the FBI probes. His administration was discredited by the revelations about the CIA and Ford's nonresponse to them. Ford, furious at CIA Director Colby for helping the Church committee and leaking information to Hersch, removed Colby and nominated George Bush. George Bush became the head of the CIA in November 1975 and helped to implement Edward Teller's Alternative B.

In the second Carter-Ford debate, which was devoted to foreign policy, Carter said "We are weak," recalling a central tenet of Kennedy's 1960 campaign. (Kennedy's election rhetoric predicted the second great post–World War II arms buildup and Carter's rhetoric foretold the third.) The second debate was probably one of many factors that in itself lost the election for Ford. Carter seemed more compelling than Ford. "As far as foreign policy goes," said Carter, "Mr. Kissinger has been the President of this country. Mr. Ford has shown an absence of leadership and an absence of a grasp of what this country is and what it ought to be." Perhaps Carter's broadside unnerved Ford. When a *New York Times* reporter said that the Helsinki accords had recognized Soviet autonomy in Eastern Europe, Ford rebutted that, in fact, Eastern European countries like Poland were indeed "autonomous" nations. In fact, this was one of the negotiated points of the Helsinki agreement, although the Soviets probably took this point to be more of an assurance that NATO, not themselves, would refrain from intervening in Eastern Europe. Post–Cold War Russian apprehensions about Poland, the Czech Republic, and Hungary entering NATO reinforce this point. (The Helsinki accords could be viewed as a reaffirmation of the post–World War II division of Europe. Mutual surveillance was agreed upon to insure a deadlock. However, the agreement also helped open up the Eastern European market. The human rights provisions in the Helsinki agreement also took on import in Jimmy Carter's foreign policy.)

Perhaps Ford meant to say that Eastern European nations had more independence than many people realized, or as much range of governmental action as a leader like himself had. Perhaps he could identify with the Soviet-dominated Eastern European leaders he had met who were somewhat independent but subject to enormous pressures. Nixonishly, he was slow to acknowledge his mistake. Never admitting that he had misspoken, he had given substance to Jimmy Carter's questioning of his leadership and momentum turned back to Carter. Interestingly, Ford had gained momentum in the first debate, which was limited to domestic affairs. In that debate, Carter revealed the lack of a clear Democratic objective.

Carter's four-year campaign for the presidency demonstrated that a presidential campaign took as long as a presidential term and further politicized the governmental process. Oddly, Carter's rise was aided by Democratic reformers who had opened the presidential selection process after the horror of the 1968 convention. In 1972, reforms that helped remove the nomination process from Washington establishments, together with the secret assistance of the Committee to Re-Elect the President, were successful in nominating George McGovern. A Democratic standard-bearer outside federal governmental processes was produced. Then in 1976 a former southern governor was elected for the first time since the Civil War. Although Nixon's most visionary initiatives may have been in his plans for revenue-sharing and the gradual withering away of the federal government, Nixon became linked with "Washington." By casting himself in competition with the Democratic Congress, Carter was indirectly opposing Nixon, and by extension Ford, a strategy that elected him. However, it was not yet clear how tenuous a Democratic working majority was in Congress, and a Democratic president who had difficulty working with a Democratic Congress reinforced the notion of Democratic inefficiency and ushered in the Reagan revolution as an antidote to a central government that was paradoxically associated with both unwanted change and the status quo. The Ford years were pivotal in a transformation from the public's high expectations of federal government to low government expectations and to its general willingness to privatize. The link between the government and the individual was weakened, and the private sphere increasingly assumed the functions of the public.

In a sense, Ford was the perfect "unpresident" for his times. When our culture seemed to stagnate, the heuristics and demographics of presidential politics changed. After the rifts of the Vietnam War, the presidency began to lose much of its power as an ideological organizing mechanism. Johnson simply could not fathom or communicate with sixties counterculture and protest groups. This culture ironically expanded together with U.S. involvement in the Vietnam War. Nixon, considering himself as a kind of savior of American hegemony, institutionalized this communication gap. Open political discourse was not an aim of his government, because it seemed to hinder the workings of a presidential administration. With Watergate, the stridency of this, to Nixon, self-evident stance was rejected. Ford's popularity suffered when his pardon of Nixon tainted him with a sense of Nixonian public-be-damned back room dealings. Like Bush later, Ford was never able to resolve his anxiety of influence with his predecessor. His calls for voluntary group involvement were met with apathy and confusion, such as his WIN effort for economic recovery, and fear and trepidation, such as his call for the public to cooperate with the free swine flu vaccination program despite its killing of dozens of Americans. Carter, too, stumbled early in his administration with his protection of political ally Bert Lance, and a seeming lack of propriety that undermined his campaign commitments to honesty and an opening of the political process. If government could not be trusted, however, it seemed to be the government's fault, and Americans rejected Jimmy Carter's suggestion that the public examine its ennui. Perhaps this ill-advised Carter strategy defined the Reagan presidency. An ideological liberal, in the English sense of being an advocate of the free market, Reagan called for Americans to follow their xenophobic, self-centered impulses. Of course, Reagan himself could reward his friends and be forgiven since that's what we are all free to do. It would all work out. There was no more malaise. At least somebody was rich. Much, however, is obviously unaccounted for. Under Ford, government lost its accountability, in the sense that we increasingly stopped trying to apply government to our lives.

Gerald Ford became a public figure as an All-American center for the University of Michigan football team in Ann Arbor. If, as Eugene McCarthy said, Walter

Mondale had "the soul of a vice president," the center plays the football position of vice presidents. The center reaches to the ground for a football and, with his or her back to the quarterback, snaps the ball back to him or her. Plays are initiated by the ball going from the least to most glamorous position. A center can then only offer him- or herself as a sacrifice to delay the other team's rush to the quarterback. The center is the sacrificial position of football, and also a team's anchor. Ford snapped America. Through Ford, the powers of American government were dispersed and aligned according to the powers of capital—the private possessions of public trust.

In *Specters of Marx,* Derrida reads the armor of the ghost of Hamlet's father as a bodiless body, a spirit, a deconstruction like the "totalitarian" yet "de-facto Communism" in Eastern Europe that he says was "the element in which what is called deconstruction developed."[184] Similarly, American deconstruction develops within the context of the unraveling of America's sense of its progress, when, as Derrida begins *Specters of Marx,* "the time is out of joint." Derrida notes that Shakespeare's trope could mean that time is not flowing in its proper order. Similarly, Ford says "the State of the Union is not good" near the beginning of his first State of the Union address. The State of the Union was not progressing; it was out of joint. Most political and social perspectives have shared this sense that progress has stopped, that the future is in the past. Clinton's 1993 inaugural address tries to reverse this rhetoric and set a stage for positive governmental action: "You have forced the spring." Clinton's difficulties with Congress and the 1994 election showed how contested this "spring" would and will be. We sense that fundamental change is inevitable, but we do not know what form this change will take. Will a consensus be formed about a positive role for government?

During the Ford administration, government aspired to get out of the government business. Why not funnel out the task to the private realm? This movement culminated in Ronald Reagan's national acceptance. Reagan did not hide his status as an actor turned politician. He probably knew that an aura of virtuality added to his appeal. Perhaps Americans were at an impasse and the act of being president was more desired than the reality behind it. And yet, as Derrida points out, Marcellus says "something is rotten in the state of Denmark" when it becomes apparent that the true Danish government is ghostly.

Marx, according to Derrida, problematized being as an inheritance, a gift, a commodity, a debt, a ghost. Marxism is a specter that reveals a specter. In this sense, David Antin's April 1981 poem notes that Reagan was also a kind of ghost who presided over a nation haunted as it had rarely been haunted before:

people disappear from the numbers of the unemployed as they
cease to be counted among the job hunting poor   who as they
are no longer counted dont count and become some kind of
indefinitely numerous ghosts   who no longer live in our
affluent or struggling economy   but trouble it mysteriously
                    nonetheless

                              and if for a long time i didn't know what it
                    meant to be haunted i begin to know it now[185]

Prior presidencies prepared us for this haunting. We could see the Ford presidency as the ghost of a commodity exchange that showed the American presidency itself as a series of such exchanges. Under Ford, the ghost of the presidency followed the ghost it exorcised.

EPILOGUE

John Ashbery's mid-seventies post–oil crisis poem, "The One Thing That Could Save America," maintains that "the juice is elsewhere." So what is the one thing that can save America? If not oil, what does the speaker offer? He is befuddled that the message of one as self-professedly "private" as he could be destined to "boom later like golden chimes / Released over a city from a highest tower." He awaits this message but it "never arrives" because it is already in everyone's political consciousness, although "its time has still / Not arrived." The message is already "ripped open," its envelope destroyed, offering notes "dictated a long time ago"—a time capsule waiting for us, an old message on an answering-machine tape.

Home answering machines, appropriately, are first widely used in the late seventies, and this book is itself a kind of playback of "answering-machine messages," many of which have not been read critically for decades. This project has attempted to survey these messages to sensitize us to our own resistance to them, to sensitize us, that is, to our own "self-surveillance."

According to the poem, a paradoxically recently sent long ago message is now "The One Thing That Can Save America": a reading of the then contemporaneous seventies, the era within which we are still psychologically stuck. We must read this "message" so that we can finally assimilate the eras surrounding it. We back away from a chronicle of how we moved from the sixties to the eighties. When Bruce Springsteen sings in 1984 of a Vietnam veteran who "spends half of his life covering up," he could be referring to the collective consciousness compulsively recounting recent history in a superficial fashion as a progression of styles and hit singles that forecloses meaningful discovery. We must understand that something happened in the seventies and grapple with the "life" of the episteme as it evolved. I have used micro-periodizing to concretize the seventies and it episteme.

We must come to grips with a concrete chronicle of the seventies, a chronicle that I inevitably have shaped selectively. There are, of course, many versions of the seventies. Many economists stress the 1972 Smithsonian Agreement to re-institute fiscal regularity, after Nixon took the United States off the gold standard in 1971, as the beginning of a worldwide decline in government spending. Certainly the 1973 OPEC oil embargo underscored America's vulnerability in the international market, asserting petroleum reserves as a new kind of gold, a "key juice," to use Ashbery's expression. Other economists posit the grain shortages of the mid-seventies, largely caused by the 1973 Soviet crop disaster, as further fueling the upsurge in global inflation spurred by the 1973 oil crisis and contributing to politically fatal dissatisfaction with all three seventies presidents—Nixon, Ford, and Carter. Of course, others might not stress economic and political trends and events. For example, a film critic might concentrate on a movement from a playful confrontation with social issues and visions of reality in American films of the early seventies—a vast improvement from most sixties films—to strategies for maximizing profits. This book has attempted to tie together various seventies chronologies by finding their tropological regularities.

Notes

Introduction

1 *Washington Post*, "Pursuit of the Presidency," 28 October 1980, p. 399.

2 See Alan Nadel, *Containment Culture* (Durham: Duke University Press, 1995) for a discussion of how the Cold War mediated post–World War II American culture.

3 *Washington Post*, "Pursuit of the Presidency," 28 October 1980, p. 399.

4 Hunter S. Thompson, *Fear and Loathing: On the Campaign Trail '72* (New York: Straight Arrow Books, 1973), 18.

5 Ibid., 20–21. As I discuss in chapter 1, this book considers "real" effects of rhetoric and textual effects of "reality." Therefore, the present tense of the literary and the past tense of the historical sometimes intermingle.

1 Rippling Epistemes

1 Fredric Jameson, *The Ideologies of Theory, Volume Two: Syntax of History* (Minneapolis: University of Minnesota Press, 1988), 208. I talk often of the benefits of periodizing. However, my manner of periodizing could also be referred to as deperiodizing because close readings break through traditional generalizations based on hard and fast notions of periods. In fact, I deperiodize the seventies as I periodize it. An opportunity is created to bypass accepted generalizations. Particularities create their own fabric. Generalizations themselves can be read as "particular" textual figures.

A genealogy of theories of periodization might trace its assuptions back to Vico and Hegel. However, there would seem to be enough of a notion of the zeitgeist embedded in Foucault's notion of the episteme to keep us closer to our own period. Foucault, like Barthes before him, used the cultural relativism of Lévi-Strauss's textualized analyses of third world cultures to gain a perspective upon Western culture.

To say that a period can be studied implies a zoning of this period so that it is in a sense spatialized. Such implicit spatialization suggests an instantaneousness of field and an apparent totalization. In order to avoid insipid repetition of the obvious, I use two tools: a diachronic rendering of a synchronic set of conditions and an account of the synchronic as a kind of public space that is negotiated between the participants and phenomena of a given epoch.

2   Marge Piercy, *Woman on the Edge of Time* (New York: Fawcett Crest, 1976), 104.

3   "Talk of the Town: The Seventies, Back and Forward," *New Yorker,* 10 October 1993, 45.

4   Fredric Jameson, *The Political Unconscious: Narrative as a Socially Symbolic Act* (Ithaca, N.Y.: Cornell University Press, 1981), 31.

5   W. J. T. Mitchell speaks about "attempts to 'picture theory'" (*Picture Theory* [Chicago: University of Chicago Press, 1994], 5). These attempts are crucial for Mitchell because he believes that we have moved from a predominantly linguistic to a pictorial era. It is no longer sufficient for criticism to decode its subjects. Such criticism implies a verbal key that explains our culture according to a hidden reality. We must now consider the nodes of our objects of study and find the places where these nodes meet.

In relation to what is apparent, this will produce uncanny criticism. Using Freud's explanation of the uncanny as a critical rather than a psychological paradigm, I use the term uncanny, as we more commonly use it now, to mean peculiar, astonishing, bizarre, and incredible, rather than spooky and eerie. For Freud "uncanny" meant a feeling of horror produced by sensing pre-birth experiences that suggest castration (see Sigmund Freud, "The 'Uncanny,'" trans. Alix Strachey, in Ernest Jones, ed., *Sigmund Freud's Collected Papers,* vol. 4 [New York: Basic Books, 1959], 368-407). I employ the Freudian sense of uncanny to suggest the production of an interpretation based upon seemingly absent links. "Uncanny criticism" conveys the wonderment at establishing links that do not seem to be there. In a reverse of Gertrude Stein's comment about Oakland, "there is no there there," there is a there nowhere. However, such rabbits out of the hat are not the products of an invisible yet coherent cause. This account of them would be too easy and not really uncanny. Rather, absent causes generate uncanny connections. Paradoxically, to delineate the political unconscious is to mark off something that is vital because it is not there. The critic traces the political unconscious—the absence that drives culture.

6   Louis Althusser, *Lenin and Philosophy,* trans. Ben Brewster (London: Monthly Review Press, 1971), 42.

7   Ibid., 222-23.

8   John Ashbery, *Nation,* 8 May 1967, 578.

9   John Ashbery, letter, *Nation,* 29 May 1967, 692.

10 Charles Simic and David Lehman, eds., *Best American Poetry 1992* (New York: Scribner's, 1992), xvi.

11 Jameson, *Political Unconscious,* 82.

12 Ibid.

13 No one more than Hayden White articulates the tropological ground for historical study. However, White's scale is different than mine. I am more prone to unpack shorter periods than White. White also stresses rhetorical modes rather than

the close reading of seemingly non-tropological, specific phenomena. Likewise, although Althusser laid a ground for a causality that links all aspects of culture, his work did not regularly cross the line between theory and an application of that theory to small and specific cultural details.

My work has many apparent analogues, such as Lucien Goldmann's concepts of homology, isomorphism, and structural parallelism. However, as Jameson notes (*Political Unconscious*, 43–48), Goldmann uses these notions within a mechanistic model. Within the similarities that Goldmann notes, there is little room for differences. In addition, Goldmann does not adequately account for a historical era's reception. Similarly, A. J. Greimas, in "The Interaction of Semiotic Constraints" (1968), posits structural categories of historical reality that do not note the importance of the changes that cultural phenomena undergo through their transcriptions and interpretations. We might also point to Bakhtin's concept of "simultaneity," which considers the role of social energies as they dialogically speak through the author.

Other analogues include Barthes's cultural analyses, reader response theories, "anti-theorist" thought, and New Historicist work. However, in order for my project to be successful it must move to apply the better known realms of theory to more specific articulations. In so doing, I address what might be considered one of the cornerstones of the veritable discipline of "theory"—the opening of Derrida's *Of Grammatology*, which suggests that language itself has entered a stage of infinite inflation. Although my text considers all things as language, the limits of language are also observed, thus facilitating, if not entirely accomplishing, theory's "deflation" and reduction to its "use value."

14 Jameson, *Political Unconscious,* 82.

15 Jacques Derrida, *Of Grammatology,* trans. Gayatri Spivak (Baltimore: Johns Hopkins University Press, 1974), lxxxix.

16 Dates of poems indicate the year of the poem's first publication. Unless otherwise noted, texts of Ashbery poems cited in this book are from John Ashbery, *Selected Poems* (New York: Penguin, 1985). Hereafter this work is cited in my text as *SP.*

17 Henry M. Sayre, *The Object of Performance: The American Avant-Garde Since 1970* (Chicago: University of Chicago Press, 1989), 64.

18 Michel Foucault, *Power/Knowledge: Selected Interviews and Other Writings, 1972– 1977,* ed. and trans. Colin Gordon et al. (New York: Pantheon, 1980), 193.

19 Michel Foucault, *The Archaeology of Knowledge and the Discourse on Language,* trans. A. M. Sheridan Smith (New York: Pantheon, 1972), 47–48.

20 Foucault, *Archaeology of Knowledge,* 28.

21 It initially bothered me that my project hinged upon close reading. Close reading would seem to imply the presence of a transcendental reality outside, or, as it were, "beneath" the text. Indeed, how certain can I be that there is a text of the mid-seventies or seventies? Are there such historical unities? How certain can we be of any textual unity? However, a positing of cultural unities would seem nearly impossible to avoid, even if such unities are always questionable. I have come to consider one's present situation at the time of writing as a kind of *langue* or un-

manifested code through which a specific text must be processed. "Subjectivity" is thus a function of related processes; "objectivity" is a problematized adherence to what appear to be the limits of a cultural text. Considering underlying cultural unities requires the texts, events, and artifacts of a given historical moment within a culture, all the phenomena of a particular time, to be filtered through a perhaps vague sense of the present. The two codes—that is, the codes of the past and the present—interact. The writer's or the historian's object of study and the writing process change one another.

22 Foucault, *Archaeology of Knowledge,* 7.

23 Ibid.

24 I apply the poetic principle of Roman Jakobson, that is to say, I apply the metaphoric axis to cultural studies, which customarily is analyzed in terms of metonymic, narrative, and causal modes. (With "micro-periodizing," I also apply the metonymic axis to the ostensibly timeless, metaphoric, synchronic realm of periodization.) The next section demonstrates that finding textual complexities on the "outside" of the text through the mediating mechanism of the episteme helps us to find the "trapdoor" in the text through which the diverse manners of many other texts can be reached. This trapdoor, which can be equated to Paul de Man's notions of allegory, opens all linguistic phenomena to one another.

25 It is important to recall that deconstruction had considerable assistance in this project. It is commonplace to maintain that deconstruction replaced New Criticism. However, this historical rendering overlooks previous challenges to New Criticism in the form of Northrop Frye's mythic analyses, political critical modes, the reader response approaches of Stanley Fish, the black protest approaches of Amiri Baraka and others, Harold Bloom's schema, the structuralist slants of American critics like Robert Scholes, the hermeneutics of Gadamer and Habermas, the left-wing influences of the Frankfurt school and of Walter Benjamin, Susan Sontag's "against interpretation" rhetoric, and feminist criticism such as *The Mermaid and the Minotaur.* As Nixon revived the traditional organizing device of the American presidency, which then became a site for further problematization and complex ideological modifications, so deconstruction has ultimately served both to problematize and to inflate "textuality."

26 Michel Foucault, *Archaeology of Knowledge,* 191.

27 To use another analogy, epistemes as they are used here are not so much like an outline as colors that mix and bleed and change according to our angle and distance from a painting. For instance, in a sheerly demographical sense, the "sixties" gather steam around the time of the Woodstock music festival and soon thereafter when mainstream America assimilates and codifies sixties mores and styles, yet, chronologically speaking, the sixties can be said to have happened in the seventies. In a sense, the upshot of the sixties is its codification. For example, singles bars accommodate impulses toward sexual liberation, and Jordache sells expensive, stylized versions of casual blue jeans. However, such "codifications" were at odds with the commercial ambivalence that was a constituent characteristic of the "sixties." This is not to say that all aspects of seventies codifications

were insignificant or bad. For example, the Clean Water Act codified sixties concerns about the environment, and this act has been surprisingly successful, but it nonetheless did not quite pack the surprise or social punch of mid-sixties civil rights legislation or the helter-skelter enactment of Great Society legislation.

28 Foucault similarly explained his method as the building up of tropological or "discursive regularities" (*Archaeology of Knowledge,* 63). In other words, Foucault looked for the semiotic consistencies within an era. However, he was usually hesitant to maintain that the tropological regularities of historical phenomena are mediated by the set of discursive forces and regularities that the author, historian, critic, or philosopher could be said to constitute. Foucault ultimately identified his "aim" as the deletion of all subjectivity from his analyses of history so as "to cleanse it of all transcendental narcissism" (Ibid., 203). Despite occasional comments concerning the thin line between fiction and history, Foucault was sensitive to accusations of naive individualism. For Foucault, the bases of "political reality" and "historical truth" precede "fiction." Perhaps Foucault's fear was a way of protecting himself from attacks such as Derrida's "Cogito and the History of Madness" (*Writing and Difference,* trans. Alan Bass [Chicago: University of Chicago Press, 1963, rpt. 1978], 31–63). Derrida maintained that Foucault's first major book, *Madness and Civilization* (1961), "runs the risk of being totalitarian" (Ibid., 57) because, Derrida argued, Foucault imposed an order upon his subject, madness, that ultimately objectifies it around Foucault's unwitting evocation of the forces of reason. According to Derrida, Foucault preserved Cartesian subject-object distinctions. "The attempt," said Derrida, "to write the history of the decision, division, difference [of madness] runs the risk of construing the division as an event or a structure subsequent to the unity of an original presence, thereby confirming metaphysics in its fundamental operation" (Ibid., 40). Derrida associates an objective viewpoint with metaphysical "operation[s]." By characterizing the approach of *Madness and Civilization* as "metaphysical," and identifying Foucault's subject as one constructed by the historical logos at his disposal, Derrida implicitly accuses Foucault of commenting on a fiction of his own making, and suggests that Foucault's book is indulgently, if indirectly, expressive and bourgeois. Foucault countered by stressing the overarching inclusivity of his discipline. "Could there be," Foucault rhetorically asked, "anything anterior or exterior to philosophical discourse?" ("My Body, This Paper, This Fire," trans. Geoff Bennington, *Oxford Literary Review* 4 [1979]: 10). Since there is nothing outside the text, no philosophical or referential object, Derrida's equating of the metaphysical with authorial expression, which causes us to stay "in" the text, could be seen as overly reductive. Foucault accuses Derrida of pedantic indulgence. His "well-determined little pedagogy" "gives" "to the master's voice the limitless sovereignty which allows it to restate the text indefinitely" (*Madness and Civilization: A History of Insanity in the Age of Reason,* trans. Richard Howard [New York: Pantheon, 1965], 27). However, Foucault seems to have been extremely sensitive to Derrida's criticisms, with their implications that Foucault was fictionalizing. In his next book, *The Birth of the Clinic* (1963), Foucault searches for the point of the real on the inside and on the

outside of the body, as if he were trying to locate an enabling irritant, something that would free him of solipsistic narcissism and the possibility of being accused of it. Interestingly, about twenty years later, Christopher Lasch's anti-narcissistic *The Culture of Narcissism* (1978) initiates Foucault's inquiry into "technologies of the self" (*Technologies of the Self*, 1988). Nonetheless, narcissism and writerliness are not the same. Epistemic reception is important because it gives us a way out of our self-surveillance, a way to negotiate with it. If rippling epistemes constitute a way of knowing ourselves, the playful writerly reconstruction of these epistemes makes us conscious and holds out the possibility of our empowerment.

29 John Ashbery, *The Double Dream of Spring* (New York: Eco Press, 1970, rpt. 1976), 13. My methodology similarly admits the inevitability of deferred action—the Freudian mechanism through which seemingly "real" subject matter is in great part produced by the telling of it—in any convincing historical narration. Critics are time travelers who cannot avoid altering by their presence the past they visit. One of the greatest fears of fictional time travelers is in fact an everyday critical occurrence. We sometimes approximate the strategies of *Bill and Ted's Excellent Adventure* and *Bill and Ted's Bogus Adventure,* in which time travel to the future and the past is adeptly used to affect the present.

As with E. H. Gombrich's figure of the duck/rabbit, in which the viewer is said to be forced to make a choice of figure and ground relations and see either the duck or the rabbit, so it is difficult for us to admit that the positings of the real and the imaginary work together in the same linguistic space. The most seemingly objective histories are at least partially sustained by their affects. Truth is always in some way generated, even when it seems indisputably true.

30 Rippling epistemes and self-surveillance are notions linked with the origins of cultural studies. Cultural studies (and perhaps "culture" itself), the "spirit of the times," the gaze, and the Industrial Revolution are all interrelated. As has become a commonplace notion of English literary studies since Raymond Williams (1958) first popularized it in the fifties, it was only with the Industrial Revolution that theories of culture and of cultural change became relevant. How had we changed? Who were we? We desired a window upon a view of our origins and ends. The concept of culture arises from the othering of our hypothetical selves and from the implicit gaze that occurs within this othering. Edward Said's *Orientalism* and *Culture and Imperialism,* like Derrida's *Of Grammatology* and Gayatri Spivak's *Other Words,* demonstrate the exploited other at the heart of the category of "culture." Culture must establish unbridgeable difference. It encodes us by valorizing us. Hence, "culture" in the modern sense of the industrial zeitgeist or episteme, breeds surveillance of itself. The examination of a "culture" is a self-regulatory enterprise.

In the sixties and seventies, there is an increase in the intensity with which we examine our culture. If the sixties can be considered a climax of the industrial and old style colonialist/imperialist cultural frame, and totalizing concepts can be linked to this episteme, of course we will see dramatically non-dramatic shifts in our perceptions of changes in culture in the seventies. The very notion of the "spirit of the time" runs aground in the seventies, and we are at a loss to explain our culture. Surveillance is jarred loose and yet is perceived as a vital constituent of a now apparently ad hoc culture. This perception is not simply a fear of a relatively remote Orwellian totalitarian future. It is a recognition that we must negotiate with culture's arbitrary and unfixed nature.

31 Edmund S. Ions, *The Politics of John F. Kennedy* (New York: Barnes and Noble, 1967), 60.

32 Ibid., 45.

33 John Ashbery and Kenneth Koch, "A Conversation," *Out of This World,* ed. Anne Waldman (New York: Crown, 1991), 19.

34 As president, Nixon wished to rule in crisis. Moreover, he wished to define the crisis he ruled within. Modeling himself on Lincoln, Nixon depicted in antiwar demonstrators the danger of a divided nation. Interestingly, the man who would have had it that he built his career on crises in his first autobiographical memoir, *Six Crises,* occupied the White House while Paul de Man, in 1970, announced that "the notion of crisis and criticism are very closely linked, so much so that one could state that all true criticism occurs in the mode of crisis" (*Blindness and Insight* [Minneapolis: University of Minnesota Press, 1983], 8). Intriguingly, our perception of the mode of crisis that de Man worked within intensified dramatically after his death.

35 The vice president made many Americans recall the warmth with which they received him after his Checkers speech performance, in which he presented himself as an average American who did not possess a slush fund. Rather, he contended that he was a relatively poor public servant whose wife wore a modest but fine "Republican cloth coat." He implied that he merely accepted an understandable subsidy from well-meaning friends that included Checkers the cocker spaniel for his daughters, and, of course, he could not return Checkers. Nixon was not glamorous but rather a sensible household man.

36 Indeed, the sheer fiction of the missile gap makes it a worthy precursor to the credibility gap, of which Nixon will become the most famous victim—it is odd how much more "celebrated" a victim that Nixon is than Johnson.

37 Immediately after his defeat, the former vice president immediately feigned political suicide (ABC presents an hour documentary entitled *"The Political Death of Richard Nixon"*) so as to draw attention away from himself by calling attention to a new enemy—the press. "You won't have Nixon to kick around anymore," he told reporters at his campaign's concluding press conference, perhaps clinching his status as someone who would always be kicked around, a kickball for the ages. Nevertheless, this maneuver helped establish rapport between him and the press-hating Goldwater right (such media attacks become a way of governing under Nixon and Agnew) and divert attention from his defeat and his political ambitions so that he could go into hiatus and, through a Republican statesman role, garner favor throughout the party and, surprisingly, much of the nation.

38 Nixon left the draft intact long enough to sustain South Vietnam until his reelection. If not for Watergate, he might have sent more American troops into Vietnam

to avoid losing the war. Certainly, he would not have been as resigned as President Ford was during the American evacuation of Saigon.

39 Walter Benjamin, *Illuminations* (New York: Harcourt, Brace and World, 1968), 241.

40 Peter Carroll, *It Seemed Like Nothing Happened: The Tragedy and Promise of America in the 1970's* (New York: Holt, Rinehart, and Winston, 1982), 231.

41 Years later, George Segal aptly commemorated the site of the Kent State shootings with a sculpture in which Abraham prepares to kill Isaac, but the sculpture was subsequently removed from the campus.

2 Mystery Tain

1 Similarly, the role of "collector" is much more problematic in *Rocky* (1976) than in *Get Shorty* (1995).

2 Slavoj Žižek, *For They Know Not What They Do: Enjoyment as a Political Factor* (New York: Verso, 1991), 90.

3 See Niklas Luhmann, *Essays on Self-Reference* (New York: Columbia University Press, 1990).

4 In this regard, Scott's presence is a cinematic tip of the cap to *Dr. Strangelove* (1963), which ends the world in nuclear catastrophe with the soundtrack of the quintessential World War II song, Vera Lynn's "We'll Meet Some Day."

5 Roland Barthes's *A Lover's Discourse* (1977) distinguishes the lover's discourse from the "love story." "The *love story*," says Barthes, is "subjugated by the great narrative Other, to that general opinion which disparages any excessive force and wants the subject himself to reduce the great imaginary current, the orderless, endless stream which is passing through him, to a painful morbid crisis of which he must be cured, which he must 'get over' ('It develops, grows, causes suffering, and passes away' in the fashion of some Hippocratic disease): the love story (the 'episode,' the 'adventure') is the tribute the lover must pay to the world in order to be reconciled with it" (7).

6 "Self-Portrait in a Convex Mirror" finds "sex" in the "sands" of the mirror's past:

> To be serious only about sex
> Is perhaps one way, but the sands are hissing
> As they approach the beginning of the big slide
> Into what happened.
> (*SP,* 202: 20–24)

The "play" of the "mirror play" of sex has been removed, as if the commodity value of a commodity were lost. In the speaker's revelry, the mirror's glass itself can be seen as mere transmuted sand.

7 As the film indicates, throughout the seventies, progressive education goes into decline.

8 We may note how the exhilaration of Nixon's "opening" of the mysterious China is coupled with the nearly extinct panda bears that he brings to America. In the eighties, this love of idiosyncratic, endangered panda-like creatures culminates (via the eccentric search of Richard Dreyfuss's character in 1977's *Close Encoun-*

ters of the Third Kind) in the wonder of *E.T.* (1982). Fantasy becomes complete and occupies a realm of its own by the early eighties. We may also note the fantastic sexual crossover of Michael (Dustin Hoffman) in *Tootsie* (1983) to preserve his authentic self as an actor. Whereas Jack Lemmon's and Tony Curtis's characters in *Some Like It Hot* (1959) pose as women to escape the mob, Michael chooses to be seen as a woman *and* to see from a woman's perspective to attain self-expression. In the eighties, a fantastic realm of the repressed Vietnam War gains credence as many conservatives believe the war would never have happened as it did if America had been allowed to be America and Reagan was allowed to be president in the sixties. This attitude finds its fullest expression in *Rambo, First Blood, Part II* (1985).

9   The plot of *Play Misty for Me* is virtually the same as the 1986 blockbuster *Fatal Attraction*, except that the latter film's hero is married, which centers *Fatal Attraction* around the dangers of infidelity.

10 Patrick McGilligan, *Robert Altman: Jumping off the Cliff* (New York: St. Martin's Press, 1989), 400.

11 Perhaps this is partially due to our difficulty in fully assimilating the verbal meaning of the Vietnam War with the pictures we saw of it. Jasper Johns's painting *Ventriloquist* (1983) seems particularly appropriate in this regard. Johns paints a world of split surfaces. A painted rendering of a Barnett Newman print, which in Newman's typical style creates a pictorial surface with a single mark that paradoxically functions as the print's background, occupies the upper right hand corner of *Ventriloquist*. Johns's version of Newman's untitled 1961 print, however, is reversed so as to match the stone from which the print was produced. Similarly, two black, green, and orange—the photographic complements of colors of white, red, and blue—American flags occupy the center of the canvas. Hence, when one adds blackness to this image by closing one's eyes, the American flags hinge into their correct colors. Fittingly, Johns has painted a pair of hinges along the vertical center of *Ventriloquist,* with a face that contains two human profiles outside its outlines on the right of the hinges. On the left, the hinges seem to support a screen with the image of the great whale Moby Dick outlined upon it. We are reminded that during the sixties Lyndon Johnson's aspirations in Vietnam were often likened to Captain Ahab's mad enterprise. The huge shadowy image of Moby Dick seems to be the camouflaged body that speaks throughout this web of reconciled eighties bifurcations between ideology and action that I discuss in the next chapter. On the "skin" of the whale are the commodities of fragile and unbalanced ceramic collectibles, touching on the tenuousness of the eighties art market.

12 Adrienne Rich, *On Lies, Secrets, and Silence: Selected Prose, 1966–1978* (New York: Norton, 1979), 110.

13 Jean Baudrillard, *The Evil Demon of Images,* trans. Philip Beitchman, Paul Foss, Paul Patton and Philippe Tanguy (New York: Power Institute Publications, 1987), 17.

1 Henry M. Sayre, "The Avant-Garde and Experimental Writing," *The Columbia Literary History of the United States,* ed. Emory Elliott (New York: Columbia University Press, 1988), 1180.

2 I discuss this claim in relation to Johns's prior use of the flagstone motif later in this chapter.

3 Distinctions that we ordinarily make between seemingly authored and non-authored work need not preclose analogies between the two. As Foucault argued, all phenomena are discourse. "What, in short," said Foucault, "we wish to do is to dispense with 'things.' To 'depresentify' them. To conjure up their rich, heavy, immediate plenitude. . . . To substitute for the enigmatic treasure of 'things' anterior to discourse, the regular formation of objects that emerge only in discourse. To define these objects without reference to the ground, the foundation of things, but by relating them to the body of rules that enable them to form as objects of a discourse and thus constitute the conditions of their historical appearance. To write a history of discursive objects that does not plunge them into the common depth of a primal soil, but deploys the nexus of regularities that govern their dispersion" (*Archaeology of Knowledge,* 47–48). In other words, a "thing" cannot be understood without a condition, context, or system, that makes its understanding possible. We need to understand the manner in which understanding is produced. In terms of a historical study, this means coming to grips with a period's prevalent ways of knowing. This is done by decoding the nexus of discursive regularities that govern the dispersion of discursive phenomena. For Foucault, a historical study seeks to comprehend the "conditions of historical appearance," that is, to understand how certain phenomena have entered the historical discourse within an epistemological system that is constitutive of our understanding of an epoch. All forms are constituents of the epistemological systems (or, in effect, enabling rules of discourse) that are at work in a given period. A basis is thus established for synchronic cultural studies and periodization.

Lacking an empirical ground, all categories are open to question and comparison. A historian can find unexpected significance in her or his objects of study. However banal it may be, however unimportant its consequences may appear to be, however quickly it may be forgotten after, however little heard or however badly deciphered we may suppose it to be, a statement is always an event that neither the language (*langue*) nor the meaning can quite exhaust (Foucault, *Archaeology of Knowledge,* 28).

From the postulation of this kind of plenitude, surplus, or inexhaustibility of meaning to be garnered from statements, the extremely close readings that we normally associate with literary criticism can be applied to all manner of cultural artifact. For Foucault, many diverse kinds of cultural output may be discussed as "documents" (*Archaeology of Knowledge,* 7).

These documents need not be considered as the work of a single consciousness, since Foucault likens documents, in the broad sense of the term as he uses it, to "archaeological" artifacts that have been abstracted from an unfamiliar culture (*Archaeology of Knowledge,* 7). This deliberately estranged perspective promotes a more adequately close "reading" of each object of study.

4   Ashbery's poetry is also an exemplar of Derrida's philosophy. Many Ashbery poems bespeak a familiarity with ideas associated with structuralist and poststructuralist thought. For example, the concluding words of Ashbery's "And *Ut Pictura Poesis* Is Her Name" (1977) might serve as a pithy description of deconstruction: "understanding / May begin, and in doing so be undone" (*SP,* 235: 29–30).

We can likewise note Derridean inferences in the following lines from the final verse-paragraph of "Self-Portrait in a Convex Mirror":

> as the principle of each individual thing is
> Hostile to, exists at the expense of all the others
> As philosophers have often pointed out, at least
> *This* thing, the mute, undivided present,
> Has the justification of logic.
>
> (*SP,* 200: 32–34; 201: 1–2)

"The mute, undivided present," with "the justification of logic," characterizes Derrida's concept of "presence" with startling efficiency. That presence is equated to "this thing" reminds us that, for Derrida, the notions of "presence" and "signifieds" imply each other. Ashbery, in the lines quoted above, makes the Derridean point that a more conventional, or structuralist, conceptualization of difference may explain "each individual thing" as an entity that is counter, or "hostile to," other individual things; however, further analysis is required to refute presence, in its Derridean sense, more thoroughly. The presence of "an individual thing" must here be understood as the absence of all other individual things. Hence, any notion that we can have of presence is severely undermined. Ashbery's speaker questions presence:

> *This* thing, the mute, undivided present,
> Has the justification of logic, which
> In this instance isn't a bad thing
> Or wouldn't be, if the way of telling
> Didn't somehow intrude, twisting the end result
> Into a caricature of itself. This always
> Happens.
>
> (201: 1–7)

The speaker finds presence wanting because he finds logic suspect. It is difficult not to recall Derrida's notion of *logos,* or the logic of egocentric presence. In these lines from "Self-Portrait in a Convex Mirror," the speaker maintains that attention to the means of articulating logic turns the products of logic against the premises that enable their production. This describes one of Derrida's characteristic means of analyzing a text, in that Derrida often exploits a seemingly inconsequential phrase, using it to overturn the pervading interpretation of a text.

Even if Ashbery had not done doctoral work in French literature at New York University (interestingly, Ashbery wrote an unfinished dissertation about the novelist Raymond Roussel, whom Foucault wrote a major student work about, and Ashbery and Foucault met at Roussel conferences), it would seem appropriate to note affinities of content, style, and structure between Ashbery and French writers who are often associated with structuralist and poststructuralist thought. This is not to disavow the crucial influences of other poets on Ashbery, but merely to say that critics, philosophers, and poets share influences.

Even when normal influence is considered, this reading seems appropriate. Although Ashbery claimed to me that he had not read Derrida at the time that he wrote "Self-Portrait in a Convex Mirror," he could not have been entirely unaware of the intellectual climate in which Derrida wrote, since Ashbery lived in Paris and served as an art critic for *the International Herald Tribune* from the mid-fifties to the mid-sixties, when many of the structuralists were newly popular figures in France.

5 Jacques Derrida, *Disseminations,* trans. Barbara Johnson (Chicago: University of Chicago Press, 1981), 32–33.

6 Rodolphe Gasché, *The Tain of the Mirror: Derrida and the Philosophy of Reflection* (Cambridge: Harvard University Press, 1986), 238.

7 Derrida, *Disseminations,* 45.

8 Ibid., 26.

9 Ferdinand de Saussure, alluding to his own comparison of signifiers and signifieds to two sides of a piece of paper, maintained that in a symbolist poem there is no signified "side of the paper." To make this analogy, Saussure employed Baudelaire's likening of his poetry to an open window. In this regard, one thinks of William Blake's previous conceit of having cleansed the windows of perception to see infinity.

10 Louis Althusser, *Lenin and Philosophy,* trans. Ben Brewster (New York and London: Monthly Review Press, 1971), 162.

11 Although the early sixties may have been the period of Clement Greenberg's "flatness," and Kenneth Noland's chevron and stripe paintings, by the late sixties the end of painting is anticipated.

12 I use the term "picture plane" in light of the heightened awareness of "flatness" from post–World War II Pollock paintings to early-sixties Noland paintings. Flatness in this mid-twentieth-century sense isolates the picture plane instead of using it to nuance or denote the three-dimensional. In the early sixties, the anti-illusionistic impulse driving painting toward the flat makes a quantum leap into sculpture. In Donald Judd's work, flatness is a perceptual illusion imposed on three-dimensional constructions, and only the most relatively unembellished materials, inevitably communicating their materiality, can serve as art.

13 John Ashbery, *Three Poems* (New York: Viking, 1972), 8.

14 I describe the pattern of *Scent* in more detail in chapter 5.

15 This pictorial impulse systematically mobilizes space at the end of the nineteenth century: however, its traces can be seen well before, with such painters as Goya and subsequently Manet.

16 Althusser, *Lenin and Philosophy,* 171.

17 Ibid., 172.

18 Carl Bernstein and Bob Woodward, *All the President's Men* (New York: Simon and Schuster, 1974), 142.

19 Ibid., 132.

20 Jean Baudrillard, *Simulations* (New York: Semiotext, 1983), 27.

21 Jonathan Schell, *The Age of Illusion* (New York: Vintage, 1975), 178.

22 The inability of the post-Watergate Congress to regulate the oil companies' windfall embargo profits signaled the exhaustion of the left.

23 Such subsidies were won with less angst in the Reagan era, when they were justified not so much because of crisis but more to facilitate the consumption of an imagined abundance.

24 The rapidity with which oil prices soon dropped in 1985 when the Saudis broke from OPEC and increased oil production revealed the extent to which the dramatic rise in oil prices, in terms of cost per barrel if not at the pumps, was psychologically driven.

25 "The One Thing That Could Save America," in *Self-Portrait in a Convex Mirror* (New York: Viking, 1975), 44, lines 6, 13.

26 One could say that the Saturday Night Massacre and the oil embargo were causally related because Nixon was too preoccupied with the tape subpoenas to cope with OPEC energy threats. However, this theory does not explain why other American governmental and industrial powers did not foresee the dangers ahead.

27 Disco, unlike seemingly cosmic sixties music, is site-specific, albeit this site is a veritable icon that reflects throughout the disco universe, a major Brooklyn disco, in Bay Ridge, with a name, Odyssey 2001, that suggests sixties infinitude. Indeed, the Bee Gees, who added songs to the film in post-production, were a sixties group enjoying a revival, filling the airwaves for months as no group since the Beatles had done. The Bee Gees' great insight was to record their rhythm tracks first and then tailor their instrumentation and vocals to their sharp grooves. Similarly, the Beatles had attained an overwhelming sense of ease by opening up their rhythms to all manner of inflection and enhancement while rarely losing their beat. Originally signed by Brian Epstein and mistaken for the Beatles by many top-forty and sixties FM radio listeners, the Bee Gees echoed the Beatles in seventies disco fashion. Appropriately, the Bee Gees, as the group most identified with disco, became straw dogs for those with American punk sensibilities who, like John Lennon near the Beatles' end, objected to overproduction and the trappings of the recording studio. Disco and punk were both site-specific: disco in dance clubs and punk in music clubs. They come from different traditions but are synchronic cultural analogues. In both cases, minimalist musical tendencies enable all manner of other musical phenomena to tag along.

1   In reading the following analysis of Ashbery's long poem, glancing back at the previous chapter's short "summary" of this infinitely complex poem may assist the reader.

2   The poem runs the gamut of ekphrastic delight, indifference, and horror. See "Ekphrasis and the Other" in W. J. T. Mitchell, *Picture Theory* (Chicago: University of Chicago, 1994), 151–82. See also my discussion of ekphrasis in terms of Baldwin in this chapter's third section.

3   Michel Foucault, *Discipline and Punish: The Birth of the Prison,* trans. Alan Sheridan (New York: Vintage, 1977), 195–228.

4   Ibid., 204.

5   Kenneth Burke, "The Virtues and Limitations of Debunking," *The Philosophy of Literary Form: Studies in Symbolic Action* (Baton Rouge: Louisiana State University Press, 1941), 168.

6   John Ashbery, "The New Spirit," *Three Poems* (New York: Viking, 1972), 3–24.

7   Jacques Lacan, *Écrits,* trans. Alan Sheridan (New York: Norton, 1966), 2.

8   Nathaniel Hawthorne, *The Scarlet Letter* (New York: Viking Penguin, 1983), 128–29.

9   Paul Breslin, *The Psycho-Political Muse: American Poetry Since the Fifties* (Chicago: University of Chicago Press, 1987), 227.

10 Ibid.

11 Ibid., 228.

12 Paul de Man, *Blindness and Insight: Essays in the Rhetoric of Contemporary Criticism* (Minneapolis: University of Minnesota Press, 1971), ix.

13 Richard Howard, "A Formal Affair," *Poetry* 127, no. 6 (March 1976): 351.

14 Laurence Lieberman, *Unassigned Frequencies: American Poetry in Review, 1964–77* (Chicago: University of Illinois Press, 1977), 59.

15 Jacques Derrida, "The Truth in Painting," *Art and Design* 6, nos. 3 and 4 (1988): 19–25.

16 Ibid., 22.

17 Ibid., 23.

18 Howard, "A Formal Affair," 351, 349.

19 Ashbery, *Three Poems,* 127.

20 David Shapiro, *John Ashbery: An Introduction to the Poetry* (New York: Columbia University Press, 1979), 4.

21 Ibid.

22 Michel Foucault, *The Order of Things: An Archaeology of the Human Sciences,* 1970, trans. A. S. London (New York: Random House, 1973), 3–16.

23 Ibid., 4.

24 Ibid., 16.

25 Jacques Derrida, *Of Grammatology,* trans. Gayatri Spivak (Baltimore: Johns Hopkins University Press, 1976), 70.

26 Toril Moi, *Sexual/Textual Politics: Feminist Literary Theory* (New York: Routledge, 1991), 135.

27 Toni Morrison, *Song of Solomon* (New York: Plume, 1977), 128.

28 Toni Morrison, *The Bluest Eye* (New York: Simon and Schuster, 1970), 42.

29 Monica Duchnowski, conversation with author, 5 May 1995.

30 John Wideman, *Sent for You Yesterday* (New York: Random House, 1983), 15.

31 Françoise Lionnet, *Race, Gender, Self-Portraiture* (Ithaca: Cornell University Press, 1989), 115.

32 Morrison, *The Bluest Eye,* 43.

33 Toni Morrison, *Sula* (New York: Plume, 1973), 112.

34 Adrienne Rich, *Blood, Bread, and Poetry: Selected Prose 1979–1985* (New York: Norton, 1985), 119.

35 Morrison, *Sula,* 66.

36 Ibid., 9.

37 Gérard Genette, *Figures of Literary Discourse,* trans. Alan Sheridan (New York: Columbia University Press, 1982), 9.

38 Patricia Hill Collins, Black History Month convocation, 21 February 1995, Franklin College, Franklin, Indiana.

39 Luce Irigaray, *This Sex Which Is Not One,* trans. Catherine Porter (Ithaca: Cornell University Press, 1985), 77.

40 Ibid., emphasis in original.

41 Ibid., 77, 79.

42 See also the third section of chapter 6, concerning Nixon's resignation speech, in which I use Irigaray's comments to elaborate upon Nixon's fear of playing with the textual and the woven and his inherent investment in covering up.

43 Adrienne Rich, *The Dream of a Common Language: Poems 1974–1977* (New York: Norton, 1978), 43.

44 Adrienne Rich, *On Lies, Secrets, and Silence: Selected Prose, 1966–1978* (New York: Norton, 1985), 73.

45 Sam Shepard, *Seven Plays* (New York: Bantam, 1981), 193–94.

46 Ibid., 168.

47 Ibid., 168–69.

48 Ibid., 200.

49 Morrison, *Song of Solomon,* 281.

50 Shepard, 173–74.

51 Julia Kristeva, *About Chinese Women,* trans. Anita Barrows (New York: Marion Boyars, 1986), 199.

52 Adrienne Rich, *Your Native Land, Your Life* (New York: Norton, 1986), 33. Further references to poems in this collection are cited in the text by page number.

53 Irigaray, *This Sex Which Is Not One,* 176–77.

54 Adrienne Rich, "When We Dead Awaken," *On Lies, Secrets, and Silence* (New York: Norton, 1979), 48–49.

55 Allen Ginsberg, "America," *Collected Poems: 1947–1980* (New York: Harper and Row, 1984), 147.

56 Ibid., 148.

57 James Baldwin, "Many Thousands Gone," *Notes of a Native Son* (Boston: Beacon, 1955), 24–25.

58 Ibid., 175.

59 Jacques Lacan, "The Mirror Stage as Formative of the Function of the I as Revealed in Psychoanalytical Experience," *Écrits,* trans. Alan Sheridan (New York: Norton, 1966), 5.

60 Wallace Stevens, "An Ordinary Evening in New Haven," *The Palm at the End of the Mind* (New York: Vintage, 1967). Hereafter cited in the text by page and line.

61 Wallace Stevens, "The Auroras of Autumn," *The Palm at the End of the Mind* (New York: Vintage, 1967). Hereafter cited in the text by page and line.

62 W. J. T. Mitchell, *Iconology: Image, Text, Ideology* (Chicago: University of Chicago Press, 1986), 47.

63 Ibid., 43.

64 James Baldwin, *If Beale Street Could Talk* (New York: Laurel, 1974), 3.

65 James Baldwin, "Sonny's Blues" *Going to Meet the Man,* (New York: Dial, 1965), 101–41.

66 Morrison, *The Bluest Eye,* 42.

67 Baldwin, *If Beale Street Could Talk,* 185.

68 Guy Debord, *Society of the Spectacle* (Detroit: Black and Red, 1977), 154.

69 Ibid., 147–64.

70 Baldwin, *If Beale Street Could Talk,* 102–3.

71 Thomas Pynchon, *Gravity's Rainbow* (New York: Viking, 1973), 647–48.

72 Ibid., 645.

73 Ibid., 3.

74 Ibid.

75 Ibid.

76 Ibid., 9–10.

77 Ibid., 647–48.

78 Pynchon, *Gravity's Rainbow,* 616.

79 Martin Duberman, *Stonewall* (New York: Dutton, 1993), 164.

80 Significantly, Robert J. Corber's study of pre-Stonewall gay culture, *Homosexuality in Cold War America: Resistance and the Crisis of Masculinity* (Durham: Duke University Press, 1997) examines the political relevance of articulating gay identity in the fifties since "masculinity" was such an important ideological support for the Cold War consensus. However, it should also be noted how easily these gay articulations were misinterpreted as apolitical or nonapplicable to the rest of American culture.

81 John Ashbery, "An Outing," *The Double Dream of Spring* (New York: Ecco Press, 1970), 60.

82 Dennis Altman, *The Homosexualization of America, The Americanization of the Homosexual* (New York: St. Martin's Press, 1982), 104.

83 Ibid., 90–91.

84 John Ashbery, *Self-Portrait in a Convex Mirror* (New York: Viking, 1975), 22–24.

85 Michel Foucault, *The History of Sexuality, Volume One, An Introduction,* trans. Robert Hurley, (New York: Random House, 1978), 43.

86 Ibid., 101.

87 Julia Kristeva, *Black Sun: Depression and Melancholia* trans. Leon Roudiaz (New York: Columbia University Press, 1979), 41.

88 John Ashbery, "Poem in Three Parts," *The Double Dream of Spring* (New York: Ecco Press, 1970), 22–24.

89 Kristeva, *Black Sun,* 51.

90 Ibid., 53.

5 Crossing Seventies Art

1 Johns emphasizes this point about his work in his comments that were displayed on the walls of his 1996 Museum of Modern Art retrospective.

2 Don DeLillo, *Libra* (New York: Penguin, 1988), 16.

3 Dorothy Miller, *Sixteen Americans* (New York: Museum of Modern Art, 1959), 22.

4 Jasper Johns, "Sketchbook Notes," *Art and Literature* 4 (spring 1965): 22.

5 David Shapiro, *Jasper Johns: Drawings 1954–1984* (New York: Abrams, 1984), 3.

6 Ibid., 38.

7 Ibid., 41.

8 Rosalind Krauss, "Jasper Johns: The Functions of Irony," *October* 2 (summer 1976): 94.

9 Ibid., 95.

10 Ibid., 97.

11 Ibid., 97–98.

12 Ibid., 98.

13 Ibid.

14 Joseph Masheck, "Jasper Johns Returns," *Art in America,* 64, no. 2 (March–April 1976): 65.

15 Jacques Derrida, "The Truth in Painting," trans. Geoff Bennington *Art and Design* 4, no. 3/4 (1988): 24.

16 Rosalind Krauss, *The Originality of the Avant-Garde and Other Modernist Myths* (Cambridge: MIT Press, 1986), 19.

17 Mark Rosenthal, *Jasper Johns: Works since 1974* (Philadelphia: Philadelphia Museum of Art, 1988), 42.

18 Barbara Rose, "Jasper Johns: Pictures and Concepts," *Arts Magazine* 52, no. 3 (November 1977): 149.

19 Ibid.

20 James Baldwin, *Another Country* (New York: Doubleday, 1960), 150.

21 Richard Francis, *Jasper Johns* (New York: Cross River Press, 1984), 66.

22 Johns, "Sketchbook Notes," 187.

23 Max Kozloff, *Jasper Johns* (Abrams: New York, 1969), 21.

24 Joseph Masheck, "Jasper Johns Returns," *Art in America* 64, no. 2 (March–April 1976): 65.

25 Ibid., 65–66.

26 Michael Crichton, *Jasper Johns* (New York: Abrams, 1977), 61.

27 Ibid.

28 Ibid., 33.

29 Charles Altieri, "John Ashbery and the Challenge of Post-modernism in the Visual Arts," *Critical Inquiry* 14 (summer 1988): 812.

30 Charles Harrison and Fred Orton, "Jasper Johns: Meaning What You See." *Art History* 7, no. 1 (March 1984): 99.

31 Conversation with Kenneth Deifik, 25 February 1991.

32 Norman Brown, *Love's Body* (New York: Random House, 1966), 159.

33 Robert Rosenblum, *Andy Warhol: Portraits of the Seventies* (New York: Random House and the Whitney Museum, 1979), 20.

34 Ibid.

35 Serge Fauchereau, *Kasimir Malevich* (New York: Rizzoli, 1992), 24.

36 Peter Brooks, *Reading for the Plot* (Cambridge: Harvard University Press, 1984), 37–61.

37 Andy Warhol, *The Philosophy of Andy Warhol (from A to B and Back Again)* (New York: Harcourt Brace Jovanovich, 1975), 26–27.

38 Sylvia Plath, *The Collected Poems* (New York: Harper and Row, 1981).

39 Warhol, *Philosophy of Andy Warhol,* 100–101.

6 Politics in the Watergate Era

1 H. R. Haldeman, *The Haldeman Diaries: Inside the Haldeman Diaries* (New York: Putman, 1994), 3.

2 Jeb Stuart Magruder, *An American Life: One Man's Road to Watergate* (New York: Atheneum, 1974), 172.

3 Ibid., 172–73.

4 Haldeman, *Haldeman Diaries,* 2.

5 Ibid., 42.

6 Roger Morris, *Richard Milhous Nixon: The Rise of an American Politician* (New York: Henry Holt, 1990), 496–97.

7 John Dean, *Blind Ambition: The White House Years* (New York: Simon & Schuster, 1976), 56–57.

8 Norman Mailer, *Miami and the Siege of Chicago: An Informal History of the Republican and Democratic Conventions of 1968* (New York: Signet, 1968), 78.

9 Ibid., 41.

10 Haldeman, *Haldeman Diaries,* 303.

11 Ibid., 53.

12 Differences between Clinton's claim of attorney-client privilege and Nixon's claims of executive privilege have gone virtually unreported. Clinton merely wished to withhold from evidence the work of lawyers who were working on his personal

problems. It never would have occurred to Watergate investigators to subpoena the meetings between Nixon and his Watergate lawyer, James St. Clair. This is the ostensible reason Clinton wanted an assurance that releasing notes taken in the meeting in which government laywers handed over the entire matter to private lawyers, a meeting in which government and private interests merged, would not create a precedent in the private realm.

13 Garry Wills, *Nixon Agonistes: The Crisis of the Self-Made Man* (New York: Mentor, 1979), 371. In 1960, as in 1968, Nixon presented himself as a markedly changed, more moderate politician.

14 Theodore White, *Breach of Faith: The Fall of Richard Nixon* (New York: Atheneum, 1975), 349. See the next section concerning Nixon's resignation speech.

15 Peter Halley, *Collected Essays: 1981–1987* (Zurich: Bruno Bischofberger, 1988), 162.

16 Ibid., 133.

17 Ibid., 163.

18 Warhol, *Philosophy of Andy Warhol*, 145–46.

19 Carl Bernstein and Robert Woodward, *The Final Days* (New York: Simon and Schuster, 1976), 190–91.

20 Ibid.

21 Warhol, *Philosophy of Andy Warhol*, 89.

22 Bernstein and Woodward, *Final Days*, 274–76.

23 Gerald Gold, ed., *The White House Transcripts* (New York: Bantam, 1974), 857.

24 Halley, *Collected Essays*, 133.

25 Marjorie Perloff, *The Dance of the Intellect: Studies in the Poetry of the Pound Tradition* (Cambridge: Cambridge University Press, 1985), 158.

26 Theodore Lowi, *The Personal Presidency: Power Invested, Promise Unfulfilled* (Ithaca: Cornell University Press, 1985), 181–82.

27 Arthur Schlesinger Jr., *America's Second Century* (New York: Public Broadcasting System, 1980).

28 Lowi, *Personal Presidency*, 180–81.

29 Ibid., 309.

30 Ibid., 212.

31 Ibid., 97–133.

32 Wills, *Nixon Agonistes*, 76–92.

33 Gold, *The White House Transcripts*, p. 857.

34 Niklas Luhmann, *Essays on Self-Reference* (New York: Columbia University Press, 1990), 4.

35 Tom Wicker, *One of Us: Richard Nixon and the American Dream* (New York: Random House, 1991).

36 Fawn Brodie, *Richard M. Nixon: The Shaping of His Character* (New York: Norton, 1981), 17.

37 Derrida, *Disseminations*, 95–116.

38 Bruce Mazlish, *In Search of Nixon: A Psychohistorical Inquiry* (New York: Basic Books, 1972), 115.

39 Ibid., xxv.

40 Ibid., 115.

41 Mary McCarthy, *The Mask of State: Watergate Portraits* (New York: Harcourt Brace Jovanovich, 1974), 4.

42 Richard Nixon, *The Memoirs of Richard Nixon* (New York: Grosset and Dunlap, 1978), 368–69.

43 Peter Carroll, *It Seemed Like Nothing: The Tragedy and Promise of America in the 1970's* (New York: Holt, Rinehart, and Winston, 1982), 3–4.

44 Brodie, *Richard M. Nixon*, 18.

45 Stephen Ambrose, *Nixon* (New York: Simon and Schuster, 1987), 87–92.

46 Barry Sussman, *The Great Cover-Up* (Arlington: Seven Locks Press, 1974), 190–92.

47 Ibid., 192–93.

48 *U.S. v. Mitchell*, 2, National Archives Nixon Project pagination.

49 Carl Bernstein and Robert Woodward, *All the President's Men* (New York: Simon and Schuster, 1974), 56.

50 *U.S. v. Mitchell*, 4.

51 Ibid., 3.

52 Ibid., 16.

53 Ibid.

54 Ibid., 7.

55 Ibid.

56 Don DeLillo, *White Noise* (New York: Vintage, 1985), 209.

57 Ibid., 12.

58 Ibid.

59 Ibid., 13.

60 *White Noise* characterizes the eighties as a kind of seventies trace. If Watergate is the seventies' high-water mark, the eighties comprise a seamless fabric of evasion and cover-up. Whereas a characteristic seventies garment is the defining container of the tight-fitting pair of designer jeans—which one can jokingly compare with a tight Watergate-like cover-up, the cooly allusive yet power-conveying jacket can be said to be the quintessential eighties article of clothing. Appropriately, the "waves and radiation" that permeate *White Noise* are more evenly distributed throughout the landscape of the novel than in any previous DeLillo book. In *Players*, for instance, the codes inherent in the pushes and pulls of the credit currents of abstract electronic currency are merely played with and tested outside of international stock and money markets. However, in *White Noise*, the waves and radiation cannot be escaped, as the airborne toxic event demonstrates. And yet the culture presented by *White Noise*, in addition to the study of culture, is based upon a blind acceptance of commodities, whether those commodities are Hitler Studies or seemingly plastic, brightly colored food. Indeed, the title *White Noise*, denoting a sound with no distinguishable background or foreground, together with the novel's association of white noise with death, suggests a world in which a deathly commodification is everywhere. The world is a value-neutral supermarket. Indeed, value is enhanced by this neutrality, as in Ronald Reagan's tacit acknowledgment and memorialization of the achievements of the Nazi SS at Bitburg

in 1984. It mattered little that Reagan ostensibly considered the graves of the SS troopers as mere background, or "white noise," meaning that, he, as the president, does not directly face these graves. In effect, Reagan is playing to the desire of some Germans to eradicate any hint of responsibility for World War II, while Reagan relies on his Teflon reputation and youthful glow to mitigate damage at home. Reagan's youthful glow intermingles power, obedience toward power, charisma, and spiritual aura. In *White Noise,* a feeling of entitlement produces an oddly spiritual if imperfect appearance. "They've grown comfortable with their money," Jack, the narrator of *White Noise,* says of privileged college students. "They genuinely believe they're entitled to it. This conviction gives them a kind of rude health. They glow a little." This glow (in DeLillo's novel, the excesses of a privileged class and the glow of nuclear waste associated with the 1979 Three Mile Island accident come together) implies a manifest privilege. (The Ramones suggest that Reagan is something like an indifferent youth in their song "Bonzo Goes to Bitburg" [1985].)

61 *U.S. v. Mitchell,* 2.
62 Ibid., 3.
63 Ibid., 8.
64 *JFK* was released after I wrote the preceding comments about Nixon's "Bay of Pigs" remarks.
65 Don DeLillo, *Mao II* (New York: Penguin, 1991), 221.
66 Sayre, *The Object of Performance,* 250.
67 Dean, *Blind Ambition,* 344.
68 *U.S. v. Mitchell,* 5–6.
69 Wills, *Nixon Agonistes,* 548.
70 Ultra Violet, *Famous for Fifteen Minutes: My Years with Andy Warhol* (New York: Harcourt Brace Jovanovich, 1988), 5.
71 *U.S. v. Mitchell,* 4.
72 Bernstein and Woodward, *The Final Days,* 96.
73 Theodore White, *Breach of Faith: The Fall of Richard Nixon* (New York: Atheneum, 1975), 29–30.
74 Raymond Price, *With Nixon* (New York: Viking, 1977), 2.
75 White, *Breach of Faith,* 114.
76 Jonathan Schell, *The Time of Illusion* (New York: Vintage, 1975), 22.
77 Ibid., 22.
78 White, *Breach of Faith,* 14.
79 Ibid.
80 Ibid., 349.
81 Ibid.
82 Philip Corrigan and Derek Sayer, *The Great Arch: English State Foundations as Cultural Revolution* (Oxford: Blackwell, 1985), 3.
83 Philip Abrams, "Notes on the Difficulty of Studying the State [1977]," *Journal of Historical Sociology* 1, no. 1 (March 1988): 58.
84 Ibid.
85 Ibid.

86 Ibid.

87 Schell, *Time of Illusion,* 51.

88 Magruder, *An American Life,* 349.

89 Schell, *Time of Illusion,* 51.

90 White, *Breach of Faith,* 349.

91 Wills, *Nixon Agonistes,* 76–92.

92 White, *Breach of Faith,* 349.

93 Gold, *White House Transcripts,* 868.

94 White, *Breach of Faith,* 349–50.

95 Ibid., 350.

96 Ibid.

97 Ibid.

98 Ibid.

99 Ibid.

100 Ibid.

101 Note the discussion of the cancer trope in the next part of this section.

102 White, *Breach of Faith,* 351.

103 Ibid.

104 Ibid.

105 Ibid., 351–52.

106 Ibid., 352.

107 Gold, *White House Transcripts,* 132.

108 Peter Rodino, *Comparison of White House and House Judiciary Committee Transcripts of Eight Recorded Presidential Conversations* (Washington, D.C.: U.S. Government Printing Office, 1974).

109 Dean, *Blind Ambition,* 131.

110 Ibid., 189.

111 Gold, *White House Transcripts,* 54.

112 Ibid.

113 Ibid., 132.

114 Ibid.

115 Ibid., 133.

116 Ibid., 134.

117 Ibid.

118 A. R. Ammons, *The Selected Poems: Expanded Edition* (New York: Norton, 1986), 43–44.

119 Gold, *White House Transcripts,* 134.

120 Ibid.

121 Ibid., 154.

122 Ibid.

123 Ibid., 160.

124 Ibid., 142.

125 Ibid., 134.

126 Ibid.

127 Ibid.

128 Ibid.

129 Ibid., pp. 134–35.

130 Ibid., 135.

131 Ibid.

132 Ibid., 137.

133 Ibid., 137–38.

134 Ibid., p. 136.

135 Ibid.

136 Ibid.

137 Ibid., 137.

138 Ibid., 146–47.

139 Ibid., 173–74.

140 Ibid., 148.

141 Ibid., 167.

142 Ibid., 172–73.

143 Ibid., 187.

144 Ibid., 188.

145 Ibid., 151.

146 Ibid., 147.

147 Ibid., 165.

148 Ibid., 158.

149 Ford Congressional Papers, Warren Commission file, folder Working Papers-Undated —2. Citations in the body of my text refer to archives at the Gerald R. Ford Library in Ann Arbor, Michigan, where I also viewed the cited news telecasts. The Gerald R. Ford Library is an amazingly rich resource for scholars of the American presidency, politics, and culture, and this section would have been impossible without a travel and research grant from the Gerald R. Ford Foundation. I am thankful to my Ford Library archivist, Jennifer A. Sternaman.

150 Jacques Derrida, *Given Time: I. Counterfeit Money,* trans. Peggy Kamuf (Chicago: University of Chicago Press, 1992), 16.

151 Derrida, *Given Time,* 115.

152 W. J. T. Mitchell, *Picture Theory* (Chicago: University of Chicago Press, 1994), 72.

153 Robert Hartmann, *Palace Politics: An Insider's Account of the Ford Years* (New York: McGraw-Hill, 1980), 259.

154 *CBS Evening News,* 5 September 1975.

155 John Robert Greene, *The Presidency of Gerald R. Ford* (Lawrence: University Press of Kansas, 1995), 193.

156 Wills, *Nixon Agonistes,* 15.

157 Ibid., 16.

158 Ibid., 17.

159 John Updike, *Memories of the Ford Administration* (New York: Knopf, 1992).

160 Gerald Ford, *A Time to Heal* (New York: Bantam, 1979), 126.

161 Mark Green, *Who Runs Congress?* (New York: Bantam, 1972), 16.

162 All of the briefings reports that I refer to can be found in the first two boxes of the Hoopes files at the Ford Presidential Library. David Hoopes was the Ford administration's deputy staff secretary. He tracked the White House paper flow, including Ford's presidential briefing papers, which are available at the Ford Presidential Library in Ann Arbor. The president's briefs are too numerous to consider in their entirety, even for a short period of time. I aim here to indicate only a sense of them.

163 Interestingly, in the last days of the Vietnam War, South Vietnam Ambassador Graham Martin cites the meat problem at home when discussing the benefits of sending cans of meat for humanitarian aid. See Graham Martin memo to Henry Kissinger, "Humanitarian Aid," National Security Council Convenience Files, Materials from U.S. Embassy, Saigon (26 April 1975, Box 5), Gerald R. Ford Library.

164 See Kenneth Rush memo, "Meeting with Economic Advisors," Gerald R. Ford Library, 9 August 1974, Ann Arbor, Michigan.

165 See Saxbe memo to Alexander Haig, *Gerald R. Ford Library* (31 July 1974).

166 See Cole memo, "Meeting with Attorney General Saxbe," *Gerald R. Ford Library* (12 August 1974).

167 See, for example, "The Story on Gold," Graham Martin to Brent Scowcroft, 4/27/75, folder Saigon to Washington, 4/9/75–4/28/75, National Security Council Convenience Files, Materials from U.S. Embassy, Saigon, Box 5, Gerald R. Ford Library.

168 *NBC Nightly News,* 27 April 1975.

169 *CBS Evening News,* 30 April 1975.

170 Robert Sam Anson, *Exile: The Unquiet Oblivion of Richard M. Nixon* (New York: Simon and Schuster, 1984), 56.

171 Ford, *A Time to Heal,* 144.

172 See Rogers B. Morton letter to the president, "Vice Presidency," Philip Buchen, *Gerald R. Ford Library* (Box 19).

173 Ford, *A Time to Heal,* 145.

174 Robert T. Hartman, *An Inside Account of the Ford Years* (New York: McGraw-Hill, 1980), 265.

175 Jacques Derrida, *Specters of Marx: The State of the Debt, the Work of Mourning, and the New International,* trans. Peggy Kamuf (New York: Routledge, 1994), 487.

176 *CBS Evening News,* 9 September 1974.

177 See H. Guyford Stever memo to Fred Slight, "Swine Flu," David Gergen, *Gerald R. Ford Library* (Box 9).

178 See Henry Kissinger and Brent Scowcroft Files, *Gerald R. Ford Library* (Box 45).

179 See Henry Kissinger and Brent Scowcroft Files, "Aid," *Gerald R. Ford Library* (21 June 1976, Box 45).

180 See Ambassador Graham Martin memo to Henry Kissinger, National Security Council Convenience Files, Materials from U.S. Embassy (9 April 1975 to 28 April 1975, Box 5), Gerald R. Ford Library.

181 See Henry Kissinger memo to Graham Martin, National Council Convenience Files, Materials from U.S. Embassy (June 1975 to January 1976), Gerald R. Ford Library.

182 Greene, *Presidency of Ford,* 143–51.

183 *CBS Evening News,* 10 September 1975.

184 Jacque Derrida, *Specters of Marx: The State of Debt, the Work of Mourning, and the New International* (New York: Routledge, 1994), 14–15.

185 David Antin, *What It Means to Be Avant-Garde* (New York: New Directions, 1993), 53.

Index

(page numbers in italics indicate illustrations)

Namath, Joe, 250

Narcissism, 144

NASA, 54. *See also* Apollo

Nashville (film), 94–97, 199

National Guard, 51, 60

Nationalism, 343

National Public Radio, 104

National security, 52, 58, 269, 277, 287–88. *See also* Foreign policy

Native Americans, 41–42, 55, 63, 75–77, 181

Neighborhood Youth Corps. *See* Youth culture

Network, 96–97, *96*, 221

Neutron bomb, 63. *See also* Nuclear arms

New Criticism, 11

New Deal, 29, 36, 39, 43, 347

New Federalism, 262–64, 343, 348–49

New Historicism, 27

Newman, Barnett, 118–20, 249

Newman, John, 238

New Spirit, The (Ashbery), 117, 149

New York Daily News, 359

New Yorker, 123

New York Herald Tribune, 302

New York Post, 125, 128–30

New York Times, 91, 265–67, 288, 360

Nicaragua, 3. *See also* Iran-Contra affair

Nichols, Mike: *The Birdcage*, 207; *Carnal Knowledge*, 82; *Catch-22*, 71; *The Graduate*, 243

Nicholson, Jack, 82, 95

Night Dances, The (Plath), 251

Night of the Living Dead, 81–82

Night at the Opera, 210

1984 (Orwell), 2

Nineties, 6, 27, 32, 49, 349. *See also* Bush, George; Clinton, Bill; Elections; Film; Music

Nixon, Richard, 16, 36–43, 49–57, 108, 259–71; and Ashbery, 110; and Checkers speech, 339, 373; and control, 321; and Ford, 334–38, 342; and *Gravity's Rainbow*, 202–4; and Gulf of Tonkin, 287; and image, 254, 283–85; and inflation, 354–55; and Justice Department, 2; and Kennedys, 290; *The Memoirs of Richard Nixon*, 287; and *Patton*, 71; and race, 198; as representative of America, 171; resignation

of, 31, 56–58, 89, 275, 299–316, 328, 332, 348; and *The Rocky Horror Picture Show*, 91; in Shepard, 173; *Six Crises*, 287; and Supreme Court, 51; and surveillance, 1. *See also* Cambodia; Campaign; China; Election; Foreign policy; Gold standard; New Federalism; Pardon; Presidency; Saturday Night Massacre; Silent majority; Soviet Union; Tape; Vietnam War; Watergate

Nixon, Tricia, 51

Nobel Peace Prize. *See* Kissinger, Henry

Noland, Kenneth, 119

North, Edmund H., 71

North, Oliver, 110, 131, 281

North American Time (Rich), 175–76

Nostalgia, 30–34; and art, 117, 121; for fifties, 59; for music, 86–87; in *Pulp Fiction*, 66; and Reagan, 3; in *Self-Portrait in a Convex Mirror*, 108, 140, 147; in *Serpico*, 86; for seventies, 2, 21, 46–47; in seventies, 260; for sixties, 77; in Warhol, 255

Notes of a Native Son (Baldwin), 189–90, 198

Not Ready for Prime Time Players, 128

Novak, Michael: *The Rise of Unmeltable Ethics*, 40

Nuclear arms: and Carter, 61; and Cold War, 36; and Ford, 334; and Nixon, 312; reduction of, 20, 57; and Soviet Union, 44, 54. *See also* Alternative B; Cold War; SALT; SALT II; Soviet Union

Nuclear reactor. *See* Protests; Three Mile Island

Obstruction of justice. *See* Impeachment

October, 45

Of Grammatology (Derrida), 159, 162

O'Hara, Frank, 23

Oil embargo, 6–13, 54–57, 63, 124–29, 366; and Ashbery, 126–27, 365–66; and Ford, 356; and gas lines, 20; and *Gravity's Rainbow*, 203; and Johns, 221

Olitski, Jules, 119

Olympics. *See* Israel

O'Neal, Ryan, 74

One Day at a Time, 32

Stephen Paul Miller is Associate Professor of English
at St. John's University.
Library of Congress Cataloging-in-Publication Data
Miller, Stephen Paul.
The seventies now: culture as surveillance /
Stephen Paul Miller.
Includes bibliographical references (p.) and index.
ISBN 0-8223-2154-8 (cloth : alk. paper).
ISBN 0-8223-2166-1 (paper : alk. paper)
1. United States—History—1969-   2. United States—
Politics and government—1969-1974.   3. United
States—Politics and government—1974-1977.
4. United States—Social life and customs—1971-
5. Popular culture—United States—History—20th
century.   6. Electronic surveillance—Social aspects—
United States—History—20th century.   7. Espionage—
Social aspects—United States—History—20th century.
I. Title.
E855.M56   1999   973.92—dc21   98-47225   CIP